The Multimodal Context of Phonological Learning

The Multimodal Context of Phonological Learning is both authoritative and practical, combining research review and a pedagogical orientation presented by a researcher and teacher whose work in second language acquisition has centrally involved the wider context in which pronunciation is situated.

The book reviews the early foundation established by speechreading studies that explored the extraction of speech information from a talker's facial movements and the interaction of auditory–visual cues in perceptual illusions. It then focuses on the role of auditory, visual, and tactile information in second-language perceptual learning and the interactional functions of eye gaze within the complex of non-verbal communication that incorporates head movements and manual gestures. The book also details an original mixed-methods study of the eye-gaze behaviour of perceivers when viewing the face of a speaker producing their first language (English) and a speaker producing their second language (French) in different stimulus conditions.

The issue of variability in speech emerges as a central theme throughout the book and is one which researchers and teachers are encouraged to exploit through their selection of multimodal materials and their approach to pronunciation teaching.

DEBRA M. HARDISON is an associate professor in the Department of Linguistics, Languages, and Cultures at Michigan State University.

Applied Phonology and Pronunciation Teaching

Series Editor – Martha C. Pennington, Birkbeck University of London

The Applied Phonology and Pronunciation Teaching series seeks to provide a forum for dissemination of knowledge in the area of applied phonology and pronunciation teaching.

The series aims to provide information and stimulate conversations that can advance knowledge, understanding, and good practice in any of the areas of applied phonology and pronunciation teaching.

Published

Voice and Mirroring in L2 Pronunciation Instruction
Darren LaScotte, Colleen Meyers, and Elaine Tarone

The Multimodal Context of Phonological Learning
Debra M. Hardison

The Multimodal Context of Phonological Learning

Debra M. Hardison

UNIVERSITY OF TORONTO PRESS
Toronto Buffalo London

Published by University of Toronto Press
Toronto Buffalo London

utppublishing.com

Printed in Canada

ISBN 978-1-4875-6950-1 (cloth) ISBN 978-1-4875-6953-2 (EPUB)
ISBN 978-1-4875-6951-8 (paper) ISBN 978-1-4875-6952-5 (UPDF)

Library and Archives Canada Cataloguing in Publication

Title: The multimodal context of phonological learning / Debra M. Hardison.
Names: Hardison, Debra, author
Description: Series statement: Applied phonology and pronunciation teaching | Includes bibliographical references and indexes.
Identifiers: Canadiana (print) 20240536401 | Canadiana (ebook) 20240536452 | ISBN 9781487569501 (cloth) | ISBN 9781487569518 (paper) | ISBN 9781487569525 (PDF) | ISBN 9781487569532 (EPUB)
Subjects: LCSH: Grammar, Comparative and general – Phonology – Study and teaching. | LCSH: Second language acquisition – Study and teaching. | LCSH: Speech perception. | LCSH: Nonverbal communication.
Classification: LCC P217 .H37 2025 | DDC 414–dc23

Cover design: Val Cooke
Cover image: Lauren Spiegel, Heatmap of French AV Condition as Head Tipped Back and Mouth Began to Open for the Utterance *bande*. For more information see fig. 5.19 on p. 126.

We wish to acknowledge the land on which the University of Toronto Press operates. This land is the traditional territory of the Wendat, the Anishnaabeg, the Haudenosaunee, the Métis, and the Mississaugas of the Credit First Nation.

University of Toronto Press acknowledges the financial support of the Government of Canada, the Canada Council for the Arts, and the Ontario Arts Council, an agency of the Government of Ontario, for its publishing activities.

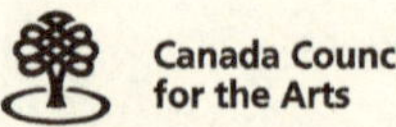

Funded by the Government of Canada | Financé par le gouvernement du Canada | Canada

To the memory of my family

Contents

Preface

My interest in the integration of auditory and visual cues in speech processing started many years ago as I watched various family members struggle to understand speech when they could not see the talker's face. They were experiencing hearing loss from military service and industrial work environments. As time passed, aging made the loss worse. Many service encounters would have been more successful if the talkers had just faced them, enunciated clearly, and used supporting gestures or visual materials.

When I became interested in linguistics and cognitive psychology, I took a graduate course on speech processing taught by Professor David Pisoni at Indiana University. Among the readings was the classic article, "Hearing Lips and Seeing Voices," by Harry McGurk and John MacDonald (1976), which presented findings on the perceptual illusion that became known as the McGurk–MacDonald effect. That short article of less than two full pages further inspired my research in auditory-visual speech processing and decades of research by many others.

I was thrilled at the prospect of hearing Harry McGurk speak in person at the International Conference on Auditory-Visual Speech Processing in Australia in early December 1998, especially because I had published a study on the McGurk effect (as it was then called) with second-language learners just 2 years earlier. Unfortunately, he passed away in April 1998. Although I missed listening to him, I have the recording of him demonstrating the McGurk effect on the conference proceedings' CD-ROM and have continued to be fascinated with that perceptual illusion.

In writing this book, I was also inspired by Peter Jusczyk's (1993) chapter titled "Sometimes It Pays to Look Back Before You Leap Ahead." As such, each chapter starts by acknowledging the important groundwork laid by early researchers before more recent developments are explored; for example, looking back on the historical roots of current issues in pronunciation teaching (chapter 7) was particularly enlightening and led me to a more in-depth knowledge of the work of Daniel Jones (1881–1967). Many issues in the field that we might think are relatively recent are actually over 100 years old!

Acknowledgments

I would like to express my gratitude to several people whose efforts have aided this research: Solène Inceoglu and Dustin Crowther for assistance in collecting the eye-tracking data, Jenie Lubick for online library search, Lily Ashburn for copy-editing, Lauren Spiegel for graphic design, Sue Lim and Sarah Manski for their statistical expertise, Alissa Cohen and Austin Kaufmann for the loan of pronunciation textbooks, and Russ Werner for much technical assistance on many projects over the years. I am also grateful to Martha Pennington for encouraging me to write this book and for assisting in its evolution from a rough draft into a final, published volume by interacting significantly with not only its form but also its content.

Series Editor's Preface

I am pleased to present Debra M. Hardison's *The Multimodal Context of Phonological Learning* as the second book in the Applied Phonology and Pronunciation Teaching series. The book is important and original, offering a fresh outlook on phonological learning that stresses the context within which speakers produce and listeners perceive speech. It is the first comprehensive treatment of phonology as a multimodal phenomenon presented from the perspective of contemporary applied linguistic research and language teaching.

Hardison's orientation to phonology and the teaching of pronunciation is groundbreaking, going considerably beyond a traditional articulatory view in its attention to perception and, in particular, to the visual context of the lips and the wider gestural complex of face and hands linked to spoken language. It is a monumental work of scholarship that incorporates the author's own research and a wide-ranging review of the relevant scholarship in applied linguistics and related fields, in addition to practical material for teaching phonology as an integrated aspect of expression involving multiple senses.

For researchers in applied linguistics and second- and foreign-language teaching, the book offers an authoritative and up-to-date review of published studies and research trends, and for language teachers, it offers suggestions and materials for pronunciation pedagogy. For both of these groups of readers, it is a rich resource for broadening and deepening their understanding of phonological learning with attention to visual and other modalities of perception and expressive channels for communication. The book stands out in giving considerable attention to various technologies used for researching and teaching pronunciation in context, including for high variability perception training (HVPT), video analysis and annotation, and the contribution made to comprehension by looking at a speaker's face.

The Multimodal Context of Phonological Learning is a significant new work – a modern and forward-looking volume that can enrich current perspectives on phonological learning and, in so doing, contribute to creating a bright future for applied phonology and pronunciation teaching.

Martha C. Pennington
Series Editor
Applied Phonology and Pronunciation Teaching

List of Abbreviations

ACTFL	American Council on the Teaching of Foreign Languages
AE	American English
ANOVA	analysis of variance
AOI	area of interest
A-only	auditory-only
AV	auditory-visual
AVn	auditory-visual with noise added
BOLD	blood-oxygen-level-dependent
CEFR	Common European Framework of Reference
CV	consonant-vowel
CVC	consonant-vowel-consonant
dB	decibel
EFL	English as a foreign language
ERP	event-related potential
FL	foreign language
fMRI	functional magnetic resonance imaging
HVPT	high variability perception training
IELTS	International English Language Testing System
IPA	International Phonetic Alphabet
L1	first language
L2	second language
MRI	magnetic resonance imaging
s	second(s)
SNR	signal-to-noise ratio
TFC	total fixation count
TFD	total fixation duration
TOEFL	Test of English as a Foreign Language
TTFF	time to first fixation
TTMC	time to mouse click
V-only	visual-only

List of Figures

List of Tables

Introduction

This book fills a need in second-language (L2) phonology research and teaching, a field that has not given sufficient attention to the visual aspect of speech communication, specifically to the facial movements and gestures associated with speech. The book differs from other approaches to phonological learning in its foregrounding of both the multimodal nature of speech and the role of stimulus and talker variability in perception and production. Multimodal (or multisensory) integration refers to the neural integration or combination of information from different sensory modalities, such as sight, sound, and touch (e.g., Holmes et al., 2009; Stein et al., 2009). Both terms (i.e., *multimodal* and *multisensory*) appear in this book, generally following the usage adopted in each study being reviewed. *Multisensory* tends to be used more in contexts that make specific reference to sensory processing as compared to modality of speech input.

While doing research for each chapter, I discovered several works that had been published many years ago but that are still relevant today. As such, each chapter begins with a look to the past to acknowledge the important early groundwork laid by researchers on the chapter's topic before exploring more recent developments. An important part of the foundation for years of research on multimodal speech was the accidental discovery by Harry McGurk and John MacDonald of "hearing by eye" (McGurk, 1988, p. 9) – the perceptual illusion that occurs when the articulation that is visible on a talker's face does not match the sound that is produced by the voice. For example, a visual /ba/ presented with an auditory /ga/ often results in the percept /da/.

With regard to pronunciation teaching, looking back on its historical roots was particularly enlightening and led to a more in-depth knowledge of the contribution of Daniel Jones, who, in his lectures around 1912, recommended to language learners that they observe the mouth movements of speakers of the target language to learn its pronunciation (Collins & Mees, 2002).

Today, many researchers regard speech as a multimodal rather than a purely auditory phenomenon. Proponents of the multimodal view have been increasing in number, which may be due, in part, to advances in digital video technology that allow us to capture, analyse, and annotate the acoustic and visual components of a speech event, as well as to advances in neuroscience, which provide new insights on speech processing through techniques such as magnetic resonance imaging (MRI).

Outline of the Book

Chapter 1 addresses the roles that visual information from a talker's face can play in a communicative interaction, including the establishment of a visual connection between interlocutors as well as the improvement of perceptual accuracy, especially, but not exclusively, in noisy environments. Despite the contribution of visual cues to speech processing in general, the auditory intelligibility and visual discernibility of speech cues are impacted by variability and a perceiver's familiarity with a talker.

Interest in the integration of auditory-visual (AV) cues in speech perception flourished after the initial publication of the McGurk–MacDonald effect in 1976 (chapter 2), and, ultimately, research on the perceptual illusion involved native speakers of several languages in addition to English and L2 learners. The discovery of the illusion had a substantial influence on the consideration of speech as a multimodal phenomenon. Like other areas of speech research, the abundance of studies exploring this illusory effect showed variability in the strength with which perceivers experienced it.

Chapter 3 continues the theme of variability in its pivotal role in the development of what became known as high variability perception training, or simply HVPT, which initially focused on auditory input. In training studies, variability was introduced in the form of multiple talkers producing the target stimuli in multiple phonetic contexts. Successful studies resulted in the development of robust perceptual categories and generalization of improved abilities to the perception of novel stimuli and unfamiliar voices. This set the stage for the use of AV input in segmental perception training with the goal of transferring improved skills to greater production accuracy and earlier identification of words beginning with the target sounds.

For a fuller understanding of multimodal speech, we need to ask where perceivers look on the face of a talker and how gaze patterns change as a speech event unfolds. Chapter 4 thus provides some background on eye-movement research with an emphasis on speech. Chapter 5 then presents original data from a study that tracked the eye movements of first language (L1) English intermediate-level L2 French learners during L1 and L2 vowel identification tasks in three stimulus conditions: AV with and without noise added, and visual-only (V-only). Identification accuracy and several eye gaze measures were calculated for both languages. This study was able to assess how much of the variability in each measure was accounted for by the independent variables of language and stimulus condition, and how much could be attributed to variability across the participants. In post-study interviews, participants reflected on their typical face-viewing behaviour during communication and their experiences during the study.

Although the face attracts attention in face-to-face communication, other elements are also important. Chapter 6 reviews a range of non-verbal cues used in communication, such as eye gaze in its interactional role (e.g., directing turn-taking) and manual gestures. As with other components of a speech event, variability exists across speakers and cultures in their gestures, and familiarity plays a role in the contribution of a speaker's gestures to comprehension, as it does for accent and topic too.

Multimodal input in phonological learning is not a recent concept. It is among several issues in the field that can be found in the writings of Daniel Jones from the early 1900s (Collins & Mees, 2002). In addition to promoting both auditory and visual input in teaching and learning pronunciation, Jones was an advocate of the importance of intelligibility as the goal of language learning, and of the importance of positive attitudes towards accents (chapter 7). These issues form part of the foundation of teacher education, which is then developed in chapter 8 in the form of suggestions for a multisensory approach to the teaching of speech sounds in a stand-alone pronunciation course and in a course more broadly focused on the development of oral communication skills.

Finally, chapter 9 concludes the book with a focus on the key theme of variability that emerges throughout the preceding chapters.

Chapter 1

Laying the Foundation for a Multimodal View of Speech

> *Phonology is largely acquired in the context of conversation, and in this context speech perception is at least a bimodal process; the individual listens with ear and with eye.*
>
> – McGurk (1981, p. 336)

*****

Background

As early as 1912, Hermann Gutzmann, a German physician, emphasized the roles of both vision and audition in speech perception when he noted the following:

> Stellt man die Verwechslungsmöglichkeiten der optischen und akustischen Perzeption für die einzelnen Konsonanten zusammen, so erkennt man deutlich, wie ausserordentlich wichtig die gegenseitige Unterstützung der beiden Sinne bei der sprachlichen Perzeption ist und wie, wenn Ohr und Auge zusammen bei der Perzeption tätig sind, eine Verwechslung geradezu ausgeschlossen wird. (p. 55)[1]
>
> [If one summarizes the possibilities of confusing the optical and acoustic perception for the individual consonants, one can clearly see how extremely important the mutual support of the two senses is in linguistic perception and how, when ear and eye are active together in perception, confusion is almost impossible.][2]

However, it took several decades after Gutzmann's (1912) comment before some researchers in the United States suggested that the prevailing view of speech perception as an auditory phenomenon might have overlooked an important source of input for the listener – the talker's face. What finally led them in that direction? To appreciate the development of the view of speech as a multimodal phenomenon (e.g., Rosenblum, 2005, 2010), we begin with some background.

In many communicative settings, listeners deal with a background of different types of noise. In those cases, as G.A. Miller and Nicely (1955) proposed, "we might learn something about speech perception and might even improve communication if we know what kinds of errors occur" (p. 338). In their study, native speakers of American English (AE) were presented auditorily with 16 AE consonants in consonant-vowel (CV) syllables containing the low, open back unrounded vowel /ɑ/ (e.g., *h<u>o</u>t*).[3] Different levels of masking noise were added to the speech signal to produce a range of signal-to-noise ratios (SNRs): −18 dB, −12 dB, −6 dB, 0 dB, +6 dB, and +12 dB. An SNR of 0 dB represents equal signal (in this case, speech) and noise levels; +6 dB represents more signal relative to the noise, whereas a negative value such as −6 dB represents more noise than signal. The higher the ratio, the better the speech signal quality; the lower the ratio, the poorer the speech signal and the greater the challenge to the listener. Noise is often added in AV perception experiments because the contribution of vision becomes clearer when auditory information is degraded in some way to reduce ceiling effects on perception; however, the auditory stimulus does not need to be impoverished for vision to be beneficial.

In the G.A. Miller and Nicely (1955) study, the consonants varied in terms of place and manner of articulation (i.e., where and how they were produced), the activity of the vocal folds in the throat (i.e., vibrating or not), and whether the sounds were produced with air expelled from the mouth (i.e., oral sounds) or the nose (i.e., nasal sounds). In the following description of the consonant pairs used in that study (which also provides a useful overview of terms that will be relevant throughout the book), the first consonant listed at each place of articulation (e.g., /p/) is voiceless (i.e., without vocal fold vibration), and the second (e.g., /b/) is voiced (i.e., with vocal fold vibration). The set of consonants included the following:

1. *Stops* (or plosives): Stops are produced by obstructing the airflow from the lungs at various places in the vocal tract and then releasing the closure. For example, the release of lip closure produces /p/ (e.g., *<u>p</u>at*) and /b/ (e.g., *<u>b</u>at*); the release of the tongue tip closure at the alveolar ridge behind the upper teeth creates /t/ (e.g., *<u>t</u>op*) and /d/ (e.g., *<u>d</u>ot*); and the release of the closure of the back of the tongue

against the soft tissue, or velum, at the back of the roof of the mouth produces /k/ (e.g., <u>c</u>*ot*) and /g/ (e.g., <u>g</u>*ot*).

2. *Fricatives*: Fricatives are characterized by audible friction that is created as air is forced through a narrow channel. For example, friction created by the airflow between the lower lip and the upper teeth produces /f/ (e.g., <u>f</u>*ine*) and /v/ (e.g., <u>v</u>*ine*), and friction created by the airflow between the tongue tip and the upper teeth when the tongue is inserted between the teeth produces /θ/ (e.g., <u>th</u>*ink*) and /ð/ (e.g., <u>th</u>*e*).
3. *Sibilants*: Sibilants constitute a subcategory of fricatives and are often described as hissing sounds. They are produced by the friction created when air passes through a narrow channel between the tongue tip and alveolar ridge, resulting in /s/ (e.g., <u>s</u>*ip*) and /z/ (e.g., <u>z</u>*ip*), or when air passes through a somewhat larger channel created a bit farther back in the mouth, resulting in /ʃ/ (e.g., <u>sh</u>*ip*) and /ʒ/ (e.g., *mea*<u>s</u>*ure*). Speakers can enhance the friction for /s/ and /z/ by widening the channel for airflow through lip spreading, and they can enhance the friction for /ʃ/ and /ʒ/ by lengthening the channel for airflow through lip rounding or protrusion.

The aforementioned oral sounds are produced with air flowing through the oral cavity or mouth, whereas nasal sounds are produced when air flows through the nasal cavity, or nose, when the velum is lowered. Two nasal sounds were included in the G.A. Miller and Nicely (1955) study: /m/ (e.g., <u>m</u>*ight*) and /n/ (e.g., <u>n</u>*ight*); both are voiced. In all, the sounds under study addressed several characteristics of consonants: place of articulation, ranging from the front to the back of the mouth; manner of articulation, including stops and fricatives; voicing (i.e., voiceless and voiced); and nasality.

G.A. Miller and Nicely (1955) determined that the characteristics of voicing and nasality were much less affected by masking noise than other features; in fact, determining if a sound was voiced or voiceless, nasal or oral, was possible at SNRs as poor as −12 dB. As a guideline for interpretation, at −18 dB, the poorest ratio used in the study, there is insufficient information for accurate auditory recognition of *spondaic* words (i.e., words with two syllables in which both are stressed, such as *downtown*) (Erber, 1969) or for identification of individual consonants, most of which are confusable at that level of noise when presented in CV syllables (Summerfield, 1987). In contrast to the features of voicing and nasality, which were affected the least by noise, G.A. Miller and Nicely determined that cues to place of articulation were affected the most and were hard to distinguish at ratios less than +6 dB. The distinction in place of articulation for the fricatives /f/ (e.g., *first*) and /θ/ (e.g., *thirst*) and their voiced counterparts of /v/ (e.g., *van*) and /ð/ (e.g., *than*) was among the most difficult for listeners. As G.A. Miller and Nicely concluded, "it seems likely that in most natural situations the differentiation depends more on ... visual observation of the talker's lips than it does on the acoustic difference" (p. 347). Although the place of articulation was the hardest to hear in noise, it was proposed as the easiest characteristic to see on a talker's face (G.A. Miller & Nicely, 1955; Summerfield, 1987).

Cues to a consonant's place of articulation are often present in the speech signal in the form of rapid transitions of a *formant* to or from an adjacent vowel (Summerfield, 1987). A formant is a resonating frequency of the air in the vocal tract that is perceived as sound – in particular, speech sound. A set of formants resonates in a way that is characteristic of a given sound, differentiating it from all other sounds (e.g., each vowel from every other vowel) and showing distinctive patterns of transition from one sound to another (e.g., between the two vowel nuclei in a diphthong or between a vowel and a neighbouring voiced consonant). For example, the difference in the formant transitions from the initial consonants [b] and [d] to the following vowel [æ] distinguishes words such as *bad* and *dad*. These transitions occur predominantly in the frequencies above 1 kHz/1000 Hz, a perceptual range that represents the greatest loss in absolute sensitivity for individuals with hearing loss that originates in the *cochlea* (i.e., the spiral cavity of the inner ear that produces nerve impulses in response to sound vibrations).[4] In contrast, cues to nasality and voicing involve the presence or absence of energy over tens of milliseconds in lower frequency regions – mainly below 1 kHz (Summerfield, 1987). Energy in the lower range is less distinctive for perception of specific sounds than energy in the range above 1kHz, which is compatible with the findings of G.A. Miller and Nicely (1955) regarding the weaker masking effects of noise on nasal sounds and on distinctions in voicing as compared to the effects on place of articulation.

At about the same time as the G.A. Miller and Nicely study, Sumby and Pollack (1954) reported research demonstrating enhancement of speech intelligibility through observation of a talker's lips and facial movements. Unlike most research conducted since that time using recorded stimuli, the Sumby and Pollack study involved a live talker located about 5 ft (1.52 m) away from participants, who listened to the speech through headphones. Stimuli were bisyllabic words with a spondaic stress pattern. Half of the listeners heard and saw the talker, and the other half only heard him. The task required listeners to identify the spoken word from a reference list. Findings revealed that identification accuracy was better in AV versus auditory-only (A-only) presentation and that the benefit increased as the SNR decreased. A decreasing SNR represented more *white noise* (i.e., noise with equal intensity at different frequencies) relative to the speech signal. Sumby and Pollack concluded that "the results suggest that oral speech intelligibility may be appreciably improved in many practical situations by arrangement for supplementary visual observation of the speaker" (p. 215).

The studies by G.A. Miller and Nicely (1955) and Sumby and Pollack (1954) are frequently cited and regarded as classic works in the field of AV speech perception, although both were specifically focused on the benefits of visual input for specific listener populations: the hearing impaired (G.A. Miller & Nicely) and those in noisy military and industrial settings (Sumby & Pollack). As time passed, there was increased recognition of the role of visual input for the general population because "communication is not often carried out in ideal acoustic environments .... It is therefore likely that speech perception will often be dependent on complementary information from the visual modality" (Dodd, 1977, p. 40). Despite findings on the contribution of visual cues to speech comprehension, many researchers continued to argue that speech was predominantly an auditory phenomenon (e.g., Easton & Basala, 1982; Wood, 1975).

A Renewed Appreciation for Visual Cues in Speech

It is also possible that some non-researchers would have agreed with the characterization of speech as exclusively or essentially an auditory phenomenon until the COVID-19 pandemic occurred. Prior to that time, it is likely that many people were only aware of vision's role in speech comprehension if they were dealing with hearing loss (e.g., Bergeson et al., 2003; Walden et al., 1977) or trying to understand speech in ambient noise (e.g., for English, Binnie et al., 1974; Rosenblum et al., 1996; Summerfield, 1979; Summerfield et al., 1989; for French, Benoît et al., 1994; Robert-Ribes et al., 1998). Summerfield (1992) estimated that skill in *speechreading* – using visual as well as auditory cues – enabled an observer to tolerate a poorer SNR, by a measure of 4–6 dB.[5] More recent work by Ross et al. (2007) demonstrated that when native English speakers were able to view a talker producing speech, their improved identification accuracy was equivalent to about a 10 dB increase in the SNR – an increase that could substantially improve the amount of speech that is understood at increased levels of noise.

When face masks became commonplace as a mitigation measure to help prevent the spread of COVID-19, broader segments of the population in a variety of communicative settings experienced the old adage *you don't appreciate what you have until it's gone* because the cues on a talker's face that were related to speech or emotional state were hidden behind a mask. So critical was the perceived importance of this visual information that early in the pandemic the need to facilitate mask-to-mask communication prompted the sale of masks with a clear panel over the mouth. One online company charged USD$350 for such a mask (deHahn, 2020). According to the company's website in March 2020, supplies were sold out. As months passed, masks that had a clear panel or were fully transparent became more readily available online from multiple vendors and for much lower prices, permitting listeners to engage their speechreading skills. Fortunately, neither hearing loss nor ambient noise is necessary for the development and use of speechreading ability, which seems to be a skill developed by hearing and non-hearing populations. Owens and Blazek (1985), for example, discovered a similar degree of skill in the V-only recognition of consonants in nonsense syllables by adults with normal hearing and those with *postlingual* (i.e., after language acquisition) hearing loss.

The Roles of Vision in Speech

Across hearing and non-hearing populations, visual cues in communicative contexts serve several purposes. In general, a visual connection between interlocutors helps to establish the rapport that is important in many cultures for successful interaction. Visual cues can also suggest the emotional state of a talker, signal when speech begins and ends, and direct turn-taking in an interaction. Visual cues may therefore be important enough that people feel uncomfortable when they are absent. In North America, people are commonly observed to move from where they are sitting or standing in order to see an interlocutor's face even if they can hear every word clearly.

In speech perception by the hearing population, Reisberg et al. (1981) observed that when participants could not see a talker's face, their eye gaze was directed towards the loudspeaker from which a word list was heard, and this improved their memory recall. In addition, Reisberg et al. (1987) discovered that speechreading significantly improved peoples' performance when shadowing a foreign language, English (their L1) spoken with an accent, or a semantically complex message (e.g., philosophical passages). Comprehension of the lyrics of a song also showed a 35% improvement when the singer could be seen (Jesse & Massaro, 2010). This finding is striking because singing can alter articulatory gestures, and thus could potentially be more obstructive to comprehension than facilitative, depending on the type of music and the strength and clarity of the singer's voice. Yet it seems that seeing a singer can provide information on consonantal place of articulation, vowel features, and the correlation between head and eyebrow movements with pitch changes (e.g., Hardison, 2018c; Munhall et al., 2004).

For individuals with acquired hearing loss who have hearing aids or cochlear implants, visual cues orient their attention to a talker, and speechreading skills maximize speech recognition (e.g., Bernstein et al., 2022). For individuals who rely on sign language interpreters because of hearing loss, a wide range of facial expressions and body movements contribute to full comprehension of the message (e.g., Kimmelman & Pfau, 2016). These movements, which serve a variety of linguistic functions, include mouth movements for lexical disambiguation or the expression of adverbial meanings, body movements to express contrast, and head movements for negation and affirmation. Eyebrow movements mark sentence type (e.g., statement versus question), topics, focal elements, and subordinate clauses of various types.

Speechreading Challenges

In many settings, environmental factors, such as noise, reduce auditory speech intelligibility and increase observers' dependence on visual cues. When their dependence on visual cues increases, observers can face challenges. Numerous reports in the early speechreading literature demonstrated that less information was communicated visually than auditorily (e.g., Woodward & Barber, 1960). The early findings on the primacy of auditory over visual information were the basis for the notion of *auditory dominance* in speech processing. As Easton and Basala (1982) concluded, "if information processed in a particular modality is more informative, it will dominate intermodal processing" (p. 570). It should be noted, however, that while in some contexts the visual modality may contribute *less* information, this does not necessarily mean *no* information; moreover, the contribution of both visual and auditory cues varies markedly across talkers and contexts.

Speechreading studies have generally focused on consonants rather than vowels. Consonants, which convey more linguistic information than vowels, are typically easier to speechread because observers can watch for more specific points of articulation. There has been no consensus on the number or composition of sets of *visemes* (henceforth, visual categories), that is, groups of sounds whose articulations are not considered visually distinctive.[6] For example, visual information alone may render indistinguishable the articulatory gestures that are involved in producing each word in the phrase *buy my pie*. This is one of the challenges experienced by individuals with hearing loss or those in a very noisy environment who need to rely on a talker's articulatory gestures for speech comprehension. Articulations that are easily confusable visually, such as the initial consonants in *buy my pie*, are often, though not always, more distinguishable in the auditory modality.[i]

Based on the results of a study in which normal-hearing participants were asked to judge visually presented CV syllables in AE as the same or different (e.g., /pa/-/pa/ or /pa/-/ka/), Woodward and Barber (1960) identified only four visually distinctive consonant categories: bilabials /p, b, m/; labiodentals /f, v/; the approximants /w, r/; and nonlabials, which is a large category incorporating interdental, alveolar (including /l/), palato-alveolar, palatal /j/ (e.g., *yes*), and velar consonants, plus /h/. Not surprisingly, consonants with some lip involvement were the most visually distinguishable. However, not all speechreading studies have drawn the same conclusion on the number or composition of visual categories; for example, in addition to bilabials, labiodentals, and /w, r/, Fisher (1968) established the velars /k, g/ as a category separate from other nonlabials.

Determining the composition of visual categories is influenced by numerous factors, including the phonetic context, an observer's viewing angle of the talker, talker characteristics (e.g., the amount of articulatory movement enhancing the visual discernibility of sounds), the length of the speech sample, the background of the observer (e.g., speechreading training), the testing conditions (e.g., lighting), and the statistical criteria used to evaluate results. The phonetic context of a consonant includes the adjacent vowel(s), the consonant's position (initial, medial, or final) in the syllable or word, and its presence as a singleton or part of a cluster.

---

i. Editor's Note: It is worth noting that distinguishability of sound ("a difference in sound") is a key criterion of phonemehood. The other key criterion, a difference in meaning, helps to decide what phoneme was intended when the sound produced is not auditorily distinguishable from one or more other phonemes, for whatever reason (e.g., poor articulation, poor hearing, interfering sounds in the environment). The context will often rule out any phoneme that does not occur in a word whose meaning fits with the surrounding context. – MCP

Although *coarticulation* (i.e., the overlapping of adjacent articulations, such as the influence of an adjacent vowel on the production of a consonant) is most extensive in connected speech (Daniloff & Hammarberg, 1973), the effect of vowels on the articulation of neighbouring consonants in isolated syllables and words must also be considered. A talker's anticipatory lip position for an adjacent rounded vowel, such as /u/ (e.g., *cool*), tends to obliterate all consonantal articulatory movements except those for bilabials (e.g., *boot*) and labiodentals (e.g., *food*) and has been associated with the most consonant errors in speechreading experiments (Benguerel & Pichora-Fuller, 1982). The coarticulatory effect of the lip rounding gesture for /u/ can extend over as many as four consonants preceding the vowel (Daniloff & Moll, 1968). This is a consistent finding: the vowel /u/ exhibits the least variability in production across native speakers of English because it has the smallest amount of width and height in the lip opening as compared to other vowels (Fromkin, 1964).

Based on identification accuracy data from an experiment using a live talker producing consonants before and following the vowels /i/, /a/, and /u/, four consonant groups met the statistical criterion to qualify as a distinctive visual category in syllable-initial position: /p, b, m/; /w/; /f, v/; and /ʃ, ʒ, tʃ, dʒ/ (e.g., /tʃ/ *church*, /dʒ/ *judge*), with /r/ close to the criterion (Berger, 1972, 1973).[7] Three groups of consonants appeared as distinctive categories in final position: /p, b, m/; /f, v/; and /ʃ, ʒ, tʃ, dʒ/. Speechreading scores for consonants preceding the low, open-jaw vowel /a/ were better than those for the other vowels. Accuracy did not depend on a 0° viewing angle (i.e., facing the speechreader); in fact, accuracy when the talker was at a 45° angle to the speechreader was slightly better as compared to a 0° angle, and definitely superior to a 90° angle. A 45° angle could have made protruding lip movements more visually salient.

In addition to the influence of vocalic environment, visual discernibility varied for consonants in initial cluster (versus singleton) position (e.g., /sm/, /spl/, /dw/, /θr/) in nonsense syllables with the vowel /ʌ/ (e.g., *hut*) produced by three talkers (Franks & Kimble, 1972). Based on responses from 275 participants, initial consonant clusters were identified with only 11% accuracy. They were more frequently misperceived as singletons (46% of responses) or as other clusters (43% of responses). Responses suggested five visual categories, each with one or two visually prominent components: /r/ or /w/; /b/, /m/, or /p/; /θ/ or alveolar articulations; /ʃ/ or /ʒ/; and /f/. A consonant's position (i.e., initial or final) in the syllable had an influence on discernibility; for example, when presented in initial clusters involving consonants articulated with the lips (i.e., the bilabial stops /p/

and /b/ or the voiceless labiodental /f/), /r/ and /l/ were visually confused with each other, but they could be distinguished in clusters with consonants produced with closure at the velum (/k, g/). The confusions did not appear to differ significantly across the three talkers in the study.

However, talker variability can exert an influence on the visual discernibility of speech sounds. In a speechreading study, observers tried to identify the syllables and sentences produced by six female talkers who varied in the ease with which their articulations could be distinguished (Kricos & Lesner, 1982). Results indicated variability in the number and composition of visual consonant categories across talkers. Responses to four out of the six female talkers pointed to a unique visual category for /w, r/. For two of the talkers, /l/ was also a unique visual category, but for the others, it was not sufficiently discernible from other alveolar segments.

In English, rhotics (i.e., /r/-like sounds) exhibit considerable variability across talkers (Lindau, 1985), including the degree to which they are visually distinguishable. This variability adds to the challenge that learners of English as an L2 often face in the acquisition of AE /r/ (Hardison, 2003). Some speechreading researchers placed /r/ and /l/ in two independent (unique) categories (e.g., Berger, 1972; Binnie et al., 1976); others, however, placed /w/ and /r/ together in one category with /l/ in its own category (e.g., Fisher, 1968; Woodward & Barber, 1960), and /l/ was also placed in a general category of alveolar and velar consonants (Woodward & Barber, 1960), and in a category with one or more other specific consonants, such as /n, l/ (Binnie et al., 1976) or /k, g, n, l/ (Owens & Blazek, 1985). The primary source of disagreement across the studies involved the less visually distinctive alveolar and postalveolar consonants, but vocalic influence also played a role. Close examination of the scores reported in Owens and Blazek (1985) for the visual recognition of /r/ and /l/ by normal-hearing adults revealed greater identification accuracy for /l/ when it was paired with /ɑ/, and for /r/ when it was paired with /ʌ/; in other words, accuracy was greater in the context of an unrounded vowel with a more open articulation.

Visible speech cues of different types are also helpful to observers for stretches of speech larger than CV syllables or spondaic words (Summerfield, 1979). In Summerfield's study, a native speaker of Southern British English was recorded while producing lists of sentences under four different AV conditions: *full video*; *lips only* (only the light reflected from luminous make-up on the lips was recorded); *dots* (a dot of luminous make-up was applied to the midline prominence of the upper and lower lips and at each corner of the mouth); and *circle* (a graphic circle, the diameter of which varied in conjunction with the amplitude of each sentence, replaced the talker's mouth on the screen). Normal-hearing observers wrote down each sentence, which was presented at the SNR of −12 dB; the noise was a segment of continuous prose. The number of main words correctly written was scored as a percentage and compared to results from an A-only condition. Baseline accuracy (i.e., no visual information) was 22.7% as compared to accuracy for the full-video condition at 65.3% and for the lips-only condition at 54%. Although the full-video and lips-only conditions offered significant improvement over the A-only baseline, observers commented that the absence of teeth and tongue movement and a non-salient lip closure in the lips-only condition led to their poorer performance. The dots display offered minimal and non-significant improvement (8%) over baseline performance, and the unfamiliar and more abstract display of the circle resulted in no improvement. This study was also a good example of the insight that can be gained following data collection by asking participants about their experience.

Using a similar approach, Rosenblum and Saldaña (1996) increased the number of luminous points in three types of *point-light* stimuli applied to one male talker in the following conditions: *lip lights* (total of 14 points/dots); *lips, teeth, and tongue lights* (total of 19); and *all lights*, which included lips, teeth, and tongue plus the chin, jaw line, cheeks, forehead, and tip and bridge of the nose (a total of 39 lights). The talker was recorded while speaking in the dark so participants would see only the moving dots. Noise-embedded sentences were dubbed with these point-light images at various SNRs. For normal-hearing participants, the lip-lights and all-lights conditions improved speech comprehension, but there was no significant difference between the lips-teeth-tongue-lights condition and the all-lights condition. In addition, participants' performance improved as they gained experience with the stimuli and became more familiar with the talker; familiarity alone may have contributed to improved speechreading ability (Berger, 1972; Walden et al., 1977).

Perceptual confusability involving consonants varies with SNRs. Binnie et al. (1974) presented stimuli consisting of 16 AE consonants preceding /ɑ/ in CV syllables to participants under eight conditions: AV and A-only each at three SNRs (−18 dB, −12 dB, and −6 dB); A-only in the clear (no noise added); and V-only. At the poorest SNR (i.e., −18 dB), at which level little speech information is perceptible, the difference between the intelligibility score in the AV and A-only conditions, interpreted as a measure of the visual component, was 41.4% and comparable to the V-only score of 43.2%. At −12 dB, the visual component was 49.8% and then declined to 35% at –6 dB, when more of the speech signal was audible. Binnie et al. speculated that this decline was the result of participants' increased use of auditory information as it became more available with a change in SNR. Results also confirmed the voicing and nasality features' resistance to masking noise. From visual information only, participants distinguished five visual categories: bilabials /p, b, m/; labiodentals /f, v/; interdentals /θ, ð/; palato-alveolars /ʃ, ʒ/; and a diverse set of nonlabials /t, d, n, s, z, k, g/. These categories differed somewhat from those established by Woodward and Barber (1960) and Fisher (1968), but they generally reflected the visual salience of articulations involving the lips. Note, however, that although the participants had normal hearing, they were enrolled in a course on the teaching of speechreading, and what they learned in this course might have influenced their performance.

Using CV syllable stimuli produced by speakers of British English and presented auditorily in white noise, Summerfield (1987) found that most consonants were confusable with others at an SNR of –18 dB; in a range of –15 to –12 dB, voiced consonants (i.e., those produced with vibration of the vocal folds) became distinct from their voiceless counterparts (e.g., voiced /b/ *b̲it* vs. voiceless /p/ *p̲it*). With improvement of the SNR, other distinctions based on manner of articulation (i.e., how sounds were produced) were possible, but only at +15 dB did listeners distinguish all of the different places of articulation (i.e., where sounds were produced) reliably. More recent studies have underscored the variability of the SNR threshold for distinguishing speech sounds. Robinson and Casali (2003) reported that an SNR of approximately +12 dB was needed to understand speech, but other data suggested lower SNRs should be adequate for normal hearing listeners (Shadle, 2007).

Although cues to nasality and voicing versus place of articulation are more resilient in the face of auditory distortions, the opposite pattern holds for visual perception, and the criteria set for statistical significance play a role (Summerfield, 1987). Adult observers with hearing loss who had been trained in speechreading were able to distinguish five different places of articulation in carefully pronounced British English CV syllables with /a/: labiodental /f, v/; interdental /θ, ð/; alveolar and palato-alveolar fricatives /s, z, ʃ, ʒ/; sounds with labial involvement /p, b, m, w, r/; and nonlabials (e.g., /l, n, t, k/). Yet they had difficulty detecting differences in voicing and nasality. With an adjustment in the criterion for statistical significance, however, nine categories were identified at 75% accuracy: /f, v/; /θ, ð/; /s, z/; /ʃ, ʒ/; /p, b, m/; /w/; /r/; /l/; and nonlabials /t, d, n, k, g, j/.

Speechreading can be enhanced by pitch information. Because the *fundamental frequency* (i.e., the acoustic correlate of pitch) of the voice is not directly visible, a speechreader may miss valuable segmental information (e.g., distinctions between voiced and voiceless segments) and suprasegmental information (e.g., intonation marking a question and placement of focal stress in a sentence) to aid comprehension. In an early study, while speechreading a talker, observers with normal hearing were presented auditorily with the pitch contour extracted from that talker's speech to approximate the experience of a person with postlingual deafness who has to rely on cochlear stimulation (Rosen et al., 1981). With the presentation of pitch, participants' speechreading rate increased, and those who performed better in the speechreading-alone condition demonstrated more improvement with the addition of pitch information than did those with worse performance in the speechreading-alone condition.

Visual Cues to Prosodic Information

Speechreaders may also extract some prosodic information from the facial gestures or head movements of a talker (e.g., Cutler & Jesse, 2021). In one study, speakers of both tonal (Thai) and non-tonal (Australian English) languages were able to discriminate between tone pairs in Cantonese based on visual information, even when they were unfamiliar with the language (D. Burnham et al., 2001). The visual cue may have been the talker's facial gestures or head movements (e.g., raised chin for raised pitch and lowered chin for lowered pitch).

Research with English speakers also showed a coordination of movements, such as eyebrow raises and eyeblinks with pitch (Birdwhistell, 1970; Bolinger, 1985; Flecha-García, 2010), and rapid head movements with stress (Hadar et al., 1983). Because of the correlation between head movement and vocal pitch or stress, visible head motion in conjunction with prosody may aid observers in segmenting the speech stream. Munhall et al. (2004), for instance, found that movements of an *animated* or *talking head* contributed to identification of words by native speakers of English when the words were presented in noise.

The range of *optical correlates*, or visual cues, to lexical stress also appears to include articulatory gestures and other facial movements (e.g., Cho, 2006; de Jong, 1995). Scarborough et al. (2009) noted that English-speaking adults in a speechreading study were able to distinguish with 62% accuracy several real noun-verb word pairs, such as *SUBject* (noun) versus *subJECT* (verb) – where upper case marks the stress – and pairs of stimuli composed of reiterant nonsense syllables, such as *FERfer* versus *ferFER*, which minimized segmental variation between the stressed and unstressed syllables. Several measures were calculated across the stimuli, including eyebrow movement, head displacement, mouth opening, and chin displacement. Measures of chin and lip displacement or movement reliably distinguished stress, as the displacement was larger or faster in stressed versus unstressed syllables. For observers, chin movements contributed to the perception of stress beyond the contribution of lip movements. As with the speechreading of segmental information, talker characteristics and familiarity were shown to influence the speechreading potential of prosodic information.

Speechreading Improvement with Training

The variability in the results of speechreading studies raised the question of whether training could increase the information value of visual cues to speech perception. In Walden et al.'s (1977) study, 31 adults with postlingual hearing loss participated in intensive speechreading training focused on 20 English consonants – /p, t, k, f, θ, s, ʃ, b, d, g, v, ð, z, ʒ, m, n, w, r, j, l/ – that were presented in CV syllables with the vowel /ɑ/. Tasks required same-different discrimination judgments between pairs of syllables and identification of the syllables. Intensive and individualized training took place over 14 hours and included immediate feedback on response accuracy with repetition of a stimulus when the response was incorrect. Post-training data indicated an increased ability to separate the consonants into distinct visual categories; nine categories ultimately were identified: /p, b, m/; /f, v/; /θ, ð/; /s, z/; /ʃ, ʒ/; /t, d, n, k, g, j/; /w/; /r/; and /l/. The largest increases in accuracy following training were for (a) visual recognition of /r/, which increased from 36.1% to 88.6% accuracy and differentiated that consonant from /w/; (b) recognition of a unique category for /s, z/ (i.e., separating these sounds from a broader pretraining category including /ʃ, ʒ/); and (c) recognition of a nonlabial category /t, d, n, k, g, j/. The targets showing the most improvement may have been the result of the participants' increased ability to recognize the lip protrusion associated with /r/ and /ʃ, ʒ/.

This study by Walden et al. is frequently cited for the successful recognition performance it produced and for several particularly notable methodological contributions it made to subsequent perception training studies, including those with L2 learners as participants (e.g., Hardison, 2003). First, Walden et al. noted that the maximum improvement took place after about 5 hours of training. Second, the methodology underscored the role of familiarity with the talker as affecting performance. The participants in the study became very familiar with the articulation patterns of the three clinicians who provided their individualized training; however, the talker in the pre- and posttest had been unfamiliar. Third, the statistical criterion used for defining a visual category was a 75% within-group response rate, which the researchers considered relatively stringent for that type of study. Finally, it was recommended that individuals with hearing loss should increase segmental visual recognition skills to an optimal level before beginning sentence, contextual, and AV integration training (see Hardison, 2005b, 2018b; chapter 3 in this volume).

In a subsequent study, a significant increase in consonant recognition was observed after 7 hours of training with consonants in the frame /ɑ_ɑ/ for two training groups with hearing loss: one group received A-only input and one received V-only input (Walden et al., 1981). For the A-only training group, mean identification accuracy for /r/ increased from 83% to 97%, and for /l/ from 75% to 89%. For the V-only group, an increase occurred in both the number of visual categories and the reliability with which they were identified, although the gains in Walden et al. (1977) had been greater – a difference that the authors attributed to differences in the characteristics of the talkers in the two studies. Specifically, although /s, z/, /w/, /r/, and /l/ each had been visually distinguishable for the adult male talker in the Walden et al. (1977) study (e.g., mean posttest rates of 88.6% for /r/ and 93.4% for /l/), in the Walden et al. (1981) study, /w/ and /r/ formed a single visual category, and /s, z/ and /l/ were not visually distinguishable from other alveolar and velar consonants produced by the adult female talker. A further finding was that the separate V-only training and A-only training at the syllable level resulted in improvement in AV sentence recognition.

Role of Variability and Familiarity in Speechreading

Variability in speechreading can have several sources, including the speechreader population, the stimuli, and the talkers. Tye-Murray et al. (2016) suggested that individual differences affect the degree to which visual information enhances speech perception and that this may indicate a reduced ability to carry out the initial stage of extracting visual information.

Although there has been some variability in the composition of visual categories, speechreading studies have generally placed the bilabials in the same visual category (i.e., /p, b, m/) based on observers' inability to discriminate them visually from one another, coupled with the observers' ability to distinguish bilabials as a group visually from other consonants (e.g., Woodward & Barber, 1960). However, the use of more recent technology determined that differences in speechreading potential might even exist among the bilabials. In the first of two experiments, Mayer et al. (2011) analysed *orofacial* motion (i.e., motion related to the mouth and face) in a video (front and profile views) when a talker produced pseudowords containing the point vowels (/i, ɑ, u/) and the bilabial consonants. Visible differences occurred in the production of the bilabials regardless of the position in the carrier sentence where the word occurred or the angle of view. The second experiment involved AV presentation to 37 participants of the bilabials produced in sentence contexts with degraded audio. Bilabial perceptual identification accuracy ranged from 20% to 30%; accuracy was the poorest for /b/. Mayer et al. suggested that the resonance for the nasal /m/ and the voiceless burst for /p/ may have been more salient than the acoustic cues for /b/ in the *pink noise* condition (i.e., noise having more power at lower frequencies and less power at higher frequencies as compared to white noise).

From research findings and general observations it is apparent that variability also pertains to the characteristics of talkers, and that variability has an impact on the auditory intelligibility and visual discernibility of speech. Kricos and Lesner (1982) were ahead of their time in suggesting that teachers and clinicians should use a variety of talkers to evaluate the speechreading ability of individuals with hearing loss and to conduct speechreading training. In fact, talker variability was later recognized as an important factor in: (a) A-only speech perception for the general population (e.g., Johnson & Mullenix, 1997; Pisoni, 1997); (b) A-only perception training for L2 learners of English (e.g., Lively et al., 1993); and (c) AV perception training for L2 learners of English (Hardison, 2003; see also chapter 3).

Following episodic models of memory, talker-specific information is encoded in memory during auditory speech perception facilitating later recognition of a word spoken by a familiar voice (Nygaard, 2005; Pisoni, 1997). Because talker familiarity plays a role in the cognitive processing of speech (Conrey & Gold, 2006), varying the talker in an auditory perception task can decrease speech intelligibility for listeners and the speed with which word identification can be made. Similarly, changing talkers within a speechreading task decreases performance as compared to using the same talker (Yakel et al., 2000). Although variability is challenging for research design, including it makes possible the investigation of the observers' ability to understand a range of talkers and provides more ecological validity for results.

Talker variability is but one source of variability in the methodological details of speech perception studies, including those involving speechreading. The many sources of variability challenge researchers' ability to compare findings across studies and draw conclusions. This dilemma is captured in the abstract of Owens and Blazek's 1985 article, in which the authors stated that the results of their study were "in general agreement with other studies with respect to the visemes identified, provided it is acknowledged that changes can occur depending on variables such as talkers, stimuli, recording and viewing conditions, training procedures, and statistical criteria" (p. 381). In listing all these variables, Owens and Blazek were making the point that there was little basis left for comparison across studies! More recent research has continued to emphasize the difficulty in comparing studies because of differences in factors such as the type of masking noise (e.g., white, pink, a background of babble), the specific speech sounds investigated, talker gender, and other talker characteristics (e.g., Apoux & Bacon, 2004).

Crucially, as with voices, there is a strong role for familiarity in the discernibility of visual speech cues. The speech patterns of familiar talkers (e.g., relatives, close friends) are generally easier to speechread than those of strangers (Berger, 1972; Yakel et al., 2000). Becoming familiar with a talker through speechreading for 1 hour allows a perceiver to better understand that talker's speech in noise (Rosenblum et al., 2007). Berger (1972) reflected that for optimal understanding, the speechreader should know the language variety of the talker, as this has implications for communicative settings such as classrooms, where students may need some time to adjust to a teacher's language variety and speech patterns.

Maximizing Auditory Intelligibility and Visual Discernibility

The variability that exists in perception studies reflects the natural language environment. Perceivers must deal with the numerous dimensions along which variability can occur, often simultaneously. Given the many dimensions of variability with which perceivers must contend, a talker's particular constellation of articulatory features may be easier or harder to process. Researchers have examined the characteristics that make speech more or less intelligible. In the auditory modality, the following talker characteristics were determined to contribute to intelligible speech based on data from 10 male and 10 female adult native AE speakers: being female; using a relatively expanded vowel space; having precise articulation, especially of the point vowels (/i, ɑ, u/); producing a low degree of phonetic reduction; and, at the sentence level, using a relatively wide range in fundamental frequency (Bradlow et al., 1996). These characteristics form part of a talker's *articulatory setting*, which has been defined as the set of postural configurations and mechanics that serve as a framework for the vocal tract articulators to produce fluent and natural speech (e.g., Honikman, 1964; see also chapter 7).

Several of the characteristics that Bradlow et al. (1996) found to make speech more intelligible are also found in the speech of mothers to their infants (so-called motherese) and of L1 speakers to non-native speakers (so-called foreigner talk). Thus, the production of acoustically more extreme point vowels, representing an expanded vowel space, characterized the speech that 10 native-speaking mothers each of AE, Swedish, and Russian used to a comparable degree when speaking to their infants as compared to when they were speaking to other adults (Kuhl et al., 1997), as well as the speech that adult L1 British English speakers used when speaking to adult non-native speakers (Uther et al., 2007). Adjustments to speech may help infants and non-native speakers alike to separate one sound from other competing sounds.

Given that articulatory settings vary across talkers, variability in the contribution of visual cues from a talker's face to speechreading is not surprising. The determination of visual categories in research studies is subject to variable talker characteristics, including movement of the articulators (i.e., tongue, teeth, and lips) and coordinated movement of orofacial muscles (e.g., Kricos & Lesner, 1982; Owens & Blazek, 1985). Maximizing the visual discernibility of speech encompasses several factors under the control of the talker, including (a) articulatory skills; (b) verbal support strategies; (c) non-verbal support strategies; and (d) supplemental input (Lesner, 1988). Each is discussed in turn below.

Articulatory Skills

Lesner (1988) outlined the following articulatory skills contributing to intelligibility: slightly slower-than-normal speaking rate; clear and precise articulation to maximize contrasts involving the more visible articulators;

natural (vs. exaggerated) enunciation; flexibility of the speech organs; and awareness of the distortions that can be produced by undershooting the target articulation and by producing coarticulatory phenomena. Coarticulatory phenomena occur frequently in natural, connected speech; for example, production of the /n/ in *ten* in the phrase *ten bikes* as the bilabial /m/ results from anticipation of the bilabial /b/ in *bikes*. Lesner also pointed out that the visual discernibility of speech sounds could be enhanced by an absence of facial hair and hair that obscures movements of the forehead, eyebrows, and cheeks in addition to the visibility of the whole face (vs. just the mouth).

Developing flexibility of speech organs as an aspect of articulatory skill has been referred to as *mouth gymnastics* – a term suggested by Daniel Jones (1881–1967), who was known for the application of phonetics to language teaching, with reference to exercising the vocal organs to prepare them to articulate another language (Collins & Mees 2002, Lecture 13). This flexibility increases the discernibility of visual speech cues and could also have a role in teacher education and language learning (see chapters 7 and 8).

Studies examining the influence of speech rate on the visual discernibility of sounds generally used an artificially slowed presentation of speech to speechreaders; in doing so, only the rate was affected. However, in natural speech, the by-products of a slower rate also include lengthening the duration of individual speech sounds and adding pauses (Picheny et al., 1986). The presence of meaningful pauses can signal the end of a phrase and offer the speechreader time to process the information gleaned to that point before speech continues (Jacobs, 1982); more efficient speechreaders timed their eyeblinks to occur during visual pauses, which helped them to avoid loss of information (Lesner & Hardick, 1982).

Verbal Support Strategies

Verbal support strategies include the use of (a) more visually salient words (e.g., *baby* vs. *infant*); (b) more predictable sentence structures that follow a subject-verb-object word order as in active versus passive voice; (c) frequently occurring words with two or more syllables; and (d) short, declarative sentences (Lesner, 1988). Speechreading ability varies across individuals, and some sentences are easier to speechread than others, specifically those produced with the verbal support strategies identified by Lesner. According to research by MacLeod and Summerfield (1987), the easier sentences tend to be composed of words beginning with visually distinctive consonants, such as /b/ and /f/. In that study, about 70% of participants with normal hearing could correctly speechread the three keywords (shown in upper case) in the sentence *A BOY FELL from the WINDOW*, although only about 7% could identify the keywords in *Some STICKS were UNDER the TREE*; both sentences were presented in white noise. In the first sentence, the initial consonant of each keyword was either the bilabial stop /b/ (*boy*), the labiodental fricative /f/ (*fell*), or the labiovelar approximant /w/ (*window*). In the second sentence, the keywords began with the alveolar sounds /s/ (*sticks*) and /t/ (*tree*), or a vowel with a relatively neutral mouth shape (*under*). The first two sounds of a word are critical in establishing the initial cohort of possible word candidates (Fort et al., 2012; Hardison, 2005b, 2018b; Skipper, van Wassenhove, et al., 2007; Tyler, 1984); therefore, distinctive initial consonants may reduce the size of the visible cohort, leaving fewer lexical alternatives and facilitating word identification (see chapter 3).

Non-verbal Support and Supplemental Input Strategies

Lesner (1988) also identified non-verbal support strategies, such as appropriate facial expression, message-related gestures, and body movements. Supplemental input strategies included the use of hand signals, electronic displays, and tactile aids. Keeping these optimal talker characteristics in mind "may aid in screening 'good' from 'poor' talkers for the selection and training of oral interpreters, teachers of the hearing impaired, and other professionals who deal with hearing-impaired individuals" (Lesner, 1988, p. 96). To that list of the beneficiaries of good talkers we could add the general population, including L2 learners.

Observers' Perspectives and Strategies in Speech Processing

So far, the consideration of what contributes to successful speechreading has focused primarily on the characteristics of the stimuli and the talker; however, there is another important participant in the speech event: the observer. Word identification accuracy for congenitally deaf adults who rely on visual speech averages 45%–50%, within a range of 0%–80% (E.T. Auer & Bernstein, 2007). In contrast, adults with normal hearing generally demonstrate less speechreading ability, with an average of 20% accuracy for identifying words presented in sentences, but also with a considerable range in accuracy – from 0% to above 60% (e.g., Bernstein et al., 2000). Individuals with cochlear implants, despite having improved auditory abilities, may maintain a higher level of speechreading ability and AV integration performance as compared to normal hearing individuals (Rouger et al., 2007). For older adults with acquired hearing loss, the ability to integrate AV speech cues may increase with age and exceed the ability of age-matched adults with normal hearing (Tye-Murray et al., 2007). The auditory experiences of adults whose deafness is postlingual may contribute to the development of a normal neural network for speechreading (Suh et al., 2009).

AV speech identification is better than just the sum of A-only plus V-only speech identification; that is, it produces a *superadditive* benefit (e.g., Dias et al., 2021). In addition, although unisensory speech identification declines with age, compensatory changes in multisensory superadditivity may preserve AV speech identification in older adults. The superadditivity observed for AV presentations may be due to the simultaneous shaping of a single lexical representation versus the combining of distinct auditory and visual speech cues (Tye-Murray et al., 2016; Sommers, 2021). Tye-Murray et al. (2016) proposed that an AV percept is shaped by *reinforcement* and *complementarity*. Reinforcement occurs when both auditory and visual cues are available, allowing one to play a disambiguating role if needed; complementarity occurs when information from only one modality is available.

The contribution of AV speech cues is also evident in *spoken word recognition*, although early research in the field focused only on auditory input. Spoken word recognition refers to the computational processes by which listeners identify the acoustic-phonetic and/or phonological form of spoken words, and may be regarded as a form of pattern recognition (Pisoni et al., 1985). In contrast, *lexical access* refers to higher-level processes that are involved in the activation of the meaning(s) of words present in the listener's mental lexicon. The meaning of a word is accessed from the lexicon after its phonetic and/or phonological form is matched with a similar representation stored in memory. The process of spoken word recognition can also be visual, as in the case of speechreading, or auditory-visual.

Recognizing a spoken word occurs as a continuous process of perceiving and analysing the incoming sound as it is produced, to the point when sufficient information has been processed to narrow down perception to one word. As more and more stimulus information is perceived, words of similar form are activated in the perceiver's mental lexicon as potential word candidates to match what is being perceived (Luce & Pisoni, 1998;

Marslen-Wilson & Tyler, 1980). The word recognition process entails a competition among the potential word candidates, and recognition occurs when one word achieves the best match to the input, even before the whole word has been produced. Auditorily, words are generally recognized faster when competition is minimized, as it is in relatively sparse *lexical neighbourhoods*. A lexical neighbourhood consists of words that are similar in form to the target word. Neighbourhoods are described as having some level of density. Auditorily, neighbourhood density is determined by the number of words that differ from a target by a one-phoneme addition, deletion, or substitution (Luce, 1986) – for example, the lexical set that includes *pip*, *pep*, *prep*, *peppy*, *preppy*, *pap*, *pappy*, *pup*, *puppy*, and so on. For the visual modality, estimates of lexical neighbourhood size are based on the visual confusability of words (e.g., *pet* and *bet* look similar). Competition among word candidates is reduced when the target is more distinctive than, or stands out from, other words in its lexical neighbourhood. Deaf adults, using only visual information, and hearing adults, using only auditory information, can identify words in sparser neighbourhoods (i.e., having fewer similar words) more accurately than words in denser neighbourhoods (i.e., having multiple similar words; e.g., E.T. Auer, 2002; Mattys et al., 2002; Strand & Sommers, 2011), suggesting that the perceptual and cognitive properties underlying word recognition are not specific to one sensory modality (i.e., they are not *domain-specific*).

Just as talkers vary in the visual discernibility of their lip movements, observers may vary in the perceptual strategies they use in comprehending speech in situations where the visual modality offers the best or perhaps the only information; and these strategies may be better suited to some talkers than to others. The question arises as to where observers look on the face of talkers for speech information with and without an auditory component. Although a talker's lip movements may be the primary source of linguistic input on the face, other areas may also contribute valuable information for speech processing. Eye-tracking data from one Japanese-speaking and one English-speaking observer showed they spent 45%–70% of each AV stimulus presentation in their respective L1s gazing at the talker's eyes, leading Vatikiotis-Bateson et al. (1998) to conclude that phonetically relevant information may be distributed on the talker's face beyond the mouth region as a result of changes in the orofacial muscles during articulation and that observers may detect "well-learned, phonetically correlated events" (p. 938; see also chapter 4).

Eye-tracking data from a speechreading task (with no audio input) involving native AE speakers showed that the observers' eye gazes were mostly directed towards the talker's mouth (Lansing & McConkie, 1999). Gazes in the middle region of the face accounted for 37% of the data – gazes that would have been assigned to one of the eye regions in the Vatikiotis-Bateson et al. (1998) study. Observers' eye gazes directed towards the nose might represent visual attention to a central feature of the face with subsequent shifts of attention to other areas as needed (Hardison, 2003).

In a later study involving V-only and AV conditions, Lansing and McConkie (2003) demonstrated that by the time a talker's face appeared on the screen, observers had often shifted their eye gazes from the centre of the screen, where the nose would appear, towards regions where they anticipated the talker's eyes or mouth would appear. The talker's eye area attracted attention before and after speaking, referred to as the *eye primacy effect*. In 30%–50% of the cases, the observers' eye gazes shifted towards the region where the talker's mouth would appear, termed the *information source attraction effect*; in other words, visual attention appeared to be drawn to a location where observers anticipated information relevant for the task. The attraction effect may be stronger in more challenging speech environments, such as those involving a degraded or missing audio signal, or situations with observers who are not familiar with the talker or are learners of the talker's language (see chapters 4 and 5).

In communicative contexts, variability is present in both the visual information available in the speech of different talkers and in the strategies observers use to attempt to process that speech information. Conrey and Gold (2006) used the technique of *ideal observer analysis* to quantify the amount of physical information available in the stimuli of a perceptual task. This measure contributed to the definition of the ideal observer as one who produces the best possible performance on a particular task given the limitation in the amount of available information (Geisler, 2004). Stimuli in the study were limited to eight familiar monosyllabic words of equal frequency in AE following a consonant-vowel-consonant (CVC) pattern: *far, gave, job, house, put, should, thought*, and *voice*. The initial consonants of these stimuli included one bilabial /p/, two labiodentals /f, v/, one interdental /θ/, two sibilants /ʃ, dʒ/, and two nonlabials: velar /g/ and /h/. Stimuli from eight talkers (four female, four male) were then presented in a V-only perception task. Observers selected the word they thought had been produced from the list of eight words and received auditory feedback to indicate if the response was correct. There was considerable variability in word identification according to the talker.

Conrey and Gold (2006) identified several possible observer strategies. One strategy was to look only at the lower half of a talker's face, including the area from the bottom of the nose to the bottom of the chin. Alternatively, observers might look only at the talker's mouth (from the top of the upper lip to the bottom of the lower lip and from corner to corner). A comparison of the performance of human observers and computer simulations using the ideal observer analysis approach revealed variability in V-only speech perception due to differences in both the physical information available across talkers and the observers' perceptual strategies, which can be more efficient for speechreading some talkers as compared to others.

If observers find that the initial target of their eye gazes towards a given talker is not sufficiently helpful, they might seek information from other areas of the face to complete a task. In this process, familiarity plays a role. In cross-cultural situations, experience with a talker's language and culture may determine the area of the talker's face that an observer predicts will be the most beneficial (see chapter 4). This area can then become the initial target of the observer's eye gaze on subsequent occasions and should thus allow more attentional resources to be directed towards understanding the speech. Gaze may also be shifted strategically towards other areas of the face as needed.

Hardison (2006) conducted a two-phase experiment to explore the influence of observers' familiarity with talkers' faces and voices on the processing of speech and retention of information in memory. In the familiarization phase, L2 speakers of English (L1 Korean) with upper-intermediate aural/oral skills viewed recorded AV presentations of female native AE speakers producing a series of frequently occurring words. During this phase, participants saw the entire face of the talkers. This process was repeated for 10 days to ensure familiarity. In the test session involving a word identification task, participants were divided into four groups, each presented with a different stimulus condition in noise (–5 dB): AV-whole face (the entire face was visible), AV-lower face (from the bottom of the nose to the bottom of the chin), AV-eyes (eyes and upper cheek areas visible from mid-forehead to the supratip of the nose), and A-only (voice only, black screen). A control group for whom all talkers were unfamiliar was assigned to each stimulus condition and participated only in the test session.

Results indicated a statistically significant effect of talker; overall, identification accuracy was greater for words produced by familiar talkers (Hardison, 2006). There was also a significant interaction between talker familiarity and stimulus condition. When the talker was familiar, a partial visual stimulus was more informative; specifically, (a) the lower face (mouth and jaw) conveyed task-related information that was comparable to seeing the whole face, and (b) more information was conveyed by the eyes and upper cheek areas as compared to the A-only condition (no visual cues).

To this point in the chapter, multimodal speech has concerned auditory and visual input; however, speech input can also be tactile (Sparks et al., 1978). The next section considers the role of the sense of touch for individuals who can see and hear, those with hearing loss who may rely on cochlear implants, those who can neither hear nor see, and those asked to use tactile information from different sources.

Speech Processing Involving Tactile Input

Although sighted individuals may not appear to need tactile input to understand speech, there is some evidence that it may offer a benefit. In a study involving visual and tactual[8] perception, Fairhurst et al. (2018) asked sighted participants to determine whether the vertical bar in inverted T-shaped stimuli (made of raised plastic bars mounted on heavy paper) was shorter or longer than the horizontal bar in both clear-cut and ambiguous cases. Vision provided a more accurate basis for perceptual judgments overall; however, despite confidence ratings being higher based on vision for clear-cut cases, the sense of touch provided a higher level of confidence in ambiguous cases – a phenomenon the authors referred to as "fact checking by touch."

Integration of auditory and tactile input appears to follow a pattern similar to that of auditory and visual input. For example, if AV cues are congruent (i.e., they represent the same sound), perceptual identification accuracy may be enhanced; however, if cues are recorded and edited to produce incongruent input, such as seeing a talker's articulatory gesture for /ga/ but hearing /ba/, a perceptual illusion (e.g., /da/) may be experienced – a phenomenon known as the McGurk–MacDonald effect (McGurk & MacDonald, 1976; see also chapter 2).[9] Similarly, manual contact with a talker's lip movements when presented with incongruent auditory input can elicit an auditory-tactual illusory effect (Fowler & Dekle, 1991). Both phenomena support the multimodal nature of speech perception.

Tactile input is also beneficial for those with hearing loss. Many cochlear implant users can understand speech in generally quiet conditions but encounter problems in the presence of background noise due, in part, to limited transmission of low-frequency sound information, especially within a frequency range of 20–500 Hz. Fletcher et al. (2018) trained normal-hearing participants to listen to speech in noise, designed to simulate a cochlear-implant experience. Concurrent *vibro-tactile* stimulation (i.e., vibration) of the fingertip provided *temporal envelope* information (i.e., a low frequency amplitude modulation conveying segmental and suprasegmental information) and voicing information extracted from the speech-in-noise material. Prior to training, the tactile stimulation had improved the intelligibility of speech in multitalker noise as compared to no tactile input. Following 3 days of training (a total of 30 min), the improvement increased.

For individuals with both vision and hearing loss, manual tactile information from placing a hand on a talker's face to glean speech information – known as the Tadoma method (Alcorn, 1932) – can be successful with training. Gick et al. (2008) used the Tadoma method to investigate the contribution of tactile information to speech perception by untrained perceivers with normal speaking and hearing skills. A total of 14 English obstruents (six stops and eight fricatives) was presented in the frame /a_a/ in two bimodal conditions: auditory-tactile (AT) and visual-tactile (VT), where the tactile information came from the experimenter's face. To use the Tadoma method, each participant (a) placed the index finger just above the experimenter's mandibular ridge (located in the front portion of the mandible or jawbone); (b) spread the other three fingers out below the ridge across the experimenter's throat; (c) placed the palm over the jaw and chin; and (d) placed the thumb lightly on the experimenter's lips. In the AT condition, the speech signal was partially obscured by white noise and participants closed their eyes. In the VT condition, the noise completely obscured the speech signal and participants kept their eyes open and looked at the experimenter. After each trial, participants repeated the stimulus aloud. Separate control trials were conducted using A-only or V-only input. Gick et al. found a significant perceptual improvement of almost 10% in both the AT and VT conditions. There was individual variability in terms of which combination of modalities was favoured. Those who benefited more from tactile information in one cross-modal condition tended to benefit less from tactile information in the other condition.

Tactile speech information may also come from other sources. Participants were more likely to identify a stop consonant in a CV syllable as aspirated if they felt light inaudible puffs of air on the back of the right hand or neck while simultaneously hearing the syllable (Gick & Derrick, 2009). The bilabial stops /p/ and /b/ were presented in white noise in one block, with /t/ and /d/ in another block. The puff of air on the skin (i.e., an aero-tactile stimulus) would be compatible with the puff of air articulated with voiceless stops in this context.

In a subsequent visual-tactile experiment, with no auditory input, participants saw videos of faces producing /pa/ and /ba/, both alone and in conjunction with puffs of air directed towards each participant's *suprasternal* notch (a visible dip or depression at the centre of the top of the sternum) (Bicevskis et al., 2016). The air puffs occurred both synchronously and at different temporal intervals up to 300 ms before and after the stop release. Overall, in a V-only condition, participants were significantly more likely to identify the syllable as /ba/; when the air puffs were present, participants were more likely to identify it as /pa/. When the visual stimulus was /pa/, the highest /pa/ response rate (65%) occurred when the stimulus onset asynchrony (SOA) was 50 ms; when the visual stimulus was /ba/, the highest rate of /pa/ response (67%) occurred at 200 ms SOA. Analysis uncovered an asymmetric temporal window for visual-tactile integration such that a significantly greater number of /pa/ responses occurred from −200 ms (tactile stimulus leads the visual stimulus) to 300 ms (tactile stimulus follows the visual stimulus) as compared to the V-only condition. This is a wider window of integration as compared to AV stimuli (e.g., 0 to 180 ms in Munhall et al., 1996; −30 to 170 ms in van Wassenhove et al., 2007) and auditory-tactile stimuli (e.g., −50 to 200 ms in Gick et al., 2010). In Gick et al. (2010), the maximum delay of 200 ms, at which integration occurred, corresponded to the maximum time window for perception of an actual speech-related puff of air (Derrick et al., 2009).

Chapter 1 in Review

Looking back to the chapter's opening epigraph, which noted that "speech perception is at least a bimodal process" (McGurk, 1981, p. 336), the phrase that should stand out to readers now is "at least." The findings of the studies reported in this chapter involved the integration of auditory-visual, auditory-(aero-)tactile, and visual-(aero-)tactile stimuli, emphasizing the impacts of stimulus, talker, and contextual factors on the contribution of sensory cues to the perceptual outcome. In contrast to early notions that speech is perceived as an auditory signal, complemented when needed (e.g., to deal with noise and/or hearing loss) by information from other modalities, Bicevskis et al. (2016) proposed that in speech "no mode is necessarily primary, but instead context and signal strength always apply" (p. 3532). Among the context factors affecting perception of speech are the facial and other non-verbal features that are interactively processed with the auditory signal.

This chapter has set the stage for a theme of variability that will continue throughout the book with implications for the improvement of L2 learners' perceptual accuracy through multimodal input and the training of language teachers to maximize that input. Chapter 2 considers the development of multimodal speech perception from infancy to adulthood for both native speakers and L2 learners.

Chapter 1 Notes

1. Gutzmann (1865–1922) was considered the founder of *phoniatrics* (Kuczkowski et al., 2015), which is the study and treatment of the organs involved in speech production.
2. I thank Professor Senta Goertler (personal communication, 19 June 2023) for checking this translation and pointing out that *optische* might be expressed today as *visuelle* (visual) in this context.
3. The phonetic symbols /ɑ/ (a low back unrounded vowel) and /a/ (a low front unrounded vowel) appear throughout the book. When reporting the findings of a study, the choice of symbol follows that used in the original publication; however, in some studies /a/ may have appeared solely because of typographical considerations and so the precise vowel sound is not known. Some American linguists do not distinguish /ɑ/ from /a/ and use either symbol for a low unrounded vowel distinct from /æ/ (e.g., *hat*) (Pullum & Ladusaw, 1996).
4. The frequency of a phenomenon, such as a sound wave, that has regular periodic variations can be expressed in Hertz (Hz). The number of Hz represents the number of cycles per second.
5. Summerfield (1992) and others recommended use of the term *speechreading* instead of *lipreading*. *Lipreading* refers to extracting speech information from a talker's articulatory gestures alone. *Speechreading* has a far broader scope and includes lipreading as well as gleaning information about what a person is saying from observation of the tongue, teeth, eyes, facial expressions, gestures, and so forth, and may include audition.
6. In the early speechreading literature, Fisher (1968) proposed that the term *viseme*, which he described as a shortened form of the phrase *visual phoneme*, could be used to refer to any set of sounds within which the articulatory movements were not visually distinguishable. In other works (e.g., Woodward & Barber, 1960), this set of sounds was described as *homophenous*; for example, the bilabial consonants /p/, /b/, and /m/ often constituted one group, and the labiodentals /f/ and /v/ constituted a separate group. However, Mills and Thiem (1980) argued that the features that differentiate the visual groups are not the same as those that differentiate phonemes, and that homophenous groups are not established according to invariable and independent criteria but rather according to statistical criteria

determined from perception experiments. Therefore, Mills and Thiem recommended the term *visual category*, which is used in this book.

7. The point vowels occupy the extreme positions of the vowel space: the high front vowel (/i/) produced with lip spreading, the low and most open-jaw vowel /ɑ/, and the high back and most rounded vowel /u/. Because of their lip positions, these vowels are often used in speechreading and other perception experiments to represent the parameters of articulatory gestures for vowels. The sounds /tʃ/ (voiceless) and /dʒ/ (voiced) are palato-alveolar affricates produced by making a closure for the stop portion (/t/ or /d/) and releasing it into a fricative /ʃ/ or /ʒ/. These sounds may exhibit visually salient lip protrusion.
8. *Tactual* refers specifically to the sense of touch, whereas *tactile* can refer to the sense of touch as well as to something tangible or perceptible.
9. In this book, I follow the example of some other recent publications (e.g., Hickok et al., 2018) in recognizing the contribution of John MacDonald to the discovery of the perceptual illusion by referring to it as the McGurk–MacDonald effect (rather than solely the McGurk effect; see also MacDonald, 2017).

Chapter 2

Multimodal Input in Language Development and Processing

Babies were to be presented with videofilms of talking heads .... In two of them [the films], lips and voices were coordinated in perfect synchrony, ba-voice/ ba-lips, ga-voice/ga-lips. The other two comprised the mismatching combinations, ba-voice/ga-lips and vice versa .... However, when we watched the films for the first time, instead of perceiving a conflict and "seeing through" the dubbed sections of film, we heard entirely new sounds! To ba-voice/ga-lips, instead of conflict, we heard "da"; to ga-voice/ba-lips we variously heard "ba" or "bga" .... We had stumbled across a previously unidentified phenomenon – hearing by eye.

– McGurk (1988, p. 9)[1]

*****

Background

One of the best-known phenomena in cognitive psychology is the McGurk–MacDonald effect. This perceptual illusion was discovered during the preparation of stimuli for experiments in a lab directed by Harry McGurk, whose early work focused on unimodal visual perception by infants (e.g., McGurk, 1972). The experiments referenced in the epigraph above were designed to see if infants would react differently to matched (congruent) versus mismatched (incongruent) AV speech stimuli. The following section, which presents different views on the development of *intermodal* relationships (i.e., coordination of information from a single event through multiple modalities) in infants, provides some background to those plans. This is followed by a description of infant responses to spatial displacement as a foundation for the discussion of the infant responses in the lab to the mismatched speech cues. After this look to the past at work focused on infants, the chapter continues with the McGurk-MacDonald effect in adult native and non-native speakers of languages, and it concludes with observations on the contributions of behavioural research and technological advances to an understanding of some of the neurophysiological processes involved in AV speech integration.

Views on Intermodal Relationships in Infants

There are different views on the development of intermodal relationships. On the one hand, the *primitive unity* position (e.g., Bower, 1974; Gibson, 1966) posits an initial unity of the senses for the human infant: perception is *amodal*, that is, it makes use of information that is common or redundant across multiple senses, such as auditory and visual (Reisberg et al., 1987). Subsequent development of the infant's perceptual skills increases sensory differentiation. In a speech event, amodal information involves changes in AV synchrony, tempo, rhythm, and intonation (intensity changes) that are common to facial movements and speech sounds and are important for perceptual accuracy (Bahrick & Lickliter, 2000). By attending to temporal synchrony, the sights and sounds involved in someone speaking convey relatively consistent sensory information to produce a unified and coherent percept. Bahrick and Lickliter proposed that amodal information is salient, influences selective attention, and develops early in infancy, contributing to perceptual and cognitive development. A commonly encountered example of amodal perception is the *ventriloquism effect*, in which a person utters sounds so that they seem to come from somewhere else. This can be observed when entertainers appear to make their voices come from a ventriloquial figure, or "dummy," whose mouth is moved manually in sync with speech uttered by the entertainer but with little to no visible human mouth movement. The effect also occurs in a movie theatre when the audience perceives the sounds as coming from the images (e.g., of actors) on the screen, not from the loudspeakers positioned around the room. Visual estimates of location are typically more accurate than auditory estimates, so vision generally determines the perception of location, consistent with the *modality-appropriate hypothesis* (Welch & Warren, 1980), which posits that the most appropriate or reliable modality for a given task will contribute more to the percept than a less reliable one.

In contrast to the primitive unity position, the *integrationist* view states that the sensory systems have independent origins and that integration develops through the coordination of sensory experiences (e.g., Birch & Lefford, 1967). Data from several perception experiments involving infants, summarized in McGurk and MacDonald (1978), tended to support the integrationist position; however, the authors proposed that because the experiments they cited had used relatively arbitrary sight-sound combinations with little ecological validity (e.g., combinations of red circles and a clicking sound, which infants would unlikely experience in their natural environment), a better test of the likelihood of primitive perceptual unity in neonates might be the presentation of naturally occurring sight-sound combinations. The human face and voice constitute a natural multimodal stimulus that is salient to the species; therefore, evidence of neonates' primitive perceptual unity might emerge in their response to violations (e.g., spatial displacement) of the expected multimodal unity of this complex stimulus.

Infant Responses to Spatial Displacement

To explore the primitive unity hypothesis, Aronson and Rosenbloom (1971) conducted an experiment in which eight infants 30–55 days old looked at their mothers who stood about 24 in. (60.96 cm) in front of them behind a glass window. The mother's voice was projected from two speakers, one on each side of the infant. In the first stage of the experiment, each mother spoke to her infant with the speakers in balance, which localized her voice in the centre of the window. In the second stage, one of the speakers was completely dominant so that the mother's voice appeared to emanate from the speaker either to the left or the right of the infant. In doing so, her voice was spatially displaced from her face, which reportedly made the infants visibly distressed. These findings were interpreted as evidence that infant perception occurs within a common AV space.

Aronson and Rosenbloom's (1971) conclusion was challenged by McGurk and Lewis (1974) in a study involving 35 infants, ages 1, 4, and 7 months, who were exposed to modifications of the normal spatial relationship between the voice of each infant's mother and her face, which was located about 49 in. (124.46 cm) away from them. All of the infants primarily oriented visually towards the mother regardless of the location of her voice. Most of the infants' head turning occurred when face and voice were spatially dislocated; however, only for the 4- and 7-month-olds was the direction of head turning significantly related to the direction from which the voice emanated. There was no reported evidence of infant distress resulting from the violations of any pre-existing expectation for face and voice to occupy the same spatial location. McGurk and Lewis concluded that their findings supported progressive development of the integration between sensory systems that are relatively independent in the initial stages of life, consistent with the Piagetian view of the onset of coordination between vision and audition at about 2–4 months of age followed by rapid development of sensory integration (Piaget, 1952).

Subsequent research in McGurk's lab also demonstrated that during the first year of life, infants could detect a change in a complex (e.g., auditory-visual) stimulus whenever a change was introduced to the information being presented to only one of the senses (McGurk, 1988). However, the question remained as to how the infants were processing the stimuli. McGurk outlined three options for the processing of the auditory and visual components of stimuli: (a) the components were processed in an undifferentiated manner; (b) the components were processed in parallel as separate but unrelated streams of information; or (c) the components were processed in a parallel and coordinated manner. McGurk concluded that in addition to testing the effects of spatial dislocation on infants, human faces and voices might also be useful stimuli to test the differentiation and integration of simultaneously presented auditory and visual information involving lip movements. Having established some background for the findings summarized in this chapter's epigraph, we now consider how the infants responded to the mismatched speech cues it described.

Infant Responses to Mismatched AV Speech Cues

The films described in the epigraph were presented to infants whose attentional and other behavioural responses were recorded (McGurk, 1988; McGurk & MacDonald, 1978). It was hypothesized that if infants could both differentiate and coördinate the auditory and visual components of speech, they would exhibit different behaviours towards matched versus mismatched stimuli. Results revealed an important effect of an infant's age on response behaviour. *Prelingual* infants (i.e., those who had not yet acquired language) were equally attentive to both matched and mismatched speech cues; that is, they did not demonstrate an awareness of the relationship between a talker's speech sounds and the associated articulations. The youngest child to provide any evidence of such an awareness was about 18 months of age and had already acquired some basic speech. By 3 years of age, children began to show lipreading ability, as evidenced by partial sensitivity to AV speech illusions, although they did not appear as susceptible to the perceptual influence of lip movements as adults. As compared to 3-year-olds, 7-year-olds showed somewhat more visual bias in processing speech but still much less than adults, and they responded mostly to what was expressed by a talker's voice rather than the talker's face. In sum, participants demonstrated relatively little sensitivity to the phonetic associations of lip movements during infancy, with awareness increasing throughout early childhood to adulthood that McGurk (1988) attributed to experience participating in interactions.

However, in a later study, prelingual infants at 5 months of age, also from an English-language environment, showed sensitivity to AV discordant speech cues (Rosenblum et al., 1997). In that study, infants were *gaze-habituated* to the AV syllable /va/; that is, the habituation stimulus was presented repeatedly until infants became disinterested, exhibiting a corresponding decline in visual attention. Then two different dishabituation stimulus combinations were presented: auditory /ba/–visual /va/ (which may be perceived by adults as /va/) and auditory /da/–visual /va/ (which may be perceived by adults as /da/). The habituation/dishabituation process depends on the tendency of infants to look longer at unusual or unexpected stimuli than familiar ones. Rosenblum et al. reported that infants' mean looking time to the dishabituation stimulus pair of auditory /ba/–visual /va/ was not significantly longer than that for AV /va/; however, their looking time to auditory /da/–visual /va/ was significantly longer as compared to AV /va/, suggesting that the infants were able to discriminate these auditory and visual cues in a manner similar to adults.

The remainder of this chapter presents evidence of infant gaze behaviour in the early stages of development, how adults process discordant speech in their native and non-native languages, and what multimodal input tells us about the neurophysiological processing of speech.

Early Development of Intermodal Processing

Some sensitivity to relationships between lip movements and speech sounds develops within the first year of life (e.g., Dodd, 1987; Meltzoff & Kuhl, 1994). Blind infants babble less than sighted infants after the first 6 months (Mills, 1987), implying that observed lip movements are an important source of stimulation. Dodd (1979) discovered an awareness of the congruence between lip movements and speech sounds in infants as young as 3 months old. They attended significantly less to an out-of-synchrony AV presentation of nursery rhymes than to an in-synchrony presentation. Between 4 and 12 months of age, infants' babbling patterns were modified by AV (vs. A-only) speech input such that those receiving AV input increased the number and length of utterances containing consonants, and some infants silently imitated lip movements; by 19 months of age, toddlers could lipread familiar words (Dodd, 1987).

Imitation of speech sounds begins early. In Meltzoff and Moore's (1977, 1993) studies, infants only 12 to 21 days old imitated adult mouth movements, such as tongue protrusion, mouth opening, and lip protrusion, leading the researchers to propose that a *supramodal* network combines information about movements (i.e., articulatory gestures) that infants see and those that they make, and that the two types of movement are subject to monitoring by *proprioception* (i.e., a talker's sense of the position and movement of the articulators in the vocal tract). In this view, neonatal imitation is mediated by an active intermodal mapping process.

In a subsequent study by Kuhl and Meltzoff (1984), using a preferential gaze procedure, 4-month-old infants demonstrated sensitivity to AV correspondences when they were shown two images side-by-side of a talker's face articulating the vowels /i/ and /u/ while the talker's voice matching one of the vowels was presented auditorily. Infants looked longer at the face that matched the sound. In a second experiment, the auditory stimuli were altered to remove the spectral information that is needed to identify the vowels. The resulting stimuli were *pure tones* (tones of a consistent frequency and amplitude) of the same duration and alignment to the visual stimulus as the original vowel. In this second experiment, the same effect on gaze duration did not occur, indicating the infants' sensitivity to the relationship between spectral information – which is dependent on articulatory changes – and visual speech information. The infants' ability to recognize AV correspondences in the articulation of speech sounds and to imitate speech sounds was taken as evidence in support of the intermodal acquisition of speech.

The above findings were replicated by Walton and Bower (1993), who presented 6- to 8-month-olds with a face articulating /u/ paired with three different sounds: /u/, which created a familiar matched combination; /i/, which created a mismatched "impossible" combination; and /y/ (a high front rounded vowel occurring in French), which created a possible AV combination but with a novel sound. Infants preferred the matched (i.e., with auditory /u/) and possible (i.e., with auditory /y/) pairs over the impossible pair (i.e., with auditory /i/). In a similar study, Legerstee (1990) presented matched and mismatched AV stimuli to different groups of 3- to 4-month-olds. Only those who had been exposed to the matched AV stimulus combinations for the vowels /ɑ/ and /u/ imitated the vowels.

Development of Visual Attention to Speech Cues and Faces

A great deal of development takes place during the first year of life in both face and speech perception. During that time, infants undergo a process of *perceptual narrowing* or *attunement* as their ability to discriminate speech stimuli beyond those in their ambient environment declines (Werker & Tees, 1984). Does the same process apply to faces, which might impact the processing of visual speech cues?

In a recent study, the ability of 50 German Caucasian infants to discriminate among Caucasian faces, Asian faces, and Cantonese speech tones was tested at 6 months and then at 9 months of age (Krasotkina et al., 2021). At 6 months of age, infants could discriminate among all stimuli (faces and tones); by 9 months, however, they could no longer discriminate among Asian faces or Cantonese tones but continued to be able to discriminate among Caucasian faces. Krasotkina et al. concluded that the infants had undergone perceptual narrowing for both faces and speech when they were 6–9 months of age, and they interpreted this as support for a domain-general, or modality-neutral, theory of perceptual narrowing in both face and speech perception.

During the first year, development also occurs in terms of gaze-following behaviour and selective attention to the visible speech cues of a talking face that help prepare the human infant for language development. There are different opinions about the age at which infants develop the ability to follow gaze. Establishing joint attention is important developmentally because it helps in understanding others' thoughts and intentions (e.g., Gustafsson et al., 2015). In addition, gaze-following behaviour has been strongly correlated with language scores for 18-month-olds (Brooks & Meltzoff, 2005). D'Entremont et al. (1997) concluded that gaze-following behaviour occurs as early as 3 months of age based on observations that 73% of infants ages 3–6 months shifted their gaze in conjunction with the movement of an adult who turned her head intermittently to talk to a puppet. Brooks and Meltzoff (2005) observed that infants 10 and 11 months of age followed adult head turns significantly more often when the adult's eyes were open versus closed, but this feature did not affect the responses of 9-month-olds.

In a study by Lewkowicz and Hansen-Tift (2012), infants' attention to a talker's mouth increased around the age of 6–8 months, coinciding with the emergence of canonical babbling, but decreased again around the end of the first year of life. By attending to the mouth of a talking face, infants gained access to visual speech cues that allowed them at 4–6 months of age to discriminate between languages; however, Weikum et al. (2007) determined that only infants in a bilingual environment retained this perceptual sensitivity at 8 months of age. Other factors might also drive children to look towards the mouth versus the eyes of a talking face. For example, Król (2018) noted that when speech was presented in noise, toddlers between 17 and 35 months of age paid more attention to a talker's mouth versus the eyes, and attention to the mouth correlated with higher word recognition proficiency.

Pons et al. (2015) investigated the influence of age and the ambient language environment on selective attention to the mouth of a talker by 4-, 8-, and 12-month-old Catalan and Spanish monolingual and bilingual infants. Monolinguals at 4 months old looked more at the eyes than the mouth but reversed this pattern at 8 months by attending more to the mouth in response to both native and non-native speech. At 12 months old, however, they looked more at the mouth than the eyes, although it was only in response to non-native speech. In contrast, infants in a bilingual environment at 4 months old looked equally at the eyes and mouth of a talking face, shifting more to the mouth than the eyes at 8 months, and continuing this pattern at 12 months. At all ages, the infants in a bilingual environment showed similar response patterns to both native and non-native speech. Because of their bilingual environment, the infants were able to exploit AV speech cues earlier and longer than monolingual infants.

In contrast, when Morin-Lessard et al. (2019) investigated the influence of children's ages (5 months to 5 years) and language background (monolinguals vs. bilinguals) on their attention to talking faces, patterns of attention were similar for monolinguals and bilinguals, and in response to a native and a non-native talker. Based on the data collected using a remote eye tracker, 5-month-olds showed balanced attention to the talker's eyes and mouth, but children up to 5 years old tended to be most interested in the mouth. Children showed large but stable individual variability in their face-scanning patterns across different talkers, and their allocation of attention to talking faces changed with age.

The ability of infants to observe talking faces is important for the development of speech perception and production. This ability was put at risk during the COVID-19 pandemic. As Lewkowicz (2021) pointed out, infants cannot access visible speech cues if talkers outside the home are wearing masks, as was required in many places during the height of the pandemic; consequently, Lewkowicz recommended an emphasis on as much face-to-face interaction as possible for infants within the home to attempt to compensate for the lost input opportunities outside the home.

The McGurk–MacDonald Effect in L1 English

McGurk (1988) observed that an awareness of the association between lip movements and speech sounds increased throughout childhood to adulthood as a result of interaction experiences. So are adults sensitive to discrepant, or mismatched, AV speech cues?

McGurk and MacDonald (1976) presented adult native speakers of British English with CV syllables produced by a female voice involving the bilabial and velar stops: /ba/, /pa/, /ga/, and /ka/. These were dubbed onto her filmed lip movements of these syllables to create matched and mismatched combinations, such as /ka/-lips and /pa/-voice. The participants' task was to watch the film and repeat what they had heard. Auditory intelligibility averaged 99%. Responses in the AV condition fell into four categories: (a) responses that matched the auditory cue (i.e., correct responses); (b) those that matched the visual cue; (c) *fused* responses (i.e., those that included a new element not present in either cue); and (d) *combination* responses (i.e., those that included elements of the auditory and visual cues). The majority of responses (81%) to /ka/-lips and /pa/-voice were *ta* (i.e., fused). In contrast, 44% of the responses to the combination of /pa/-lips and /ka/-voice represented a combination, such as *paka*, and 37% matched the visual cue *pa*. A similar pattern of responses occurred for the voiced consonants.

The McGurk–MacDonald effect also occurred at the sentence level (McGurk, 1988). When McGurk's voice uttering *My bab pope me pu brive* was dubbed onto his lip movements for *My dad taught me to drive*, the AV percept was reported as *My dad taught me to drive.*[2] In that sentence, the consonants that differed between modalities were the stops (e.g., /b/ in *bab* matched with /d/ in *dad*), similar to the CV stimuli used in McGurk and MacDonald (1976).

A similar visual bias was observed in the identification of vowels presented in a synthesized /bVd/ continuum (i.e., on which the vowel progressed from /i/ to /a/ and then to /u/) modelled on the speech of an adult male speaker of British English who also provided the recordings for the visual component (Summerfield & McGrath, 1984). Participants were instructed to report what they heard. Responses showed a bias towards identifying the acoustic vowel as one that was more like the visual articulation; for example, when the visual component was *booed* /bud/, the average response favoured the *booed* end of the continuum. Visual bias occurred even for perceivers who reported detecting intermodal conflict. The size of the effect was related to the amount of physical difference between the visible configuration of the talker's lips and the configuration that would be expected to accompany the acoustic vowel that was presented.

Around the same time as the publication of McGurk and MacDonald (1976), Dodd (1977) reported the ability of 12-year-olds to repeat CVC words presented to them in white noise under different stimulus conditions: AV in synchrony; AV out of synchrony; A-only; V-only; and mismatched AV input. Visual information in matched AV syllables resulted in fewer errors for bilabial, labiodental, and interdental consonants than for other more posteriorly articulated consonants. When AV inputs were mismatched, more errors occurred than in the unimodal conditions, resulting in some responses that combined information from both modalities, such as *towel* in response to the presentation of auditory *tough* and visual *hole*.

Welch and Warren (1980) proposed that experimentally induced intersensory discordance reduces or eliminates redundancy between the modalities; in doing so, it tags the information from each modality in order to help evaluate its contribution to the perceptual outcome. However, there are limits to the integration of discrepant cues. The next section describes the conditions that can affect the occurrence of the McGurk–MacDonald effect.

Factors Affecting the McGurk–MacDonald Effect

Since the publication of the first McGurk–MacDonald effect study in 1976, decades of studies have uncovered variability in the strength with which individuals experience the illusion. In fact, the pattern of responses in the first study differed somewhat from that of the second study (MacDonald & McGurk, 1978). If the results of the second study are separated into two groups according to consonantal place of articulation – labials /p, b, m/ and nonlabials /t, d, n, k, g/ – there were no significant perceptual errors for stimuli in which the visual and auditory cues were taken from the same group. For example, 70% of responses to the stimulus /ka/-lips and /pa/-voice were *pa* (i.e., correct); however, this stimulus pair had produced primarily *ta* responses in the first study. The stimulus pair of /pa/-lips and /ka/-voice in the second study elicited 82% correct *ka* responses and only 9% each of *pa* responses and the combination response *pka*, although these latter two were the predominant responses to this stimulus pair in the first study. Similar differences between the two studies emerged for the voiced stops.

The different pattern of findings in MacDonald and McGurk (1978) raises the issue of *stimulus compellingness*, or the degree to which an AV discrepancy can be perceived as a single event. The higher the compellingness of the discordance as a single event, the greater the contribution of the visual cue (Easton & Basala, 1982; Warren et al., 1981). When the discrepancy is too great (i.e., the compellingness of the event is too low), the single-event assumption can no longer be maintained and perceivers might attempt to attend differentially to the two sources of information. Reisberg et al.'s (1987) precondition on integration stated that "the perceptual system must first be persuaded that the visual and auditory inputs 'belong' to each other" (p. 107) and emphasized that such a stipulation was consistent with the notion of a unity of the senses (e.g., Marks, 1978). Therefore, in Reisberg et al.'s (1987) terms, a low compelling condition would not adequately persuade the perceptual system that the inputs constitute a single event.

The determination of what constitutes stimulus compellingness might be somewhat illusory. When Green et al. (1991) dubbed a male voice onto the video image of a female talker, and vice versa, using the CV syllables /ba/ and /ga/, there was no significant reduction in the McGurk–MacDonald effect. In addition, Dekle et al. (1992) found a strong effect when monosyllabic words presented auditorily did not match the observed words in terms of consonantal place of articulation.

Over the years, the potential influence of numerous other factors on the McGurk–MacDonald effect was investigated, including the degree of intermodal asynchrony, auditory signal level, adjacent vowel, talker familiarity, level of image detail, angle of view, language and cultural issues, auditory intelligibility, presence of noise, amount of exposure to the language, individual variability, and type of response format. These factors shed some light on the AV integration process and are addressed here in turn.

It would be reasonable to assume that asynchronous auditory and visual cues might disrupt the perception of a unitary event; however, even if the cues are out of synchrony by roughly ± 180 ms, an observer's perceptual system may still attempt to organize the input as a single experience for analysis – although more synchronous AV stimuli do tend to elicit more responses that are indicative of visual bias as compared to less synchronous AV stimuli (e.g., Munhall et al. 1996; Remez et al., 2001).

In addition, variable visual effects may depend on the auditory signal level (Kuhl et al., 1988). When presented with a stimulus combining /ga/-lips and /ba/-voice, the number of illusory *da* responses significantly increased as the auditory signal level increased from "soft" (45 dB) to "moderate" (58 dB) and from "moderate" to "loud" (66 dB) although

Kuhl et al. noted that this finding might be somewhat counterintuitive. Green et al. (1988) pointed out that the adjacent vowel is also a source of variability in participants' responses to a CV stimulus mismatching visual /gV/ and auditory /bV/. The number of illusory *d*V responses was highest when the vowel was /i/, moderate for /a/, and almost non-existent for /u/. Because rounded vowels can obscure lip movements that distinguish consonants, the rounding of /u/ might have led participants to report the bilabial stop /b/ as the percept, which would have been the correct response in this type of task (see chapter 1).

Walker et al. (1995) have also demonstrated that familiarity with a talker's face influences the effect of lip movements independent of familiarity with the voice. In that study, when participants were shown matched face-voice pairs (i.e., from the same talker) and mismatched pairs (i.e., from different talkers), those who were familiar with the faces, and thus the association between the talker's articulatory gestures and speech sounds, were less susceptible to visual bias than those who were not familiar with the faces.

Given the amount of variability in speechreading performance among hearing and hard-of-hearing populations, MacDonald et al. (2000) conducted a series of studies to determine how much detail needed to be extracted from a visual speech cue in order for it to contribute to a percept and result in the McGurk–MacDonald effect. Normal-hearing adults were presented with CV syllables produced by a female native speaker of British English. The consonant was a voiced or voiceless stop or a nasal paired with /a/. The visual stimulus was an image of the talker's face in which the level of detail was systematically varied. As the coarseness of the image increased, the illusory effect systematically decreased. However, even at the coarsest level (11.2 pixels/face), the illusion did not completely disappear; interestingly, the participants who did not experience the illusion showed the effects of AV interaction in their clarity ratings of the auditory cue. MacDonald et al. concluded that the visual information typically being extracted reflects relatively gross features of movement versus fine-level detail.

Perceivers do not need to fixate exclusively on the talker's mouth in order to perceive speech information (e.g., Paré et al., 2003). Only when participants' gaze fixations were displaced beyond 10°–20° from the centre of the talker's mouth was the McGurk–MacDonald effect significantly reduced, and only when gaze was directed 60° from centre did it become negligible. Paré et al. concluded that these results demonstrate the strength of the influence of visual speech information on perception and the substantial spatial range of visible speech processing (see also chapters 4 and 5).

The McGurk–MacDonald Effect in Languages Other Than English

In addition to English, a robust McGurk–MacDonald effect was reported for German and Spanish speakers (Fuster-Duran, 1996) and for Italian speakers (Bovo et al., 2009); however, several studies reported weak illusory effects for native speakers of some other languages. In a study involving Japanese speakers, Sekiyama and Tohkura (1991) observed that the occurrence of the illusion depended on the auditory intelligibility of the stimuli and the presence of noise. In that study, stimuli included voiced and voiceless stops, /w/, /r/, and the nasals /m, n/. When presented in the clear (i.e., no noise), visual effects occurred mostly with auditory /p/, /w/, and /t/, for which auditory intelligibility had been slightly less than 100%. For the auditory labials /p/ and /w/, effects were significant when paired with visual nonlabials. In noise, the McGurk–MacDonald effect was stronger and more widespread; perception of auditory nonlabials was significantly affected by visual labials sharing manner of articulation. Similarly, auditory labial stimuli, when combined with visual nonlabials, produced significant visual effects and a predominance of nonlabial responses.

In a subsequent study, Sekiyama and Tohkura (1993) explored the occurrence of the McGurk–MacDonald effect with Japanese speakers listening to 10 AE syllables and AE speakers listening to 10 Japanese syllables. The Americans had not studied Japanese nor lived in Japan, although the Japanese participants had studied English grammar and reading before attending university. The native AE speakers' responses showed a stronger effect of incongruent visual cues as compared to the Japanese speakers' responses, and each L1 group showed more of an effect of visual cues in the stimuli from the non-native language. Auditory intelligibility of AE /r/ at 67% showed no improvement when the matched visual cue was added – a finding that Hardison (1996) later explored (see below). To summarize the results, Sekiyama and Tohkura (1993) argued that perceptual processing was "vision-independent" for Japanese speakers in contrast to AE speakers, and that Japanese speakers incorporate visual cues only when auditory information is insufficient for speech perception (p. 442).

Taking a different approach, Massaro et al. (1993) presented adult Japanese, Spanish, and AE speakers with stimuli synthesized along an auditory /ba/-/da/ continuum with corresponding articulatory gestures on a computer-animated face. All participants were university students; the Japanese speakers, who resided in Japan, had received an average of 8 years of English instruction focused on reading and writing. All participants demonstrated the McGurk–MacDonald effect in both a two-alternative forced choice task (i.e., choose /ba/ or /da/) and a more open response format. Massaro et al. concluded that the magnitude of the influence of visible speech was approximately the same across the three language groups.

In another study, Sekiyama (1997) reported a relatively weak visual effect for 14 Chinese speakers who had been living in Japan for 4 months to 6 years. Participants' proficiency in Japanese varied and most did not speak English. In that study, stimuli consisted of 10 consonants in CV syllables with the vowel /a/ produced by a Japanese speaker and an AE speaker. Each auditory syllable was dubbed onto each visual syllable produced by the same speaker. Participants who had been in Japan for more than 3 years tended to experience a stronger McGurk–MacDonald effect for both the English and the Japanese stimuli than did those who had been there for a shorter period of time. Both languages were unfamiliar to the participants. Sekiyama drew two conclusions. First, since Chinese is a tonal language, native speakers of Chinese might have developed a strong dependence on auditory (vs. visual) speech information, which was compatible with a face-avoidance or auditory-dominance hypothesis. Second, the correlation between the magnitude of the effect and the amount of time the Chinese participants had spent in Japan could signal that even people who had not been accustomed to using visual speech cues might utilize them in learning a second language.

With a focus on potential changes in visual effects across the lifespan, Sekiyama and Burnham (2008) discovered weaker visual effects on the perception of /ba/, /da/, and /ga/ by adult Japanese speakers as compared to adult English speakers. These CV syllables were produced by talkers in the participants' respective languages. The same stimuli were then presented to children in three age groups (6, 8, and 11 years old) within each language. Results showed that the degree of visual influence was low but equivalent for the 6-year-olds in both language groups. Although the visual influence was not greater among the 8- and 11-year-old Japanese-speaking children as compared to the 6-year-olds, there was an increase in visual influence associated with the age of the English-speaking children, especially for those between 6 and 8 years old. Based on reaction time data, the English-speaking adults and older children processed visual speech information relatively faster than auditory information, whereas there was no difference between the modalities for the Japanese participants.

To explore further the effect of L1 background on the use of visual cues in speech perception, Wang et al. (2009) used A-only, V-only, and AV (congruent and incongruent) presentations of English CV syllables to 15 L1 Korean, 20 L1 Mandarin, and 15 L1 English university students in Canada. The non-native English speakers had been in Canada for 1–4 years. The syllables consisted of the vowels /i/, /a/, and /u/ combined with fricatives varying in place of articulation: labiodentals /f/, /v/ (both non-existent in Korean); interdentals /θ/, /ð/ (both non-existent in Korean and Mandarin); and /s/, /z/ (present in all L1s). For labiodentals, the L1 Korean perceivers showed lower V-only accuracy as compared to the L1 English and L1 Mandarin perceivers, but they achieved native-level perception in the A-only and AV conditions. For interdentals, the L1 Korean and Mandarin perceivers had lower A-only accuracy as compared to the L1 English perceivers, and they benefited from visual information, resulting in improved performance in the AV condition. Among the non-native groups, the L1 Mandarin perceivers showed poorer A-only and AV identification of the interdentals and greater fused responses with the incongruent AV stimuli. Although the results support the ability of non-native perceivers to use visual speech cues, their success may vary according to the status of the target sounds in the L1.

To investigate visual bias in speech perception using greater within- and between-talker variability, Hazan et al. (2010) presented the CV syllables /ba/, /da/, and /ga/ produced by five Australian English and five Mandarin speakers to listeners from several language backgrounds: 18 Australian English, 17 British English, and 15 Mandarin Chinese. Participants were university students who were tested in their L1 environments. Stimuli were presented in several conditions: A-only, V-only, and congruent and incongruent AV, either in the clear, in noise, with blurring, or with combined AV degradations. Results indicated that L1 background influenced the weighting of auditory and visual cues, as noted by Wang et al. (2009). Cue weighting was also influenced by individual talker characteristics and, notably, by individual perceiver strategies.

Mallick et al. (2015) discovered that both perceivers and the type of response format were sources of variability in the occurrence of the McGurk–MacDonald effect. Within a sample of 165 English-speaking adults, there were substantial differences in how frequently they perceived the illusion (from 0% to 100%) and in how frequently the illusion was perceived across different stimuli (from 17% to 58%). Moreover, despite the amount of variability across participants and stimuli, there was little change in the frequency of the effect between the initial testing of 40 of the participants and their 1-year retest (a mean change of only 2% with a test-retest correlation, $r = .91$). In a second experiment exploring the difference between an open versus closed (or forced-choice) response format, the forced-choice format resulted in an estimated 18% greater frequency of the effect but with similar levels of variability across individuals. Mallick et al. argued for the importance of considering individual variability in the McGurk–MacDonald effect versus just group statistics and emphasized that regardless of this variability, the effect can still be considered a stable measure of AV integration.

Studies concerning the McGurk–MacDonald effect use discrepant auditory and visual cues and may also degrade the acoustic signal (e.g., through the addition of noise). However, Reisberg et al. (1987) pointed out that visual cues are routinely used in the understanding of speech, not solely when auditory cues are degraded or unavailable, although the contribution of visual cues to a perceptual outcome may be more evident when the auditory signal is not at ceiling levels. This observation was explored in several experiments. In the first experiment, native speakers of English who had studied French for 4 years listened to a total of 14 passages from a French textbook recorded by a native French speaker, each about 60 s in duration. For half of the passages, participants saw the face of the speaker (AV condition); in the other half, there was no visual information (A-only condition). The AV and A-only conditions were presented in alternating trials. Following shadowing training using English with visual input, participants were instructed to shadow each French passage. Shadowing accuracy was significantly better in the AV condition.

Reisberg et al. (1987) considered the possibility that the AV condition in the first experiment might have resulted in better performance based solely on the tendency of a visual target to hold perceivers' attention. To confirm the hypothesis that lip movements were the critical component of the visual stimulus, a second experiment was conducted comparing an AV condition with one in which the lips and chin of the talker's face were hidden but the remainder of the face was visible. As with the first experiment, the participants were native speakers of English, but this time, the target language was German, which the participants had studied for about 2 years. Other procedural details were the same. Shadowing performance was significantly better when the talker's lip movements could be seen.

In a third experiment, native speakers of English listened to the speech of a native English speaker who recorded 10 passages having more complex philosophical content, each about 60 s in duration. Shadowing performance again was significantly better when the talker's lip movements were visible. Reisberg et al. (1987) argued that visual speech information is not merely a "back-up" system that comes into play only when audition is insufficient. Even though the auditory signal was intact in their experiments, the use of a less familiar language or a complex message allowed the benefit of visual information to become clear.

In concluding their article, Reisberg et al. (1987) described anecdotal comments from L1 Chinese and L1 Japanese speakers learning English as an L2 who reported that they found lip movements to be distracting instead of helpful in understanding English.[ii] Comments such as these set the stage for further investigation of the contribution of a talker's lip movements to the perception of L2 sounds by learners who were actively engaged in learning the language in order to communicate well with native speakers (Best & Tyler, 2007).

The McGurk–MacDonald Effect in L2 Learners

Hardison (1996) presented a total of 115 L2 learners of English of four L1s (Japanese, Korean, Spanish, and Malay) and 20 native AE speakers with both matched and mismatched auditory and visual CV syllables involving the consonants /p/, /f/, /w/, /r/, /t/, and /k/ with the vowel /ɑ/ produced by a female native AE speaker. The learners were enrolled in an intensive English program at an upper-intermediate proficiency level based on a series of in-house tests. They had been in the US for about 2–6 months. Stimuli were presented in the clear and in noise. For learners, significant visual effects occurred even without noise. The most informative cue contributed the most to the percept, and the determination of a cue's information value was influenced by the learners' L2 perceptual categories. For example, the L1 Spanish speakers' identification of auditory /f/ declined from 62% to 7% when combined with visual /p/ and improved little when the visual cue was /f/. The perceptual confusion of the labials for the Spanish speakers may have been influenced by aspects of their L1

ii. Editor's Note: Japanese students that I have taught at American universities have often remarked how much more demonstrative in their facial and bodily gestures Americans are than Japanese and that these more demonstrative gestures would be considered inappropriate in Japan. – MCP phonology, which includes unaspirated /p/, /f/, and /b/ (which is produced as a voiced bilabial [β] intervocalically) (Hualde, 2005).

For all L1 groups, the influence of visual /p/ when combined with auditory /t/ was evident, especially for the Korean speakers, who had only 67% correct *ta* responses; the remainder were *pa*. For the Japanese speakers, the addition of visual /r/ and /f/ improved identification accuracy of their respective auditory cues, rising significantly from 65% to 87% for /r/ and from 56% to 70% for /f/. The increase in identification accuracy for /r/ contrasts with the absence of improvement for /r/ reported by Sekiyama and Tohkura (1993). This could be the result of greater L2 English exposure and interaction experience for the English as a Second Language (ESL) learners in the US as compared to the Japanese speakers in Japan who had studied only English grammar and reading in the study by Sekiyama and Tohkura. In contrast to the L2 learners, the native AE speakers in Hardison (1996) experienced significant visual effects only in noise, which may have been due to the composition of the stimulus set; that is, it included three stops, a fricative, and two approximants, which native speakers of English were able to perceive accurately in the absence of noise, reducing the likelihood that their perceptual systems would regard discrepant AV stimuli as a unitary event.

To explore the hypothesis that a more compelling stimulus set (i.e., less discordance between auditory and visual cues) would increase the assumption of a unitary perceptual event, especially for native AE speakers with more stable perceptual categories for L1 English than L2 speakers, Hardison (1996) conducted a second experiment using only the stops /p, t, k/ presented with and without noise. Although the L2 learners' responses in Experiment 1 had revealed significant visual effects, the question arose as to whether the influence of visual /p/ combined with auditory /t/ and /k/ would occur if another labial cue (i.e., /f/), close in articulation to /p/, were removed from the stimulus set. In other words, would the information value of /p/ change for the learners if potential confusion were eliminated? In Experiment 2, participants were native AE speakers, along with L1 Japanese, Korean, and Spanish learners of L2 English at the same proficiency level and in the same English program as those in Experiment 1.

Results of Experiment 2 demonstrated significant visual effects for the native speakers both in noise and in the clear for the labial and nonlabial cues, supporting a role for stimulus compellingness in deriving a unitary percept (Hardison, 1996). For the L2 learners, visual nonlabials produced a significant visual effect, but the effect of visual /p/ differed according to the L1. For L1 Spanish speakers, the influence of visual /p/ may have resulted from the absence of the other competing labial cue (/f/) that was included in the stimulus set of Experiment 1. For the L1 Korean speakers, the influence of visual /p/ increased when combined with auditory /t/ and /k/, while for the Japanese, visual /p/ remained a weak visual cue. In sum, the most informative visual cue (labial articulation) contributed the most to the perceptual outcome, and the participants' L1 played a role in determining a cue's informativeness.

The Metamodal/Supramodal Brain

Although the discovery of the perceptual illusion known as the McGurk-MacDonald effect was accidental, it had a pivotal impact on the consideration of speech as a multimodal phenomenon and challenged traditional views of perception as a modular function based on the independent operation of different sensory modalities (Shams & Seitz, 2008; Shimojo & Shams, 2001). Subsequent behavioural and brain imaging studies demonstrated that cross-modal interactions were the norm in perception and cortical pathways were not sensory-specific but were modulated by signals from other modalities. Sams et al. (1991) discovered that visual input specifically from lip movements influenced activity in the auditory cortex. In a functional magnetic resonance imaging (fMRI) study, Calvert et al. (1997) also found that the primary auditory cortex was activated when a talking face was viewed in the absence of sound. The activation was observed specifically when viewing speech-related lip movements but not nonlinguistic facial movements (e.g., twitches in the lower part of the face).

To address the discovery of cross-modal interactions, Pascual-Leone and Hamilton (2001) hypothesized that the brain might represent a *metamodal* structure. The metamodal hypothesis was advanced based on several experiments with different populations. Using serial fMRI studies, Pascual-Leone and Hamilton discovered that the visual cortex in early blind and congenitally blind individuals could be activated by tactile stimulation of the fingers. In an earlier study, Pascual-Leone and Torres (1993) had determined that the sensory and motor representations in the brain related to the index finger that is used to read Braille are significantly larger for Braille readers than for blind non-Braille readers or sighted persons. In another of the experiments by Pascual-Leone and Hamilton (2001), sighted individuals who had been blindfolded for 5 days described experiencing visual hallucinations, perhaps the result of modifications made by the visual cortex in processing both tactile and auditory information when it was deprived of visual input. After the blindfold was removed and visual input was experienced for 12–24 hours, all changes induced by blindfolding disappeared. Because of the short timeline in that experiment, establishment of new neural connections was not possible; therefore, Pascual-Leone and Hamilton concluded that tactile and auditory input to the visual cortex was present in all participants. They characterized the visual cortex as a metamodal structure that receives visual, auditory, and tactile stimuli that can be activated and gain functional relevance when needed.

Based on these experiments, Pascual-Leone and Hamilton (2001) proposed that the brain is made up of *metamodal operators*, which are local neural networks defined by a given computation that is applied regardless of the sensory input that is received; in other words, the neural networks are built around operators instead of sensory modalities. Pascual-Leone and Hamilton's proposed architecture was based on several hypotheses: (a) different brain regions are best at performing particular functions; (b) these regions compete for the ability to perform a set of tasks; and (c) the competition leads to functional specialization of brain regions and the determination of the inputs that are best suited for them. Each region tends to win the competition for those functions for which its structure makes it well suited. The metamodal structure consists of two types of networks: *expert* networks, which compete with each other to learn training patterns, and a *gating* network, which mediates the competition. The winning expert network receives the information and learns about the current training pattern, which contributes to greater success in the next similar competition and forces other networks to develop expertise with other inputs. In sum, the processing of sensory information beyond the traditionally recognized cortical boundaries for a particular sensory modality may represent the workings of an efficient metamodal brain, which uses inputs to those cortical regions (operators) that seem best suited to carry out the computations successfully.

Several years later, Rosenblum et al. (2017) put forth the supramodal hypothesis supported by research on multisensory speech perception. Like metamodal responses, supramodal responses do not depend on a specific sensory modality but rather on the distinct content and task invoking a response. The supramodal architecture implies that the senses have some degree of perceptual equality and that cross-sensory integration occurs early and completely. Cecchetti et al. (2016) asserted that a lack of vision leads to a structural and functional reorganization within primarily visual brain areas, a phenomenon known as *cross-modal plasticity*, and that "supramodal is what takes place *despite* the lack of vision, whereas *cross-modal* is what happens *because of* the lack of vision" (p. 1). Therefore, some authors (e.g., Heimler et al., 2015) refer to *task-specific sensory-independent* activity to characterize how supramodal brain areas respond to a given perceptual task, independent of the specific sensory modality that conveys the input to the brain.

Speech as a Multimodal Phenomenon

Beauchamp (2016) proposed that the McGurk–MacDonald effect resulting from the presentation of incongruent stimuli provides strong evidence that speech perception is multisensory. Rosenblum and Dorsi (2021) described multisensory speech perception as ubiquitous and automatic (see also van Wassenhove, 2013). However, Soto-Faraco et al. (2019) argued that if multisensory integration were entirely automatic and unavoidable (e.g., Bertelson & Aschersleben, 1998), real-world environments, cluttered with unrelated sensory inputs, would result in constant perceptual illusions. Cross-modally congruent events are not necessarily the salient ones in cluttered environments. According to Soto-Faraco et al. (2019), some top-down mediation of multisensory processes plays a role in real-life scenarios, influencing how the brain decides what to integrate out of all possible sensory combinations. For example, in multi-speaker scenarios, one speech stream can be singled out from several others by selecting the corresponding articulatory gestures, but localizing the source of the sound may require attentional control to organize the input (Alsius & Soto-Faraco, 2011). In response, Rosenblum and Dorsi (2021) argued that "to date, it is unclear whether outside attention can truly penetrate the speech *integration* function or instead simply distracts from the extraction of the visual information for a McGurk effect" (p. 31).

In evaluating multisensory integration, some authors (e.g., Rosenblum & Dorsi, 2021) recommended an emphasis on neurophysiological studies. The next section thus reviews some key findings in the study of the neuroarchitecture of AV integration.

The Neuroarchitecture of AV Integration

Hickok et al. (2003) used fMRI to identify human auditory regions having both sensory and motor response properties. In the sensory phase of the

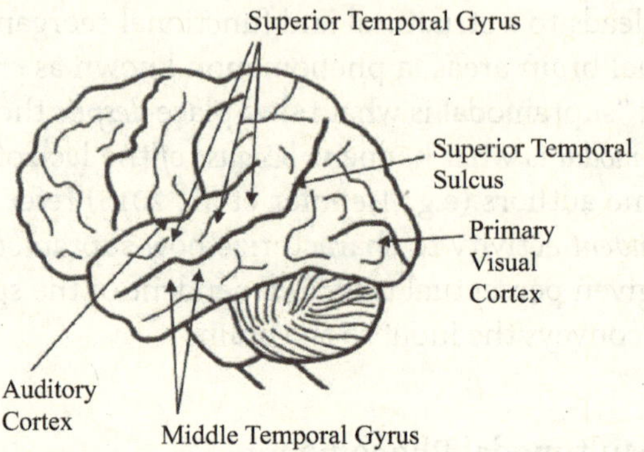

FIGURE 2.1 Primary Regions in the Speech Network

task, participants listened to speech (nonsense sentences) or music (novel piano melodies); in the motor phase, they performed covert rehearsal (e.g., humming) of the auditory stimuli. A brain region that exhibits both auditory and motor response properties (area Spt) showed particularly robust responses to both phases of the task. Hickok et al. suggested that a predominantly left hemisphere network enables acoustic-phonetic input to guide the acquisition of language-specific articulatory gestures and underlies phonological working memory in adults.

A commonly used technique for examining human brain function and multisensory speech is blood-oxygen-level-dependent (BOLD) signals detected in fMRI, which reflects changes coupled to underlying neuronal activity (Friston, 2009). Beauchamp (2016) outlined some limitations in the use of the BOLD signal, an indirect measure of neural activity with limited temporal precision; however, a speech network is identifiable with fMRI and includes different cortical regions (see Figure 2.1). Beauchamp's description of the most consistent activations in three regions can be summarized as follows:

1. The visual cortex, especially the lateral *extrastriate* motion-sensitive areas, processes the motion signals produced by a talker's face motion and forms a representation of visual speech. *Extrastriate* refers to the visually responsive regions located outside the primary visual or striate cortex. Ozker et al. (2018) found enhanced visual cortex responses to V-only speech by recording responses from small populations of neurons in individuals implanted with subdural electrodes. This enhancement was specific to regions of the visual cortex with *retinotopic* representations (i.e., visual input mapped from the retina

to neurons) of the talker's mouth. Connectivity was strong between the frontal cortex and the mouth regions of the visual cortex but weaker between the frontal cortex and non-mouth regions of the visual cortex or auditory cortex; this is compatible with an important role for the frontal cortex in AV speech perception through top-down selection of visual information from a talker's mouth.

2. The auditory cortex and auditory association areas on the superior temporal gyrus contribute to processing complex auditory information needed to form a representation of speech sounds. Beauchamp (2016) described these representations as those of key phonemic features of speech that allow perceivers to integrate AV cues from an unfamiliar talker.
3. Multisensory areas in the posterior superior temporal sulcus (pSTS) appear to integrate the visual and auditory speech representations to determine the most likely percept.

Determining the percept is challenged by the fact that the information value of each modality varies across time; therefore, perceivers need to weight each modality according to its reliability and must do so dynamically (Beauchamp, 2016). For example, in noisy environments, visual information may be more reliable than auditory information and deserve more weight, whereas in poorly lit environments, perceivers may need to rely more on auditory information. Using BOLD fMRI, Nath and Beauchamp (2011) examined the neural mechanisms involved in the dynamic weighting of sensory information by adding masking noise to degrade the auditory input and blurring an image to degrade the visual input. *Functional connectivity* (i.e., the degree to which activity between a pair of brain regions covaries or correlates over time; Stephan & Friston, 2009) was observed between the superior temporal sulcus (STS) – a multisensory area – and the auditory association areas and the lateral extrastriate visual cortical areas, but not between the STS and the primary auditory or primary visual cortex. The connectivity increased between the STS and the extrastriate visual cortex when the visual modality was more reliable or informative even when changes in its reliability were rapid during presentation of successive words. Changes in STS functional connectivity may underlie speech perception in challenging settings and may be important for AV training (e.g., Powers et al., 2012).

Is the McGurk–MacDonald Effect a Proxy for AV Integration?

Studies were also conducted to investigate individual variability in the McGurk–MacDonald effect from a neural perspective. In a BOLD fMRI study, Nath and Beauchamp (2012) divided young adults into two groups based on the strength of the McGurk–MacDonald effect they had experienced in a pre-scanning experiment. The first step involved identifying the STS for each participant by presenting A-only and V-only words (vs. AV syllables); this was followed by measuring responses in the STS to individual AV syllables during passive viewing (i.e., no active response). The STS in both groups responded identically to congruent AV syllables; however, the participants who had experienced a stronger pre-scanning McGurk–MacDonald effect exhibited greater BOLD responses to the incongruent stimuli during the scan. There was a positive correlation between how often they had perceived the illusion and the amplitude of the BOLD fMRI response of the STS but no other brain region.

What is the neuronal architecture of the STS that produces the McGurk–MacDonald effect? High-resolution fMRI and other studies showed that the cortex in the STS contains a patchy distribution of neurons that respond to A-only, V-only, or AV stimuli (Beauchamp et al., 2004; C.D. Dahl et al., 2009). Analysis of BOLD fMRI data demonstrated that activity in a region that includes the STS could discriminate between individual auditory syllables (e.g., /ba/ vs. /da/; Formisano et al., 2008; Raizada et al., 2010). In an architecture in which the STS contains small patches of neurons that respond to specific syllables, activity across multiple syllable patches would result in the most active patch determining the percept (Beauchamp et al., 2004, 2010). Each patch might receive input from neurons in visual and auditory association areas coded for specific visual categories and phonemes. Beauchamp et al. (2010) proposed that during presentation of congruent AV speech, input from auditory and visual neurons would be integrated, improving sensitivity; however, presentation of incongruent AV stimuli could result in unexpected percepts. For example, if an STS patch representing /da/ received input from both auditory /ba/ and visual /ga/ neurons (i.e., a McGurk-type stimulus), Beauchamp et al. (2010) predicted that the /da/ patch would exhibit a large response, producing a *da* percept. They further predicted that disrupting activity in the STS would eliminate this multisensory integration.

Several studies combined the use of BOLD fMRI with transcranial magnetic stimulation (TMS), which is a technique that allows active interference with brain function to (a) investigate the relationship between cortical activity and behaviour; (b) trace the timing at which activity in a particular cortical region contributes to a given task; and (c) map the functional connectivity between brain regions (Pascual-Leone et al., 2000; Walsh & Cowey, 2000). Beauchamp et al. (2010) employed both techniques to demonstrate the necessity of activity in the STS for the McGurk–MacDonald effect to occur. First, BOLD fMRI was used to identify the multisensory region of the STS in each of the participants who had strongly perceived the illusion in pre-screening. A locus of activity was identified in the posterior STS that responded to both auditory and visual speech. Then, to disrupt activity in the STS, single pulses of TMS (<1 ms duration) were delivered as participants were presented with incongruent CV syllables (i.e., auditory /ba/ + visual /ga/, or auditory /pa/ + visual /ka/ or /na/) and control stimuli (i.e., auditory /ba/ with no visual cue, or auditory and visual /pa/). Without TMS, the illusory percept was reported where expected on nearly every trial; however, with TMS there was a significant reduction in the likelihood of the illusion, although TMS did not interfere with perception of the control stimuli. When TMS disrupted the McGurk–MacDonald effect, the most common experience (reported 66% of the time) was a percept similar to that in the A-only trials. TMS of another location used as a control did not influence perception of either the McGurk–MacDonald effect or the control stimuli.

Beauchamp et al. (2010) also reported that disrupting the perceptual illusion with a single-pulse TMS was effective only within a narrow temporal window extending from 100 ms before the acoustic onset of the syllable to approximately 100 ms after its onset. This 200 ms window supported the notion that TMS disrupted a specific neural computation in the STS (i.e., AV integration) that was time-locked to stimulus presentation. This finding was consistent with behavioural results showing that the illusion is robust to AV asynchronies within an approximately 200 ms integration window (van Wassenhove et al., 2007), and with results from electrophysiological recording demonstrating strong responses in STS beginning about 100 ms after stimulus presentation (Canolty et al., 2007; Puce et al., 2007). Because temporary disruption of the STS interfered with the McGurk–MacDonald effect, which depends on the interaction of the auditory and visual modalities, the results were interpreted as support for the critical role STS plays in this effect as a proxy for the AV integration of speech (Beauchamp et al., 2010; for an alternative view, see Alsius et al. 2018). As predicted, perception was not affected by TMS disruption of the STS after the auditory and visual syllables had been integrated.

To examine patterns of activation within STS, Venezia et al. (2017) used BOLD fMRI to measure activation in native English speakers to a range of unimodal and multimodal speech and nonspeech stimuli. The A-only, V-only, and AV stimuli produced the largest effects in the anterior, posterior, and middle STS (mSTS), respectively. Within the mid-posterior and mSTS regions, response preferences changed gradually from visual to multisensory and then to auditory moving from posterior to anterior. The mSTS also exhibited preferential responses to AV stimulation as well as to speech versus nonspeech stimuli. These results suggest that auditory and visual speech representations are elaborated gradually within anterior and posterior processing streams, respectively, and might be integrated within mSTS.

In sum, the variability present in the methodological details and findings of studies on the McGurk–MacDonald effect make it challenging to compare them and draw conclusions. There are also differences in how the issue of variability is interpreted. Rosenblum and Dorsi (2021) commented that "extreme" variability in methodology across studies might account for some of the variability in the findings while noting that "finding evidence of the effect under such different conditions does speak to its durability" (p. 32). Recall that in one of the largest studies (165 participants), responses within individuals between an initial test and a 1-year retest differed by only 2%, although there were substantial differences in the frequency with which the illusion was perceived across participants and stimuli (Mallick et al., 2015). In other words, the effect within individuals was consistent over time. However, Sommers (2021) observed that "although the McGurk effect is reliable, it may be a relatively poor measure of auditory-visual integration" (p. 523), a view that is in contrast to the view of Beauchamp et al. (2010) on the effect as a proxy for AV integration of speech. Research will likely continue on this issue.

Event-Related Potentials

In contrast to fMRI, studies using electrical and magnetic measurements can directly measure neural activity with high temporal precisions (for an outline of other measurements, see Beauchamp, 2016). Event-related potentials (ERPs) can be recorded; these represent transient changes in the brain's electrical activity that occur in response to the presentation of a stimulus – for example, responses to AV syllables display peaks between 100 ms and 200 ms after the onset of the stimulus (Bernstein et al., 2008).

ERPs were used to investigate the timing and localization of the cortical processes underlying a different type of illusory effect (Mishra et al., 2007). Although the best-known cross-modal effects are those of vision influencing other modalities, as in the McGurk–MacDonald effect, visual perception can also be altered by other modalities. Visual illusions can be induced by sound even when there is no ambiguity in the visual stimulus. For example, in each trial in the Shams et al. (2002) study, there were 1–4 flashes of light accompanied by 0–4 auditory beeps. Participants had to determine the number of flashes they saw on the screen. When a single flash of light was accompanied by multiple auditory beeps, the single flash was perceived as multiple flashes. The temporal window of the AV interaction was about 100 ms.

Mishra et al. (2007) determined that the overall pattern of cortical activity associated with an illusory flash of light differed from the pattern evoked by a real second flash. The illusion of the double flash was associated with short latency ERP activity localized to the auditory cortex and polymodal cortex of the temporal lobe, along with gamma bursts in the visual cortex.[3] Perception of the illusory second flash may have resulted from very rapid dynamic interaction between auditory and visual cortical areas triggered by the second sound.

The Role of Causal Inference

Magnotti and Beauchamp (2017) proposed that the fundamental issue in integrating speech cues is *causal inference* – the brain's calculation of the likelihood that a specific pair of auditory and visual syllables is from a single talker (vs. multiple talkers). The brain must infer the likelihood of each causal scenario and then combine the representations from each scenario, weighted by their likelihoods. The final result of causal inference is the average of the integrated multisensory representation, which assumes a single talker, and the auditory representation, which assumes separate talkers, weighted by the likelihood that the face and voice arise from a single talker versus separate talkers.

Magnotti and Beauchamp (2017) developed a simplified model using causal inference to provide a computational framework that would be able to predict the percept from combinations of auditory and visual speech inputs. Models with and without causal inference made comparable predictions for congruent AV stimuli; however, differences appeared when incongruent stimuli were used. The model incorporating causal inference better predicted the behavioural data collected from 60 participants than the model without causal inference. For example, in response to auditory /ba/ + visual /ga/, participants reported a *ba* percept on 57% of the trials and *da* on 40% of the trials, as compared to the predictions of 51% and 49%, respectively, by the model with causal inference; however, the model without causal inference predicted almost all *da* responses. For the stimulus combination of auditory /ga/ + visual /ba/, participants reported *ga* on 96% of the trials, which compared favourably to the prediction of 97%

by the model with causal inference; however, the model without causal inference again predicted almost all *da* responses.

Chapter 2 in Review

This chapter considered the role of visible speech cues in perception from infancy to adulthood, addressing such issues as where infants look in the early stages of development, how adults process discordant speech cues in native and second languages, and what multimodal speech and technology contribute to our understanding of the neurophysiological processing of speech.

A critical focal point in this discussion was the McGurk–MacDonald effect – arguably the best-known perceptual illusion in speech research. The abundance of studies exploring this effect over many years uncovered illusory effects that were relatively common across perceivers as well as variable effects that emerged through investigation of an increasingly large number of factors, including the degree of intermodal asynchrony, talker familiarity, angle of view, language and cultural issues, and individual variability, among others. Despite the variability in the occurrence of the effect across individuals and stimuli, many researchers (e.g., Beauchamp, 2016; Mallick et al., 2015) concluded that it is still a stable measure of AV integration, although others expressed some reservations (e.g., Rosenblum & Dorsi, 2021; Sommers, 2021).

Exploration of the McGurk–MacDonald effect involving L2 learners showed a critical role for the most informative cue in establishing the AV percept. As Shams and Seitz (2008) noted, "It is likely that the human brain has evolved to develop, learn and operate optimally in multisensory environments" (p. 411). Chapter 3 explores the factors influencing the improvement of the information value of L2 speech cues through focused training, with an emphasis on the use of AV input.

Chapter 2 Notes

1. In the epigraph, "we" included John MacDonald, a co-author on several articles with Harry McGurk, including those involving the McGurk–MacDonald effect.
2. Participants at the International Conference on Auditory-Visual Speech Processing held in Australia in 1998 received a CD-ROM of the proceedings, which included recordings of Harry McGurk demonstrating the perceptual illusion using the sentence. I watched and listened to the sentence and heard *My dad taught me to drive*. To satisfy my curiosity, I listened to the file with my eyes closed

and then watched the video without audio, confirming that the auditory and visual cues were indeed different. As observed by McGurk and Buchanan (as cited in Alvin M. Liberman, 1982), listeners are *usually* not aware of the bimodal conflict. A more recent demonstration of the McGurk–MacDonald effect by another speaker can be found in a BBC Horizon video clip from 2010 (see sixesfullofnines, 2016).

3. Cortical gamma oscillations occur alongside perceptual processes and in proportion to perceptual salience; they involve synchronized discharges of neural assemblies and emerge over a fast timescale consistent with that of perception (Sedley & Cunningham, 2013).

Chapter 3

Multimodal Input in L2 Perceptual Learning

> *All these effects [e.g., the McGurk-MacDonald effect, the ventriloquism effect] emphasize the strong effect of visual signals on the other modalities, consistent with the commonsense notion that human is primarily a vision-dominated animal.*
>
> – Shimojo & Shams (2001, p. 506)

*****

Background

Many years ago, Trubetzkoy (1939/1969), a Russian linguist and historian, provided an early view of the processing of sounds in a foreign language and the speech perception-production link when he wrote the following: "When learning a foreign language . . . it is not enough to get one's vocal organs accustomed to a new articulation. One must also get one's phonological consciousness accustomed to interpreting such new articulations correctly" (p. 64). Trubetzkoy viewed the phonological system of a language as a series of sieves through which heard speech passed. Features that were needed to identify phonemes remained in the first sieve; the rest fell into another sieve in which details "of appeal" to the listener were retained (p. 52).[1] A third sieve retained features that characterized the speaker's expression. This system of sieves was said to be different across languages. Individuals would acquire the system of their L1, and then the sounds of a foreign language would be "strained through the phonological sieve" of the L1, resulting in some errors in interpretation and pronunciation (p. 52). Trubetzkoy proposed that difficulties could be overcome in time, although an accent might remain.

Differences between the L1 and L2 phonological systems continue to be a consideration in the assessment of learners' L2 perception and production challenges. To L1-L2 differences, researchers have added a number of variables, such as age at the onset of learning, the nature of L1 phonetic categories, and the amount of L2 use and continued L1 use (for an overview, see, e.g., Flege & Bohn, 2021); quantity and quality of input and of interaction opportunities (e.g., Gass, 2017); stimulus variables, such as the influence of a target sound's position in a word (henceforth *word position*); and the characteristics of a talker's voice (e.g., Lively et al., 1993). Notably absent from many studies on the adult acquisition of novel L2 sounds was the contribution of the visual modality.

However, the importance of visual input from a talker's face for children's L2 phonological development was not lost on the medical community, especially during the height of the COVID-19 pandemic. When face-to-face communication in many settings, including in-person instruction, was replaced by mask-to-mask, a pediatrician and former acting director of the Centers for Disease Control and Prevention in the US, Dr. Richard Besser, made the following comment in a television news interview: "For children who speak another language . . . [w]hen will they be able to see a teacher's mouth so that they can more easily learn a language?" (as cited in Berman, 2022).

So for adults, how do we reconcile the auditory dominance in the L2 literature with the behavioural and neurophysiological findings presented in previous chapters and the epigraph by Shimojo and Shams (2001) that opens this chapter on the role of vision in perception? This chapter will focus on the contributions of the visual modality to L2 phonological learning for adults, beginning with a review of some A-only perception training studies followed by the findings of AV training studies, the transfer of improved perceptual abilities to earlier word identification in connected speech, and, finally, the contributions of cognitive and neurophysiological research to understanding multimodal learning.

Early Auditory Dominance of L2 Speech Perception Training

Early research in auditory perception demonstrated successful training of adults to discriminate some non-native contrasts. In a study by Pisoni et al. (1982), after a single training session native English speakers could identify a new voice-onset-time (VOT) category for consonants.[2] In a later study, Morosan and Jamieson (1989) aimed to maximize a different temporal contrast using a *perceptual fading* technique to improve L1 French speakers' identification of the English interdental fricative contrast /θ/-/ð/ in CV syllables with the vowel /ʌ/ in two training sessions (90 min). In the perceptual fading technique, the friction of the consonant in synthesized CV syllables was initially exaggerated and then gradually decreased. Identification of synthetic tokens improved, but there was no generalization to different word positions or to a /ð/-/d/ contrast. Results showed that participants could identify a voiced fricative /ð/ only when the alternative stimulus was its voiceless counterpart /θ/ (i.e., a temporal difference) but not /d/.

Exaggerated stimuli were also used by McCandliss et al. (2002) to improve L1 Japanese speakers' perceptual accuracy of /r/ and /l/. Synthesized *rock-lock* and *road-load* continua were used with exaggeration of the critical acoustic cue differentiating /r/ and /l/: an AE /r/ is characterized by a lower third formant (F3) frequency distinguishing it from /l/ and /w/ (Lindau, 1985). Japanese speakers performed as well as Americans in discriminating differences in the F3 transition with nonspeech stimuli in isolation; however, these populations differed when the F3 transition served as a phonetic cue in combination with first (F1) and second formant (F2) patterns related to the perception of /r/ and /l/ (Alvin M. Liberman et al., 1973). In the McCandliss et al. (2002) study, *adaptive training* and *fixed training* were compared. Adaptive training exaggerated the /r/-/l/ contrast with progressive reductions in exaggeration based on a participant's success on eight tokens in a row; fixed training involved good examples of /r/ and /l/ taken from each continuum. For each training type, the presence or absence of feedback was also tested. Participants were trained on one of the continua and tested on both using identification and same-different discrimination tasks. Comparison of the training groups' overall performance revealed the following ranking: fixed training with feedback (the best results), adaptive training with or without feedback, and fixed training without feedback (little improvement).

There were several limitations to McCandliss et al.'s (2002) experimental approach, including the absence of variation in the target sounds' word position, its adjacent vowel, and the talker's voice. Exaggerated stimuli may draw attention to critical cues by making them more perceptually salient and less frustrating for learners. Although this focusing of attention on one critical cue may offer faster gains, it may not be as efficient in producing robust perceptual categories that result in better generalization performance. Broader generalization requires broader training, and more variation in experimental stimuli better approximates the natural language environment.

In general, contrasts based on temporal characteristics (e.g., VOT) are easier to acquire than those based on *spectral* cues (i.e., cues related to the component frequencies that make up a sound during a given time interval), such as the contrast between /r/ and /l/ (e.g., Bohn, 1995). The following section outlines the challenge of distinguishing /r/ and /l/ for some L2 English speakers and the training that has been used.

The Challenge of /r/ and /l/

Based on decades of published L2 speech studies, two of the most popular target sounds for research have been the AE liquids /r/ and /l/, historically considered obstacles for many Japanese and Korean speakers, among other L1 groups (for L1 Japanese, see Miyawaki et al., 1975; Mochizuki, 1981; Yamada & Tohkura, 1992; for L1 Japanese & L1 Korean, see Ingram & Park, 1998). The learners' challenge may stem, in part, from phonological conflicts between the L2 and the L1. Japanese has a voiced apical flap in the dental or alveolar region that occurs in utterance-initial and intervocalic positions and has acoustic, articulatory, and perceptual similarities to the AE flap (Price, 1981). The Japanese flap shows context-dependent variability and does not appear adjacent to other consonants, but it may occur in the environment of all Japanese vowels (Tsujimura, 2013). Although a lower F3 frequency distinguishes AE /r/ acoustically from /l/ (Lindau, 1985), Yamada (1995) discovered that L1 Japanese listeners tended to focus on a different formant: they used F2 frequency values to distinguish /r/ and /l/ in an identification task using synthesized speech stimuli (a *right-light* series) whose F2 and F3 onset and transition frequencies and F1 transition duration had been manipulated.

L1 Korean speakers may also experience difficulty perceiving and producing the AE liquids. Korean phonology includes a voiced alveodental flap intervocalically (or between vowel and glide) and a voiced apicoalveolar non-velarized (clear) /l/ in syllable-final position, where AE tends to velarize the /l/ (Kim-Renaud, 1974; see chapter 8). Challenge in the perception of /r/ and /l/ may also stem from variability within the class of rhotics (/r/-like sounds) across languages and varieties of one language, including AE.

Auditory Perception Training of /r/ and /l/

Early perception training studies to enhance identification accuracy of /r/ and /l/ were limited to the auditory modality. For example, Strange and Dittman (1984) tested L1 Japanese speakers in the US with natural speech stimuli comprising 16 minimal pairs that contrasted /r/ and /l/ in initial, medial, and final positions, and then administered an auditory discrimination task using 10 synthesized stimuli in a *rock-lock* series over

14–18 training sessions. Following training, testing with a synthesized *rake-lake* series resulted in improved performance but with poor generalization to natural speech containing word-initial liquids.

Subsequent auditory training studies modified several methodological issues in the Strange and Dittman (1984) study. Logan et al. (1991) used natural (vs. synthesized) speech and a large number of minimal pairs contrasting AE /r/ and /l/ across five word positions (i.e., initial singleton and cluster, medial/intervocalic, final singleton and cluster) produced by five different talkers in a training study for L1 Japanese learners of English in the US. A forced-choice identification (vs. discrimination) task was used before and after 3 weeks of training (15 sessions). Identification tasks promote recognition of between-category differences, whereas discrimination tasks require attention to small within-category differences manifested in low-level acoustic information in sensory memory (Pisoni, 1973). During perception training in the Logan et al. (1991) study, stimuli were presented individually for identification, participants selected a response, and then participants received feedback on the accuracy of their response. Feedback is particularly important under conditions involving a high degree of within-category variability (Homa & Cultice, 1984), which is characteristic of AE /r/ and /l/. Results of the identification tasks showed significant improvement from pretest to posttest with an increase in mean accuracy from 78% to 86%; most improvement occurred between the first and second weeks. The individual talker had a significant effect on accuracy. Although the generalization phase involved few participants, they demonstrated good identification performance with novel words produced by both a familiar and a new talker. In the Logan et al. (1991) study, the initial and medial word positions of the liquids, especially initial clusters, were the most difficult for Japanese speakers; however, using a similar stimulus set and training approach, Yu and Jamieson (1993) found that the final cluster position was the most challenging for five Korean speakers. The consistent finding across the latter two studies was that liquids in clusters proved the most challenging.

In a subsequent study, Lively et al. (1993) divided L1 Japanese learners of English in the US into multiple-talker and single-talker training groups. Testing stimuli were drawn from Logan et al. (1991), and training (15 sessions) was limited to the most difficult word positions identified in that study: initial singleton and cluster, and intervocalic. For the multiple-talker training group, moderate but reliable improvement was noted in identification accuracy (mean pretest = 79.96%, posttest =

85.57%), with decreases in response latency. Talker identity and word position of the target sounds produced significant effects. Learners generalized their improved performance to novel words produced by a familiar and unfamiliar talker (mean accuracy = 88% for both). For the single-talker training group, the overall change in performance over time was not significant, although accuracy improved for /r/ and /l/ in initial clusters.

A third study, that of Lively et al. (1994), addressed another issue in perception training, specifically, retention of improved abilities. Participants were L1 Japanese learners of English as foreign language (EFL) in Japan. The same stimulus set, identification task, and multiple-talker procedure were used as described in Lively et al. (1993). Identification accuracy during training in the 1994 study showed a significant effect of talker and word position and improvement after 3 weeks. To address retention, the posttest and tests of generalization were administered again 3 months following training with only a 2% loss in posttest accuracy. Subsequent auditory perception training studies with the same stimulus set also demonstrated improvement in production ability following perception training for EFL learners in Japan, although with substantial individual variation, and these abilities were retained at a 3-month follow-up test (Bradlow et al., 1999).

Hallmarks of Successful Auditory Perception Training

Comparison of the Strange and Dittman (1984) methodology with the subsequent series of studies described above supports the following hallmarks of successful perception training:

1. compatible testing and training stimuli with verified intelligibility;
2. natural versus synthesized speech;
3. multiple exemplars of one or more target sounds in a range of phonetic environments to facilitate generalization to new stimuli;
4. stimuli produced by multiple talkers (i.e., voices) to promote robust perceptual category development and generalizability;
5. an identification (vs. a discrimination) task;
6. relatively implicit training with feedback;
7. generalization to improved perception of novel stimuli and unfamiliar voices;
8. transfer of skill to other tasks, such as production in the absence of explicit production training; and
9. retention of improved abilities.

Other L2 A-only studies focusing on other sound contrasts also incorporated multiple exemplars. For example, in a study by Wang et al. (1999) in which American listeners were trained to perceive Mandarin tones, there was a 21% overall improvement in identification accuracy, with significant improvement in each of the four tones. There was no significant effect of talker, and improvement generalized to new stimuli and voices, with retention of improvement when tested 6 months later. In addition, participants felt they had improved at least to a moderate degree. In a follow-up study by Wang et al. (2003), improvement in tone identification transferred to production. Post-training tone contours approximated native norms to a greater degree than pretraining contours. Pitch height was more resistant to improvement than pitch contour, especially for the low-dipping Tone 3, which was easier to perceive than produce.

Cognitive Perspectives on Auditory Perception Training

Variable performance across phonetic contexts and talkers is consistent with an episodic view, in that memory encoding of speech involves storage of the attended perceptual details of individual episodes that preserve both contextual features and the indexical properties of speech that pertain to talker identity (e.g., voice quality, national or regional accent, ethnolinguistic variety) and to the talker's current physical and emotional state (e.g., tired or energetic, angry or happy) (Goldinger, 1997; Johnson & Mullennix, 1997; Nygaard et al., 1995). Language learners may rely on context-dependent exemplars (vs. abstract prototypes) as memory representations to which input can be matched for identification (Lively et al., 1993) rather than an abstract description of the category (prototype concept) to which they belong. Incorporating (vs. discarding) sources of variability in the speech signal during training promotes the development of perceptual categories robust to the variability present in natural speech. Training shifts incorrectly focused attention to relevant cues. These shifts have been described as the stretching and shrinking of perceptual distances in psychophysical space to make sounds from different categories (e.g., /r/ and /l/) appear less similar, and within-category variants (e.g., non-velarized and velarized /l/) appear more similar (e.g., Nosofsky, 1986).

However, Pierrehumbert (2016) proposed that a hybrid model of phonological representation is needed, including (a) an abstract level of representation at which phonetic details and contextual features are disregarded, and the existence of which would support the rapid processing of both novel words and familiar words in novel contexts through reuse of existing categories; and (b) a richly detailed level of representation compatible with experimental evidence that shows that contextual details and indexical properties of speech are retained in memory and used for future processing (e.g., Hardison 2006, 2012; Johnson & Mullennix, 1997; Pisoni, 1997).

Visual Cues in L2 Perceptual Learning

In addition to the importance of visual cues in the speechreading literature (see chapter 1), there was some early mention of their role in aiding L2 speech learning. When referring to the difficulty that L1 Japanese speakers experienced in identifying and producing AE /r/ and /l/, Goto (1971) described the auditory presentation of the sounds as a disadvantage because the learners could not read the lips of the talker. A few years later, McGurk and MacDonald (1976) published research findings on what came to be known as the McGurk–MacDonald effect, which was followed by numerous studies investigating the perceptual illusion, including some using stimuli in a non-native language and one by Hardison (1996) using AE stimuli presented to speakers of four L1s actively engaged in learning the L2 (see chapter 2). Hardison's study included congruent as well as incongruent AV stimuli. Results showed higher identification accuracy of /r/ and /f/ when the L1 Japanese and Korean learners could see the talker's articulations while hearing her voice, suggesting an important contribution of visual information to the percept. Therefore, based on the findings of Hardison and the studies demonstrating successful auditory perception training, the next step was to explore how the information value of a talker's facial speech cues could be maximized, following the procedures of successful perception training, to increase their contribution to the perceptual outcome.

AV Perception Training

The influence of modality of training (AV vs. A-only), talkers' articulatory gestures, phonetic environment (vocalic context and word position), and talker familiarity was investigated by Hardison (2003) in the training of Japanese and Korean learners in the US to identify AE /r/ and /l/. Participants were tested on their perception of /r/ and /l/ in AV, A-only, and V-only conditions, and they took 3 weeks (15 sessions) of either AV or A-only perception training. A forced-choice identification paradigm was used in testing and training. Training involved multiple natural exemplars contrasting /r/ and /l/ in different word positions (initial singleton and cluster, medial, final singleton and cluster) with adjacent vowels varying along dimensions of height, backness, and rounding. Training stimuli were produced by a total of five talkers (three female, two male), although each training session involved only one talker because a visual change in talker involves a corresponding slight reduction in performance independent of intelligibility differences as perceivers adapt to the new talker (e.g., Heald & Nusbaum, 2014). Feedback was included.

In the Hardison (2003) study, within each L1 group, the perceptual accuracy of the A-only stimulus condition for the AV-training group was compared to the accuracy of the A-only training group; the A-only stimulus condition was the only condition that the training groups shared, and thus the only one that could be compared. Both L1 groups demonstrated significantly greater improvement in identification accuracy with AV versus A-only training. Visual input from facial cues contributed the most to the bimodal percept for the more difficult phonetic environments: initial word positions for the Japanese speakers and final positions for the Korean speakers. There were significant effects of talker and phonetic environment. Identification accuracy by both L1 groups was better for one of the female talkers who exhibited greater movement of the lips and a wider oral aperture as compared to the other talkers. Greater degrees of articulatory movement enhance the visual distinctiveness of sounds (e.g., Lesner, 1988). In general, for the Japanese and Korean speakers, identification accuracy scores were lower for word-initial /r/ and /l/ followed by /u/ (e.g., *broom-bloom*); for the Korean speakers, accuracy was lower in final positions following the high front vowel /i/ (e.g., *hear-heal*). The effect of phonetic environment could have been due to a combination of factors, such as L1 phonotactic constraints, including the absence of consonant clusters in Japanese (Tsujimura, 2013) and avoidance of syllable-final clusters in Korean (Kim-Renaud, 1974). In addition, some degree of visual distinctiveness is lost between /r/ and /l/ in contexts with rounded vowels (Owens & Blazek, 1985).

Training transferred to production improvement for both L1 groups in the Hardison (2003) study, especially for those who received AV training and who were often observed to imitate silently the training talkers' articulatory gestures during the sessions. Production results also showed some similarities with the perception findings; for example, initial clusters and contexts with rounded vowels were more difficult for the Japanese speakers. A direct comparison of multiple- versus single-talker training was possible for the Korean speakers and showed only a marginally significant benefit of multiple-talker training on accuracy in tests of generalization to novel words, and this occurred only in the AV condition.

Hazan et al. (2005) carried out a pretest-posttest study testing 39 Japanese learners of British English on their perception of the /v/-/b, p/ distinction in AV, A-only, and V-only conditions and administered 10 sessions of either AV or A-only perception training. AV training was more effective than A-only in improving perception. In a second experiment in the same study, 62 Japanese speakers were similarly tested on their perception of the /r/-/l/ contrast and took 10 training sessions using either AV stimuli with a natural face, AV stimuli with a synthetic face synchronized to natural speech, or A-only stimuli. Participants' perception of the /r/-/l/ contrast improved overall, and AV training was not more successful than A-only. Training with the natural versus the synthetic face provided better results (see also Massaro & Light, 2003). Hazan et al. (2005) attributed the findings to the observation that the /r/-/l/ contrast was "less visually distinct than the labial/labiodental contrast" (p. 368). However, visual salience is variable and depends on the talker, the phonetic environment, the recording conditions, and other factors.

As compared to Hardison (2003), there were several methodological details in Hazan et al. (2005) that could explain the contrasting findings: (a) Hazan et al.'s participants were a mix of 40 university students in Japan who reported little experience interacting in English and 22 students who were attending a short-term English course in the United Kingdom; (b) the articulatory gestures of the Southeastern British English talkers may not have provided the same level of visual discernibility as that of the talkers from the upper Midwest in the US; (c) a shorter training period (10 sessions) was used; and (d) the stimuli were different in the two studies. Specifically, Hazan et al.'s testing stimuli embedded /r/ and /l/ in nonsense words in initial and medial positions as singletons or in clusters with /k/ and /f/, and in the context of the point vowels /i, ɑ, u/. However, training stimuli were minimal pairs (real words) containing /r/ and /l/ in initial singleton and cluster positions and in medial singleton and cluster positions (no final position), with various vowels.

Hazan et al. (2006) did not find an advantage for a talker's facial speech cues for L1 Spanish speakers trying to identify British English /p, b, v/ embedded in nonsense words. In their study, mean identification accuracy in AV perception (78.1%) was very similar to A-only (77.3%). More specifically, participants who performed poorly in distinguishing /b/ and /v/ did so in both AV and A-only conditions; similarly, those who could distinguish the sounds did so regardless of modality. Several factors could account for the lack of compatibility of the Hazan et al. findings with those of other studies. Among them is the discernibility of articulatory gestures associated with different Spanish sounds produced with labial involvement (see Hardison, 1996), and the differences in discernibility between bilabial and labiodental articulations in British English, to which the participants in the Hazan et al. (2006) study were exposed, and those articulations in American English, which were used in Hardison (1996).

Factors other than phonetic environment and talker may impact perceptual accuracy. To investigate whether age influenced the efficacy of training, Shinohara (2021) provided both adults (university students ages 18–23 years) and children (ages 7–12 years) with 10 sessions of AV perceptual identification training on /r/ and /l/. The adults had started learning English at about age 12, and the children knew some basic English words from school; neither age group spoke English in their daily lives. Testing before and after training was conducted in AV, A-only, and V-only conditions and revealed more improvement in identification accuracy in the AV condition than in the single-modality conditions, with no clear benefit for one age group. Both groups showed a similar amount of improvement in the auditory discrimination of the critical acoustic cue (F3) for /r/.

Kawase et al. (2014) investigated the contribution of facial speech cues to Canadian English listeners' perceptions of English consonants in CV syllables produced by both native Japanese and native English speakers. Consonant contrasts included /b/-/v/, /θ/-/s/, and /l/-/r/ in AV, A-only, and V-only conditions. Auditory identification accuracy of the Japanese speakers' productions of /b, s, l/ was better than for /v, θ, r/. The addition of visual cues significantly improved intelligibility for /v/ and /θ/ but not /r/; the Japanese speakers' articulatory gestures lacked the lip protrusion present in native English speakers' productions of /r/ and thus were not as beneficial.

In a perception training study focused on the identification of French nasal vowels, Inceoglu (2014) assigned L2 French learners (L1 AE) to one of three groups: AV training, A-only training, and control (no training). These vowels can be placed along a lip-rounding continuum ranging from the hyper-rounded [ɔ̃] to the slightly rounded [ɑ̃] and unrounded [ɛ̃] (see chapter 5). Similar to the findings in Hardison (2003), both AV and A-only training groups in the Inceoglu study showed significant improvement. Although the AV group in Inceoglu's study did not show overall a statistically significant advantage over the A-only group in perceptual identification accuracy, the results per vowel indicated greater improvement following AV versus A-only training. In addition, evaluation of the effects of perception training on production revealed significantly greater production accuracy for the AV as compared to the A-only group.

Cognitive Perspectives on AV Perception Training

In an adaptation of multiple-trace memory theory (e.g., Hintzman, 1986), Hardison (2003, 2012) proposed that the exemplars of episodic models and the prototypes of an abstractionist approach could coexist, as Pierrehumbert (2016) later suggested. Multiple-trace memory theory states that the memory encoding of a perceptual event involves storage of attended details as episodes or traces, preserving aspects of variability. In processing, a retrieval cue or probe contacts all stored traces in long-term memory simultaneously in parallel, activating each to a greater or lesser degree based on similarity to features of the probe. In AV speech perception, the features that comprise the preliminary representation that probes memory depend on the attention given to the auditory and visual attributes of a stimulus relevant for a given task. Jusczyk (1993) considered the extraction of auditory features in infant speech input as part of the human auditory system's guided learning mechanism that served an attention-weighting role by giving prominence to the critical features involved in L1 perceptual attunement. For L2 learners, perception training can serve to focus attention to critical stimulus attributes for the L2. The probe is said to return an echo or response to primary memory. For learners, the goal is to have the echo from an aggregate of clearly defined L2 traces overshadow (i.e., be greater in terms of strength of activation) that from any similar L1 traces. As a result, new L2 traces should be less ambiguous in content and at greater psychological distance to L1 traces.

In this model of memory, at the time information is retrieved, abstract knowledge can be derived from a composite of episodic traces. Thus, a perceptual category is an aggregate of individual exemplars (i.e., episodic traces) activated together at the time of information retrieval. The prototype concept, as a representation of the shared features of multiple traces, captures the advantage of redundancy. Although exemplars preserve detailed relevant information of an event, they may be forgotten over time; in contrast, the prototype concept is retained longer. During training, the more exemplars of a category that are stored, the more likely one or more will generalize to the probe and influence its classification. Goldinger (2007) provided computational evidence of a reciprocal neural network (i.e., a complementary learning systems approach) that included interdependent episodic and abstract representations involved in word perception. This approach combines the advantage of a fast-learning network and a more stable network.

Role of Variability in Perception Training

The success of some perception training studies has been attributed, in part, to the use of a highly variable stimulus set, leading to the frequent use in the literature of the acronym HVPT (high variability perception training). However, unlike the variability in natural language, the variability in studies is controlled. The testing and training environments typically involve only one talker at a time, sound-attenuated conditions, stimuli that do not vary along multiple dimensions simultaneously, and other kinds of controls. This level of control helps to focus participants' attention on critical cues for AV or A-only speech perception.

Some variability in perception training that incorporates exposure to multiple voices and faces is beneficial for the achievement of a number of objectives, including (a) the development of perceptual categories robust to the variability in the natural language environment; (b) generalization to new stimuli and novel talkers; and (c) transfer to improved production ability as shown by the results of auditory training studies (e.g., Bradlow et al., 1999; Lively et al., 1993) and AV training studies (Hardison, 2003, 2005b, 2018b).

However, the incorporation of variability in input may be overwhelming for some learners. The appropriate amount of variability and the ideal timing of its introduction in the learning process are not likely to be the same for every learner. A notable study by Leather (1990) on the perception and production of Chinese tone by Dutch speakers was published just prior to the auditory training studies of Pisoni and colleagues (e.g., Lively et al., 1993). As Leather (1990) concluded:

> The present perceptual learning data underline the need for the learner to have access to sets of exemplars which collectively span an appropriate range of inter-speaker variation. Too much or too little variability at too early a stage may prevent the learner from discovering with sufficient accuracy the prototypical forms that exemplars expound. (p. 96)

There may be an advantage to learners of a relatively early introduction to a controlled amount of variability. Studies have shown that much perceptual development for most late L2 learners situated in the target environment occurs within the first 6–12 months of immersion, and that little perceptual benefit occurs from additional experience beyond the initial year (e.g., Flege & Liu, 2001; Jia et al., 2006). For example, English vowel intelligibility for both L1 Mandarin and L1 Slavic speakers improved significantly from about 64% to 74% accuracy within their first year in Canada, with most of the improvement occurring during the first 6 months (Munro & Derwing, 2008). Variability in perception training often contributes to production improvement, but it also has implications for L2 learners' ability to identify words earlier in connected speech.

Transfer of Segmental Training to Earlier Word Identification

Early research demonstrated the transfer of segmentally focused perception training to better word identification in connected speech. Walden et al. (1981) determined that L1 English adults with diminished hearing whose English consonant identification improved with AV training also exhibited better word identification in sentences. They surmised that such training reduced the number of alternatives from which the perceptual system had to choose in order to recognize words in continuous speech.

In addition, research with a normal-hearing population demonstrated that articulatory gestures often precede the associated acoustic signal (Munhall & Tohkura, 1998), and that such temporal precedence could serve a priming role for a perceiver in the AV speech recognition process. Skipper, van Wassenhove, et al. (2007) proposed that visible articulatory movements allow the perceiver's brain to reduce the set of potential targets the speaker will likely produce. The more informative visual cues (e.g., those for bilabials /p, b, m/) offer the ability to make more precise predictions. However, for L2 learners, a priming role depends on the salience and information value of the visual cue and the perceiver's language experience (e.g., Hardison, 2005b, 2005c, 2018b).

The original auditory gating paradigm (Grosjean, 1980) was extended in research by Hardison (2005b, 2005c) to AV speech in order to investigate the transfer effects of AV and A-only segmental perception training of /r/, /l/, /p/, and /f/ to earlier spoken word identification by L1 Japanese and Korean learners of AE. In gating, successively increasing increments of a speech stimulus are presented, each representing a gate, until the target is correctly identified. In the Hardison (2005b, 2005c) research, AV and A-only gated stimuli were presented to match the modality of the participant's perception training. Stimuli were familiar bisyllabic content words from low-density lexical neighbourhoods, beginning with /p/, /f/, /r/, /l/, and nonlabials /s, t, k/, all with initial-syllable stress, combined with

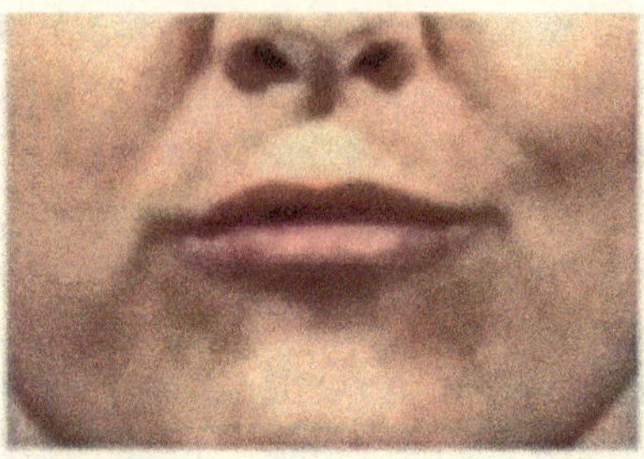

FIGURE 3.1 Lip Shape for American English [ɹ]

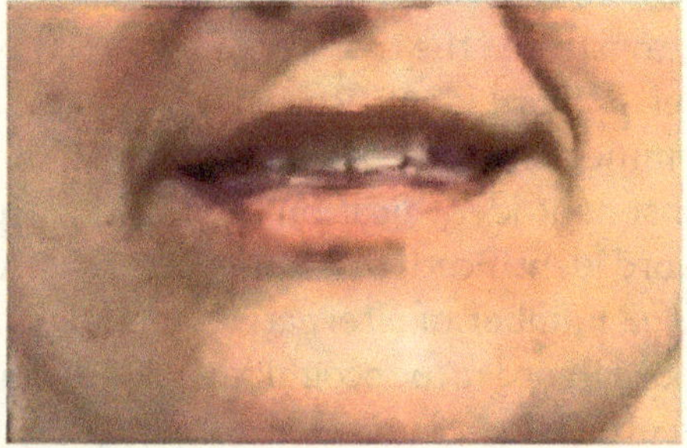

FIGURE 3.2 Lip Shape for American English [l]

high, low, and rounded vowels. One gate was composed of two frames of recorded speech. The identification point of a word was the gate at which the word was correctly identified (and not subsequently changed).

Findings in Hardison (2005b) supported the priming role of visual cues in AV speech processing. For example, in the AV and A-only conditions, L1 Japanese learners required less information in order to identify gated words that began with the CV sequence of /r/ + a low vowel (e.g., *rocket*) or the low vowel as the first element in a diphthong (e.g., *writer*) as compared to those sequences with a rounded vowel (e.g., *ruler*, *robot*). In phonetic contexts with a low versus a rounded vowel, there was a more visually salient articulatory gesture for consonants, consistent with other studies (e.g., Owens & Blazek, 1985). The L1 Korean learners in Hardison (2005b) also demonstrated earlier identification of words following perception training with visual cues. Results for the Korean speakers followed patterns similar to those of the Japanese speakers with regard to the influence of the adjacent vowel. Figures 3.1 and 3.2 show the lip shape of the talker from the study in the process of producing [ɹ] at the beginning of *reason* and [l] at the beginning of *leather*, respectively.

The gating paradigm was also used to investigate the effects of perception training, visual cues, and preceding sentence context on spoken word identification by L2 learners (72 L1 Japanese, 88 L1 Korean) and 66 native AE speakers in Hardison (2018b). For the learners, parallel word identification tasks were administered before and after segmental perception training using the stimuli and methodology of Hardison (2003, 2005a). Learners were assigned to one of four groups: AV or A-only, which were each subdivided into word-in-sentence context and excised-word conditions for the gating tasks. The sentence fragments preceding the target words were designed to be relatively short and appropriate syntactically, semantically, and pragmatically. In addition, the fragments were tested with native speakers and a peer group of learners to ensure that the participants in the study would be unlikely to guess the target word without using any of its acoustic-phonetic (and visual) properties. A female native AE speaker recorded familiar bisyllabic words from low-density neighbourhoods, beginning with /p/, /f/, /r/, /l/, and nonlabials /s, t, k/, followed by three visually salient vowels. Participant groups for the gating tasks received modality-matched perception training.

Analysis of learner data in the Hardison (2018b) study involved a mixed-effects model with the following fixed factors: modality (AV, A-only); stimulus condition (i.e., gated word presented with preceding sentence context vs. excised from the sentence); initial CV sequence of the target word; and time (pre- and post-training). Trials and participants were random factors. For the Japanese speakers, the gating tasks revealed significant main effects of modality (earlier identification with AV), condition (earlier identification with context), time (earlier identification following training), and the target words' initial CV sequence. There was a significant interaction involving modality, time, and CV sequence, indicating that the advantage of AV over A-only input was more accentuated for some sequences as compared to others following perception training. Further analysis identified the CV sequences as those with /r/ and /l/. For example, for words beginning with /r/ followed by an unrounded vowel (e.g., *rocket*), the amount of input needed for accurate identification declined from a mean of about 95% in the AV pretest to 63% in the AV posttest (data collapsed here across stimulus conditions). In contrast, in the pretest A-only conditions, these words were not identified prior to their acoustic offset; however, following training, a mean of about 77% of a word was sufficient for identification. Words beginning with /r/ and a rounded vowel (e.g., *robot*) were not identified before their acoustic offset in the AV or A-only pretest, but in the posttest, identification was possible based on about 80% (AV) or 90% (A-only) of the target words.

Data from the Korean speakers in Hardison (2018b) revealed significant main effects of modality, condition, and time. Word identification was earlier with visual cues, preceding sentence context, and following training. In contrast to the Japanese speakers, there was no significant main effect of the initial CV sequence; however, further analysis of interactions involving this factor showed that sequences with /r/ and /l/ benefited more from AV input and training as compared to other sequences. For example, identification of words beginning with /f, r, l/ showed a greater AV (vs. A-only) advantage. About 95% of each word beginning with /r/ or /l/ in the two AV conditions (context vs. no context) was required for identification prior to training, regardless of the adjacent vowel. In the posttest, this figure dropped to about 68%. In the A-only conditions before training, identification was not made prior to the acoustic offset of the words; following training, however, about 79% of each /r/-initial word and 84% of each /l/-initial word was needed for identification. In all, the four main factors (modality, stimulus condition, training, initial CV sequence) accounted for about 63% of the variance in the L1 Japanese data and about 53% in the L1 Korean data. For both learner groups, the effects of contextual and visual cues remained statistically independent and may have competed for attention across trials and participants. In sum, word identification was earlier for both learner groups following perception training, which alone accounted for 42% of the variance for the Japanese speakers and 36% for the Korean speakers.

For the native AE speakers in the Hardison (2018b) study, like the L2 learners, there were significant main effects of modality (earlier identification with AV) and condition (earlier identification with context) with interactions involving the target words' initial CV sequence, showing that words beginning with /r/ and /l/ benefited more from AV input as compared to other CV sequences, but only in the sentence condition. Unlike the learner data, there was a significant Modality x Condition interaction such that only 63% of a word was needed for identification when both visual and contextual cues were present as compared to about 82% for either the AV word (no context) or A-only sentence (no visual) conditions, and 93% for the A-only word.

In sum, to the list of the hallmarks of successful training mentioned earlier we can add the presence of talkers' facial speech cues, an extended view of the composition of the phonetic environment of a target sound to include the adjacent vowel, and consideration of transfer of perception training to tasks other than production, such as the earlier identification of words in isolation and connected speech (Hardison, 2005b, 2005c, 2018b).

The AV Temporal Integration Window

Behavioural evidence across studies supports a temporal precedence of articulatory gestures over the associated acoustic signal that could serve a priming role for perceivers in speech recognition by reducing the set of potential targets that the talker being observed will likely produce (Hardison, 2018b; Munhall & Tohkura, 1998; Skipper, van Wassenhove et al., 2007). Cortical areas supporting speech production serve a predictive role by providing information about the relationship between articulatory gesture and sound. This information can speed up cortical processing of auditory signals by native speakers within 100 ms of signal onset (van Wassenhove et al., 2005). More informative visual cues (e.g., bilabial consonants) offer more precise predictions.

However, claims involving the visual precedence of articulatory gestures might be an oversimplification of a complex process (Schwartz & Savariaux, 2014). Gestures of different kinds have components or phases. For example, in a manual gesture sequence, the first phase is preparation, when a speaker's hand-arm begins to move (Kendon, 1972; see also chapter 6). For an articulatory gesture, the first phase or event is also preparatory; for example, to produce [p] at the beginning of an utterance, the speaker's lips come together. The second event is the closure release, and synchronous with the visual closure release is the auditory release for [p]. Therefore, for AV stimuli, there is a period of asynchrony between the onset of the visual preparatory gesture and the offset for the auditory event. Some researchers have assigned a measure in the range of 100–300 ms to this period of asynchrony (e.g., Chandrasekaran et al., 2009); however, Schwartz and Savariaux (2014) argued that this assessment might be valid only for CV syllables produced in isolation or in utterance-initial position, as are typical of stimuli used in perception studies, but not for syllables "chained in sequences," which are often encountered in natural speech (p. 3). The claim that vision leads audition does not take coarticulatory effects into account. For example, in a gating experiment using French in which the task was to identify the final vowel in the gated sequences [zizi] ([i] is a high front unrounded vowel) and [zizy] ([y] is a high front rounded vowel), identification was affected by the anticipatory rounding gesture associated with [y], which occurred during the last 40 ms of the talker's production of the vowel [i] (Troille et al., 2010).

Natural coordination between sound and image can produce instances of both lead and lag for the visual input. In van Wassenhove et al. (2007), audio recordings of CV syllables were dubbed onto video recordings, producing incongruent auditory /pa/–visual /ka/ and auditory /ba/–visual /ga/ pairs, typical of perceptual illusion stimuli (e.g., McGurk & MacDonald, 1976; see chapter 2). Asynchronies ranged from –467 ms (auditory lead) to +467 ms (auditory lag). An identification task by L1 English speakers revealed illusory fused responses (i.e., *ta* or *da*) for bimodal asynchronies from –30 ms (auditory lead) to +170 ms (auditory lag). Results pointed to a 200 ms duration window for integration.

Schwartz and Savariaux (2014) recorded six repetitions of eight syllables /pa, ta, ka, ba, da, ga, ma, na/ produced by a French speaker either as isolated CV syllables with a 500 ms silent period between each syllable, or as a series of VCV sequences (e.g., /apa/) with no silence between the sequences. The complex temporal relationship between auditory and visual cues resulted in an integration window ranging from a 30–50 ms auditory lead to a 170–200 ms auditory lag. Schwartz and Savariaux proposed that the perceptual system internalizes this range through experience, compatible with Welch and Warren's (1980) unity hypothesis. According to this hypothesis, perceivers naturally integrate multisensory stimuli referring to the same event, and this leads to both fused percepts and a decreased ability to detect temporal asynchronies (Vatakis & Spence, 2007).

The plasticity in the size of this temporal integration window was investigated by Powers et al. (2009) using a perceptual learning paradigm in which participants were given feedback during a two-alternative forced-choice AV simultaneity judgment task. Training resulted in a substantial narrowing of about 40% in the size of the window. Such findings have implications for L2 perceptual learning; in fact, Navarra et al. (2010) reported that language experience appeared to influence the integration of AV speech cues. In that study, English and Spanish speakers, with little prior experience with Spanish and English, respectively, were asked to judge the simultaneity of the bimodal presentation of spoken sentences in each language. Results indicated that perception of simultaneity required the visual speech stream to lead the auditory stream by a significantly larger interval in the native versus non-native language; however, this difference tended to disappear with increasing amounts of experience with the non-native language. Navarra et al. concluded that linguistic experience modifies the constraining role that visual information plays in the temporal alignment of AV speech cues.

Neurophysiological Perspectives on the Perception–Production Link

It is likely that exposure to visual speech during language acquisition establishes the neural circuitry linking visually perceived gestures to the speech motor system (e.g., Lewkowicz & Hansen-Tift, 2012). The behavioural and neuropsychological data suggest that such circuitry remains active in adulthood, as is the case for auditory speech (Hickok & Poeppel, 2000). Using BOLD fMRI, Venezia et al. (2016) identified a visuomotor circuit/pathway for speech production as participants perceived and covertly rehearsed CV syllable sequences presented in A-only, V-only, or AV conditions. The motor act of rehearsal produced different patterns of sensorimotor activation when cued by V-only or AV speech as compared to A-only speech such that a network of brain regions, including the left posterior middle temporal gyrus (pMTG) and several frontoparietal sensorimotor areas (see Figure 2.1), were more strongly activated during rehearsal that was cued by a visible talker. Some of these brain regions responded exclusively to rehearsal cued by V-only or AV speech. Venezia et al. maintained that increased activation was likely produced through recruitment of a visual speech–specific network of sensorimotor brain regions, and that the left pMTG was crucial in the visual-to-motor speech pathway. Other studies also found activation in the left pMTG during perception of V-only or AV speech (e.g., Callan et al., 2003; Calvert & Campbell, 2003; Sekiyama et al., 2003). In addition, research demonstrated a localized area that is selective for visual speech versus nonspeech facial gestures and that showed tuning to visual (vs. auditory) phoneme categories; this was dubbed the *temporal visual speech area* in the posterior temporal cortex, located ventral and posterior to the multisensory pSTS (Bernstein et al., 2011; Bernstein and Liebenthal, 2014). The pSTS is known to respond when perceivers are asked to report the speech of a talker they either see or hear. This activation is enhanced when perceivers have had some AV experience with the talker (von Kriegstein et al., 2005), a finding that has implications for exposure to multiple talkers in perception–production training.

Implications for Instruction

Multisensory input can enhance learning in several ways (Shams & Seitz, 2008). At a basic level, it appeals to individuals with different learning styles (e.g., visual vs. auditory learners). At a processing level, it offers multiple channels of congruent input and appears to be superior in terms of retention of information in memory. The foundation of speech processing as a mechanism that is not linked to information from a single sensory modality is not a new idea (e.g., Reisberg et al., 1987; Summerfield, 1987). This concept of multisensory speech has been referred to as *amodal* (Reisberg et al., 1987), *modality-neutral* (e.g., Rosenblum, 2005), and *supramodal* (e.g., Fowler, 2004; Rosenblum & Dorsi, 2021). The supramodal theory posits a speech mechanism that is sensitive to phonetically relevant information embodied in multiple sensory modalities rather than linked to information from a specific modality. This notion is consistent with the *metamodal* theory of multisensory perception, which argues that function and task, rather than a specific sensory modality, guide perceptual processes (e.g., Pascual-Leone & Hamilton, 2001; see chapter 2).

The *supramodal* learning hypothesis (Rosenblum & Dorsi, 2021) proposes that during bimodal speech-related perceptual experiences, perceivers learn talker-specific articulatory properties that can then enhance subsequent processing of that talker's speech regardless of the modality of the input. This hypothesis is consistent with the finding that AV training for L2 learners also improves unimodal (i.e., A-only and V-only) perceptual accuracy (Hardison, 2003; Hazan et al., 2005; Leather, 1990).

The findings of other studies also support the importance of multimodal input in L2 instruction. For example, Macedonia and Kepler (2013) advocated sensorimotor encoding as a natural way to learn L2 vocabulary in order to maximize the benefit of word storage in networks in the brain. Several brain imaging studies determined that reading a word with a meaning that is associated with a sensory perception or with movement of one or more parts of the body activates brain regions in the motor cortex that are related to the meaning. For example, in research by Hauk et al. (2004), reading words such as *pick*, *kick*, and *lick* activated cortical regions related to the movements of the hand and arm, foot, and face, respectively. In a study by Carota et al. (2012), words for food elicited activity in the area of the motor cortex that controls tongue movements and a region in the forebrain related to the perception of taste. Carota et al. also discovered that words related to tools activated the area in the motor cortex that processes finger movements.

Given the connection in multimodal networks between words and the experiences that are related to their meanings, Macedonia and Kepler (2013) advocated for these meaning-action and meaning-perception connections to be part of foreign language instruction. The implication is that L2 vocabulary learning should involve all of the senses and body movements associated with specific word meanings; this is consistent with the view that multisensory learning is more effective than unisensory (e.g., Shams & Seitz, 2008), and with views that gestures facilitate retention of verbal information (e.g., Engelkamp & Krumnacker, 1980; see chapter 6). Imitation was also proposed as an essential aspect of language learning because mirror neurons are part of the neurobiological basis for imitation, which includes silent rehearsal of talkers' articulatory gestures, as observed in AV perception training (e.g., Hardison, 2003).

Chapter 3 in Review

This chapter outlined the experimental findings that demonstrate the hallmarks of effective A-only perception training, the role of HVPT, and the transfer of perception training to production improvement. To this foundation were added a number of other features of effective perception training based on a review of relevant research showing the benefit of seeing a talker's facial speech cues; the value of considering the adjacent vowel in addition to word position as part of a sound's phonetic environment; and the transfer of training to earlier identification of a word presented in isolation and following sentence context.

Proposed explanations of L2 perceptual challenges ranged from Trubetskoy's (1939/1969) notion of L2 sounds being "strained through the phonological sieve" of the L1 (p. 52) to exemplar-based models of the encoding of speech in memory in order to preserve perceptual details for later processing (e.g., Johnson & Mullennix, 1997), and to the merging of exemplars and prototypes in an adaptation of multiple-trace memory theory (e.g., Hardison, 2003, 2012; Pierrehumbert, 2016).

Neurophysiological findings were reviewed that support AV integration, the link between speech perception and production, and the use of multimodal input in language instruction. Having established the importance of more than one modality of input in speech processing, chapter 4 pursues the question of where perceivers look for speech information on dynamic (i.e., talking) faces in the examination of the important perceptual role of eye gaze.

Chapter 3 Notes

1. In Nikolai Trubetzkoy's (1890–1938) view, every utterance had three aspects: an expression of the speaker, an appeal to the listener, and a representation of the topic being communicated.
2. Voice-onset-time (VOT) is the length of time between the release of a stop consonant and the onset of voicing for the following vowel.

Chapter 4

The Perceptual Functions of Eye Gaze

> *Well, it often happens that people with good eyesight fail to see what is right in front of them. They have too much to take in, I suppose. Whereas people who cannot see (or see very little) have to take in only the essentials, whatever registers tellingly on their remaining senses.*
>
> – Bond (2014 , p. 2)

*****

Background

The phrase *the ayes have it*, referring to a majority of affirmative responses following a vote, has been part of the English language for many years. The word *aye*, meaning "yes," has an uncertain etymology, although Anatoly Liberman (2014) has suggested an origin in the sixteenth century. This chapter is interested in the phrase's homophonous version, perhaps a pun – *the eyes have it* – which appeared as the title of at least two popular works of fiction originally written in the 1950s. In the first, a short story by Ruskin Bond (2013), a man whose eyes were sensitive only to light and darkness was travelling on a train in India when he met a young woman with whom he chatted briefly. It was only after she left the train and another passenger who had entered the compartment made a comment that he realized the woman was also blind. Through other senses, the two of them had been aware of and had chatted about their surroundings.

In the second work, Philip K. Dick (1953) satirically recounted reading a story, purportedly discovered in a paperback found on a bus, in which several expressions involving the eyes took on a literal, though bizarre, meaning in the science fiction context of belonging to lifeforms from another planet. As Dick read the passage "his eyes moved from person to person," he imagined quite literally that "the eyes had clearly come apart from the rest of him and were on their own" (p. 128)!

Beyond its appearance in a romantic short story and a science fiction tale, the phrase *the eyes have it*, either in that or a similar form, has appeared in the title of a variety of publications. More recently, in the research literature, it has been used with reference to the perceptual and interactional roles the eyes play in face-to-face communication (e.g., Emery, 2000). For example, in the medical community, an internal medicine specialist posted the following reflection on the role of the eyes as a gateway to a patient's mind:

> When I am looking for the answer, I have learned through more than fifty years of experience, the eyes have it. They can tell you about diabetes, hypertension, obstructive liver disease, a stroke or brain tumor and much more from a physical perspective, but looking a patient directly in the eyes can also tell you something about what they are really thinking deep in the soul. (McGowen, 2012)

In addition, and with specific relevance to the current chapter, some authors of eye-movement studies (e.g., Võ et al., 2012) have turned the phrase into a question to ask if the eyes really do have it; that is, do they prevail as the part of a talker's face that attracts the attention of a perceiver? Not surprisingly, perhaps – it depends.

The research described in previous chapters implied a benefit, to varying degrees, of AV input in L1 and L2 speech processing, with a particular focus on a talker's mouth area as the source of input and presumably the primary target of a perceiver's eye gaze. The question arises as to whether perceivers also look to other areas of a talker's face during speech in their L1 and/or L2. This chapter begins with a discussion of cultural influences on eye gaze followed by an overview of eye movement basics and a review of the relevant literature on the perceptual roles of eye gaze, including studies related to L2 speech. This will set the stage for chapter 5, which reports the findings of an eye-tracking study conducted to investigate the influence of task difficulty on the eye movements of L1 English learners of L2 French in a speech perception task.

Cultural Influences on Eye Gaze

The literature on non-verbal communication – which includes facial expressions, eye contact, body movements, gestures, and other kinds of non-verbal communicative behaviours[iii] – often makes reference to

iii. Editor's Note: Among these other behaviours are pantomimed actions as well as conventionalized, meaningful, but nonlinguistic sounds, such as the tongue-clicking sound indicating disapproval that is often written as *tsk-tsk* or the sound termed in

differences in eye gaze behaviour between cultures, especially the American and Japanese. Many Americans might question the character of an individual who does not make a certain amount of culturally appropriate eye contact, especially with an interlocutor in face-to-face communication (e.g., Argyle, 1967). American children are taught to do so; Japanese children are taught to direct their gaze to the throat or tie knot (e.g., Morsbach, 1982).

Hattori (1987) investigated whether 2 years of experience communicating face-to-face with Americans while studying abroad in the US had influenced the communication behaviour of 45 Japanese high school students. Before returning to Japan, the students completed a survey focused on their non-verbal communication in the US. These students, whom Hattori considered bilingual and bicultural, had used English to communicate with their friends while in the US. On the survey, the majority of them stated that they gazed more (40% *much more*, 36% *a little more*) at an interlocutor's eyes as compared to their Japanese friends who had lived only in Japan. During conversations with other Japanese speakers who avoided making eye contact, 42% of the students perceived their interlocutors as somewhat unfriendly, 74% considered them impolite to varying degrees (e.g., 36% *very impolite*), and 53% considered them disrespectful to varying degrees (e.g., 20% *very disrespectful*). Hattori suggested that early in their stay in the US when they had difficulty understanding English, the students "had to catch as much information as possible from their interlocutor [and] therefore the amount of gaze increased" (p. 115). The students might also have adopted the American custom of looking at the face of an interlocutor.

Although Hattori's survey items specifically addressed only eye gaze behaviour, the findings also raised the question as to whether the students were focused solely on the eyes of their interlocutors given that the mouth area contributes speech information, as described in earlier chapters. When AV cues are present in a speech event, there may be competition for a perceiver's attention between the auditory modality and the visual modality as well as between different parts of the visual modality. The most informative gaze target in a given situation may not be readily apparent to a perceiver and may vary across the stimulus as it moves. A talking face is a dynamic stimulus. In the case

---

slang a "raspberry," which the *Merriam-Webster Dictionary* online defines as "[short for raspberry tart, rhyming slang for fart]: a sound of contempt made by protruding the tongue between the lips and expelling air forcibly to produce a vibration . . . *broadly*: an expression of disapproval or contempt" (https://www.merriam-webster.com/dictionary/raspberry). – MCP

of language learners who are looking at the face of a talker producing the L2, speech processing can be influenced by learner variables such as the L1, proficiency with L2 aural skills, knowledge of the relationship between articulatory gestures and speech sounds, and the amount of exposure to a range of L2 speakers in communicative situations (e.g., Hardison, 1996, 2003).

Cultural norms are also a factor in attention directed towards a talker's face. An eye-tracking study involving East Asian and Western Caucasian observers discovered that when the task was to learn and then recognize faces, a cultural contrast emerged (Blais et al., 2008). When looking at a recorded face on a monitor, the Western Caucasian observers consistently fixated the eye regions and partially the mouth, described as a triangular scan strategy; however, East Asian observers fixated the central region of the face more.[1] Observers in the study did not change their perceptual strategy according to the race of the person they saw.

The next section provides some basic information about eye movements and visual attention, followed by a review of the relevant eye-movement literature.

Eye Movement Basics

Of primary importance in a discussion of eye movements in speech perception are the concepts of fixations and saccades.

Fixations

A *fixation* is a period of time when the eye is relatively still (Holmqvist & Andersson, 2017). Following the strong version of the *eye-mind hypothesis*, originally developed in reading research, measuring a fixation also measures the attention paid to that target (Just & Carpenter, 1980; Reichle et al., 2006). In the real world, however, fixating something does not necessarily entail close attentive processing and does not guarantee a trace in working memory of the fixated target (Triesch et al., 2003).[2] Highly salient objects are more frequently fixated as compared to those with low salience (Nuthmann et al., 2020).

Galley et al. (2015) proposed four different ranges of fixation durations, each of which reflects a different cognitive process: (a) very short fixations (<90 ms), which are not controlled by conscious cognitive operations; (b) *express fixations* (90–150 ms), which may reflect simple cognitive processes, such as movement to anticipated locations; (c) *cognitive fixations* (151–900 ms), which allow for complex operations; and (d) very long fixations (>900 ms), which fall outside of the cognitive window and are reported to be rare. Galley et al. emphasized the complexity of the relationship between fixation durations and cognitive processes – a relationship that cannot simply be deduced from measurements such as the duration of fixations and the frequency of movements from one fixation to another (i.e., *saccades*; see below).

When looking at an image, optimal image quality is achieved if the target is directly fixated (i.e., eye movement is paused) in such a way that the image falls on the small central *fovea* – a small depression in the retina of the eye also known as the centre of the field of vision – where acuity is the greatest (Bruce & Green, 1985). Outside of the fovea, in the parafoveal area, the image gradually becomes blurrier. The larger part of the visual field, the peripheral area, is better adapted to low-light vision but can detect movement as well as contrasts between colours and shapes. It provides much less detailed information; therefore, fixating ensures a better quality of information about the target for the brain to process.

Saccades

The rapid movement of the eye from one fixation to another is called a *saccade*, a type of movement that perceivers often use to inspect visual stimuli. A saccade typically takes 30–80 ms to complete; however, the decision to make a saccade is made roughly 60–70 ms before the saccade is executed (Holmqvist & Andersson, 2017). After the onset of a target for a saccade, which may be the movement of an already fixated target, it takes about 200 ms for eye movement to begin (e.g., Purves et al., 2004, chapter 19). During this delay, the position of the target with respect to the fovea is computed (i.e., how far the eye has to move), and the difference between the initial and intended position, or movement error, is converted into a motor command that activates the extraocular muscles to move the eyes the correct distance in the appropriate direction.

Saccadic eye movements are considered *ballistic* because the saccade-generating system cannot respond to subsequent changes in the position of the target during the course of the eye movement (Purves et al., 2004, chapter 19). If the target moves again during this time (about 15–100 ms), the saccade will miss the target, and a second saccade must be made to correct the error. Saccades can be voluntary but are also made unconsciously because they do not require a stimulus.

In contrast, perceivers also make a slower movement called a *smooth pursuit*, which often, but not always, involves following something because it is driven by a feedback loop that checks gaze position against the stimulus position. Smooth pursuit movements are much slower tracking movements of the eyes designed to keep a moving stimulus on the fovea. Such movements are under voluntary control in the sense that the observer can choose whether or not to track a moving stimulus (Purves et al., 2004, chapter 19).

Visual Attention

When we move our eyes to focus on a specific area of an image or object, we are placing the foveal region of the eye on that area to maximize visual processing resources by providing the brain with the best possible image. Even though we usually prefer to move our eye gaze to follow a shift in attention (i.e., *overt* attention), we can also attend to the peripheral areas of the visual field without eye movements (i.e., *covert* attention; see, e.g., Hunt & Kingstone, 2003). The location of a fixation can indicate the focus of overt attention, and the duration of a fixation can imply the processing effort directed towards that location. One fixation can last from tens of milliseconds to several seconds. Under normal light conditions, the retina requires exposure of about 80 ms to a new image before it registers that image; however, the speed with which we perceive something also depends on what is being observed (Rayner et al., 2009). Because the brain integrates the visual images that we acquire through successive fixations and attention to a visual scene or object, the more complicated the features are, the more time we need to process them. The needed extra processing time is gained through an increased duration of fixation.

Attention to an area may be in response to relatively low-level stimulus-related phenomena, such as motion or the abrupt appearance of an object (Findlay, 1982; Kramer et al., 2001) or spatial contrast (Reinagel & Zador, 1999). Such attention may also be a means of retrieving specific information to meet a task-related goal (i.e., a higher-level cognitive reason) and/or to fulfil a sociopragmatic obligation in situations involving face-to-face communication (Posner, 1980; Yantis, 1998).

Shifts in attention do not necessarily entail an overt shift of the eyes although spatial attention and the eyes often move in tandem (Posner, 1980). Posner et al. (1984) proposed several distinct operations in the control of attention: disengagement, shift, and allocation. Deubel and Schneider (1996) argued for an alignment of saccade programming and visual attention to a common target; by the time a perceiver executes a saccade to a target, however, attention has preceded it by 70–150 ms (Holmqvist & Andersson, 2017). A shift in overall attention may be initiated by covert attention followed by a shift in overt attention with the corresponding eye movements; for example, an abrupt appearance of something or someone in the visual periphery can reflexively capture both attention (Yantis & Jonides, 1984) and eye movement (Theeuwes et al., 1998). Attention may be drawn by the salience of distinctive (i.e., bottom-up) features of a target, such as its colour, motion, and size (e.g., Wolfe & Horowitz, 2004), or to goal-driven (i.e., top-down) factors, such as searching for a particular element to complete a task. Participants may fixate task-irrelevant but salient features at first; however, as the task begins, fixations to irrelevant objects decline in favour of those relevant to the task (Hayhoe & Ballard, 2005; Land & Hayhoe, 2001). When the task ends, the eyes may again be attracted by bottom-up (*pre-attentive*) salient features.

A momentary release of attention during cognitive behaviour may be provided by eyeblinks. Nakano et al. (2013) discovered that eyeblinks occurred synchronously across participants watching a video at a point when salient events were most unlikely to occur, differing from the implicit breakpoints represented by spontaneous eyeblinks. Wohltjen and Wheatley (2021) showed that attention may also be altered by a break in eye contact between interlocutors during natural conversation. In that study, eye contact was positively correlated with pupillary synchrony (a consequence of shared attention) and ratings of engagement by the interlocutors. Eye contact signalled when shared attention was high. It might also serve a corrective role in disrupting shared attention (i.e., reducing synchrony) when needed to allow independent contributions to a conversation.

As an alternative to the dichotomy of stimulus- or goal-driven attentional control, Vecera et al. (2014) proposed a continuum of *experience-based attentional tuning*, with attentional control ranging from stimulus-driven at the one extreme to increasingly goal-driven at the other. Attention can be deployed based on both stimulus factors and goals. With task experience, control becomes more goal-directed. Other factors might impact the influence of experience, including perceptual load or object complexity.

Potential Targets of Eye Gaze During Speech

There is variability in terms of where people look when viewing a human face. People often tend to direct their gaze towards the eyes or the mouth as the most expressive and informative elements of the face, respectively (e.g., Argyle & Cook, 1976; Kendon, 1967; Rossano, 2013). "People and faces invariably draw the eyes" and "motion is likely to bring about reflexive eye movements towards it, irrespective of what is moving" (Holmqvist & Andersson, 2017, p. 49).

Gaze Preference: Leftward Bias

The centre of the face (i.e., the nose) might be the most optimal gaze target for facial recognition following social norms and the most efficient for integrating information holistically, similar to the central fixation bias for scene viewing (Tatler, 2007). Buchan et al. (2007) found that when noise was present, perceivers who adopted a centralized vantage point on a talker's face showed a reduction in the frequency of fixations to the eyes, with a lengthening of the fixation duration to the nose and mouth.

Another pattern, however, was also observed. When looking at the human face, adults, infants, monkeys, and dogs demonstrated a leftward bias – that is, preferential fixation to the right side of a face (Everdell et al., 2007; Guo et al., 2009). Guo et al. (2009) defined this bias as the side of the face "inspected first and/or for longer periods" (p. 409). Using a preferential-looking paradigm to measure gaze preference, the eye position and head movements of adults and 6-month-old infants were recorded during a free viewing task while they looked at a range of objects and facial images with neutral expression.[3] In terms of the human faces as gaze targets, infants and adults consistently showed a left gaze bias as measured by the side of the face that was inspected first and longest (over 59% of viewing time for infants and 50%–55% for adults). In a later study, Guo et al. (2012) recorded adult participants' eye movements while they explored facial images in different tasks (free viewing, judging familiarity, and judging facial expression). Based on first fixation and the proportion of overall leftward fixations, there was a consistent left gaze bias in face-viewing regardless of the task demands. Guo et al. (2012) proposed that left gaze bias was an automatic reflection of hemispheric lateralization in face processing.

Similar leftward gaze preference by perceivers (i.e., preferential fixation to the right side of a talker's face) was observed in an AV speech perception task involving dynamic faces, static faces, and face-like objects, although participants exhibited a stronger leftward preference while viewing the dynamic faces as compared to the static faces or face-like objects, especially when gaze was directed towards the talkers' eyes (Everdell et al., 2007). However, viewing bias did not predict correct perception. Overall, the distribution of gaze fixations reflected participants' viewing preference, but AV integration during speech did not appear to depend on the area of the face where an observer's gaze was being directed.

Importance of a Talker's Mouth Movements to Perceivers

The face is crucial to speechreading (see chapter 1) and to L1 speech development, drawing infants' attention to facial movements and their association with vocalizations (e.g., Meltzoff & Moore, 1993; see chapter 2). Attention to a talker's eyes is common among infants up to about 6 months of age, when the eyes begin to share attention with the talker's mouth and then yield to the mouth as the dominant target around 8–10 months of age, at about the same time as *canonical* babbling – the production of syllables involving a clear consonant, full vowel, and smooth transition, as in *bababa* – begins (Lewkowicz & Hansen-Tift, 2012). Then, around 12 months of age, when infants are presented with native AV speech, attention to the mouth shows a general decline, although it increases if infants are presented with non-native speech.

The role of mouth movements as visual speech cues is also evident in the perceptual outcome of the McGurk–MacDonald effect for L1 speakers (e.g., McGurk & MacDonald, 1976) and L2 speakers (e.g., Hardison, 1996; see chapter 2). This effect can occur when the auditory and visual speech cues do not match and may produce a percept that does not match either cue. In addition, facial as well as auditory speech cues offer benefits to learners in L2 perception training (e.g., Hardison, 2003) and earlier word identification in connected speech (Hardison, 2005b, 2005c, 2018b; see chapter 3).

In most eye-movement studies, adults' gazes shifted away from a talker's eyes and towards the mouth in response to some type of challenging speech processing task. These challenges included the absence of sound, which created a speechreading task (e.g., Lansing & McConkie, 1994, 1999), the presence of masking noise (e.g., Vatikiotis-Bateson et al., 1998), the reduction of sound intensity (Lansing & McConkie, 2003), the introduction of a new talker (Buchan et al., 2008), segmentation of artificial speech (Lusk & Mitchel, 2016), and having to report the words that a talker produced (Buchan et al., 2007). In addition, tracking of eye movements in A. Yi et al.'s (2013) study revealed that in a high SNR condition (i.e., more speech signal than noise), participants were able to shift their gazes within 10° of the centre of a talker's mouth without compromising identification accuracy of words in low-context sentences. This range is similar to the range within which perceivers can still experience the McGurk–MacDonald effect (Paré et al., 2003; see chapter 2). However, in a low SNR condition (i.e., more noise than signal) or with visual distractors, such as two images of the same talker's face on the screen, gaze patterns fixated primarily on points within 2.5° of the centre of the talker's mouth.

Where Perceivers Look on Dynamic Faces

The movable articulators that produce speech (i.e., lips, jaw, and tongue) influence the shape and motion of visible orofacial behaviour. "Indeed, the face below the eyes is the visible surface of the vocal tract" (Vatikiotis-Bateson et al., 1998, p. 927), although lip shape and motion information may be distributed over a large region of the face (Vatikiotis-Bateson & Yehia, 1996). To investigate where perceivers look on a speaker's face, Vatikiotis-Bateson et al. (1998) recorded participants' eye movements during AV presentations of a series of conversational monologues (each about 35–45 s) of different image sizes, ranging from life size to five times life size, and with different levels of masking noise (i.e., a background of multilingual voices and music). The monologues were produced by one American English speaker and one Japanese speaker (Tokyo dialect). The images of the faces were divided into five areas of interest (AOIs), also known as regions of interest. The first two were the areas on each side of the vertical midline of the face above the brow line. The third and fourth involved the areas around each eye, extending up to the brow line and down to a horizontal boundary across the supratip of the nose. The fifth area was the lower face including the mouth.

Eye movements were recorded while five native speakers of English and five native speakers of Japanese watched an L1-matched talker and answered multiple-choice questions about the content using hand gestures to reduce head movement. In the highest noise condition, participants scored 25%–40% correct. They gazed more at the mouth as masking noise levels increased, but still spent 45%–70% of each stimulus gazing at the eyes. Vatikiotis-Bateson et al. (1998) commented that perceivers were able to utilize changes in the speakers' orofacial muscles that accompany articulatory movements, and they speculated that observers detect "well-learned, phonetically correlated events" from areas of the face beyond the mouth as facial muscles change during articulation (p. 938). Articulatory movements might also have been detected sufficiently by peripheral vision to perform the task (e.g., Massaro, 1998; Paré et al., 2003).

Linguistic and cultural experiences may also influence looking behaviour, which Hisanaga et al. (2016) suggested was a consequence of the development of unique neural systems for AV speech perception. In that study, one native speaker each of English and Japanese was recorded while producing the syllables /ba/ and /ga/. Native English and Japanese listeners were then presented with L1-matched stimuli in a syllable-identification task in AV and A-only stimulus conditions to collect ERP data, and in the AV condition for eye-tracking data.[4] ERP data revealed that English speakers processed AV speech more efficiently than A-only, whereas Japanese speakers showed the opposite pattern. The eye-tracking data showed a gaze bias to the mouth for English speakers, especially before the onset of the acoustic signal, but not for the Japanese speakers, who had looked at the mouth much less than the eyes and nose before the acoustic onset.

Eye-tracking data from a speechreading task (no audio input) involving native English speakers showed that the observers' eye gazes were directed mostly towards the talker's mouth, which would be expected given the absence of auditory information; however, gazes also occurred to other areas of the face (Lansing & McConkie, 1999). For analysis, the face was divided into the following areas: upper (forehead and both eyes), mid (nose and both cheeks), and lower (mouth and chin). Gazes to the eyes ranged from 14% to 40% of the data. Gazes to the middle region of the face accounted for 37% of the data and were interpreted by Lansing and McConkie as indicators of visual attention to the face as a whole. The latter were gazes that would have been assigned in the study by Vatikiotis-Bateson et al. (1998) to one of the eye regions, that is, to one of the areas around each eye that extended from the brow line down to the nose.

To explore the influence of different experimental conditions on eye gaze behaviour, Lansing and McConkie (2003) used a binocular eye tracker to record the sequence and duration of participants' fixations to different areas of a face. They tracked the gaze of 16 native English speakers with demonstrable speechreading ability during a task involving short-term recall of the exact wording of unrelated sentences presented by a video-recorded face either with sound at a low-intensity level (vs. with noise added) or with no sound (i.e., using only speechreading). The focus was whether perceivers would still gaze at the talker's eyes under the different conditions. If so, it could indicate that they were not sacrificing access to speech information because (a) sufficient task-related information was distributed broadly over the face, as Vatikiotis-Bateson et al. (1998) had suggested; and/or (b) adequate information could be derived from the talker's mouth through peripheral vision (i.e., covert attention) without a change in eye position (e.g., Paré et al., 2003; Posner, 1980; Posner & Raichle, 1994). A shift in gaze away from the eyes to the mouth movements of the talker could indicate the need for specific phonetic information, or it could indicate the detection of movement in the periphery when the gaze was directed towards the eyes, which then prompted redirection of the gaze.

For analysis, the talker's face was divided into seven AOIs: forehead, eyes, left cheek, nose, right cheek, mouth, and chin. Findings demonstrated that the perceivers' eyes were active prior to and following the speech period, often looking at the talker's eyes. More fixations were directed to the eyes than any other region during silence, which was labelled the eye primacy effect (Lansing & McConkie, 2003). Because there were fixations to the eyes prior to the speech period, the eye primacy effect appeared to be the result of a pre-existing tendency to look at the eyes for social or communicative purposes. In contrast, while the talker was speaking, the perceiver's gaze was drawn to the mouth, which was labelled the information source attraction effect. In 30%–50% of the cases, a perceiver's eyes shifted towards the region of the talker's mouth even before mouth motion began, perhaps the result of strategies developed for successful perception. Some perceivers in that study were able to identify words correctly in the speechreading condition while gazing only at the talker's eyes, supporting the observation that some speech cues may be obtained from peripheral vision (e.g., Massaro, 1998; Paré et al., 2003).

The information that could be obtained through peripheral vision was controlled in a study by Hardison (2006) in which the visible areas of a talker's face in different stimulus conditions were limited through digital video editing. In one condition, participants were able to gaze only at the region around the talker's eyes from the mid forehead to the supratip of the nose; everything else was blacked out. In another condition, participants could see only the mouth and lower jaw. In a third condition, the whole face was visible, and in the fourth condition, there was no visual information (A-only). Word identification accuracy in noise was significantly greater for the condition in which the eyes and upper cheek areas were seen as compared to the A-only condition – but only when the talker was familiar. In addition, accuracy was comparable for the condition in which only the mouth area was seen and the condition in which the entire face was seen – but again, only when the talker was familiar. The findings suggested that when attending to areas of a talker's face to process speech-related information, familiarity plays a role. Initial processing of unfamiliar faces may be more global, allowing observers to preserve as many details as possible in memory to facilitate subsequent processing of information that may be partial or degraded.

Võ et al. (2012) challenged the suggestion of a general prioritization of the eyes when viewing moving faces. In their study, the eye movements of 44 participants were monitored while they watched a short video (about 2 min) featuring close-ups of pedestrians on a city sidewalk engaged in interviews. Two versions of the videos were created: (a) *vocal* – with audio, including speech (dialogue) and background music; and (b) *mute* – with music but no speech. AOIs on the faces were defined as follows: (a) a horizontally elliptical region for each eye (considered one region for analysis); (b) a vertically elliptical region for the nose; and (c) a rectangular region including the mouth. The participants' task was simply to rate on a 4-point scale how much they liked the video; speech comprehension was not involved.

In contrast to a general preference to fixate the eyes of a talker, results revealed that gaze was directed towards the eyes, nose, or mouth in response to a specific event. Võ et al. (2012) argued that gaze allocation was driven by function. In the "vocal" version, gaze was dynamic but fixations to the eyes increased when the speaker made eye contact with the camera; fixations to the mouth increased when speech was produced, although comprehension was not necessary to complete the task. When a face moved quickly, fixations focused on the nose, perhaps as a central point from which gaze could be directed strategically. In the "mute" version, there was a decrease in fixations to faces generally, and to the mouth area specifically.

Using a *face-to-face paradigm*, Gullberg and Holmqvist (1999, 2006) observed that interlocutors with wearable eye trackers paid far more attention to the talker's face, especially the nose bridge and eye area, than to the talker's gestures, which were the original focus of the study (see chapter 6).[5] They suggested that the face might have dominated because of the natural attraction faces hold and the level of attention to the face required by the task; that is, instead of engaging in a conversation with the talker, the participants had to memorize the story being told in order to retell it.

Individual Differences in Eye Gaze Behaviour

Both consistency and variability exist among individuals in their eye gaze behaviour. A preference to fixate the mouth or eye region of a face was found for both static and dynamic faces and occurred consistently across faces (Gurler et al., 2015) and testing sessions as long as 18 months apart, demonstrating stable and unique scanning patterns not consistent with the purportedly typical triangular shaped pattern (i.e., eye to eye to mouth) that Mehoudar et al. (2014) suggested might represent a trait established in early development. However, as was noted early by Yarbus (1965/1967), individuals viewing identical images can make very different eye movements.

Individuals also vary in terms of their face-viewing behaviour as a result of factors such as task instructions (Kanan et al., 2015) and task type (e.g., Hayhoe & Ballard, 2005). For example, speech-related tasks prompted fixations to the mouth (e.g., Buchan et al., 2008; Lansing & McConkie, 2003; Vatikiotis-Bateson et al., 1998), but gender-identification tasks tended to drive fixations to the eyes (e.g., Armann & Bülthoff, 2009). To estimate the relative contributions of individual differences and of task and stimulus effects, Wegner-Clemens et al. (2019) examined the face-viewing behaviour of 41 individuals under different stimulus, task, and exemplar conditions. The tasks were simple, requiring only identification of the CV syllable /ba/ or /ga/ (i.e., the "speech task") and talker gender (male or female). Conditions were AV speech stimulus + speech task, AV speech stimulus + gender task, and static face stimulus + gender task. Results showed that task condition accounted for 41% of the variance, individual differences accounted for 28%, and stimulus exemplar for less than 0.4% of the variance.

Rennig et al. (2020) also explored individual differences in eye gaze behaviour and identification accuracy in AV speech. A total of 102 L1 English speakers participated in two tasks. The primary eye-tracking measure was the fixation time spent on the talker's mouth as a percentage of total viewing time. In the first task, identification of CV syllables spoken in the clear (i.e., with no noise) had a mean accuracy of 98% (*SD* = 1%), similar to an A-only task; however, there was substantial variability in the time that participants spent fixating the mouth (range: 3%–98%).

In the second task in the Rennig et al. (2020) study, participants had to repeat sentences presented either A-only in noise at a very challenging SNR of −16 dB or paired with a video of the talker's face (i.e., an AV condition). Few words were identified in the A-only (*M* = 9%, *SD* = 4%, range:

1%–20%) versus AV condition (*M* = 38%, *SD* = 14%, range: 4%–74%). The large AV range is compatible with the considerable amount of individual variability reported in other studies (e.g., K.W. Grant et al., 1998; Sommers et al., 2005; Tye-Murray et al., 2016; van Engen et al., 2014, 2017). Participants who spent more time fixating the talker's mouth when it was not necessary (i.e., in clear speech) made better use of that visual information when it was necessary (i.e., in noise). Interestingly, fixating the mouth when it was important during noise provided less benefit to participants who had not fixated the mouth when it was not important, suggesting development over the course of the study of individual patterns and preferences in viewing a face. Some study participants had developed stronger skills associating the talker's auditory and visual speech cues. Beyond the context of this study, Rennig et al. (2020) speculated that people who tend to fixate the mouth of a talking face might develop better comprehension of speech in noise over a lifetime of experiences. This observation is reminiscent of the suggestion by Vatikiotis-Bateson et al. (1998) regarding the learning of phonetically correlated events on the face over a period of time, and also of findings demonstrating the role of talker familiarity in AV speech processing (e.g., Hardison, 2006).

Cross-Language Eye Movement Studies

The above findings raise the question of differences in eye gaze behaviour in instances where there are no specific task requirements. For example, in Barenholtz et al. (2016), L1 English speakers attended equally to the eyes and mouth of a talker in the absence of an explicit speech-processing task; however, attention to the mouth increased in response to a task requiring perceivers to compare and identify AV speech utterances, especially when the language was unfamiliar (i.e., Spanish or Icelandic).

In the eye-tracking study of Birulés et al. (2020), participants did not complete a specific task while viewing and hearing a talker recounting three children's stories (each 60 s) in Catalan, Spanish, and English, but they were told they would be asked questions about the stories at the end of the session. The talker was described as a Catalan-Spanish-English trilingual. Participants were monolingual English speakers and bilingual Spanish and Catalan speakers; each language group reported very little to no knowledge of the non-native language. Three AOIs were identified: a rectangular area around the mouth (excluding the lower jaw), a rectangular area including both eyes, and the whole face extending from just above the brow line to just above the chin. Birulés et al. calculated the proportion of total looking time to the eyes and mouth by dividing the total amount of time spent looking at these AOIs by the amount of time spent looking at the face as a whole. Findings revealed that perceivers in both language groups attended more to the talker's eyes than mouth when speech was in their native language; however, in the non-native language, they attended more to the talker's mouth.

A second experiment by Birulés et al. (2020) was designed to explore the potential influence of the level of L2 English proficiency on the selective attention of native Spanish and Catalan bilinguals. Three new videos were created involving an AE speaker reciting monologues (each 20 s) that included anecdotes and opinions on social topics; these were considered more challenging than the original videos. The distribution of attention, defined in the study as the amount of time looking at different AOIs, depended on proficiency level. Native English speakers attended more to the talker's eyes than mouth, and the L2 English participants attended equally to the eyes and mouth regardless of English proficiency.

In a conceptual replication of the second of Birulés et al.'s (2020) experiments, Grüter et al. (2023) divided 83 participants into two groups: 38 self-identified as native English speakers, although the authors classified 13 of them as early bilinguals with English as the dominant language, and 45 self-identified as non-natives with varying L1s (36 Japanese, 7 Chinese or Korean, 1 Dutch, and 1 Italian). Eye gaze was recorded while participants watched two short videos of a talker producing a memorized script, each about 1 minute in duration, and then responded to comprehension questions. One video involving a female native AE speaker was an adaptation of an L2 listening comprehension test. The listening passage in the second video featured a male talker self-identified as a Chinese-American native English speaker and was more similar in content to casual speech with a slower speech rate as compared to the first video. Both groups of participants rated the second talker overall as less native-like.

Three AOIs were designated in the Grüter et al. (2023) study: (a) a rectangular area involving the eyes, extending from approximately mid forehead down to the supratip of the nose; (b) a rectangular area involving the mouth extending to the bottom of the lower jaw when the mouth was in a closed neutral position; and (c) the entire face. The nose was not designated as a separate AOI. For analysis, the total dwell time (fixation duration) to the eyes and mouth, respectively, was divided by the total dwell time to the face to derive a proportion of fixation time. For each video, a mixed-design analysis of variance (ANOVA) was conducted with participant group as the between-groups factor and two AOIs (eyes and mouth) as the within-group factor.

Grüter et al. (2023) reported substantial variability among the participants in both groups and videos. The L2 listeners reported that the first video was difficult to understand. In the second video involving casual speech, the L2 listeners paid more attention to the talker's mouth as compared to the L1 listeners. Among the lower proficiency L2 listeners, there were more fixations to the mouth, which were referred to as indicators of "L2 proficiency modulated attention" (p. 1). The authors proposed that L2 listeners with more limited proficiency may be especially reliant on visual cues, a suggestion that is compatible with some other speech perception findings; however, to be beneficial in speech processing, the cues must be informative for learners (e.g., Hardison, 1996, 2003; see chapter 3).

Several important issues arise here. As noted above, although eye movements and attention often function in tandem, they are not one and the same. Perceivers can demonstrate eye gaze to a target and not process the details (Triesch et al., 2003); similarly, they can perceive information through peripheral vision without fixating the target (e.g., Massaro, 1998). In addition, within-group research designs are recommended because of the idiosyncratic nature of eye-tracking measures, such as fixation duration; that is, every participant has a unique baseline setting for a measure (Holmqvist & Andersson, 2017).

Chapter 4 in Review

This chapter focused on the perceptual functions of eye gaze, especially during speech, with an emphasis on variability across perceivers and task conditions. Studies demonstrated that perceivers' attention is often directed towards the eyes of a talker as captured in the expression *the eyes have it*. This attention serves different purposes across cultures, being particularly important in American culture, but perhaps less so in Japanese culture. The eye primacy effect was proposed as a general prioritization of fixations to a talker's eyes prior to a speech period, with shifts of eye gaze to the talker's mouth in anticipation of speech (i.e., the information source attraction effect; Lansing & McConkie, 2003). Võ et al. (2012), who challenged the eye primacy effect, suggested that gaze allocation was driven by function in response to a specific event.

Various areas of a talker's face may be fixated by perceivers at different times and under different circumstances, although the existing research points to a tendency for perceivers to exhibit a leftward gaze bias when viewing a face, especially a dynamic face (Everdell et al., 2007). In general, the mouth tends to attract the most attention when a speech-related task is involved.

Most eye-movement research has involved native speakers of a language; however, it is evident from research findings reported in previous chapters that visual cues from a talker's face can offer speech-related information to help perceivers who are learning the talker's language. Chapter 5 reports the details of an original study using eye tracking to investigate where L1 AE speakers learning L2 French looked on the face of a native speaker of the L2 and a native speaker of the L1 in speech perception tasks, with stimuli presented in three conditions: AV, AV with noise added, and V-only.

Chapter 4 Notes

1. The use of *fixate* in this book follows the usage in the eye-movement research literature; that is, the verb is not followed by the preposition *on* as would be typical in common parlance.
2. For a discussion of the eye-mind link in some non-reading tasks, see Reichle et al. (2012).
3. The preferential-looking paradigm measures the differential visual fixation of images (e.g., Golinkoff et al., 1987).
4. Event-related potentials (ERPs) are very small voltages generated in certain brain structures in response to specific events or stimuli (Blackwood & Muir, 1990).
5. Different paradigms (e.g., reading, visual search, visual world, social interaction) and eye-tracking equipment are used to conduct eye-movement studies (for an overview, see Holmqvist & Andersson, 2017).

Chapter 5

Tracking Eye Gaze Behaviour in L1 and L2 Speech Perception

Individual observers differ in the way they think and, therefore, differ also to some extent in the way they look at things. . . . Depending on the task in which a person is engaged, i.e., depending on the character of the information which he must obtain, the distribution of the points of fixation on an object will vary correspondingly, because different items of information are usually localized in different parts of an object.

– Yarbus (1965/1967, p. 192)

*****

Background

Alfred L. Yarbus (1914–86) is considered one of the founders of modern eye-movement research (e.g., Tatler et al., 2010). He developed a method for accurately recording eye movements using a cap attached by suction to the human eye and devices that allowed presentation of images to move with the eyes so that a stabilized retinal image could be presented.

In Yarbus' book *Eye Movements and Vision* (first published in Russian in 1965), there were several primary themes that emerged from his research: (a) observers exhibited a strong preference to look at the eyes of a face more than any other feature; (b) for extended viewing, there was a clear tendency to make repeated cycles of fixations between the key features of a face; and (c) the instructions given to an observer influenced looking behaviour. This last theme resulted from a classic study in which observers viewed a painting from the 1880s of a complex social scene, depicting a man unexpectedly visiting a family in the living room of a home in Russia.[1] Each observer viewed the painting seven times, each time following a different task instruction. Instructions included (a) making a series of judgments about the scene (e.g., inferring the wealth of the family, what they had been doing, their ages); (b) remembering details of the scene (e.g., the clothing the people wore, the location of people and objects in the room); and (c) free viewing. Results showed similar but not identical patterns of eye movements across observers. There was also intra-observer variability, but not to the same degree as that found between observers. Importantly, results also showed the influence of cognitive factors (i.e., different task instructions) on observers' viewing behaviour.

The findings reported by Yarbus inspired much eye-movement research, including a study by Tatler et al. (2010) in which observers viewed a portrait of Yarbus (i.e., showing his face, collar, and the lower part of his hat) in contrast to the complex scene in the painting used in the Yarbus study. Observers were given the same instructions. In the free viewing condition, there was a strong tendency for observers to look at the left eye and the mouth of the face in the portrait. This contrasts with the leftward gaze bias (i.e., bias towards viewing the right side of the face) reported in recent studies of face viewing (e.g., Everdell et al., 2007; Guo et al., 2009; see chapter 4); however, leftward bias might have been disrupted in the case of the portrait because Yarbus's right eye was in a relative shadow (see Figures 6 and 9 in Tatler et al., 2010), perhaps accounting for its small fraction of the overall fixation time. Across all conditions, except when asked to remember the clothes worn in the portrait, observers looked more at the facial regions than other regions. Gaze allocation depended on the assigned task; that is, the typical tendency to view the eyes and mouth of a face and to cycle between these features was not universal and could be altered by the task instructions.

Introduction to the Current Study

The remainder of this chapter reports an original study I conducted exploring the application of some of the major themes of the work of Yarbus and others to the analysis of the eye movements of L1 AE learners of L2 French as they viewed a native AE and native French speaker in a speech perception task, with a specific focus on the learners' (a) leftward bias when looking at a talking face (Everdell et al., 2007; Guo et al., 2009, 2012); (b) tendency to make saccades between key features of a face depending on task conditions (Yarbus, 1965/1967); (c) preference for looking at a talker's eyes (Lansing & McConkie, 2003; Yarbus 1965/1967); and (d) tendency to fixate a talker's mouth as the primary source of information (Hardison, 2003; Lansing & McConkie, 2003). Two sources of task difficulty were included: (a) language – L1 AE, L2 French; and (b) stimulus condition – AV, AV with masking noise added (AVn), and V-only (i.e., speechreading). The task involved perceptual identification of visually salient vowels produced in monosyllabic words by the native speaker of the relevant language. Quantitative data involving several eye-movement measures and qualitative data from a questionnaire and interview were collected.

Research Questions

The study was designed to address the following research questions (RQs):

RQ1: Is there evidence of leftward bias (e.g., Everdell et al., 2007; Guo et al., 2009) when viewing a talking face in the L1 and/or L2 during a vowel identification task?

RQ2: How do fixation durations to the eyes, mouth, and nose as a percentage of viewing time in the L1 and L2 compare to other studies?

RQ3: To which AOI on a talker's face did participants look first and did this differ by stimulus condition and language?

RQ4: Which AOI on a talker's face attracted the most attention in terms of total fixation duration and did this differ by stimulus condition and/or visual category (i.e., labial/produced with lip involvement, or nonlabial/produced without lip involvement) of the initial sounds within the stimulus set?

RQ5: Did vowel identification accuracy differ by stimulus condition and/or visual category of the initial sounds within the stimulus set?

RQ6: Did decision time differ by stimulus condition and/or the visual category of the initial sounds within the stimulus set?

RQ7: What was the relationship between decision time and identification accuracy?

RQ8: Which response option in each language attracted the most attention?

In the case of the L1 English talker, participants' gazes were expected to shift to different areas of the face in the AV and AVn conditions but focus more on the mouth in the V-only (speechreading) condition. In terms of the L2 French talker, participants were expected to direct their gazes primarily towards the mouth area in all stimulus conditions because of the challenge that identifying French nasal vowels poses to L1 AE speakers (e.g., Inceoglu, 2014). In Inceoglu's study, learners in an AV condition demonstrated more accurate perceptual identification of the hyper-rounded vowel [ɔ̃] as compared to [ɑ̃], which has some lip protrusion and narrowing of the oral aperture (Zerling, 1989), and to the unrounded [ɛ̃], which is more open than the oral vowel [ɛ] (Martinet, 1988; see Figure 5.1a–c). In a V-only condition, Inceoglu (2014) found that the vowel [ɔ̃] remained the best identified of the three, but learners identified [ɛ̃] more accurately than [ɑ̃], which may stem from the presence of some lip protrusion associated with [ɑ̃] in contrast to its oral counterpart with which the learners were familiar. In addition, for both languages, it was hypothesized that an initial labial (vs. nonlabial) consonant might impede vowel identification accuracy in both languages (e.g., Hardison, 2003, 2005b; see chapter 3). Participants were also expected to exhibit variability in their gaze behaviour (e.g., Yarbus, 1965/1967).

Participants

A total of 32 native AE speakers (29 female, 3 male) from a fourth semester French course at a university in the US participated. The course focused on the development of listening, speaking, reading, and writing skills. Participants were ages 18–24 years (M = 19.81, SD = 1.28) who reported having begun French study at ages 13–18 years (M = 14.34, SD = 1.58). Three were majoring in French and 14 were minoring in French. None had taken a phonetics course or had studied in a French-speaking country. Interactions in French were generally limited to the classroom. Demonstrable skill in speechreading (e.g., Lansing & McConkie, 2003) was not considered a necessary qualification for participants based on previous L2 studies (e.g., Hardison, 2005b, 2018b; Inceoglu, 2014), and speechreading skill was not tested prior to the experiment.

Preparation of Materials

A total of 84 monosyllabic CVC stimuli were presented in each of three stimulus conditions (AV, AVn, and V-only) in English and French. The selection of stimuli and the presentation of response options for French were challenging and thus guided the selection of the English materials. Therefore, this section begins with the description of the French stimuli.

French Stimuli

For French, the focus was nasal vowels, which differ along the visually salient dimension of lip rounding and pose a perceptual challenge for L1

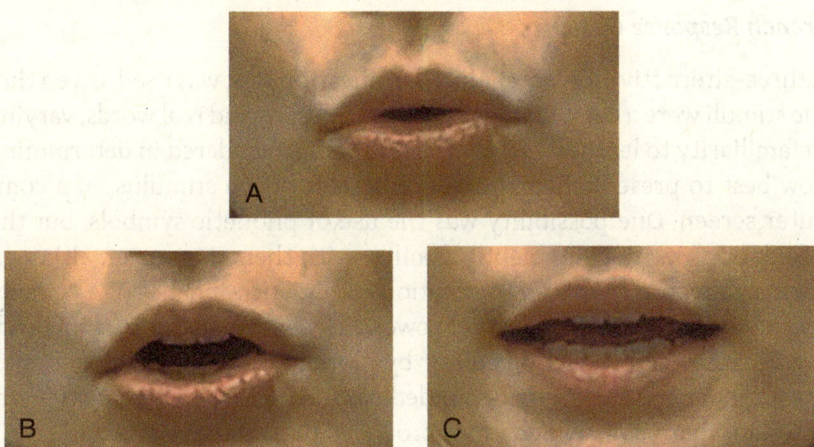

FIGURE 5.1 (a) Lip Shape for French Nasal Vowel [ɔ̃]; (b) Lip Shape for French Nasal Vowel [ɑ̃]; (c) Lip Shape for French Nasal Vowel [ɛ̃]

English learners (e.g., Inceoglu, 2014). Historically, French distinguished four nasal vowels [ɑ̃, ɔ̃, ɛ̃, œ̃], a distinction that still exists in some varieties of the language, including Southeastern French (Violin-Wigent, 2006) and Quebec French (Léon, 1983; Martin et al., 2001). However, since the mid-twentieth century, [œ̃] has been progressively replaced by [ɛ̃] in Standard French and Parisian French, resulting in the general use of three nasal vowels (Carton, 1974; Walter, 1977). The three standard French vowels (see Figure 5.1a–c) were used in the current study.

In order to construct minimal triplets to contrast the three nasal vowels, a combination of real (e.g., *banque* [ɑ̃], "bank") and nonsense words (e.g., *bonque* [ɔ̃], *beinque* [ɛ̃]) was used.[2] Because the task in the study involved vowel perception (vs. word identification), the words served only as carriers of phonetic context for the target vowels. The visual influence of the preceding consonant on vowel identification was taken into consideration; therefore, stimuli were divided into two categories: 42 began with a visually salient labial consonant, and 42 began with a nonlabial consonant. Within the labial category, five triplets contrasting [ɔ̃], [ɑ̃], and [ɛ̃] began with a bilabial stop (e.g., [b] *bonde, bande, beinde*), five with a labiodental fricative (e.g., [v] *vonte, vente, veinte*), and four with a palato-alveolar fricative (e.g., [ʒ] *jonde, jande, jeinde*). Within the nonlabial category, five triplets began with a dental stop (e.g., [d] *donte, dante, deinte*), five with an alveolar fricative (e.g., [s] *sonte, sente, sainte*), and five with a velar stop (e.g., [g] *gonde, gande, gueinde*).

French Response Options

A three-alternative forced-choice identification task was used. Given that the stimuli were a combination of nonsense words and real words, varying in familiarity to learners, several factors were considered in determining how best to present the response options for each stimulus on a computer screen. One possibility was the use of phonetic symbols, but the population was not sufficiently familiar with them. Moreover, although each nasal vowel shares an International Phonetic Alphabet (IPA) symbol (excluding the tilde) with an oral vowel, the symbol similarity is misleading because the productions differ by more than nasality; for example, the articulation of the hyper-rounded nasal vowel [ɔ̃] is closer to the oral vowel [o] than to [ɔ], which is not produced by some AE speakers.

Another possibility was the use of a sample word for each vowel. Each of the three French nasal vowels constitutes a real word: [ɔ̃] may be represented orthographically as *on*, a collective "we/they"; [ɑ̃] as *an*, "year," and as *en*, "in/to"; and [ɛ̃] as *un*, "one" or "a" (indefinite article). These vowels can also be represented by other graphemes as parts of words; for example, [ɔ̃] may appear as *om*; [ɑ̃] as *am*; and [ɛ̃] as *in*, *ain*, and *ein*. Therefore, the words *on*, *an*, and *un* were used in addition to a highly familiar word placing each nasal vowel in a CV syllable, similar to the stimuli in the experiment. Participants clicked on the option that represented the vowel sound in the word the talker had produced. The response option screen appeared as shown below (*mon*, "my"; *quand*, "when"; *fin*, "end"):

on	an	un
(as in "mon")	(as in "quand")	(as in "fin")

This approach worked successfully in an earlier training study involving the perception of nasal vowels by a peer group of L2 learners (Inceoglu, 2014).

English Stimuli

In contrast to French, English does not have nasal vowels that distinguish meaning, and the overall degree of rounding among the rounded back vowels is generally much less as compared to the rounding continuum for French vowels. For some AE speakers, there are three rounded back vowels: *boot* [u], *foot* [ʊ], and *boat* [oʊ]. For other speakers, there is a fourth vowel: the open *o* as in *caught* [ɔ], creating a vowel contrast with *cot* [ɑ]. Because the purpose of using the L1 and L2 in this study was to consider the effects of task difficulty on eye movements, not, per se, to evaluate the perceptual identification accuracy of vowels, a clearer visual dimension of variability was chosen for the English stimuli. A total of 84 real monosyllabic (C)VC words formed 28 minimal triplets contrasting the front vowels [i], [eɪ], [æ], which vary by visually discernible differences in jaw height and thus oral aperture.

Guided by the categorization of the French stimuli and to facilitate analysis, English stimuli were also divided into two categories based on the initial sound. The stimuli contrasted [i], [eɪ], and [æ] as follows: 30 began with a labial consonant and 54 began with a nonlabial consonant or a vowel. Within the labial category, two triplets began with a bilabial stop (e.g., *beat, bait, bat*), one with a bilabial nasal (e.g., *meat, mate, mat*), one with a labiodental fricative (e.g., *feet, fate, fat*), three with a palato-alveolar fricative or affricate (e.g., *chief, chafe, chaff*), and three with [ɹ] (e.g., *wreak, rake, rack*). Within the nonlabial category, five triplets began with an alveolar stop (e.g., *team, tame, tam*) or fricative (e.g., *seem, same, Sam*), two with a velar stop (e.g., *keep, cape, cap*), four with [l] (e.g., *lead, laid, lad*), and seven with either [h] (e.g., *heat, hate, hat*) or a vowel (e.g., *eat, ate, at*).

English Response Options

The approach used to present the response options for French was not possible for English as only one of the vowel sounds (i.e., [æ]) constituted a word (i.e., the indefinite article *a*). Because all of the English stimuli were real words familiar to the participants, the words were used as the response options (e.g., *teak, take, tack*).

Recording and Editing

A female native speaker of French in her early 30s was video recorded in a quiet, well-lit research room. She spoke the standard variety of French and exhibited the aforementioned three nasal vowels in her speech, both scripted and unscripted. During the recording, she was instructed to look at the camera and produce a series of real and nonsense words containing nasal vowels as naturally as possible (e.g., without hyperarticulation). The series ended with the repetition of the last utterance to control for list-final intonation. The camera captured a full-sized image of the speaker's head and lower jaw drop. A female native AE speaker in her late 20s was similarly recorded producing the English stimuli. Recordings were monitored carefully to ensure consistency in pronunciation (e.g., release of all final stop consonants). All materials were tested for auditory intelligibility with native speakers of each language.

To create the AVn condition, several SNRs were tested before selecting –12dB to provide an adequate amount of masking noise to reduce ceiling effects and to represent a noisy environment without completely blocking auditory speech information. To create the V-only condition, the audio was deleted.

Five AOIs were designated on each face as follows: (a) a rectangular area on the forehead; (b) two elliptical areas, one covering each eye; (c) an elliptical area covering the nose; and (d) a rectangular area encompassing the mouth and lower jaw. These AOIs were dynamically adapted as needed throughout the trials to ensure adequate margins that avoided overlaps.

Data Collection Procedure

Participants were tested individually in a quiet lab. They were reminded of the study's purpose and the three stimulus conditions. Participants were told not to be concerned if they didn't know some of the words since the focus was vowel identification. An informed consent statement was reviewed with each participant and any questions were addressed. Data collection took about 1–1.5 hours per participant. Upon completion of all tasks, each participant received USD$15.

A high-resolution Tobii TX300 remote eye tracker was used that permitted participants to sit comfortably in a chair to look at a 25-in. (63.5 cm) monitor (1920 × 1080 pixel screen resolution) without the need to use a chin and forehead rest to immobilize the head or wear any apparatus on the head. The camera was hidden in a dark ledge below the monitor. Gaze data were collected at a 300 Hz sampling rate (i.e., 300 data points per second).

Prior to any data collection, the computer mouse was placed on the right side of the tabletop to accommodate the participants (all were right-handed). They were advised that a camera would record their eye movements while they looked at the screen, so it was important to (a) find a comfortable position in the chair in order to avoid moving around; (b) keep the hand on the mouse in order to move it easily without having to look at it; (c) keep the head still and move only the eyes in order to look at different places on the screen; and (d) adjust the headset for comfort before beginning the task. The researcher, who sat behind and to one side, was able to see a participant's eye movements in real time on a laptop while monitoring data collection.

The initial step was a calibration procedure to provide measurements of the characteristics of each participant's eyes that contributed to the software's calculation of gaze data. This was followed by a practice trial, and then the recording started. The first still frame of each image was presented for about 1.3 s followed by the remaining frames at normal speed. The eye tracker recorded gaze behaviour from the onset of the face (i.e., the appearance of the talker's face) on each trial, and from the onset of each presentation of response options until a selection was made. The presentation sequence of the two languages and the sequence of two of the stimulus conditions (AV and AVn) within each language were counterbalanced across participants; the V-only condition was presented last. Within each condition there were several sequences of stimuli presented in different orders across participants. All trials for one language and one condition were presented in the same block so participants did not move back and forth between languages or conditions. Task instructions were reviewed with each participant prior to the presentation of the relevant stimulus condition and language. There were practice trials for each language. Participants could take breaks as needed.

For each trial, a life-sized image of the talker's head appeared in the centre of the screen at a distance of about 26 in. (66.04 cm) from the participant's face, similar to normal conversation. Participants were instructed to imagine they were engaged in a conversation with the talker on the screen. As such, the study might be described as a *simulated face-to-face paradigm* – a modification of the in-person paradigm used by Gullberg and Holmqvist (1999, 2006; see chapters 4 and 6).

After each word was produced, participants saw a screen with the response options in large black letters on a white background. Using a mouse click, participants selected a response. For English, it was the word they heard; for French, it was the sample word containing the same nasal vowel as in the word they heard. This was not a timed task; the mouse click triggered the next trial. Data were saved automatically.

Immediately following data collection, participants completed a questionnaire about their face-viewing behaviour in general and during the experiment, and then they participated in an interview with the researcher. During the interview, they were encouraged to elaborate on the eye-tracking experience.

Types of Data Collected

This section provides a description of the measures obtained for each participant. The first two measures were related to the videos of each talker's face, and the last two were related to the response options. Temporal measures were recorded in seconds.

Faces: Time to First Fixation

Time to first fixation (TTFF) is the time from the start of a task until a particular AOI is fixated for the first time. A short TTFF indicates that the AOI was discovered and fixated quickly. This may be the result of the target's strong bottom-up visual salience relative to other areas during early processing, which is not cognitively controlled by the participant (Galley et al., 2015). A longer TTFF may indicate that the AOI is not as salient as others. The AOI may also have been discovered by conscious visual search driven by top-down factors such as task relevance or cultural practice.

Faces: Total Fixation Duration

Total fixation duration (TFD) represents the total duration of all fixations within a given AOI over a trial. Fixation duration (or dwell time) *may* indicate the level of interest in an area and/or its informativeness. Although measures such as fixation duration can be insightful, eye-tracking data alone do not reveal what people think. Despite several attempts made by researchers to infer intent (e.g., interest, processing difficulty, or confusion) from eye movements, "none of them could be directly and systematically linked to specific cognitive processes" (Holmqvist & Andersson, 2017, p. 353). For example, a shorter duration to an AOI, when compared to other AOIs of a similar size and information density, can signal a decision to shift attention to other areas because of interest or the need to seek information. A prolonged gaze to an area may signal a high level of interest or degree of confusion, perceived task relevance, or stimulus complexity; it may also indicate that participants were thinking about something else (e.g., Hyrskykari et al., 2008).

The following measures were collected for the response options:

> ***Responses: Time to Mouse Click (TTMC)***
> TTMC indicates how long it takes before a participant clicks on a response (i.e., decision time). Accuracy was determined from this measure.
>
> ***Responses: Total Fixation Duration (TFD)***
> Each response option was designated as an AOI. Similar to the TFD measure for the faces, for the response options, TFD represented the sum of the duration of all fixations within a given AOI.

Visualizations

The following two visualizations were produced for the faces and response options: gaze plots and heatmaps.

Gaze Plots

Gaze plots provide a visualization of how the eye physically moves through space. Circles are used to indicate fixations; the larger the circle, the longer the fixation. Each circle has a number that represents its place in the order of fixation. Lines between the circles indicate saccades. A gaze plot representing information for one to perhaps three participants (each represented by a different colour) can provide a meaningful demonstration of saccades between fixation points; displays for a larger number of participants can become too cluttered.

Heatmaps

Heatmaps use different colours to highlight the areas of an image where participants fixated. They represent the spatial distribution of data (i.e., where participants looked), and, as such, they can exemplify eye movements and suggest stimulus characteristics that attracted attention (Bojko, 2009; Holmqvist & Andersson, 2017). Heatmaps can indicate areas where the participants either fixated for a long time or on many occasions, but not why. Red indicates the highest number of fixations or the longest time, and green indicates the least, with varying degrees in between represented by yellow. Incremental analysis of heatmaps can characterize general viewing behaviour with regard to participants' eye movements in relation to a talker's facial movement, especially articulation-related movement.

Results

Results are presented in the following order: (a) evidence of leftward bias; (b) fixation durations to AOIs as a percentage of viewing time; (c) visualizations; (d) targets of initial fixations; (e) total fixation durations to AOIs; (f) vowel identification accuracy; (g) decision time; (h) relationship between decision time and identification accuracy; and (i) response option preference.

Leftward Bias

RQ1 investigated the possibility of leftward bias when participants viewed a talking face, specifically a native speaker of the L1 and a native speaker of the L2 during a vowel identification task. Following Guo et al. (2009, 2012), two fixation measures were calculated; however, in contrast to Guo et al., instead of treating each *side* of the face as a target area, the current study designated each *eye* of the talker as a more precise AOI. The results for the eye fixated first in each stimulus condition (AV, AVn, and V-only) in each language are followed by the results for mean fixation duration to each eye as a percentage of total viewing time per stimulus (Table 5.1). These data are presented as percentages to allow some comparison with other studies. Gaze plots and heatmaps were also examined for a broader view of gaze preference to the face.

Bias as Measured by First Fixation to Each Eye

For the English stimuli, more participants exhibited a leftward bias by fixating the talker's right eye first as compared to the left eye, although this difference reached statistical significance only in the AVn condition, $\chi^2(1) = 6.53, p = .011$. For the French stimuli, there was no clear pattern of preference. Only in the French AVn condition did more participants (i.e., 18 vs. 14) fixate the talker's right eye first. In the AV and V-only conditions, more participants fixated the talker's left eye first, and the comparison approached significance only in the V-only condition, $\chi^2(1) = 3.125, p = .077$.

Bias as Measured by Mean Fixation Duration to Each Eye

In contrast to first fixations, mean fixation duration to each eye as a percentage of the total viewing time per stimulus provided a clearer picture of a possible gaze preference. Although the viewing time per stimulus was similar across the dataset for each language (i.e., a range of 3.033–3.204 s for English and 3.077–3.129 s for French), proportions were calculated following previous research (e.g., Guo et al., 2009).

As shown in Table 5.1, mean fixation duration to the talker's right eye (i.e., leftward gaze by the perceiver) consistently represented a larger proportion of the total viewing time as compared to the talker's left eye across all stimulus conditions in both languages. The minimum and maximum values of the range for each mean are provided for comparison with other studies. Based on the L1 English stimuli, there was greater variability in the current study as compared to Guo et al. (2009), which reported a very narrow range for leftward bias of 50%–55% of viewing time.

Fixation Durations Across AOIs as a Percentage of Viewing Time

RQ2 addressed how the fixation durations to the eyes (combined), mouth, and nose as a percentage of viewing time in the L1 and L2 compared to

TABLE 5.1 Mean Fixation Duration to Each of the Talker's Eyes as a Percentage of Viewing Time

	English				French			
	Right Eye		Left Eye		Right Eye		Left Eye	
Stimulus Condition	*M* (*SD*)	Min Max	*M* (*SD*)	Min Max	*M* (*SD*)	Min Max	*M* (*SD*)	Min Max
AV	27.11 (4.70)	17.76 35.15	20.31 (3.91)	11.81 29.96	23.75 (3.87)	15.41 39.81	20.06 (3.60)	12.23 29.63
AVn	27.74 (6.00)	15.77 50.44	19.43 (6.53)	5.92 46.08	22.15 (4.12)	14.57 37.54	18.29 (3.67)	11.82 26.85
V-only	17.08 (5.66)	8.59 37.40	14.11 (7.63)	3.82 45.90	10.98 (2.90)	5.47 18.36	9.97 (2.67)	5.15 17.31

Note. The designation of right and left eye is from the talker's perspective. AV = auditory-visual; AVn = auditory-visual with noise added; V-only = visual-only. Min and Max = minimum and maximum values of the mean (i.e., the range), respectively.

other studies, although such comparisons are made cautiously because of critical differences in the drawing of AOIs, variables, tasks, and other factors. For comparison purposes, data presented here are combined for both eyes.

For the English stimuli (see Table 5.1), participants directed their gazes to the eyes (combined) a mean of 47.42% (range: 12%–35%) and 47.17% (range: 6%–50%) of the viewing time in the AV and AVn conditions, respectively; this viewing time declined to 31.19% (range: 4%–46%) in the V-only condition. The range for the AVn condition was lower than the 45%–70% range reported in Vatikiotis-Bateson et al. (1998) for a noise-added condition involving an L1-matched talker; the range for the V-only condition of about 4%–46% was comparable to the 14%–40% range reported in Lansing and McConkie (1999) for a speechreading task (i.e., V-only condition).

For the French stimuli, there was a similar pattern of findings but with lower percentages, with a total of 43.81% (range: 12%–40%) and 40.44% (range: 12%–38%) of the viewing time spent fixating the eyes (combined) in the AV and AVn conditions, respectively; this viewing time declined substantially to 20.95% (range: 5%–18%) in the V-only condition. In sum, in the more challenging contexts (i.e., L2 French and/or the V-only condition), less time proportionately was spent looking at the talker's eyes.

TABLE 5.2 Mean Fixation Duration to the Talker's Mouth as a Percentage of Viewing Time Across Stimuli

Stimulus Condition	English		French	
	M (*SD*)	Min–Max	*M* (*SD*)	Min–Max
AV	45.13 (5.38)	26.33–58.67	41.72 (3.92)	31.18–52.68
AVn	56.74 (4.46)	48.27–68.41	49.30 (4.64)	35.63–58.90
V-only	62.99 (4.90)	50.03–75.23	60.05 (3.85)	53.38–69.81

Note. AV = auditory-visual; AVn = auditory-visual with noise added; V-only = visual-only. Min and Max = minimum and maximum values for the mean (i.e., the range), respectively.

As shown in Table 5.2, participants directed their gazes to the English talker's mouth, arguably the most informative AOI for a speech perception task, about 45% of the time (range: 26%–59%) in the AV condition. This range was considerably narrower than the 3%–98% (*M* = 49%) reported by Rennig et al. (2020) for an English AV condition. The current study's AV range for L2 French (42%–60%) was comparable to that for English. When the audio was degraded (AVn), these percentages increased to about 49% for French and about 57% for English; the latter was considerably lower than the 92% reported by Rennig et al. In the current study, gaze to the mouth when the audio was absent (V-only) constituted the largest percentage of viewing time.

The final AOI to be considered in this measure is the talker's nose. Previous research did not always designate the nose as a specific AOI. Although the nose is not linguistically informative, per se, it is a central feature of the face from which perceivers can obtain a global perspective of the target (e.g., Buchan et al., 2007), perhaps glean some information through peripheral vision, and then strategically shift gaze to try to obtain specific information that may be necessary for a task.

As shown in Table 5.3, the mean fixation duration to the nose as a percentage of total viewing time was very similar for both languages at approximately 20% in the AV and AVn conditions, declining slightly to about 16% in the V-only condition. Ranges were largest for the noise-added condition. For some comparison, fixations to the middle region of the face in the speechreading task (i.e., V-only condition) in Lansing and McConkie (1999) constituted 37% of their data, although that region was broader (included both cheeks), which might have offered an expanded vantage point for peripheral vision.

TABLE 5.3 Mean Fixation Duration to the Talker's Nose as a Percentage of Viewing Time Across Stimuli

	English		French	
Stimulus Condition	***M* (*SD*)**	**Min–Max**	***M* (*SD*)**	**Min–Max**
AV	21.48 (3.76)	12.32–32.82	19.98 (3.37)	13.18–28.42
AVn	19.20 (6.27)	12.67–65.06	20.27 (4.36)	8.63–33.72
V-only	15.51 (3.12)	7.63–24.87	16.73 (3.71)	9.96–28.29

Note. AV = auditory-visual; AVn = auditory-visual with noise added; V-only = visual-only. Min and Max = minimum and maximum values, respectively.

Visualizations

Gaze Plots

Using gaze plots, the eye movements of participants, a few at a time, were observed throughout each stimulus by moving the mouse incrementally through the video produced by the software. For illustration purposes, the gaze patterns of three participants for select stimuli in each language were chosen to demonstrate common patterns. Screenshots were then taken at several key points: initial fixations, immediately before discernible movement, first indication of movement, the peak of the vowel (relevant for the task), and the end of the utterance. The figures below were created from these screenshots.[3]

Figure 5.2 shows the initial fixations of the participants viewing the face of the talker who was about to produce the stimulus *read* ([i]) in the

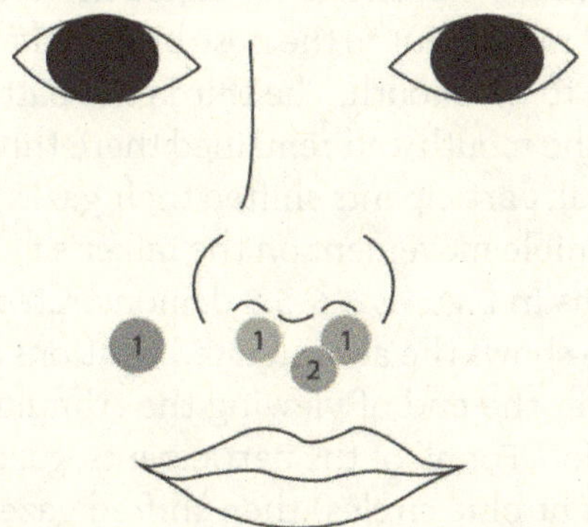

FIGURE 5.2 Gaze Plots for Three Participants in the English AVn Condition Showing Initial Fixations Prior to the Utterance *read*

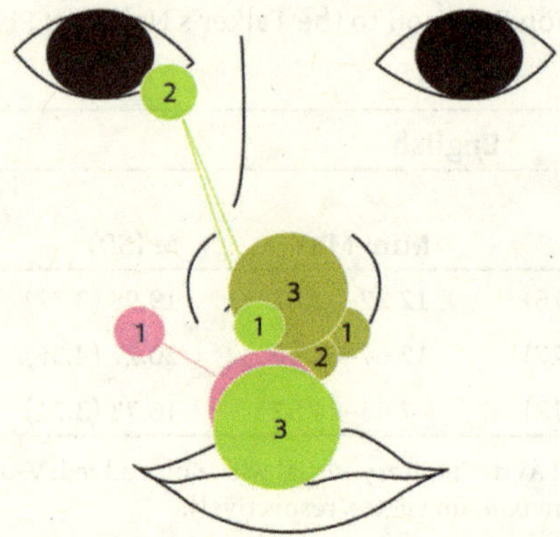

FIGURE 5.3 Gaze Plots for Three Participants in the English AVn Condition as Lip Protrusion Began for [ɹ] in *read*

English AVn condition. At this point, there was no movement, and all fixations were centrally located at the talker's nose. Figure 5.3 shows the gaze pattern of the same three participants when lip protrusion was beginning for [ɹ] (i.e., the first discernible movement). One participant (circles shown in purple) had shifted gaze to the mouth, another (light green) to the talker's right eye and then down to the mouth, and the third (olive green) remained at the nose throughout the rest of the utterance.

Figures 5.4 and 5.5 show the changes in gaze patterns for the three participants viewing the face of the talker at different stages in the articulation of the word *read* in the English V-only condition. Figure 5.4 shows the initial fixations, two of which are at the nose and the third is at the talker's left cheek. The screenshot for Figure 5.5 was taken at the beginning of lip protrusion for [ɹ]. By this time, the gaze of one participant (purple circles) had moved to the mouth and remained there. Another (light blue) showed a pattern of movement to the nose bridge, then to the talker's left eye, and ultimately to the mouth. The third gaze pattern (yellow) moved from the cheek to the mouth and remained there through the end of the utterance. In general, participants shifted their gazes in response to even the slightest discernible movement on the talker's face.

The visualizations in Figures 5.6–5.8 demonstrated variability in gaze patterns. Figure 5.6 shows the accumulated fixations and saccades of the three participants at the end of viewing the stimulus *panze* ([ɑ̃]) in the French AVn condition. For all of the participants, gaze began at the nose. One participant (light blue circles) then shifted gaze to the nose bridge followed by a back-and-forth pattern between the eyes, ultimately ending at the mouth. The other participants moved to the mouth area earlier. (Note that some lines are hidden by circles in gaze plots.)

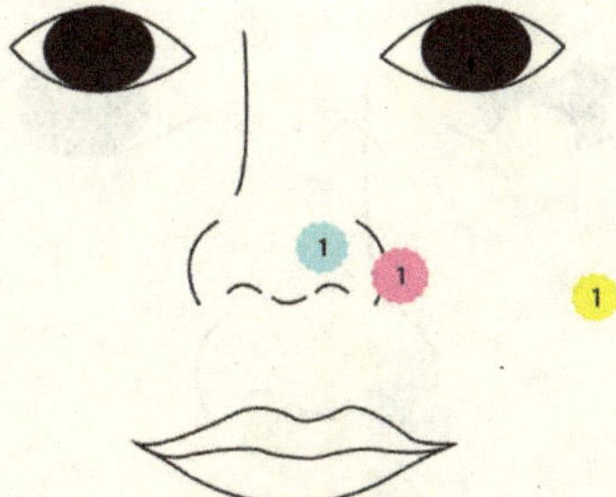

FIGURE 5.4 Gaze Plots for Three Participants in the English V-only Condition Showing Initial Fixations Prior to the Utterance *read*

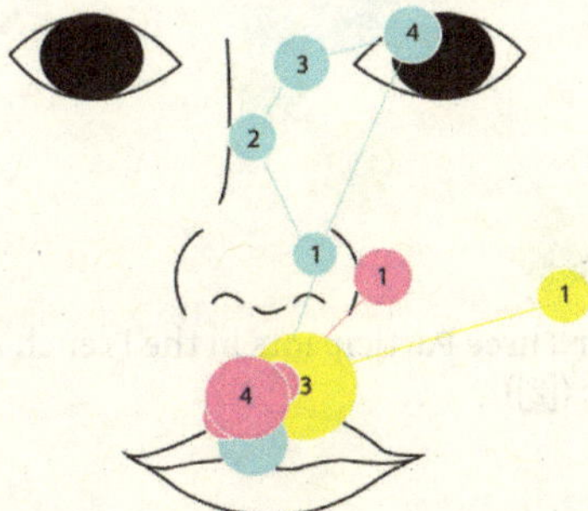

FIGURE 5.5 Gaze Plots for Three Participants in the English V-only Condition as Lip Protrusion Began for [ɹ] in *read*

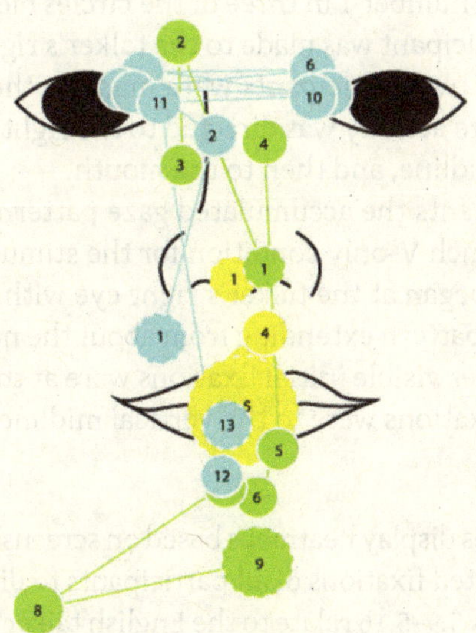

FIGURE 5.6 Gaze Plots for Three Participants in the French AVn Condition at the End of the Utterance *panze* ([ã])

FIGURE 5.7 Gaze Plots for Three Participants in the French AVn Condition at the End of the Utterance *zync* ([ɛ̃])

Figure 5.7 shows the accumulated fixations and saccades of the three participants at the end of viewing the stimulus *zync* ([ɛ̃]) in the French AVn condition. The number 1 in three of the circles means that the initial fixation of one participant was made to the talker's right eye, and the fixations of the other two participants were made to the nose. After these initial fixations, gaze activity was directed to the right side of the talker's face, the vertical midline, and then to the mouth.

Figure 5.8 represents the accumulated gaze patterns of the three participants in the French V-only condition for the stimulus *jeinde* ([ɛ̃]). One participant's gaze began at the talker's right eye with subsequent movements in a vertical pattern extending from about the nose bridge down to the mouth. The other visible initial fixations were at the nose followed by the mouth. Most fixations were to the vertical midline of the face.

Heatmaps

The following figures display heatmaps based on screenshots showing changes in the accumulated fixations of all participants to different areas of the talker's face. Figures 5.9–5.16 relate to the English talker's production of the word *read* at different points in the three stimulus conditions. In Figure 5.9,

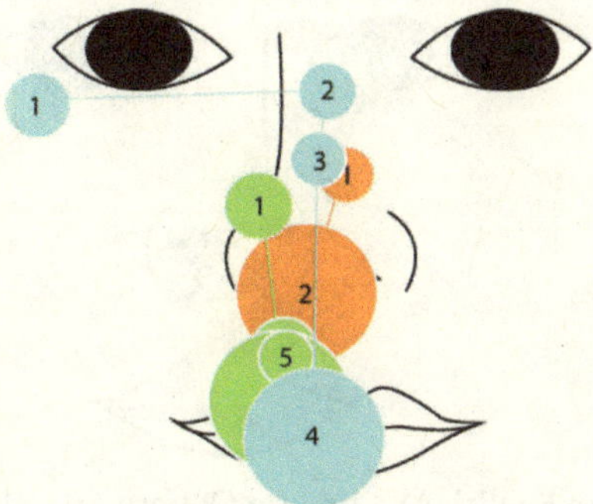

FIGURE 5.8 Gaze Plots for Three Participants in the French V-only Condition at the End of the Utterance *jeinde* ([ɛ̃])

FIGURE 5.9 Heatmap of English AV Condition Showing Initial Fixations Prior to the Utterance *read*

initial fixations in the AV condition were distributed primarily to the facial midline and the right side of the face, with concentrations around the nose. In Figure 5.10, immediately before the first sign of movement, fixations were directed primarily to the facial midline and the talker's right eye, with concentrations near the mouth. Fixations did not change as the mouth began to open. Figure 5.11 shows fixations concentrated at the mouth during the vowel [i] peak; these did not move throughout the rest of the utterance.

In the AVn condition as shown in Figure 5.12, initial fixations were directed to the talker's right eye and nose, with some to each side of the nose. As the jaw began to lower slightly (Figure 5.13), fixations were primarily directed to the mouth and remained there as the mouth started to open. At the peak of the vowel [i] (Figure 5.14), some fixations were directed to the nose and the right eye, but most were concentrated at the mouth and remained there throughout the rest of the utterance.

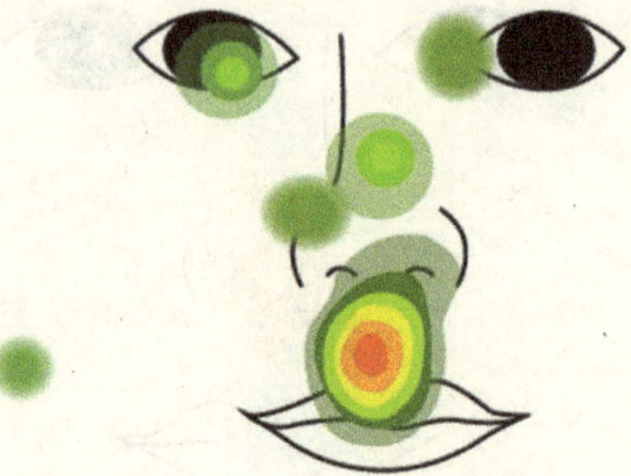

FIGURE 5.10 Heatmap of English AV Condition Before Articulatory Movement for the Utterance *read*

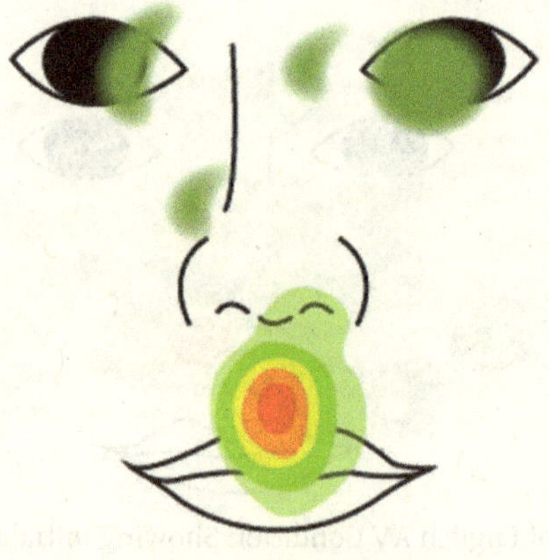

FIGURE 5.11 Heatmap of English AV Condition During the Vowel Peak for the Utterance *read*

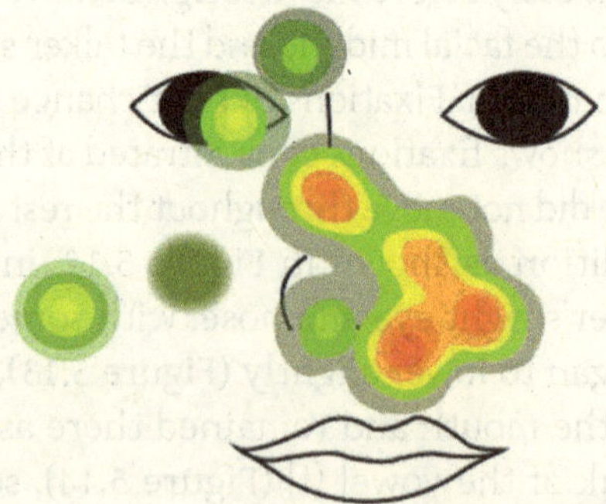

FIGURE 5.12 Heatmap of English AVn Condition Showing Initial Fixations Prior to the Utterance *read*

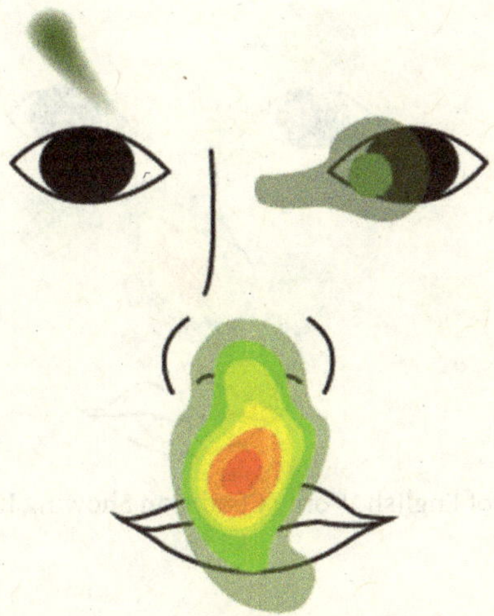

FIGURE 5.13 Heatmap of English AVn Condition as the Mouth Began to Open for the Utterance *read*

FIGURE 5.14 Heatmap of English AVn Condition During the Vowel Peak for the Utterance *read*

In the V-only condition, initial fixations were primarily to the right side of the talker's face with concentrations around the nose, shown in Figure 5.15. Immediately before discernible movement (Figure 5.16), fixations were concentrated at the mouth and remained there throughout the utterance.

FIGURE 5.15 Heatmap of English V-only Condition Showing Initial Fixations Prior to the Utterance *read*

FIGURE 5.16 Heatmap of English V-only Condition Before Articulatory Movement for the Utterance *read*

In sum, the heatmaps for L1 English in the AV and AVn conditions demonstrated that after initial fixations, most gaze movement occurred in anticipation of articulation, then in response to the slightest indication of articulatory movement (e.g., lip protrusion), and finally at the vowel peak; the vowel was the focus of the task. In the V-only condition, in which vowel identification was entirely dependent on speechreading, fixations were concentrated at the mouth earlier than in the AV and AVn conditions.

The following figures display heatmaps showing changes in the accumulated fixations of all participants to the different areas of the

FIGURE 5.17 Heatmap of French AV Condition Showing Initial Fixations Prior to the Utterance *bande*

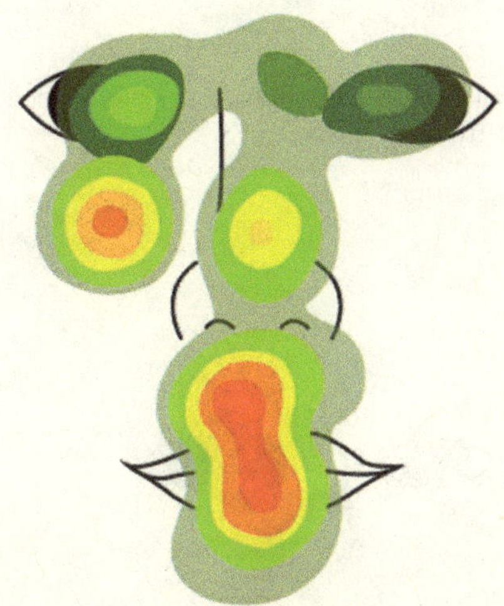

FIGURE 5.18 Heatmap of French AV Condition Before Articulatory Movement for the Utterance *bande*

French talker's face. Figures 5.17–5.25 relate to the talker's production of the word *bande* [ɑ̃], a noun meaning "band/strip," at different points in the three stimulus conditions.

Initial fixations in the AV condition (Figure 5.17) were primarily at the nose, extending horizontally to the left and right sides of the nose, and to the mouth. Prior to any discernible movement (Figure 5.18), fixations were directed to each eye, to the nose, the mouth, and the talker's right cheek below the eye. In response to the slight tipping back of the talker's head and slight movement of the mouth (Figure 5.19), fixations were primarily

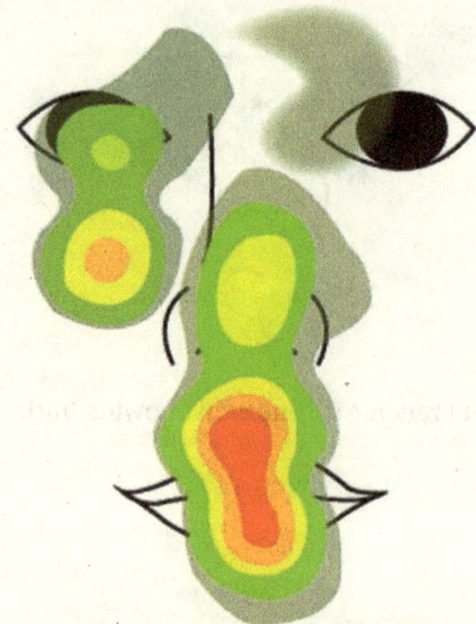

FIGURE 5.19 Heatmap of French AV Condition as Head Tipped Back and Mouth Began to Open for the Utterance *bande*

FIGURE 5.20 Heatmap of French AV Condition at the Vowel Peak for the Utterance *bande*

directed to the right side of the face and the mouth. At the peak of the vowel [ã] (Figure 5.20), most fixations were directed to the eyes and the vertical midline extending from the supratip of the nose down to below the mouth, and they remained there throughout the rest of the utterance.

FIGURE 5.21 Heatmap of French AVn Condition Showing Initial Fixations for the Utterance *bande*

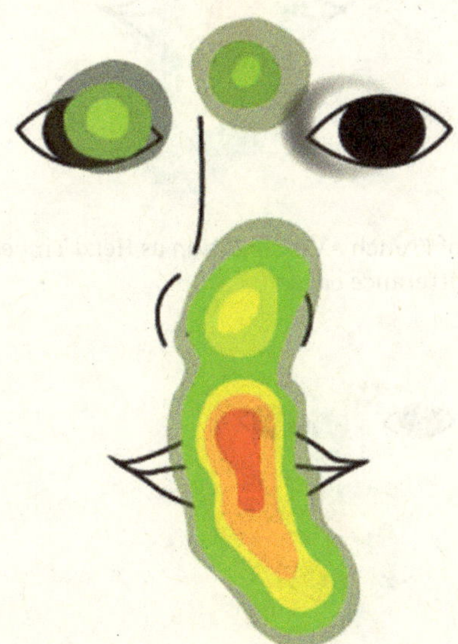

FIGURE 5.22 Heatmap of French AVn Condition Before Articulatory Movement for the Utterance *bande*

In the AVn condition, initial fixations (Figure 5.21) were concentrated at the nose bridge and an area extending horizontally to either side of the nose. Prior to any movement (Figure 5.22), fixations were directed to the talker's nose bridge, right eye, nose tip, and mouth. As the talker's head tipped back slightly and the lips started to move (Figure 5.23), fixations increased to the nose and mouth and remained in these areas.

In the V-only condition, initial fixations (Figure 5.24) were at the facial midline and the left side of the talker's face from the nose bridge down to the mouth. Prior to movement, fixations were concentrated at the mouth (Figure 5.25) and remained there throughout the rest of the utterance.

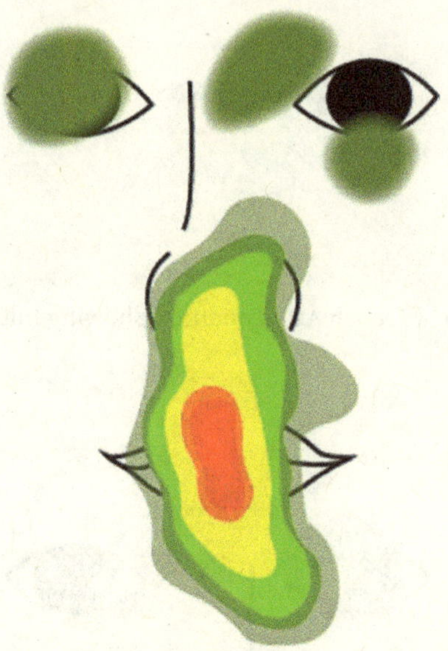

FIGURE 5.23 Heatmap of French AVn Condition as Head Tipped Back and Mouth Began to Move for the Utterance *bande*

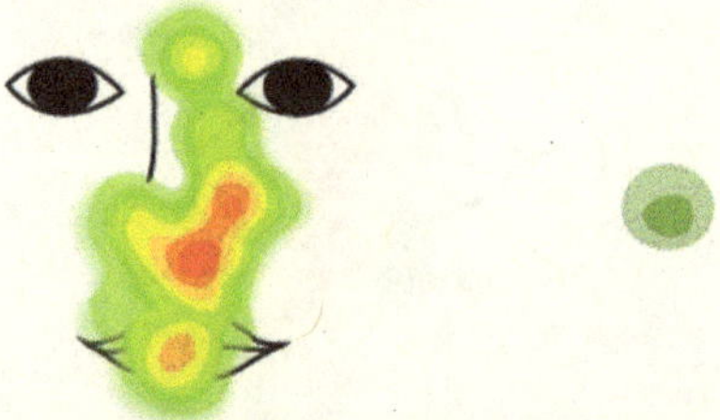

FIGURE 5.24 Heatmap of French V-only Condition Showing Initial Fixations for the Utterance *bande*

In sum, the heatmaps for L2 French demonstrated that fixations often began at the vertical midline, including the nose and eye level, but shifted to the mouth in anticipation of articulation and generally remained there throughout the utterance. Even the slightest movements, such as starting to open the mouth (Figure 5.25) or to tip the head back, triggered a shift in participants' eye gazes.

First Fixations to AOIs

RQ3 asked to which AOI on a talker's face participants looked first and if this differed by stimulus condition and/or language. The metric of TTFF

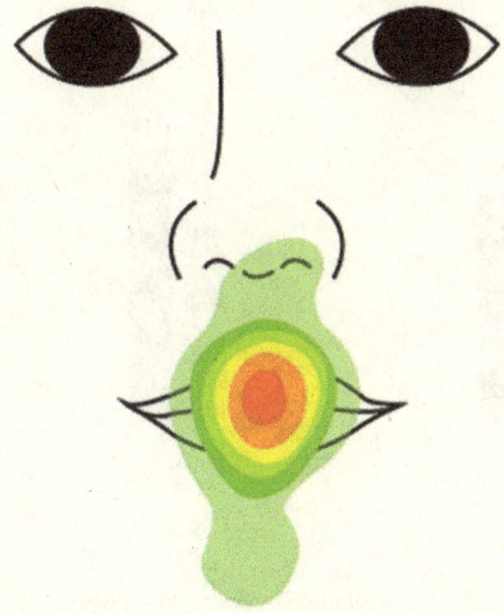

FIGURE 5.25 Heatmap of French V-only condition Before Articulatory Movement for the Utterance *bande*

was used to address this question. Figure 5.26 shows the number of trials in which each AOI was fixated first per stimulus condition in L1 English (top) and L2 French (bottom). Across conditions in English, first fixations were to the mouth, followed by the nose, eyes, and forehead; the number of first fixations to the nose and mouth were very close in the AV condition. In the French AV and AVn conditions, first fixations were to the talker's eyes in more trials than to the other AOIs, followed by the nose, mouth, and forehead. In the V-only condition, first fixations were to the mouth, followed by the nose and then the eyes.

For analysis, the predictor (or independent) variables were language (English, French) and stimulus condition (AV, AVn, V-only); the outcome (or dependent) variable was TTFF to each AOI, with participants as random effects. Because the outcome variable was categorical with more than two levels, multinomial logistic regression modelling was appropriate.[4] The data for the forehead as an AOI in the English AV and V-only conditions were below the recommended threshold of 10 events for this type of analysis (Peduzzi et al., 1996), therefore the forehead was excluded. The mclogit package in R (Elff, 2013) was used to fit two mixed-effects multinomial logistic regression models: a model with only language as the predictor (Model 0), and a model with language, condition, and the interaction of the two variables as predictors (Model 1). The Akaike information criterion (AIC) for Model 1 was lower than that for Model 0 (ΔAIC = −1075.09 points), indicating a better model fit (K.P. Burnham et al., 2011).

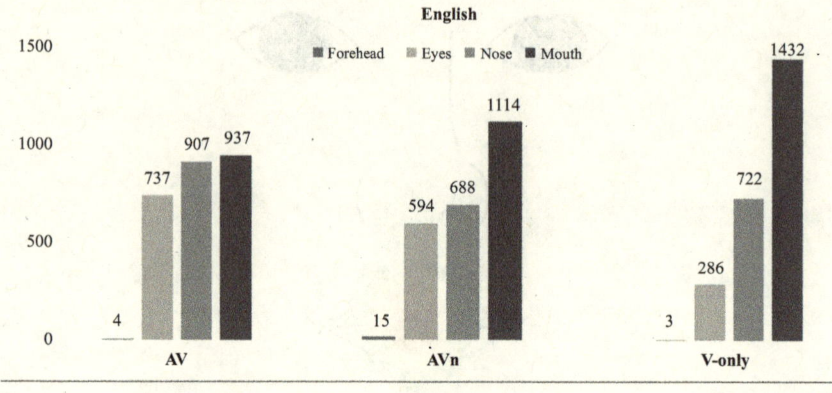

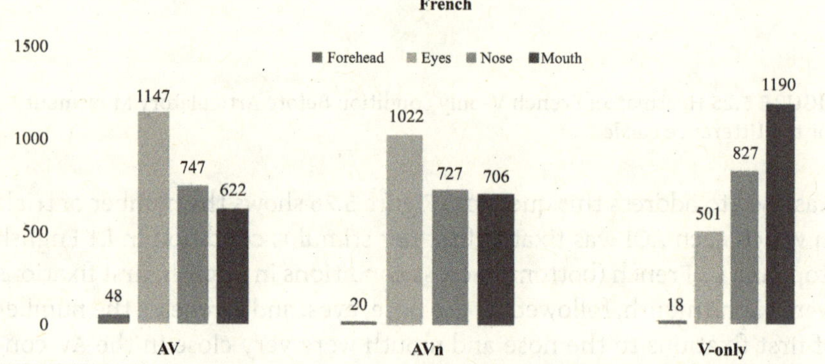

Note. AV = auditory-visual, AVn = auditory-visual with noise, V-only = visual only.

FIGURE 5.26 Number of Trials in Which Each Area of Interest Was Fixated First

The parameter estimates (fixed effects) of Model 1 are shown in Table 5.4. For this type of analysis, one group from each variable was set as the reference (baseline) group as follows: eyes for AOI, English for language, and AV for stimulus condition. The intercept coefficients in Table 5.4 refer to the log odds of first looking at the given AOI (e.g., mouth for rows 1–6) versus the eyes (the reference group) when participants were exposed to English language stimuli in the AV condition.[5] The other coefficients refer to the difference in log odds of first looking at the given AOI (i.e., the mouth or nose) versus the eyes (i.e., the reference group) for the given levels of language and/or stimulus condition as compared to the English AV condition (i.e., the reference groups for the language and condition variables). For ease of interpretation, the log odds estimates were converted to odds ratios (OR), which are closely linked to probabilities (Akiva M. Liberman, 2005).[6]

TABLE 5.4 Multinomial Logistic Regression Parameter Estimates (Fixed Effects) for AOI Fixated First

			95% CI for OR			
AOI	**Predictor**	***b*** **(*SE*)**	**Lower**	**OR**	**Upper**	***p***
Mouth	(Intercept)	0.436 (0.251)	0.945	1.547	2.532	.082
Mouth	Language: French	-1.171 (0.080)	0.265	0.310	0.363	<.001
Mouth	Condition: AVn	0.484 (0.081)	1.385	1.623	1.902	<.001
Mouth	Condition: V-only	1.749 (0.092)	4.800	5.750	6.888	<.001
Mouth	Language: French; Condition: AVn	-0.153 (0.113)	0.688	0.858	1.071	.175
Mouth	Language: French; Condition: V-only	0.172 (0.123)	0.934	1.188	1.511	.159
Nose	(Intercept)	0.470 (0.201)	1.078	1.600	2.375	.019
Nose	Language: French	-0.872 (0.075)	0.361	0.418	0.484	<.001
Nose	Condition: AVn	-0.009 (0.081)	0.845	0.991	1.163	.915
Nose	Condition: V-only	1.004 (0.093)	2.273	2.729	3.278	<.001
Nose	Language: French; Condition: AVn	0.174 (0.110)	0.960	1.190	1.475	.112
Nose	Language: French; Condition: V-only	0.256 (0.122)	1.017	1.292	1.642	.036

Note. b = coefficient, log odds; *SE* = standard error; CI = confidence interval; OR = odds ratio; AVn = auditory-visual with noise added; V-only = visual-only.

As an example of the interpretation of the intercept and predictors, start with row 7 "Nose (Intercept)" in Table 5.4. The OR of the intercept is 1.600, which means that the odds of participants looking first at the nose versus the eyes (i.e., the reference group for AOIs) when presented with English AV stimuli (i.e., the reference groups for language and condition) were 1.600:1, which represented significantly greater odds of fixating the nose first versus the eyes in the baseline condition of English AV. Converting the odds to probability, there was a 39% chance that a participant exposed to the English AV condition would first fixate the nose.

The ORs of the subsequent rows (8–12) represent the change in the ORs of first fixating the nose versus the eyes for different combinations of language and condition as compared to the reference group of English AV. For example, the OR of 0.418 in row 8 (Language: French) shows that the odds of participants first looking at the nose versus the eyes decreased with exposure to the French AV condition as compared to English AV. The

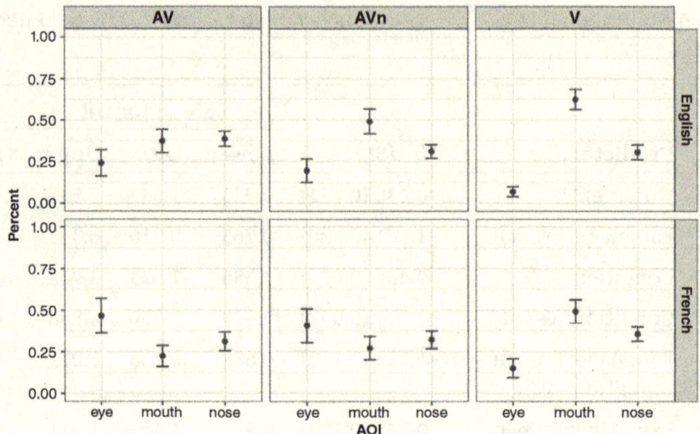

FIGURE 5.27 Predicted Likelihood of First Fixations per Area of Interest Across Languages and Conditions

likelihood of first fixating the nose in the French AV condition would be about 36% (see Figure 5.27). Figure 5.27 provides the predicted likelihood of the AOI fixated first across languages and conditions, calculated with the emmeans package in R (Lenth, 2023) using the coefficients from the model (Table 5.4). The predicted likelihood of first fixating the nose did not vary much across the language and condition combinations, but the predicted likelihood of first fixating the eyes or mouth did vary.

To quantify the amount of variance in the dependent variable explained by the random effects (i.e., differences across participants), separate binary logistic regression models were fit for the mouth versus the eyes as well as the nose versus the eyes; the eyes served as the reference AOI category. Because the multinomial model fit for Model 1 is a baseline-category logit model, which simultaneously fits a set of logistic regression models (i.e., mouth vs. eyes, nose vs. eyes), fitting separate binary logistic regression models approximates the results of the multinomial model. The performance package in R (Lüdecke et al., 2021) was used to calculate the conditional R^2 statistics (i.e., variance explained by both the fixed and random effects) and the marginal R^2 statistics (i.e., variance explained by the fixed effects only) for these separate logistic regression models based on Nakagawa's method (Nakagawa et al., 2017). The difference between the conditional and marginal R^2 values represents the proportion of total variance explained by the random effects.

Results revealed that approximately 45.5% (conditional R^2) of the variance in TTFF to the mouth (vs. the eyes) was explained by the regression model, with 15% (marginal R^2) of that variance explained by the fixed effects (i.e., differences between language, stimulus condition, and their interactions) and 30.5% by the random effects (i.e., differences across participants). Approximately 36.6% (conditional R^2) of the variance in TTFF to the nose (vs. the eyes) was explained by the regression model, with 9.6% (marginal R^2) explained by the fixed effects and 27% by the random effects.

Total Fixation Durations to AOIs

RQ4 asked which AOI on a talker's face attracted the most attention as measured by TFD and if that AOI differed by stimulus condition and/or visual category of the initial sounds within the stimulus set. For analysis, the predictor variables (fixed effects) were language (English, French), stimulus condition (AV, AVn, V-only), and visual category (labial, non-labial); the outcome variable was TFD for each AOI on a talker's face. Both condition and visual category were nested under language. The random effect was participants. Because the outcome variable was a categorical variable with more than two levels, the same statistical package was used as for RQ1 to fit multiple mixed-effects multinomial logistic regression models to reveal the patterns in the variables. Among them, the model with language and condition as main and interaction predictors had the lowest AIC and Bayesian information criterion (BIC) values, indicating the best fit for the data.

Figure 5.28 shows the number of trials for which each AOI had the longest TFD across the language and stimulus combinations. In the AV and AVn conditions in both languages, the mouth had the longest TFD, followed by the eyes and then the nose. In the V-only condition, the mouth clearly dominated, followed by the nose and then the eyes.

The parameter estimates of the model are shown in Table 5.5. The interpretation of the coefficients and ORs is similar to that for the previous model, but with the outcome as the AOI with the longest TFD. In all but one condition, the data for the forehead were below the recommended threshold of 10 for this type of analysis (Peduzzi et al., 1996), therefore the forehead was excluded. The same reference categories were used for this analysis: eyes for AOI, English for language, and AV for stimulus condition.

Figure 5.29 shows the predicted likelihood of the AOI with the longest TFD across language and condition combinations. In all, participants were most likely to fixate the mouth the longest, and the likelihood increased as the audio signal quality declined (AVn) or disappeared (V-only).

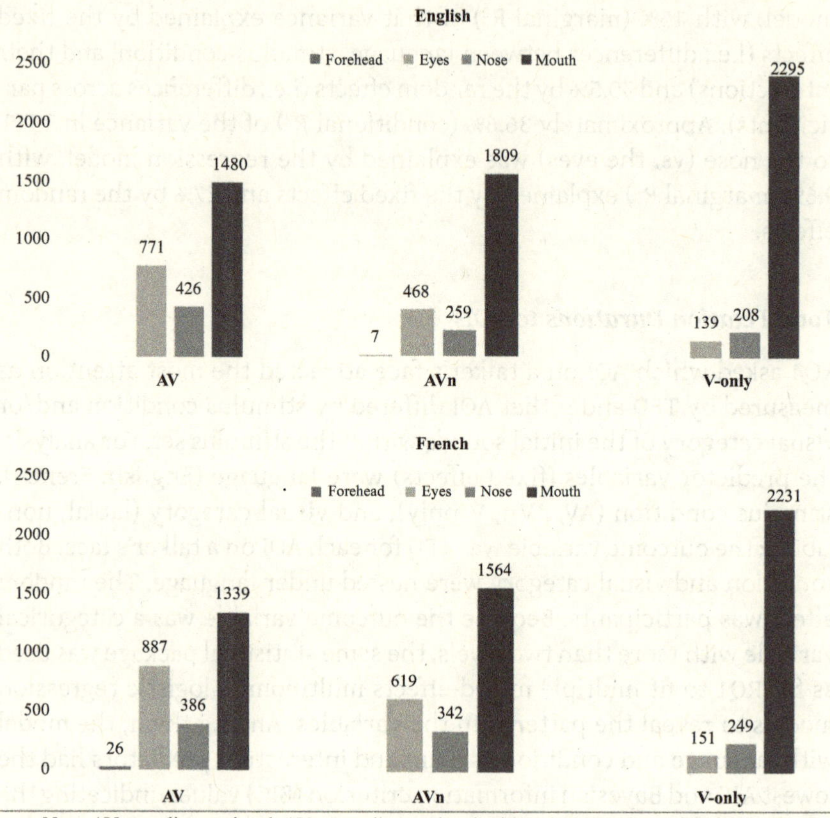

Note. AV = auditory-visual, AVn = auditory-visual with noise, V-only = visual only.

FIGURE 5.28 Number of Trials in Which Each Area of Interest Had the Longest Total Fixation Duration

The method used in RQ3 to calculate the conditional and marginal R^2 statistics was also used to calculate separate logistic regression models for the analysis of RQ4. Results revealed that approximately 60% (conditional R^2) of the variance in TFD to the mouth (vs. the eyes) was explained by the regression model, with 18.2% (marginal R^2) of that variance explained by the fixed effects (i.e., differences between language, stimulus condition, and their interactions) and 41.8% by the random effects (i.e., differences across participants). Approximately 60.9% (conditional R^2) of the variance in TFD to the nose (vs. the eyes) was explained by the regression model, with 6.1% (marginal R^2) explained by the fixed effects and 54.8% by the random effects. Therefore, similar to the analysis of TTFF (RQ3), most of the variance in TFD that was explained by the model was due to random effects (i.e., differences across participants). Table 5.6 summarizes the

TABLE 5.5 Multinomial Logistic Regression Parameter Estimates (Fixed Effects) for AOI with Longest Total Fixation Duration

			95% CI for OR			
AOI	**Predictor**	***b* (*SE*)**	**Lower**	**OR**	**Upper**	***p***
Mouth	(Intercept)	1.116 (0.329)	1.600	3.052	5.821	<.001
Mouth	Language: French	−0.406 (0.075)	0.575	0.666	0.772	<.001
Mouth	Condition: AVn	0.948 (0.081)	2.203	2.582	3.025	<.001
Mouth	Condition: V-only	2.708 (0.109)	12.102	14.996	18.582	<.001
Mouth	Language: French; Condition: AVn	−0.158 (0.111)	0.686	0.854	1.062	.155
Mouth	Language: French; Condition: V-only	0.307 (0.149)	1.015	1.359	1.820	.039
Nose	(Intercept)	−0.626 (0.354)	0.267	1.535	1.071	.077
Nose	Language: French	−0.386 (0.097)	0.562	0.680	0.823	<.001
Nose	Condition: AVn	0.125 (0.110)	0.914	1.133	1.405	.253
Nose	Condition: V-only	1.296 (0.137)	2.793	3.653	4.778	<.001
Nose	Language: French; Condition: AVn	0.332 (0.150)	1.038	1.393	1.869	.026
Nose	Language: French; Condition: V-only	0.539 (0.187)	1.188	1.714	2.474	.003

Note. b = coefficient, log odds; *SE* = standard error; CI = confidence interval; OR = odds ratio; AVn = auditory-visual with noise added; V-only = visual-only.

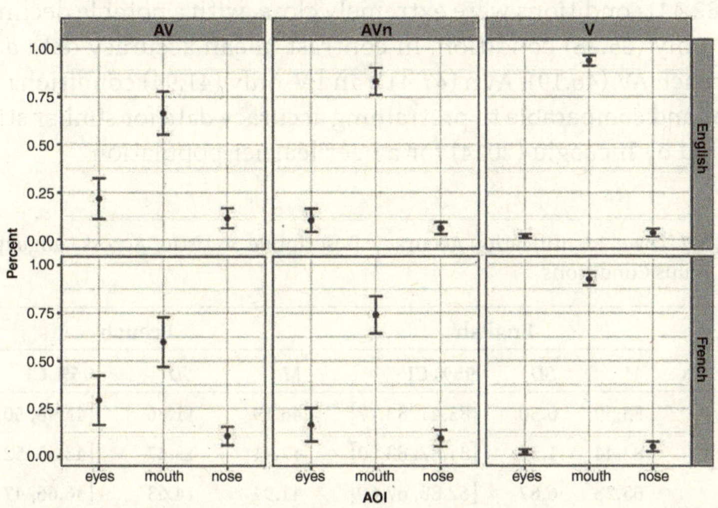

FIGURE 5.29 Predicted Likelihood of Longest Total Fixation Duration per Area of Interest Across Languages and Conditions

TABLE 5.6 Summary of Approximate Proportions of Variance Explained by Fixed and Random Effects in Models for Time to First Fixation and Total Fixation Duration Measures

	Time to First Fixation		Total Fixation Duration	
Statistics	**Mouth (vs. Eyes)**	**Nose (vs. Eyes)**	**Mouth (vs. Eyes)**	**Nose (vs. Eyes)**
Marginal R^2 (Fixed Effects)	15.0%	9.6%	18.2%	6.1%
Conditional R^2 (Fixed and Random Effects)	45.5%	36.6%	60.0%	60.9%
Random Effects	30.5%	27.0%	41.8%	54.8%

Note. Fixed effects represent differences in language, condition, and their interactions; random effects represent differences across participants.

approximate proportions of variance explained by the model statistics for the analyses of RQ3 and RQ4.

Vowel Identification Accuracy

RQ5 asked if vowel identification accuracy varied according to stimulus condition and/or the visual category of the initial sounds within the stimulus set. Table 5.7 provides the descriptive statistics for mean identification accuracy across languages and stimulus conditions (total number correct = 84). The accuracy means for the English AV (83.59) and AVn (82.44) conditions were extremely close, with a notable decline for the V-only (65.28) condition. In contrast, mean accuracy data across the French AV (46.19), AVn (47.41), and V-only (41.94) conditions were similar and comparable to pretraining accuracy data for similar stimuli reported by Inceoglu (2014) for a peer learner population.

TABLE 5.7 Vowel Identification Accuracy: Descriptive Statistics Across Languages and Stimulus Conditions

Stimulus	English			French		
Condition	***M***	***SD***	**95% CI**	***M***	***SD***	**95% CI**
AV	83.59	0.50	[83.41, 83.77]	46.19	11.66	[41.98, 50.39]
AVn	82.44	1.56	[81.87, 83.00]	47.41	13.47	[42.55, 52.26]
V-only	65.28	6.67	[62.88, 67.69]	41.94	14.63	[36.66, 47.21]

Note. Total possible correct was 84. AV = auditory-visual; AVn = auditory-visual with noise added; V-only = visual-only; CI = confidence interval.

Based on the similarity in identification accuracy between the French AV and AVn conditions, the latter involving a degraded audio signal, and the very slight decline in the V-only condition, essentially a speechreading task, the visual modality may have been the most informative input source, contributing the most to the percept in all conditions. Across the languages and conditions, as the stimuli became more challenging, either from a difference in language (i.e., the L2 vs. the L1) or the degradation or absence of the audio signal, the standard deviation increased, indicating increasing variability in the participants' response accuracy, similar to the findings of Rennig et al. (2020) for L1 English.

To address RQ5, analysis involved the predictor variables of language (English, French), condition (AV, AVn, V-only), and visual category (labial, nonlabial), as well as the outcome variable of identification accuracy expressed categorically as correct or incorrect. Because the outcome variable was categorical with only two levels, the lme4 package in R (Bates et al., 2015) was used to fit several mixed-effects logistic regression models, including one involving the variable of visual category; however, the model with only language and condition had the best fit for the data and was selected for this analysis. The parameter estimates (fixed effects) for the model are shown in Table 5.8.

The OR of the intercept 230.046 (row 1) denotes the odds of participants accurately identifying the target in the English AV condition as a 99.6% likelihood of accurate identification. The OR of 0.005 in row 2 (Language: French) means the odds of correctly identifying the target significantly

TABLE 5.8 Logistic Regression Parameter Estimates (Fixed Effects) for Vowel Identification Accuracy

		95% CI for OR			
Predictor	***b*** **(*SE*)**	**Lower**	**OR**	**Upper**	***p***
(Intercept)	5.438 (0.285)	131.474	230.046	402.522	<.001
Language: French	-5.228 (0.276)	0.003	0.005	0.009	<.001
Condition: AVn	-1.364 (0.307)	0.140	0.256	0.466	<.001
Condition: V-only	-4.128 (0.277)	0.009	0.016	0.028	<.001
Language: French; Condition: AVn	1.426 (0.312)	2.259	4.163	7.672	<.001
Language: French; Condition: V-only	3.913 (0.282)	28.790	50.060	87.045	<.001

Note. b = coefficient, log odds; *SE* = standard error; CI = confidence interval; OR = odds ratio; AVn = auditory-visual with noise added; V-only = visual-only.

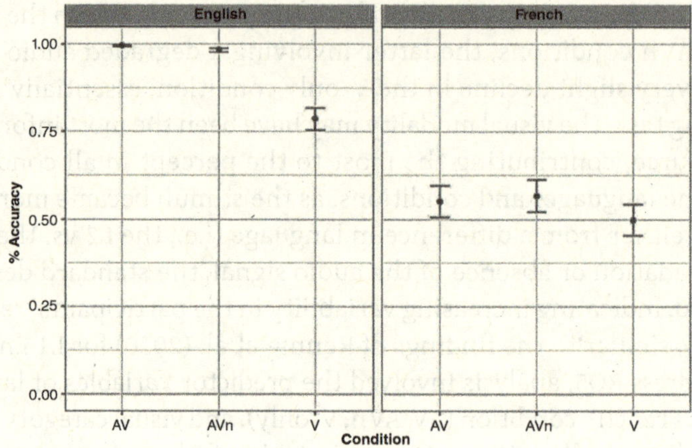

FIGURE 5.30 Predicted Likelihood of Identification Accuracy Across Languages and Conditions

decreased for the French AV stimuli as compared to English AV (i.e., language reference group); in probability terms, the likelihood of correct identification decreased to approximately 55.2%. The ORs in rows 5–6 of Table 5.8 show interaction effects. For example, the likelihood of correct identification in the French AVn condition was approximately 56.8%. Figure 5.30 illustrates the predicted likelihood values for correct identification across languages and stimulus conditions.

Although much of the variance in the AOI that was fixated first (RQ3) and showed the longest fixation duration (RQ4) was attributable to differences across participants (i.e., random effects; see Table 5.6), very little of the variance in identification accuracy was due to these individual differences. Results showed 58.7% (conditional R^2) of the variance in identification accuracy was explained by the model (i.e., fixed and random effects), and of that amount, 55.9% (marginal R^2) was explained by the fixed effects (i.e., differences in language, condition, and their interactions). Therefore, only 2.8% of the variance was attributable to the random effects. Apparently, the variability in gaze behaviour (i.e., in first fixations and fixation durations) did not come at the expense of accuracy.

Decision Time

RQ6 asked if decision time – that is, time to mouse click (TTMC) – differed by stimulus condition and/or the visual category of the initial sounds within the stimulus set. This analysis involved the predictor variables of condition (AV, AVn, V-only) and visual category (labial, nonlabial), and the outcome

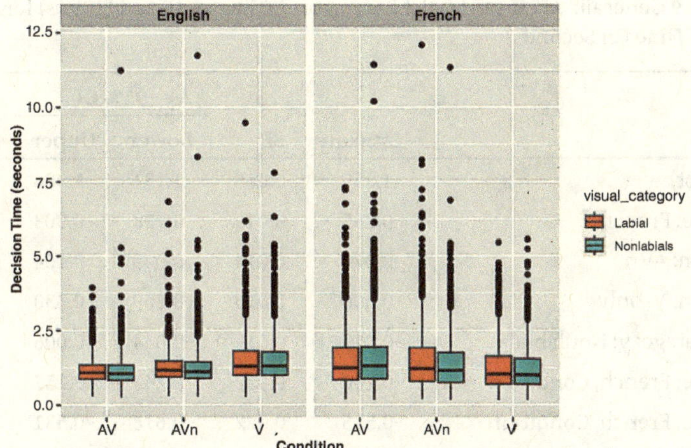

FIGURE 5.31 Decision Time by Language, Condition, and Visual Category

variable of TTMC (in seconds). This outcome variable is a continuous variable with a *gamma* distribution (i.e., a continuous probability distribution that models right-skewed data). The glmer package in R was used to fit multiple mixed-effects generalized linear models with gamma distribution. The model with all three variables and two interactions (i.e., Language x Condition + Language x Visual category) as predictors had the best fit for the data. The likelihood ratio test also showed that this model performed better than the one with only language and condition as predictors, $\chi^2 = 7.485$, $p = .023$.

Figure 5.31 shows the distribution of TTMC by language, condition, and visual category. The quartiles (Q) are denoted by the Q1, Q2, and Q3 points. The Q1 and Q3 points are represented by the edges of each box; 25% of the data points are below Q1, 50% below Q2 (i.e., the median of the distribution indicated by the horizontal line within the box), and 75% are below Q3. Across languages and stimulus conditions, the median TTMC was clearly less than 2.5 s.

Table 5.9 shows the parameter estimates (coefficients) of the model for this analysis. Reference groups were as follows: English for language, AV for condition, and labial for visual category. The coefficient for the intercept (row 1) shows the mean TTMC for the English labial stimuli in the AV condition. The coefficients for the main effect terms (rows 2–5) represent the change in the mean TTMC as compared to the intercept. The coefficients for the interaction terms (rows 6–8) are adjustments to the main effects based on the presence of the interaction between predictors. For example, the coefficient 0.265 for the second row (Language: French) signifies that the mean TTMC was 1.524 s (i.e., 1.259 + 0.265) when participants were presented with French stimuli beginning with a labial

TABLE 5.9 Generalized Linear Model Parameter Estimates (Fixed Effects) for Decision Time (in Seconds)

Term	*Estimate*	*SE*	95% CI Lower	95% CI Upper	*p*
(Intercept)	1.259	0.065	1.131	1.386	<.001
Language: French	0.265	0.019	0.228	0.303	<.001
Condition: AVn	0.076	0.014	0.049	0.104	<.001
Condition: V-only	0.300	0.016	0.269	0.330	<.001
Visual Category: Nonlabials	−0.019	0.013	−0.044	0.006	.131
Language: French; Condition: AVn	−0.200	0.022	−0.243	−0.157	<.001
Language: French; Condition: V-only	−0.575	0.022	−0.618	−0.531	<.001
Language: French; Visual Category: Nonlabials	0.010	0.018	−0.045	0.026	.592

Note. SE = standard error; CI = confidence interval; AVn = auditory-visual with noise added; V-only = visual-only.

consonant in the AV condition. The coefficient −0.200 for row 6 (Language: French; Condition: AVn) indicates that the mean TTMC was 1.4 s (1.259 intercept + 0.265 French language + 0.076 AVn condition − 0.2 coefficient) when presented with French stimuli beginning with a labial consonant in the AVn condition, which is slightly shorter as compared to the French AV condition (1.524 s). There were no significant differences based on the visual category of the initial sound of the stimuli.

Because the interaction effects involving language and condition were significant, they were used to produce Figure 5.32, which shows the predicted TTMCs across languages and conditions. The model accounted for about 16.5% of the variance in TTMC, of which the fixed effects explained 4.8% and the random effects explained about 11.7%.

Relationship Between Identification Accuracy and Decision Time

RQ7 addressed the nature of the relationship between TTMC and identification accuracy. A mixed-effects logistic regression analysis was conducted involving the predictor variable of TTMC and the outcome variable of identification accuracy. For this model, a random slope and a random intercept were incorporated to address the possibility that the relationship between TTMC and identification accuracy could differ by participant.

Only 9.3% of the variance in identification accuracy was explained by TTMC (i.e., the fixed effect) plus the differences across participants

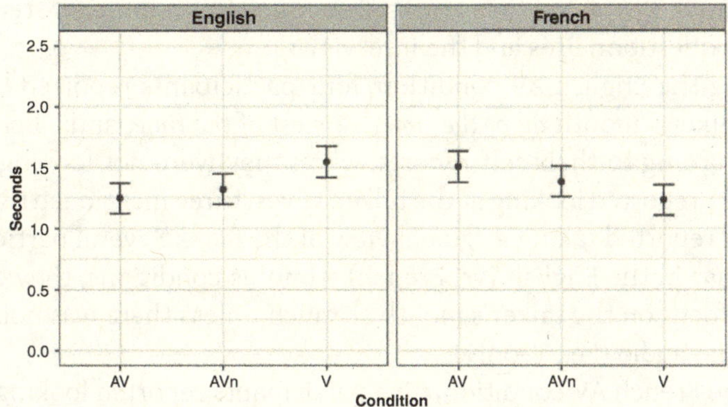

FIGURE 5.32 Predicted Decision Time by Language and Condition

(i.e., the random intercept and slope), and only 1.1% of that variance was explained by TTMC alone. Analysis also showed that as decision time increased by 1 s, the odds of a participant accurately identifying the target decreased (0.786:1).

Response Option Preference

RQ8 addressed the issue of which response option in each language attracted the most attention. For English, stimuli with the mid vowel [eɪ] attracted the most attention across trials as indicated by the highest percentage of trials with the longest TFD (40.14%), followed by [i] (33.73%), and then [æ] (26.13%). The vowel [eɪ] occupied the middle position among the response options on the screen; this could represent a central fixation bias similar to that observed in scene viewing (Tatler, 2007).

Among the French nasal vowels, the vowel [ɑ̃] had the highest percentage of trials with the longest TFD (41.72%), followed by [ɔ̃] (34.63%), and then [ɛ̃] (23.65%). The vowel [ɑ̃] also occupied the middle position on the response-option screen for French, and on the lip-rounding continuum of nasal vowels between the hyper-rounded [ɔ̃] and unrounded [ɛ̃] (Zerling, 1989). Attention to [ɑ̃] might have represented uncertainty (Hyrskykari et al., 2008); [ɔ̃] and [ɛ̃], which occupy the extreme positions on the lip-rounding continuum, tended to be easier for a peer group of learners to identify (Inceoglu, 2014).

Questionnaire and Interview

Immediately following data collection, each participant completed a questionnaire and brought it to an interview with the researcher. All 32 participants completed these tasks. The following comments stem from both the questionnaires and the interviews.

During the English AV condition, four participants reported looking at the talker's mouth *all of the time*, 14 *most of the time*, and 14 *occasionally*. According to their self-reports, when they were not looking at the mouth, 21 reported looking at the talker's eyes, three mentioned the nose, and four reported taking a "global view of the face." Several participants stated that in the English (vs. French) stimulus conditions, they did not need to focus on the talker's mouth as much unless there was noise (i.e., AVn) or no audio (i.e., V-only).

For the French AV condition, nine participants reported looking at the talker's mouth *all of the time*; however, the majority (19/32) reported looking at the talker's mouth *most of the time*, and four reported looking at it *from time to time*. Several said they tended to look only at the mouth in the AVn and V-only conditions. When they weren't looking at the mouth, 14 reported looking at the eyes and four mentioned the nose. A commonly reported scenario involved looking at the eyes initially and shifting to the mouth when they thought speech was about to begin. Several participants reported that it was easier to identify the vowel in all L2 French stimulus conditions by relying solely on the visual information; for them, the sound was more of a "distraction" because they did not think it was as informative. This account is compatible with the similar identification accuracy present across the stimulus conditions in French, suggesting that the visual cue, which was the consistent input source across conditions, contributed the most to the percept, even when both cues were present.

General Discussion

In this study, eye tracking offered a way to see how participants' eye gazes changed in relation to the articulation-related movements of an L1 English and an L2 French talker in a vowel identification task in three stimulus conditions (AV, AVn, V-only). The results of the eye-tracking measures, behavioural data from perceptual identification accuracy, and the questionnaire and interview responses provided important information.

The first analysis explored the possibility of perceivers' leftward bias (i.e., gaze directed towards the right side of the talker's face) as reported in the literature (e.g., Everdell et al., 2007). Unlike Guo et al. (2009, 2012), who examined fixations to each side of a talker's face for possible gaze bias, the current study designated each eye as an AOI. Only one of the two measurement criteria used by Guo et al., total fixation duration, clearly supported leftward bias. Results for first fixations were more variable.

There were also mixed results for the eye primacy effect (Lansing & McConkie, 2003), referring to fixations to a talker's eyes before speech begins. In the present study, the initial 1.3 s approximately of each trial was a still image (i.e., no visible movement on the screen); therefore, fixations to any AOI during this period reflected general communication practices versus attention to motion. TTFF measures plus gaze plots and heatmaps demonstrated participants' interest in fixating the eyes, but the eyes were not always the first targets. First fixations varied by language and stimulus condition. Overall, in L1 English, participants were more likely to fixate the mouth, especially in the V-only condition, followed by the nose. In L2 French, the likelihood of first fixating the eyes was greater than that for the other AOIs, except in the V-only condition, when first fixations were more likely to be diverted to the talker's mouth.

Lansing and McConkie (2003) also proposed an information source attraction effect. Perhaps this could be relabelled the *informative* source attraction effect, as this may better capture a requirement placed on an area of the face in order for the perceiver to use it to complete a task, especially in an L2 situation. If articulatory gestures are not sufficiently informative, perceivers may look elsewhere. In the current study, participants were most likely to have the longest fixation to the mouth in the L1 and L2 AV and AVn conditions in terms of TFD, with the eyes in second place. In the V-only conditions, beyond the mouth, fixation duration to the nose exceeded that for the eyes. Although the L2 talker's mouth was not fixated first as often as the eyes or nose in the AV condition, the mouth was the AOI with the longest fixation durations across conditions. The amount of information that could have been gleaned from peripheral vision by participants in this task is not known, but gaze plots and heatmaps demonstrated that some participants were content to fixate the nose throughout the task in both languages, although others fixated the vertical midline anywhere from the nose bridge to the chin in anticipation of task-related information.

For both languages, neither the masking noise nor the visual category of the initial sound of a stimulus had a significant impact on identification accuracy. Using visual cues only was more successful in English as compared to French, although V-only accuracy in French was just slightly lower than AV and AVn accuracy, suggesting, as noted earlier, that the visual cue was contributing the most to the percepts, compatible with participants' interview comments. A basic principle in AV integration is that the most informative cue contributes the most to the percept. When a cue ceases to be informative, it is reasonable to infer that it no longer holds the same amount of attention, and as a result, gaze may be redirected either to continue to search for information or to rest from the cognitive load of processing information from one area.

As noted earlier, variability is present throughout the findings of studies on face-viewing behaviour as a result of task instructions (Kanan et al., 2015; Yarbus, 1965/1967) and task type (e.g., Hayhoe & Ballard, 2005; Wegner-Clemens et al., 2019). Rennig et al. (2020) reported substantial variability in the amount of time participants spent fixating a talker's mouth as a proportion of total viewing time (i.e., a range of 3%–98%), compatible with the observation of Holmqvist and Andersson (2017) that every participant has a unique baseline setting for a measure.

Few studies have reported the contribution of differences across participants to their results. In one exception, Wegner-Clemens et al. (2019) estimated the relative contributions of the fixed and random effects in their study involving different stimuli, tasks, and exemplar conditions. Of the variance in their results, task condition explained 41%, individual differences 28%, and stimulus exemplar less than 0.4%.

In the current study, more of the variance in the AOI on a talker's face that was fixated first and showed the longest fixation duration was attributable to the random effects (i.e., individual differences or the differences across participants) versus the fixed effects (i.e., differences in language, condition, and their interactions). In contrast, very little of the variance in identification accuracy was due to random effects. Therefore, variable gaze behaviour did not impact accuracy (Everdell et al., 2007).

A Neurophysiological Foundation

Rennig et al. (2020) commented that "a lifetime of viewing faces provides a large training set on which to learn the correspondence between visual and auditory speech features" (p. 75). This learning process has a neurophysiological foundation. Perceiving biological motion activates distinct regions in the brain. To explore whether a topography exists in the human cortex during perception of biological motion, Pelphrey et al. (2005) used fMRI to focus on participants' responses to observed movements of the eyes and mouth by animated characters. The characters shifted their gazes to the left or right and back to the midline and opened and closed their mouths, each movement lasting 1 s. Findings supported the existence of distinct cortical regions that were more responsive to viewing eye movements versus mouth movements.

In addition, the areas of the human cortex in and around the pSTS are considered critical to speech perception (e.g., Zhu & Beauchamp, 2017). The pSTS responds to both the visual and auditory modalities. Rennig and Beauchamp (2018) used fMRI to measure the brain activity of participants during free viewing of talking faces and recorded their eye movements. The regions that showed a preference for participants' fixations to the talker's mouth responded more strongly to A-only and AV speech; the regions that preferred fixations to the talker's eyes did not. "Mouth-looking experience might strengthen synaptic connections between neurons in the mouth-preferring regions of posterior temporal cortex representing seen mouth movements and neurons representing heard speech sounds" (Rennig et al., 2020, p. 76).

Chapter 5 in Review

This chapter explored the perceptual role of eye gaze, specifically where and for how long L2 learners of French (L1 AE) directed their gazes when viewing a talking face in their L1 and their L2 in a speech perception task. Consistent with research findings involving speechreading, the McGurk-MacDonald effect, and perception training studies presented in earlier chapters, variability was also a theme in this chapter. Participants' interview comments were helpful in understanding the eye-movement findings, especially the perception of the greater information value of visual versus auditory cues for French nasal vowels.

Exposure to the correspondences between talkers' visual and auditory speech cues, whether through interaction experiences over time and/or focused multiple-talker perception training, may prepare perceivers to generalize what they have learned to an unfamiliar talker. The results of the current study along with those of AV perception training studies (see chapter 3) strongly suggest that a focus on facial speech cues in L2 learning is beneficial. Chapter 6 next addresses the interactional role of eye gaze behaviour as one of several forms of non-verbal communication.

Chapter 5 Notes

1. For this painting by Ilya Repin, see https://en.wikipedia.org/wiki/File:Ilya_Repin_Unexpected_visitors.jpg or Figure 3 in Tatler et al. (2010).
2. The spelling of the nonsense words in French follows common orthographic conventions.

3. To protect talker identity and improve the quality of the original Portable Network Graphics (PNG) screenshots, a graphic designer used Adobe Illustrator and Photoshop to create a generic outline of a face, which was overlaid on the original image such that the location of all features (e.g., eyes, nose, mouth) stayed exactly the same. The original image was then removed, leaving the generic face with the overlaid gaze plot or heatmap.
4. The regression analyses in this chapter were carried out by Sue Lim, who was affiliated with the neuroscience lab in the Department of Communication and served as a statistical consultant at the Center for Statistical Training and Consulting (CSTAT) at Michigan State University, and Dr. Sarah Manski, a research associate at CSTAT, with input from Dr. Steven J. Pierce, Associate Director of CSTAT.
5. The intercept (sometimes called the "constant") in a regression model represents the mean value of the response variable when all of the predictor variables in the model are equal to zero; in other words, the y-intercept indicates the y-value when the x-value is 0. A *log odds* is *the logarithm of the odds ratio.* Odds are likelihood ratios, which indicate how likely it is that something specific will happen.
6. In this analysis, the OR is the ratio of the odds of participants looking first at one particular AOI as compared to another. An OR of 1 would indicate that the odds of an outcome were equal for both. The larger the OR, the greater the odds. Odds can be converted to probability (p) using the formula p = odds/(odds + 1). For example, if odds = 2:1, then the probability would be 2/(2+1) = 2/3 (≈ .67).

Chapter 6

Non-verbal Communication: Broadening the Scope of Visual Input

> *Gestures are interactional phenomena with rich semiotic affordances to all interlocutors involved. . . . Gestures therefore also constitute input – to NSs [native speakers], teachers and learners alike – both in- and outside the classroom.*
>
> – Gullberg (2006, p. 115)

*****

Background

Thus far, the discussion of sources of visual information available to interlocutors in a face-to-face speech event has indeed focused on the face, especially a talker's mouth. However, beyond the lip movements discussed in earlier chapters, the visual affiliates of a speaker's message include such features as facial expressions, brow movements, eye gaze as an interactional (vs. perceptual) resource, body position, gestures, and head nods.

For centuries, the eyes have been recognized as the windows of the soul (for a historical overview of the role of eye gaze in social interaction, see Emery, 2000). Gratiolet (1865) noted that in face-to-face interaction, rejecting a proposition was often signalled by closing the eyes and/or turning away the face; accepting a proposition was signalled by nodding the head and opening the eyes widely. In recognizing the eyes as guideposts of emotions, Darwin (1872/1899) noted, "Painters can hardly portray suspicion, jealousy, envy . . . except by the aid of accessories which tell the tale; and poets use such vague and fanciful expressions as 'green-eyed jealousy'" (chapter III).[1] Of gesture, Darwin (1872/1899) further observed the following:

> Perplexed reflection is often accompanied by certain movements or gestures. At such times we commonly raise our hands to our foreheads, mouths, or chins; but we do not act thus, as far as I have seen, when we are quite lost in meditation, and no difficulty is encountered. (Chapter IX)

The scope of the word *gesture* has not always been clear, as Kendon (1981) observed. Does an adjustment in posture or patting one's head represent a gesture?

> The modern word "gesture" is derived from a Latin root *gerere* which means to bear or carry, to take on oneself, to take charge of, to perform or to accomplish. It derives more immediately from a Mediaeval Latin word "gestura" which means "way of carrying" or "mode of action" (Partridge, 1959) and in its earliest uses in English it referred to the manner of carrying the body, bodily bearing or deportment. Somewhat later it came to be used in Rhetorical treatises to refer to the way in which the body was to be employed in the making of speeches and this usage included, of course, the specific actions of the limbs and face that, nowadays, we usually have in mind when the term "gesture" is used. It is probably through a specialization of this usage that the modern meaning derived ... any distinct bodily action that is regarded by participants as being directly involved in the process of deliberate utterance. (Kendon, 1981, p. 153)

Using Kendon's terms, eye gaze could be similarly defined. "Gaze should be perceived as bodily action invested with meaning," Brône and Oben (2018) wrote, "both on the part of speakers and their addressees, relevant for the joint action that is human-human (or even human-computer) interaction" (p. 5).

This chapter addresses the social interactional nature of eye gaze, hand-arm gestures, and head nods with a focus on their roles as elements of non-verbal communication in the L2 environment. Topics include (a) overviews of eye gaze and gestures as non-verbal communication; (b) dimensions and structure of gestures; (c) temporal relationships between gestures and speech; (d) research findings addressing the impact of speakers' visual cues on L2 listening comprehension; (e) potential interaction of visual cues and speaker accent in L2 listening comprehension; (f) contribution of visual cues to the processing of segmental features, to discrimination of tone, and to foreign word learning; (g) gestures in interaction; (h) head movement and speech; and (i) some pedagogical implications.

Eye Gaze as Non-verbal Communication

As Rossano (2013) noted, "Looking at someone's face is interactionally more relevant than looking anywhere else during a conversation" (p. 309). Eye gaze serves a variety of communicative functions in face-to-face communication (Brône & Oben, 2018; Kendon, 1967). It contributes to the success of a communicative event by establishing it as *joint action* (Clark, 1996). The direction of an interlocutor's gaze is analysed rapidly and automatically along with head orientation and pointing gestures, which trigger a reflexive shift in an observer's visual attention (Langton et al., 2000). For English speakers, smiles that precede turns in conversation often initiate a positive or humorous attitude that may carry over to lexical, prosodic, and/or gestural components of the subsequent interaction (Kaukomaa et al., 2013). Even during silence when one interlocutor is engaged in searching for a word, visual cues may occur between interlocutors; a hand movement in addition to a shift in eye gaze or change in lip shape may indicate that word search is occurring, and the recipient may signal acknowledgment with a nod (Goodwin & Goodwin, 1986).

In dyadic situations, people tend to look at an interlocutor's face more when they are listeners than speakers (Nielsen, 1962). Eye gaze indicates attention and engagement, signals turn-taking, plays a role in speech monitoring, prevents and repairs conversation breakdowns, and can clarify meaning (for a review, see Degutyte & Astell, 2021). In an interaction, if a speaker looks at an interlocutor's face while producing a target word, it significantly increases the probability that the interlocutor will use that word later in the interaction (Oben, 2018). On the other hand, if a speaker looks at an interlocutor's face while performing a target gesture, no prediction can be made regarding the interlocutor's subsequent gesture production. However, Oben commented that if an interlocutor looked at a gesture the speaker made, that gesture was more likely to be used by the interlocutor later in the interaction (vs. a gesture that was not fixated). In a three-party interaction, gaze also functioned as an invitation to the interlocutor whom the speaker was focusing on at the end of the interaction turn to become the next speaker (P. Auer, 2018). As a discourse signalling device, a speaker's fixation on an object may indicate to listeners the content or focus of the upcoming verbal message (Staudte & Crocker, 2018).

Interactionally, the eyes also play an important role in other cultures, such as the Japanese culture, in which they help to regulate the flow of communication in conversations (Herlofsky, 1985). As Masao (1976) explained:

> Forms of unspoken communication such as *haragei* (the art of subtle communication) and *me wa kuchi hodo ni mono o ii* (the eyes say as much as the mouth) are in constant use, and they work to support our esthetic ideal. (p. 272)

In Korean culture, *nun-chi* is a communication skill. As a cultural concept, *nun-chi* can be translated as "eye measuring" or "perceptiveness or sensitivity with eyes" and refers to an ability to understand a situation without verbal explanation, to read between the lines, and to "hear between sounds" (Yum, 1987, p. 80).

Non-verbal behaviour may be more successful than verbal information in conveying emotional states, such as anxiety level (Gregersen, 2005), but although non-verbal communication can be informative, it does not always play a positive role and can lead to misunderstanding. In Faraco and Kida's (2008) classroom study, a teacher avoided eye contact while correcting a learner's phonological mistake, considering it as a way of softening the correction; the learner, however, considered the absence of mutual eye gaze to be ambiguous – should she confirm the correction or restart the discourse?

Gestures as Non-verbal Communication

Gestures are part of the field of non-verbal communication. They include multiple communicative movements primarily, but not always, involving the hands and arms (McNeill, 2006). They appear spontaneously during infancy (e.g., Özçalişkan & Goldin-Meadow, 2005), support L1 acquisition (Gliga & Csibra, 2009), and play an emotional role in communicative contexts (Kelly & Tran, 2023). Gestures even facilitate comprehension for experienced simultaneous interpreters (Arbona et al., 2023).

As Goldin-Meadow (1999) observed, "Gesture serves as both a tool for communication for listeners, and a tool for thinking for speakers" (p. 419). The ability of listeners to glean information from a speaker's gestures is evident when the gestures convey information that was not available in the speaker's words (Cook & Tanenhaus, 2009). Further underscoring the gesture–speech relationship is that incongruence between them leads to greater processing difficulty (Kelly et al., 2010). For speakers, gesturing reduces the demand on their working memory (e.g., Goldin-Meadow et al., 2001) and activates knowledge they have but do not or cannot express (Broaders et al., 2007). Even individuals who have been blind since birth move their hands when they talk (Iverson & Goldin-Meadow, 1998), suggesting gesturing and speaking indeed go hand in hand. In an interaction, gestures may regulate turns, mark agreement, and direct attention. They may specifically benefit the speaker by aiding lexical retrieval and enhancing the meaning of the intended message (for overviews, see Kendon,

2004; McNeill, 2005); gestures also facilitate lexical retrieval for L2 learners (Krauss & Hadar, 1999).

In addition, Kelly et al. (2009) showed that co-speech gestures aided recall of words in Japanese by L1 English observers with no prior knowledge of the language. Based on memory tests and ERPs, Kelly et al. suggested that co-speech gesture "deepens the imagistic memory trace for a new word's meaning in the brain" (p. 330).[2] In the academic environment, viewing instructors' gestures may help to improve L2 listening comprehension (e.g., Kellerman, 1992; Lazaraton, 2004).

For L2 speakers of English and some other Western languages that have been investigated who tend to produce more gestures in the L2 than the L1 (Gregersen et al., 2009; Gullberg, 1998), gesture production may serve to compensate for lexical, grammatical, and fluency-related issues (e.g., Gullberg, 1998; Hadar et al., 2001). Gregersen et al. (2009) investigated the relationship between learners' L2 proficiency and their frequency and type of gesture use. A total of 75 college-level learners of Spanish were video recorded while interacting in dyads, first in Spanish and then in English. Based on observer responses to the recordings, advanced learners used significantly more speech-related, meaning-enhancing gestures as compared to beginning and intermediate learners.

In face-to-face interactions, non-verbal communication serves functions beyond a compensatory role (Gullberg, 2011). Learners who gesture and engage their interlocutors may also be perceived as more proficient than those who do not (e.g., Gullberg, 1998; S. Jenkins & Parra, 2003; Neu, 1990). Neu (1990) pointed out that the culturally appropriate non-verbal behaviours, including head position and facial expressions, used by an Arabic-speaking learner of English increased the perception of his L2 proficiency; in contrast, the perception of proficiency was lower for a Japanese-speaking learner of English who did not use any non-verbal communication strategies but demonstrated better verbal performance.

The presence of non-verbal cues may also impact the perception of L2 interactive competence. Crowther (2018) observed that native English-speaking raters' scores for L2 English learners' accentedness (i.e., degree of difference between a learner's speech and the target variety) and comprehensibility (i.e., ease of understanding) did not predict their assessments of the learners' performance on an interactive task in contrast to the findings for monologic tasks. Because the assessment procedure for the interactive task included a video, raters may have been influenced by elements of non-verbal communication, such as gesture, facial expression, and body language (e.g., Jewitt, 2014).

Gestures may also serve as a scaffolding tool for instructors. The more simplified style of *teacher talk* lends itself to an increased use of gestures. Instructors also benefit from the use of other elements of non-verbal communication, including eye contact, body position, and facial expression, to help convey ideas and add emphasis. The presence of these visual cues is associated with positive attributes such as students' perceptions of rapport and immediacy (e.g., Bailey, 1982) and have contributed to higher student evaluations across cultures (S. Jenkins & Parra, 2003; McCroskey et al., 1995). International teaching assistants and other proficient L2 speakers can also use emphatic and rhythmic gestures to enhance the meaning of their speech (Gregersen et al., 2009; Hardison, 2018c; McCafferty, 2002).

Dimensions of Gesture

There are different ways to classify hand-arm gestures, many of which are produced in conjunction with utterances and linked to them semantically and prosodically (McNeill, 1992), or pragmatically (Kelly et al., 1999). The early reference in the literature to a classification scheme with four *categories* of gesture – *iconic, metaphoric, beat*, and *deictic* (e.g., McNeill, 1992) – was later revised to refer to them as *dimensions* in order to accommodate gestures that overlap categories (McNeill, 2006). Iconic gestures, associated with meaning, often occur with a speaker's description of something specific. Similarly, metaphoric gestures create visual representations but relate to abstract ideas or concepts. Representational (i.e., iconic and metaphoric) gestures tend to be used more when an interlocutor can be seen, whereas beat gestures may occur at comparable rates with or without an audience (Alibali et al., 2001). Beats or movements of the hand (e.g., up and down) are associated with the rhythm of speech and may aid a speaker in controlling the pace of speech (Morrel-Samuels & Krauss, 1992). They have been described as "simple" hand movements because they are often thought to lack the propositional content and motor complexity of representational gestures (e.g., McNeill, 1992, p. 15), but this apparent simplicity may be misleading. Beat gestures may also have imagistic qualities. For example, in Algana and Hardison's (2024) study, a speaker, while describing how to glaze a ceramic pot, moved his hand up and down (beat gesture) with the rhythm of the utterance while his index finger and thumb were placed very close together, coinciding with the phrase *least amount*, emphasized in the sentence, *You have to use the* LEAST AMOUNT [emphasis] *of water as possible.*

Deictics are pointing gestures that may refer to specific objects or may be more abstract in referring to a non-specific time or location. Based on the observation that representational and deictic gestures can also display a rhythmic behaviour, Prieto et al. (2018) proposed that all non-referential gestures be initially classified as forms of beats and labelled according to their form, temporal association with prosodic prominence, and pragmatic meaning.

Structure of Gesture

Gestures exhibit a structure, which is important for the analysis of the gesture–speech relationship. A gesture phrase (G-phrase) generally has several components or phases: preparation, stroke, and retraction (Kendon, 1972). The peak effort in a speaker's G-phrase is in the stroke, especially the apex (e.g., the maximum extent of the movement). This phase is often the most meaningful and visually salient to observers. Hardison (2018c) provides an example:

> Consider the utterance "a HUGE tree came down." Before the speaker began, her arms had started to move away from her side (preparation). She then raised both arms in synchrony up over her head (stroke phase) and then lowered them to her side (retraction). The arms reached their highest point (apex) when she uttered "huge," which received the greatest stress and exhibited the highest pitch. (p. 233)

Given the myriad functions for gestures (for a review, see Kelly et al., 2008), this chapter will focus on their co-occurrence with speech primarily as input to L2 learners.

Temporal Relationship Between Gesture and Speech

Gestures and speech exhibit a semantic and often temporal coordination (e.g., Kendon, 1972; McNeill, 1992; McNeill et al., 1990). The temporal relationship of one's own gestures and speech constitutes *self-synchrony* in contrast to *interactional synchrony*, in which gesture patterns may change as a result of an interlocutor's movements (Condon, 1976). A speaker's beat gestures often move in synchrony with the stressed units in a language, such as syllables in English, and in conjunction with prosodic emphasis (e.g., McNeill, 1992). In fact, Tuite (1993) proposed that every gesture contains an underlying rhythmic pulse or beat. At a discourse level, the gesture–speech synchrony serves a cohesive discourse function (McNeill et al., 2015).

There is a temporal relationship between the G-phrase and a tone group in speech; the tone group is defined as the "smallest grouping of syllables over which a completed intonation tune occurs" (Kendon, 1972, p. 186). Kendon (1972) observed that the apex of a gestural stroke or beat coincided with or slightly preceded the nuclear syllable in a tone group, and that it occurred at fairly regular intervals or pulses, which McNeill (1992) referred to as the "phonological synchrony rule" (p. 26). The nuclear syllable as the peak of the tone group and the apex as the peak of the G-phrase together form "peaks of energy output" (Tuite, 1993, p. 97).

Similar types of pulses have been observed with other body movements, such as finger or foot tapping (Fraisse, 1982). Studies revealed coordinated movement of eyebrow raises and eyeblinks with vocal pitch in English (e.g., Flecha-García, 2010); head movement in conjunction with prosodic peaks in English (Hadar et al., 1983); correlation between head movement, voice amplitude, and fundamental frequency (the acoustic correlate of pitch) in Japanese (Munhall et al., 2004); and longer word duration with beat gestures in Dutch (Krahmer & Swerts, 2007). Krahmer and Swerts (2007) asked L1 Dutch speakers to produce a four-word sentence, *Amanda gaat naar Malta* (Amanda goes to Malta), in several different ways. *Amanda* and *Malta* were treated as the first and second target words, respectively. Speakers were instructed to utter the sentence with a visual beat consisting of a hand gesture, a head nod, or a rapid eyebrow movement on either the first or second target word, and with a pitch accent (i.e., single tone or bitonal movement in a stressed syllable) on one or none of the target words. Results showed that acoustic effects such as a longer duration occurred with words that were accompanied by some type of visual beat. In addition, the words with a visual beat and corresponding acoustic effect seemed more prominent to perceivers, especially when the beat was a hand gesture.

Visual and acoustic correlates of prominence, such as beat gestures in English, often signal the importance of their lexical affiliate (word or phrase) in the overall discourse. Periodic patterns of beats make up rhythmic groups, which play a role in attracting and retaining the attention of perceivers. When attention is synchronized to a periodic pattern of beats or rhythm (e.g., M.R. Jones, 1986), it serves as the basis for anticipating a subsequent series of beats (London, 2012). Perceivers focus their attentional energy on anticipated points in time to track events, such as a series of beats (Large & Jones, 1999), and integrate information across sensory modalities (e.g., Merker et al., 2009).

Dimitrova et al. (2016) investigated the influence of beat gestures in participants' allocation of attention to *focal* (important) information in an audiovisual recorded dialogue. In a discourse context, beat gestures would be expected to accompany the focal points of the message. To test whether verbal and non-verbal cues would interact in the processing of information, both focal and non-focal words were accompanied by beat gestures, other hand movements, or no gestures. Results of ERPs revealed that focal words were processed more attentively, supporting the focusing function of beat gestures in multimodal settings. Additional support came from the processing difficulties experienced by participants when beat gestures occurred with non-focal information.

In face-to-face interactions, gestures can serve as visual highlighters of important information, especially through the dynamic temporal relationship between beat gestures and pitch-accented vowels in English (Hardison, 2018c). However, Gullberg et al. (2010) demonstrated that this highlighting role of gestures did not sufficiently increase the salience of Mandarin words for Dutch speakers with no prior exposure to Mandarin to help them segment the speech stream in order to correctly recognize a Mandarin word.

The roles of beat gestures and contrastive pitch accent were examined by Morett and Fraundorf (2019) to see how these cues to prominence affected memory for information. This study encompassed two experiments, the first of which had two stages. In the first stage of the initial experiment, participants watched a video of a talker who emphasized some of the words that were critical to the interpretation of the discourse by using a beat gesture. In some cases, these critical words were also accompanied by either *contrastive* accenting, which directs listeners' attention to an element that contrasts with a specific previous referent, or what Morett and Fraundorf referred to as *presentational* accenting, which directs listeners' attention to new information. The researchers provided the following example to illustrate the types of accents:

(1a) [S1] What did Marjorie have for lunch?
(1b) [S2] She had a salad.
(2a) [S1] Did you say she had a sandwich?
(2b) [S2] No, I said she had a SALAD. (p. 1516)

In (1b), *salad* is new information that a speaker would probably produce in this discourse with a presentational high-pitch accent at the beginning of the word. In (2b), *SALAD* contrasts with the previous referent (i.e., *sandwich*) and would probably be produced with a contrastive accent, consisting of a preceding low pitch followed by a sharp rise to a high level on the initial accented syllable.

This first stage of the initial Morett and Fraundorf (2019) experiment was followed by a recognition memory test. When critical words in the first stage had been accompanied by a beat gesture, the odds of participants remembering them in the recognition test were 1.67 times greater (a significant difference) if the words (e.g., *salad* in the above example) had also been produced with contrastive versus presentational pitch accents. However, when no beat gestures were used with any critical words in the first stage, there was no significant difference in the odds of participants correctly remembering them based on the type of pitch accent.

In the second experiment in the Morett and Fraundorf (2019) study, the talker in the video did not produce any beat gestures. In the subsequent memory recognition test, the critical words that had been spoken with contrastive accenting were remembered more accurately than the words produced with presentational pitch accenting. To reconcile the results of the two experiments, the researchers surmised that in situations in which beat gestures are present only sometimes, as in their first experiment, perceivers may consider pitch accenting to be important if the talker also signals the importance of some of the content by using a beat gesture. However, when beat gestures are never produced in a given situation, as in the second experiment, perceivers may infer that the talker has placed some importance on the use of contrastive pitch accenting and may direct more attentional and memory resources to it.

In contrast, using an online task in which participants' eye movements were tracked while they resolved the correct referent in the discourse, Morett et al. (2021) discovered that beat gestures and contrastive accent exerted independent influences on spoken discourse processing. They used a visual-world paradigm, an eye-tracking technique in which participants listen to a spoken utterance as they look at a visual scene containing various objects while their eye movements are tracked. In the study, the objects varied in colour and shape and consisted of four types: the context object (i.e., the referent of a context referring expression: e.g., *blue triangle*); the target object (i.e., the referent of a critical referring expression: e.g., *red triangle*, which formed a colour contrast, or *red square*, which formed a shape contrast); the competitor object (i.e., an object with the same colour but an alternate shape relative to the target object: e.g., *red square*, which formed a color contrast, or *red triangle*, which formed a shape contrast); and the distractor object (i.e., an object with the remaining combination of colours and shapes from other objects in the set: e.g., *blue square*). The presence of the competitor object created a temporary referential ambiguity between the target and competitor objects with the utterance *Now click on the red . . .*, allowing an examination of how cues to contrast affected gaze fixations on the objects when it was temporarily unclear which one was the referent.

Morett et al. (2021) discovered that when the critical referent did not contrast in colour with the context referent, the use of contrastive accenting on the colour adjective could misdirect visual attention to a colour-contrast competitor. However, when there was a genuine colour contrast, the absence of contrastive accenting on the colour adjective did not affect eye gaze. In other words, contrastive accenting necessarily indicated a contrast and was misleading when it was not used to emphasize contrastive information; however, a noncontrastive accent did not necessarily indicate the absence of a contrast, so it did not affect comprehension, even when it occurred in a contrastive context. Beat gesture also functioned as a cue to contrast. Using a beat gesture to emphasize a colour adjective when there was no colour contrast impaired comprehension. Morett et al. emphasized that online interpretation of these cues depended on whether the cues had reliably conveyed contrast within the discourse context.

Gesture and Speech: An Integrated System

As noted earlier, the temporal relationship between gestural and acoustic beats was described as one of synchrony (e.g., McNeill, 1992). The apex of a gestural beat and a pitch accent often appear to align. Pitch accents, duration, and intensity are cues to prominence in English. The occurrence of phonological synchrony was proposed as support for the claim that gesture and speech arise from a common cognitive origin – the basis of McNeill's (1992) *growth point theory* – and both are involved in the initial stage of producing a sentence. Loehr (2007) proposed a rhythmic relationship between hand gesture, head movement, and voice that he speculated was further evidence of the shared cognitive origin of gesture and speech as supported by various researchers (e.g., Kendon, 1972; McClave, 1994; McNeill, 1992). Treffner et al. (2008) also suggested that the entrainment of gestural and speech rhythms may result from their joint production.

Much neurocognitive research supports the position that gesture and speech comprise an integrated system during language production and comprehension. Based on fMRI studies, Broca's area plays a role in integrating the semantic content of gestures and speech during sentence comprehension (Skipper, Goldin-Meadow, et al., 2007; Willems et al., 2007).[3] Other brain regions may also be involved in the comprehension of verbal and gestural utterances, including multimodal integration sites such as the superior temporal sulcus (STS) in the left hemisphere, parts of the mirror neuron system, and emotional centres such as the cingulate cortex (e.g., Holle et al. 2008).[4] The STS is implicated in processing both sound-based representations of speech (Hickok & Poeppel, 2000) and goal-directed hand movements (Bonda et al., 1996). The semantic content of a gesture also influences the processing of accompanying speech. Kelly et al. (2004) presented participants with gesture–speech pairs that were congruent (e.g., saying *tall* while gesturing the height of a tall container) versus incongruent (e.g., saying *tall* while gesturing the height of a short container), finding that incongruent gestures produced a larger N400 effect (a specific type of ERP response) to speech than congruent gestures, suggesting semantic integration of the congruent gesture–speech pairs.[5]

Zhang et al. (2021) investigated the contribution of multimodal cues (e.g., mouth movements and gestures) to processing load in listening comprehension by native English speakers. A native British English-speaking actress was video recorded while she produced passages from television scripts in two ways: one with no gestures, and one in which she was instructed to gesture freely. Participants watched the videos and answered yes/no questions while their electroencephalographic (EEG) responses were recorded, with a specific focus on N400. Measures included (a) the probability of a word given its preceding context; (b) gesture type, coded as meaningful (iconic or deictic) or beat (rhythmic movement without clear meaning); (c) prosody (quantified as mean fundamental frequency); and (d) informativeness of lip movements determined by individuals guessing the word in a speechreading task.

Results in the Zhang et al. (2021) study indicated that brain responses to words were affected by the informativeness of multimodal cues. Interactions between cues suggested that the impact of each cue dynamically changed based on the informativeness of the others. N400, a key neurophysiological marker of cognitive load and prediction in language comprehension, was modulated by the informativeness of the cues. Pitch accent and meaningful gestures, occurring either individually or together in the same context, reduced the N400 amplitude overall, especially for highly predictable words. In contrast, the presence of beat gestures without a semantic component to reduce the cognitive processing load increased the N400 amplitude, especially for highly predictable words. Informative mouth movements participated in complex interactions involving other cues and exhibited a facilitative effect when either meaningful or beat gestures were present.

Pre-listening preparation involves using prior knowledge and contextual information to formulate a distribution of probabilistic hypotheses of the upcoming input (Kuperberg & Jaeger, 2016). The distribution is updated with new information, and this process recurs for subsequent events. N400 is linked to this updating process: a smaller N400 is associated with more accurate prior predictive hypotheses. Zhang et al.'s (2021) findings implied that these predictive hypotheses and updating operations respond to multimodal cues, such as mouth movements, prosody, and gestures. Neuroanatomical models that consider language in context can accommodate the results. In the natural organization of language and brain (NOLB) model, each multimodal cue is processed in different but partially overlapping subnetworks (Skipper, 2015). Different subnetworks have been associated with gestures and mouth movements, each weighted differently across listening contexts (Skipper, Goldin-Meadow, et al., 2007; Skipper et al., 2009). These distributed subnetworks are assumed to provide constraints on possible interpretations of the acoustic signal, thus enabling fast and accurate comprehension. The findings of Zhang et al. (2021) involving multiple interactions between cues are compatible with this view, thus suggesting that multimodal prediction processes are dynamic, reweighting each cue based on the status of other cues.

Other Rhythmic Patterns Between Gesture and Speech

Although beat gestures often align with stressed units in English, other rhythmic patterns also occur. In proposing the *rhythm hypothesis*, McClave (1994) discovered that beats showed a rhythm independent of speech; specifically, the beats occurred on both stressed and unstressed syllables, on function words, and during pauses. Data were obtained from two recorded dyadic conversations by native speakers of English. In some rhythm groups, the intervals of time between beats were roughly equal; in others, the intervals were suddenly halved or doubled. Despite variability, McClave still reported observing a periodic pattern and proposed that the nucleus of the tone unit was the anchor point for the beats.

The relationship between sequences of visual (e.g., gestural) and acoustic beats was examined by Hardison (2018c) in the natural speech of native and advanced non-native speakers of English with a focus on polyrhythmic sequences – that is, different rhythmic patterns present simultaneously, one for gestural beats and one for acoustic beats – to determine

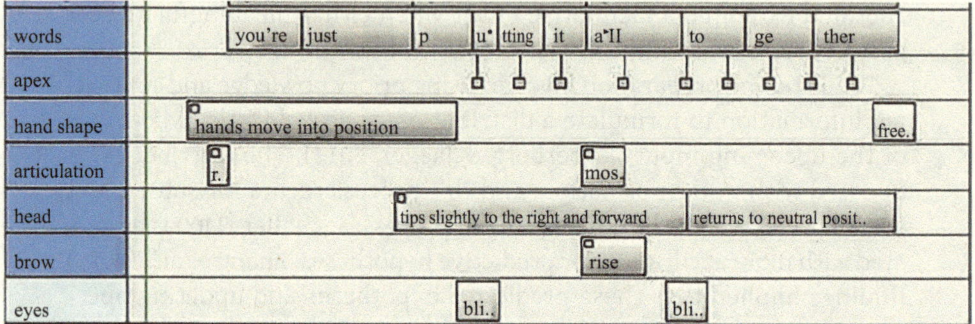

FIGURE 6.1 The Annotation Board in Anvil for the Utterance *you're just putting it all together*

their discourse role in an academic context. The first of three stages in the study analysed audiovisual recordings of native and advanced non-native English-speaking instructors at a university in the US. A frame-by-frame analysis of time-aligned annotations of the instructors' G-phrases, including polyrhythmic sequences, was conducted using Praat (Boersma & Weenink, 2022), a phonetic analysis tool, and Anvil (Kipp, 2001), a video annotation tool. Annotations were made of notable features, such as each beat's apex within intonation phrases, especially those that carried important discourse-level emphasis.[6] Analysis showed several points of convergence, representing temporal alignment of features such as the speaker's head movement, eyebrow raise, pitch peak, and some gestures (Hardison, 2018c).

As an example of this convergence, Figure 6.1 shows the gesture-relevant tracks from the annotation board in Anvil for the utterance *you're just putting it all together* in Hardison (2018c). This utterance was produced by an instructor who was trying to emphasize the need for students to integrate information (i.e., the referent for *it*) from different sources in their papers yet also calm tensions among the students by using the downgrader *just*. These tracks are labelled on the left side of the figure, starting at the top, as follows: (a) "words" – utterance in standard orthography; (b) "apex" – apex of gestural beats; (c) "hand shape" – position of the instructor's hands; (d) "articulation" – information about mouth shape relative to different points in the utterance; (e) "head" – position and movement of the head; (f) "brow" – movement of the eyebrows; and (g) "eyes" – eyeblinks during the utterance. Asterisks mark the pitch-accented vowels in the first syllable of *putting* and *all*. The instructor had begun to move his hands into position prior to saying *you're*, and they remained active until the end of the utterance (*free* is the visible part of *freeze*). With his fingers together, the instructor extended his hands in front of him with the fingertips of the left hand making contact repeatedly with the palm of the right hand as a metaphor for intersecting elements. The apex (marked as a square on the "apex" track) of the first beat coincided with the pitch-accented vowel in *putting*.

Overall in the Hardison (2018c) study, the series of apices occurred at a somewhat regular interval in the speech except within intonation phrases that carried important discourse-level emphasis where a second rhythmic pattern emerged. The intervals between beats were longer surrounding the pitch-accented vowels. In this example, the longer intervals surrounded the important word *all*, which was produced with a longer duration and exhibited a pitch peak at the end of the word. There were several points at which gestural elements converged surrounding the word *all*. Convergence is represented by vertical alignment of elements on the tracks. These elements included movement of the head, which tipped slightly to the right and forward, brow raise, and an eyeblink ("bli" on the track) before and after *all*.

In sum, longer temporal intervals occurred between beat apices surrounding pitch-accented vowels in polyrhythmic sequences (Hardison, 2018c). These polyrhythms can violate perceivers' anticipation of a regular rhythmic pattern, which may require a refocusing of their attention; however, on the positive side, this refocusing can serve as a perceptually salient highlighter of important information. In other words, the apparent simplicity of a beat gesture may be deceptive.

The second stage of the Hardison (2018c) study explored students' perceptions of the discourse role of a selection of the gesture sequences analysed in the first stage. Following Bull and Connelly (1985), students were asked to watch selected sequences of the recordings without audio, stop the playback when they thought the instructor was emphasizing something, and select a number on a 10-point scale to indicate how much attention they likely would have given the lexical content if they had been taking notes, preparing a paper, or studying for an exam. None of the students had prior exposure to the materials or the instructors. Based on the ratings, greater importance was attributed to recordings which showed a change in tempo of the hand movements in polyrhythmic sequences.

In the third stage of the Hardison (2018c) research, 10 international teaching assistants were recorded and their gestures analysed. A multistep presentation skills program was implemented, including practice with Praat, to enhance verbal and non-verbal communication skills. Suggestions were made to the teachers on the use of (a) gestures to convey emphasis; (b) body movement to create an impression of involvement with the class; (c) eye gaze directed towards the class periodically; and (d) appropriate facial expressions (e.g., McCafferty, 2002; McCroskey et al., 1995). Results of instructor and student surveys at the end of the program demonstrated improvement in the instructors' confidence and in student perceptions of increased teaching effectiveness and the ability to communicate important points.

Visual Cues and L2 Listening Comprehension

There has been a growing interest in the effects of non-verbal cues on L2 listening comprehension (e.g., Rohrer et al., 2020), although studies have provided mixed results. Some reports have demonstrated improved comprehension (e.g., T.I. Dahl & Ludvigsen, 2014; Sueyoshi & Hardison, 2005), but others have not (e.g., Algana & Hardison, 2024; Gullberg et al., 2010; Kamiya, 2022). The basis for comparison is limited, however, as many important variables differ across the studies.

Sueyoshi and Hardison (2005) investigated the influence of learner proficiency on the use of a talker's visual cues to comprehend a lecture on an unfamiliar topic. In that study, both low-intermediate and advanced L2 learners of English in the US were randomly assigned to three stimulus conditions: AV-gesture-face (lecturer's gestures and face were visible), AV-face (no gestures visible), and A-only. Scores were significantly better for both proficiency levels when visual cues were present, but differences occurred according to proficiency. For the higher proficiency groups, the AV-face condition produced higher scores; for the lower proficiency, the AV-gesture-face condition was more informative. Questionnaire responses showed positive attitudes overall towards visual cues in communicative settings. The higher proficiency learners provided a higher rating for the value of facial cues as a source of information in L2 listening, and they had a significantly more positive evaluation of the facial cues of the lecturer in the study. More proficient L2 learners may be more aware of and better able to use facial cues such as lip movements, which have a phonological association, because of L2 interaction experience. The low-intermediate proficiency learners' collective performance was better in the AV-gesture-face condition, consistent with their general preference for seeing gestures and their perception of the talker's gestures as more informative than her facial cues alone.

Visible gestures also appeared to be an advantage for younger learners (T.I. Dahl & Ludvigsen, 2014). Participants (ages 12 and 13 years) who were either L1 English speakers in the US or EFL learners in Norway were shown a video of an English speaker describing a cartoon image the participants could not see. Half of the participants in each L1 group could see the speaker's gestures while the other half could not. Based on the description, all participants were asked to draw a picture, which was then coded for recall of information. The L1 English participants produced the most accurate drawings with or without having seen gestures. For the EFL learners, those who saw gestures produced drawings within the range of the native speakers.

Recently, Kamiya (2022) investigated the effects of visual cues on L2 English listening comprehension for L1 Japanese speakers at two proficiency levels based on the Common European Framework of Reference (CEFR): 30 at the B2 (*Independent User*)/C1 (*Proficient User*) levels, and 22 at the A1/A2 (*Basic User*) levels (Council of Europe, 2001). A within-group design (i.e., all participants were exposed to all conditions) was selected to attempt to control for the influence of participants' variable sensitivities to non-verbal cues; however, this approach necessitated the creation of different tasks. An L1 English speaker from South Africa recorded six listening tasks that were accompanied by comprehension questions in Japanese. Independent variables were text difficulty (easy or hard), modality of presentation (whole body, face, or A-only), and attempt (first or second; tasks were completed twice). Although participants reported a preference for the whole-body view, there was no significant effect of modality of presentation on scores, a finding which may have resulted from the lack of examination of differences between proficiency levels, since modality effects have been shown to vary for learners at different levels (Sueyoshi & Hardison, 2005). There were, however, significant effects for text difficulty and attempt; higher proficiency participants received higher comprehension scores, especially with the easy texts on the second attempt.

Visual Cues and Accent in L2 Listening Comprehension

Several factors may impact the contribution of visual cues to listening comprehension. Among them, listeners' negative attitudes towards an accent (Lippi-Green, 2012) and stereotyping of accents (Kang & Rubin, 2014) may reduce the comprehensibility of an accented speaker (Major et al., 2005). Can visual cues facilitate comprehension of a speaker with a strong foreign accent? Few studies have investigated the effects of both visual cues and speaker accent on listening comprehension. In a study by H-G. Yi et al. (2013), L1 English listeners correctly identified more keywords in English sentences produced in noise by both L1 and L2 English (L1 Korean) speakers when facial cues were present; however, the L2 speakers were rated as more strongly accented in the AV versus A-only condition.

In a similar study involving a lecture given by an L1 and an L2 English (L1 Portuguese) speaker to L1 English college-level students, de Barros (2010) reported only marginally better comprehension for participants in the AV versus A-only condition, although those in the A-only condition reported having more difficulty comprehending the L2 speaker without visual cues, despite having a familiarity with Portuguese. Topic familiarity also appeared to contribute to comprehension, especially of the L2 speaker's lecture (Gass & Varonis, 1984).

Taking a mixed-methods approach, Algana and Hardison (2024) investigated the effects of visual cues and the English nativelikeness of a speaker's accent on 120 Arab university students' listening comprehension of video-recorded lectures delivered by an L1 AE speaker with an upper-Midwestern accent and an L2 English speaker with a strong L1 Vietnamese accent. In contrast to Kamiya (2022), Algana and Hardison used a between-groups design (i.e., every participant experienced only one condition). Participants were distributed across three stimulus conditions – AV-gesture-face, AV-face, and A-only – nested within two speaker-accent conditions (L1 and L2 English). It was important for the content of the lectures presented by both speakers and across all stimulus conditions (AV-gesture-face, AV-face, A-only) to be the same because content affects the type and number of gestures. A between-groups approach avoided the carryover effect that would have occurred if participants had heard the same content presented by more than one speaker and/or in more than one stimulus condition. The potential influence of variables, such as length of residence in an English-speaking environment and English listening proficiency, was addressed in two ways: assignment of participants to groups to balance different lengths of residence, and treatment of listening proficiency as a covariate in statistical analyses. In addition, the students' assessments of the English nativelikeness of the speakers' accents and comprehensibility were collected using 9-point scales. Students' perceptions of and preferences for visual cues in communication were obtained using the "Speaker's Accent and Visual Cues" questionnaire designed for the study. Individual interviews were conducted following data collection.

Algana and Hardison (2024) carried out analyses of covariance (ANCOVAs) on the scores from the multiple-choice listening comprehension task, and on the ratings for English nativelikeness of accent and comprehensibility with the students' listening proficiency as the covariate. Results revealed significant effects of the speaker's accent and the covariate such that comprehension scores were higher for the lecture delivered by the L1 English speaker and for the students with higher listening proficiency scores. Those who had higher listening proficiency also tended to recognize the L1 English speaker's accent as nativelike. However, the students' listening proficiency was not significantly related to their assessment of either speaker's comprehensibility. Seeing the L1 English speaker's gestures was associated with higher comprehensibility ratings; however, seeing the L2 English speaker's gestures was associated with perception of a strong non-native accent. Notably, there was no significant effect of visual cues on listening comprehension scores, although questionnaire responses pointed to a general preference for facial cues and gestures in communication.

Algana and Hardison's (2024) thematic analysis of the interviews offered considerable insight into the apparent contradiction between the students' generally favourable perceptions of visual cues, such as gestures, and the lack of a significant effect of such cues on their listening comprehension scores. During the interviews, neither the L1 nor the L2 English speaker's gestures were uniformly praised. Some of the students who saw the L1 English speaker's gestures described them as annoying, and some who saw the L2 speaker's gestures described them as uninformative. In both cases, there was a conflict between the students' evaluations of the gestures produced by the speakers in the study and the gestures they were accustomed to seeing in their home cultures. The gestural patterns within a speech community may serve as a basis of comparison when gestures are produced by an unfamiliar person from outside the community. In the Algana and Hardison study, the L2 English speaker's gestures were less rapid, generally less salient, and produced in a more limited gesture space as compared to the L1 English speaker's or those typical of Arabic speakers (Alsubhi, 2017). Although individuals vary in the number of gestures they produce, they tend to show consistency within a speech community in terms of when and how they gesture in specific communicative situations (Gullberg, 2006).

While AV cues might lessen perceivers' cognitive demands by augmenting their ability to make predictions of upcoming information (Peelle & Sommers, 2015), this potential clearly depends on the cues' informativeness from the *perceivers'* perspective. Receptiveness to cues, such as gestures, and assessment of their informativeness are influenced by attitudes and depend on perceivers' knowledge of and familiarity with them. In addition to the cross-cultural differences in gesture use, the students in the Algana and Hardison (2024) research recounted having to divert their attention to the task of understanding the L2 English speaker's Vietnamese accent, which they described as "frustrating," "overwhelming," and "stressful," leaving insufficient resources to process unfamiliar gestures.

In general, the findings of the Algana and Hardison (2024) study underscored the influence of the variability that exists across cultures in terms of gestures and the role that familiarity plays in the contribution of a speaker's gestures to listening comprehension, similar to its role in the influence of accent and topic (e.g., Gass & Varonis, 1984). The lack of cross-cultural agreement on visual cues and their significance emphasizes the need to incorporate non-verbal communication into academic curricula for international participants (e.g., students and instructors) to help build familiarity. Non-verbal cues may also have a role in language testing given the better performance shown by learners on L2 listening tests that use video texts, which, in turn, reflect the use of more authentic materials (e.g., Batty, 2021; Wagner, 2010).

Visual Cues and Perception of Segmental Features and Tone

In addition to investigating the contribution of a speaker's facial cues and gestures to listening comprehension, several studies considered their influence on the perceptual accuracy of segmental duration in languages, such as Japanese, in which durational differences affect word meaning. Hirata and Kelly (2010) explored whether a Japanese speaker's hand movements and/or mouth movements would aid perception of Japanese vowel length contrasts by L1 English speakers with no prior exposure to Japanese. Perception of the distinction between long and short vowels in Japanese is important because it can contrast meaning between pairs of words such as the long vowel *obaasan* (grandmother) and the short vowel *obasan* (aunt). A pretest-training-posttest design was used. The pretest and posttest involved only audio input. Four training conditions were created: (a) audio; (b) audio + mouth (speaker's mouth movements visible); (c) audio + hands (face obscured but hands visible); and (d) audio + mouth + hands (all movements visible). Training involved four sessions. Participants were told that the speaker's short vertical and long horizontal hand movements (i.e., symbolic gestures) corresponded to short and long vowels, respectively. Results revealed improvement for all training groups, but only the comparison of perceptual accuracy between the audio + mouth and audio-only conditions was statistically significant with mouth movements providing important information.

In a subsequent study by Hirata et al. (2014), L1 English participants either observed or produced the gestures. Similar to the Hirata and Kelly (2010) study, a pretest-training-posttest design was used by Hirata et al. (2014), with training stimuli that consisted of pairs of Japanese words contrasting vowel length in the first or second syllable produced by a native speaker of Japanese. Words with short vowels were accompanied by two short downward hand movements, which Hirata et al. referred to as *syllable-rhythm*. Words with long vowels were accompanied by either (a) one long horizontal movement that dips and then rises, followed or preceded by a short vowel associated with a short downward movement (also described as syllable-rhythm); or (b) a series of downward chopping movements corresponding to the number of morae in each word (described as *mora-rhythm*).[7] Along with auditory input, training involved one of the following conditions: (a) observation of the syllable-rhythm gesture; (b) production of syllable-rhythm with the instructor; (c) observation of the mora-rhythm gesture; or (d) production of the mora-rhythm gesture with the instructor. Results showed improvement in auditory perception of vowel length for all types of training; however, observing the gesture described by Hirata et al. (2014) as being associated with syllable-rhythm, which is typical of English (the participants' L1), produced the most improvement across word-initial and word-final vowels.

Morett and Chung (2015) explored whether hand gestures could facilitate English speakers' ability to discriminate between Mandarin words differing only in lexical tone. English monolinguals with no knowledge of Mandarin were assigned to one of three learning conditions in which the video of a Mandarin speaker varied according to gesture use as follows: pitch gesture (hand motions conveyed pitch contours); semantic gesture (hand motions conveyed word meaning); and no gesture. A pretest-learning-posttest sequence was used in which participants were instructed to view a series of video clips, and after each one they repeated aloud the word the speaker had said and its English translation while re-enacting any action they saw. Tone identification accuracy increased significantly from pretest to posttest in the pitch-gesture condition and the no-gesture condition, but not in the semantic gesture condition.

Morett and Chung concluded that the semantic gestures had interfered with the phonological processing of learned words during retrieval from memory by eliciting representations of the meanings. This same issue did not occur in a tone identification task using novel words, which would not have had any meanings stored in the lexicon.

In a series of three studies, Baills (2022) investigated the potential of auditory-visual-kinesthetic training techniques to improve L2 perception and production. In the first study, L1 Catalan speakers showed enhanced recognition and recall of tones if they had been trained with pitch-related gestures. In the second study, L1 Catalan intermediate learners of French showed improvement in accentedness and production of suprasegmental features if they had been trained with L2 prosody-related gestures. In the third study, L1 Catalan speakers, without prior knowledge of French, demonstrated improved accentedness and production of final syllable lengthening if they had been exposed to the visual and acoustic highlighting of the rhythmic properties of French words by means of handclapping. In all three studies, different types of gestures facilitated the learning of a prosodic element.

Visual Cues and Foreign Word Learning

Studies have demonstrated that training protocols involving multisensory input are optimal for learning (Shams & Seitz, 2008). The use of iconic or symbolic gestures during word learning is known to facilitate memory recall (Kelly et al., 2009). Engelkamp and Krumnacker (1980) found that while participants were reading or listening, those who produced a gesture illustrating a word or phrase experienced a superior effect on memory, referred to as the *enactment effect*, or the *self-performed task (SPT) effect* (Cohen, 1981). Three theoretical approaches were proposed to account for the enactment effect. According to Engelkamp and Zimmer (1994), the physical component of the gesture leaves a motor trace in memory. In the second view, the effect is related to the creation of a motor image or a mental representation of the action that was associated with the word during the memory encoding process (e.g., Denis et al., 1991). In the third approach, the enactment effect is driven not by motor information but by increased self-involvement of the participant when producing a gesture accompanying a word (Helstrup, 1987).

To investigate the enactment effect further, Macedonia et al. (2011) used a within-group design to explore the impact of enacted iconic gestures versus meaningless gestures (i.e., simple motor activities, such as touching the leg) on word learning using novel concrete nouns in an artificial language. L1 German participants were shown videos of an actress performing the gestures to be imitated in four stimulus conditions: (a) iconic gesture with face visible; (b) iconic gesture without face; (c) meaningless gesture with face; (d) and meaningless gesture without face. The target word appeared at the bottom of the screen followed by a German translation and was played aloud. Participants were instructed to perform the gesture as they said the word and to remember as many words as possible. Memory performance was assessed daily with a written translation task.

In the Macedonia et al. (2011) study, iconic gestures provided significantly better memory performance. After training, brain activity was measured using fMRI while participants performed a word recognition task. Brain activations to words learned with iconic gestures revealed activity in the premotor cortices.[8] In contrast, words learned with meaningless gestures elicited a vast neural network in both hemispheres associated with metacognitive processes, suggesting that participants attempted to reconcile the gesture and the word. Macedonia et al. interpreted the findings as an indication that memory for newly learned words was not driven by the motor component per se, but by the motor image that matched the underlying representation of the word's meaning. Overall, verbal information was retained better when enriched with a motor trace created through enactment, reminiscent of the total physical response (TPR) approach to language learning (Asher, 1966).

Using an interactive word learning task in Hungarian, Morett (2014) investigated the effect of gesture production and viewing on communication, encoding (in memory), and recall. Participants, who were unfamiliar with Hungarian, were assigned to one of two roles: *explainer* or *learner*. Explainers saw 20 Hungarian words with English glosses on a computer screen. In half the trials, words were presented with videos showing a native Hungarian speaker producing the words with appropriate representational gestures. Explainers then taught the words individually to the learners using whatever means they thought would work best. Covert video recording was used. Participants were then tested on their recall of target words. Similar to the findings of Macedonia et al. (2011), both gesture production and gesture viewing showed comparable enhancement of word encoding, but gesture viewing was not as effective as gesture production in promoting novel word communication and failed to promote word recall. This may be because of the sensorimotor encoding of words and the experiences that are related to their meanings (e.g., Macedonia

& Kepler, 2013) – a benefit that gesture producers (i.e., the explainers in the study) would have had, but listeners (i.e., the learners in the study) would have not.

Gestures in Interaction

In an interactive setting, where there are numerous potential targets for attention, do observers attend to a speaker's gestures and, if so, how much attention do (non-facial) gestures command relative to the face? Based on research, two principles emerge that drive the allocation of visual attention (Posner, 1980; Yantis, 1998; see also chapters 4 and 5). On the one hand, the visual system often attends to movement. Eye-gaze fixations can be precipitated by stimulus-based, low-level perceptual phenomena (bottom-up processes), such as motion, an abrupt onset, or an apparent contrast. On the other hand, task-related strategies linked to higher cognitive processes, such as the need to retrieve specific information, can drive observers' attention. In addition, culture-specific social norms that govern eye gaze may draw attention away from gestures and towards the face, especially in a live face-to-face interaction. In a speech setting, there is potential competition between gestures that encode information related to speech and the face as a source of linguistic-phonetic information (e.g., Lansing & McConkie, 2003; Vatikiotis-Bateson et al., 1998). The winner of the competition depends on the observers' goals and the properties of the target of attention. In addition, shifts in attention may be strategic choices by observers, thus indicating *endogenous* control, or they may be automatic, in which case attention is drawn to the most salient element across stimulus dimensions, indicating *exogenous* control (Theeuwes, 1993).

In a study using head-mounted eye-tracking equipment, Gullberg and Holmqvist (2006) investigated where native speakers of Swedish looked in a live face-to-face setting as compared to a video condition. Over 90% of the time, fixations (measured as fixations of at least 120 ms) were directed towards the face, regardless of whether it was on video or live. Only 0.5% of the time was spent fixating gestures, especially in the video versus live situation, although the difference was not significant. The face dominated as the "default locus of visual attention" (Gullberg & Holmqvist, 2006, p. 68), especially the nose bridge and eye area, a finding compatible with the findings of Vatikiotis-Bateson et al. (1998). Only a minority of gestures in the study attracted fixations, which Gullberg and Holmqvist

(2006) attributed to the fact that gestures are common background elements in interactions (see J.M. Henderson & Hollingworth, 1999). Of the gestures that attracted fixations, two types were identified: *holds*, that is, a temporary halting of movement in a gesture (Kendon, 1972); and gestures that the speakers themselves fixated and that then attracted observers' fixations for social reasons.

Gullberg and Holmqvist (2006) concluded that facial dominance was the result of a sociocultural norm and its status as a unique stimulus and biologically inherent focus of attention. Findings could also represent a task-based effect, specifically, the task was to memorize the story the speaker was telling and then retell it (vs. engage in a conversation). That type of task was compatible with the tasks used by Lansing and McConkie (2003), who proposed the information source attraction effect to explain fixations to the speaker's mouth area as a linguistically informative source (see chapters 4 and 5).

Head Movement, Facial Expression, and Speech

Another non-verbal device used by interlocutors is the head nod, or "clearly visible vertical head movement which accompanies at least one occurrence of lowering the head, immediately followed by a movement of raising the head approximately back to the starting position" (Maynard, 1989, p. 161).[9] In native-speaker interactions, head nods with vocalizations such as *mmm-hmm* (Bavelas et al., 2002) or those accompanied by frowns, postural changes, eyebrow movement, smiles, and laughter (Knapp et al., 1987) aid communication in conjunction with backchannels.

McDonough et al. (2019) investigated (a) an L1 English listener's visual cues (e.g., head nods, eyeblinks, facial expression) in instances of understanding versus nonunderstanding of L2 English speech; and (b) sensitivity of observers/raters to the listener's visual cues in video-recorded interactions when assessing the extent of the listener's nonunderstanding. The L2 English speakers had a variety of L1s and were estimated to be at the B2 (*Competent User*) CEFR level. A total of 21 episodes were identified in which the listener expressed nonunderstanding of an L2 speaker's utterance by requesting clarification (e.g., *a what?* or *huh?*), followed by the L2 speaker's reformulation of the utterance with a subsequent signal of comprehension from the listener. For comparison, 21 length-matched episodes of understanding were also identified. The episodes showed the listener's upper body (torso, arms, and face) while he was listening to the L2 speaker's utterance. Findings uncovered an association between episodes of nonunderstanding and *holds*, defined as occurrences during repair initiation turns "when relatively dynamic movements are temporarily and meaningfully held static" until the nonunderstanding has been resolved and dynamic movements resume (Floyd et al., 2016, p. 176). The listener's visual cues, specifically head nods and blinking, occurred to a greater extent in episodes of nonunderstanding versus understanding. Multilingual English speakers who observed the video clips evaluated the L2 speaker's comprehensibility on a rating scale, and the speaker's intelligibility through transcription. Raters provided lower ratings of the listener's comprehension (i.e., related to the speaker's comprehensibility and intelligibility) when the raters had access to the listener's face.

Head Nods in Japanese Culture

The frequency and pattern of distribution of head nods vary across cultures (e.g., Kita, 2009; Kogure, 2007; Maynard, 1986, 1993; McClave, 2000). They are often associated with Japanese speakers and occur almost three times more often in natural conversation tasks involving Japanese versus AE speakers. In Maynard's (1993) study, both speakers' and listeners' nods contributed to the frequency data, although nodding was more common by the speaker in the Japanese conversations.

Some studies in the Japanese context suggested that head nods should be considered a non-verbal form of *aizuchi*, often used interchangeably with the word *backchannel*, which characterizes the listener's use of brief utterances such as *oh* or *uh huh* in English and *hai*, *un*, or *aa* in Japanese in response to a speaker's speech. Mizutani (1982) translated *aizuchi* as "mutual hammering" to suggest a mutual effort in conversation to create something valuable, such as cooperation or harmony, between interlocutors. Although verbal *aizuchi* and head nods often occur simultaneously, some researchers have considered these features separately (Hanzawa, 2012).

In Japanese dyadic casual conversation, head movement serves multiple conversational management functions, as Maynard (1987) has observed. On the phonological level, head movement co-occurs with prominent segments and may mark emphasis or a request for clarification. Repetitive movements appear to contribute to the tempo of a conversation. Syntactically, head movement serves as a clause boundary marker. As an interactional device, head movement is performed by speakers and listeners in pragmatic contexts. It functions as a "continuer and transition filler on the listener's part; clause boundary, emphasis, affirmation, turn-end marker, transition period filler, and (pre-) turn claim on the speaker's part" (Maynard, 1987, p. 601). *Aizuchis* and nods can form a *loop sequence*; the participants may even nod simultaneously (Kita & Ide, 2007). In addition to verbal *aizuchi*, Kogure (2007) emphasized that silent head nods and smiling play an important role in the loop sequence. Efficient conversation management is not the only purpose of *aizuchis* and head nods; exchanging them in Japanese conversations "seems to be coordination for the sake of coordination," which establishes a social bond between the participants of a conversation, embodying the cooperation and consideration for others that is important in the culture (Kita & Ide, 2007, p. 1250).

Head Nods and Japanese Word Learning

Is there a relationship between a Japanese teacher's head and/or hand movements and speech in an instructional setting? Hardison (2023) conducted two experiments to investigate the temporal coordination of head movement, hand movement, and vowel duration produced by native-speaking Japanese teachers, as well as the influence these movements had on perceptual accuracy for L1 English speakers learning Japanese.

The first experiment in Hardison (2023) focused on naturally occurring gestures (i.e., head and hand movements), along with pitch accent and segmental duration (consonants and vowels) produced by three female native-speakers of Japanese (Tokyo dialect) while teaching beginning-level adult L1 English learners of Japanese in Japan. The teachers, unaware of the study's focus, chose target vocabulary for their classes from an extensive list of Japanese words including minimal pairs, each contrasting consonant length (e.g., *kata* [form] and *katta* [bought]) or vowel length (e.g., *toi* [a question] and *tooi* [far]).

Using the speech of teachers in a beginning-level class offered several advantages in the Hardison (2023) research. The teachers often uttered words in isolation versus in connected speech and at a slower rate, both of which allowed target words to be excised more easily from the recordings for analysis. It was also possible to control for several potential confounding variables that occur in conversational interactions in Japanese, including the various interactional functions of head nods described earlier. Words uttered in isolation also controlled for the influence of context (e.g., occurring from morpheme attachment) on pitch accent (Oshima, 2014).

In Hardison's (2023) first experiment, audiovisual recordings of each teacher were annotated and analysed using Anvil (Kipp, 2001). Analysis was limited to utterances involving eye gaze directed towards the class and excluded exaggerated speech. From those utterances, minimal pair stimuli were isolated and coded per teacher according to the type of natural gesture: head nods, hand gestures, combined head and hand movement, and no gesture. The frequency of occurrence of gestures related to consonant duration was insufficient across teachers for analysis; however, all three teachers produced words contrasting vowel length, primarily involving /i/, /a/, and /o/. Findings showed that teachers tended to use either a head nod or a hand gesture when teaching. A likelihood ratio analysis revealed a significant relationship between gesture type and vowel duration for each teacher. For one teacher, 82.8% of her head nods occurred with a long vowel, and 68.8% of her hand gestures occurred with a short vowel. For another teacher, 71.4% of her head nods occurred with a long vowel, and 66.7% of her hand gestures occurred with a short vowel. The predominant gesture for the third teacher was head nods, 80.8% of which occurred with a long vowel. In general, head nods tended to be associated with long vowels, and hand gestures were associated with short vowels. In addition, for all teachers, analysis of the recordings demonstrated a coordination of peaks such that the peak or apex of the head movement coincided with the peak of the syllable and the peak of the pitch contour.

The second of Hardison's (2023) experiments explored whether the association of teachers' head movements and vowel duration would influence L2 Japanese learners' perceptual identification accuracy of durational differences, and whether learners would notice anything about the teachers' movements. Participants were 30 beginning-level L1 English learners at a university in the US; all were familiar with contrastive duration in Japanese but unfamiliar with the teachers in the recordings. Minimal pairs contrasting vowel duration were selected from the recordings in the first experiment and presented on a monitor using ScreenFlow (Telestream, Inc., 2020), a screencasting and video-editing software. Four stimulus conditions were used as follows: (a) AV (auditory-visual with visible facial cues but no head movement); (b) AVH (auditory-visual with facial cues and head movement); (c) A-only (black screen); and (d) V-only (no audio). The order of conditions was counterbalanced. Participants were asked to circle the word on response sheets in a forced-choice two-alternative task. Accuracy was the highest in the AVH condition followed by AV, A-only, and then V-only.

During the interview following data collection in the second Hardison (2023) experiment, participants commented that vowel duration was more difficult to identify in word-final versus word-medial position. They were shown several AV and AVH trials for each teacher's recordings and asked where they had been looking during the experiment. They were also asked about the visual cues they paid attention to in their regular Japanese classes. The majority of participants mentioned the teacher's lip movements in the recordings and stated that they regularly paid attention to those cues in class. Two participants mentioned that they paid attention to a teacher's entire head in the recordings versus just the mouth area. Head movement may be a relatively implicit input feature for learners, especially in terms of its information value as compared to mouth movements, but findings also pointed to its role in the perception of vowel duration.

Other Pedagogical Implications of Gesture Use

Consider the following question: "Is 'foreign gesture' as detectable – and as disturbing – as foreign accent?" (Gullberg, 2006, p. 116). Based on the findings of Algana and Hardison (2024) involving observers who watched two culturally foreign speakers, the answer appears to be "yes" in some cases. The interview responses at the end of Algana and Hardison's study provided insightful comments on some strategies that participants used, such as trying to pay attention to gestures on a daily basis whenever possible in an attempt to do what one participant described as "semantically map the word or sentence they were hearing to the gesture they were seeing." However, in the listening comprehension task, when their attentional resources were stretched to capacity to deal with the L2 English speaker's challenging accent, it was far more difficult to derive any benefit from the unfamiliar gestures.

Negative impacts of unfamiliar accents and gestures may be mediated by raising awareness and building familiarity. During the interviews in the Algana and Hardison (2024) study, participants reported having used several strategies to deal with unfamiliar accents in academic settings. Among them was spending more time listening to the speaker in order to become familiar with the accent (Moussu, 2010). The reported strategies suggested a willingness to make an effort to understand unfamiliar accents and visual cues despite challenges. Raising awareness of cross-cultural differences in gestures and building familiarity with accents is consistent with the view that speech and gesture can be regarded as a "composite signal" (Gullberg, 2006, p. 108).

Building familiarity may also help to avoid confusion about the meaning of some gestures (Sime, 2008). In a study of learners' perceptions of teachers' gestures during interactions in an EFL classroom, Sime (2008) uncovered both similarities and differences in learners' perceptions of the same gestures. The teachers were L1 English speakers with EFL teaching experience, and the learners, primarily from Japan, Spain, and Italy, were described as low- to upper-intermediate in proficiency. All learners thought the teachers' gestures conveyed meanings in certain contexts and contributed to classroom interaction. Learners thought the teachers used gestures for lexical items they anticipated would be difficult for learners given their proficiency level because some gestures enhanced comprehension by illustrating words or ideas, emphasizing important words, or marking contrasts and comparisons. However, for some learners, a particular gesture appeared superfluous, although for others, it helped to focus their attention. Sime attributed these different perceptions to different learner needs and the influence of previous experiences.

To understand and use language appropriately in a range of contexts, speech and gesture need to be recognized by L1 and L2 speakers (von Raffler-Engel, 1980). In the academic context, the speech–gesture relationship offers instructors the opportunity to improve teaching effectiveness by using gestures to draw students' attention to and enhance the meaning of important content as well as raise awareness of suprasegmental features (e.g., speech rhythm, word stress) in L2 pronunciation. For example, Smotrova (2017) used reiterative gestures, or *catchments* (e.g., a counting gesture or clapping to represent the number of syllables in a word), to help students visualize otherwise intangible phenomena.

Classes that are focused on the development of L2 oral skills can go beyond considerations of the accuracy and fluency of speech to a consideration of its expressive function as language used for communication by incorporating gestures as part of a multifaceted contextualized speech event. Hardison and Sonchaeng (2005) advocated shifting the focus of learner attention to their speech in stages from the physiological to the linguistic, and then to the discourse level where the components of a speech event are integrated. Activities can include video shadowing (i.e., imitating another's speech production), pantomime, and then mirroring (i.e., expanding the imitation to include a speaker's posture, facial expression, gestures, and other movements along with speech). The number of mirrored elements chosen and their sequence depend on learners' objectives and proficiency level. Ultimately, monologue and dialogue are practised in communicatively meaningful contexts to enhance the effectiveness of learners' performance in L2 interactive situations. As Celce-Murcia et al. (2010) observed, "By encouraging gestures and body movements with all speaking and pronunciation activities, teachers can help learners rehearse an essential component of authentic speech" (p. 338).

Chapter 6 in Review

Many elements in face-to-face communication are multifunctional. Body movements, head nods, gestures, facial expressions, eye gaze, and interpersonal distance convey messages (e.g., Kellerman, 1992), and the messages may vary across cultures (e.g., Pennycook, 1985). Movements of the eyes, orofacial muscles, and brows compose facial expressions such as smiles and frowns that can set the tone for a subsequent interaction, even before speech begins.

In L2 environments, Algana and Hardison (2024) determined that gestures were neither universally beneficial for listening comprehension nor universally well received by observers. Seeing a speaker's gestures did not have a significant facilitating effect on L2 listening comprehension, although questionnaire responses did indicate participants' general preference for visual cues in daily interactions and the activities they chose to use to develop their English oral communication skills. Resolution of this apparent contradiction through interviews was insightful and underscored the value of a mixed-methods research approach. As with other components of a speech event, gesture variability exists across speakers and cultures. Familiarity plays a role in the contribution of a speaker's gestures to comprehension, as it does for accent and topic (e.g., Gass & Varonis, 1984; Perry et al., 2018). In addition, other elements such as speaker accentedness may interact with gestures' potential benefits.

In the Algana and Hardison (2024) study, the attentional demands that were needed to understand a speaker with a strong unfamiliar accent reduced the resources available to students to process the unfamiliar gestures. Such a finding should not suggest that there is no role in the classroom for gestures as a component of multimodal input, but it should encourage raising awareness of cross-cultural differences and building familiarity. Chapter 7 thus outlines the preparation of teachers to maximize multimodal input in language teaching.

Chapter 6 Notes

1. Darwin (1872/1899) is an online document that does not have any page numbers. The chapter number is given for reader reference.
2. Event-related potentials (ERPs) are short segments of electroencephalographic data that are time-locked to particular events of interest; electroencephalography (EEG) is a continuous measure of electrical brain activity (Blackwood & Muir, 1990; Light et al., 2010).
3. Functional magnetic resonance imaging (fMRI) measures the changes in blood flow that occur with brain activity and may be used to observe the parts of the brain that execute specific functions (Glover, 2011). Broca's area of the brain coordinates the transformation of information processing across the cortical networks involved in the sensory representations of words in the temporal cortex and the corresponding articulatory gestures in the motor cortex that are involved in the spoken word production process prior to articulation (Flinker et al., 2015).
4. Mirror neurons are active when a person performs or watches another person perform a series of movements. The activation of mirror neurons while watching another person's movement may allow us to "tap into our own advanced motor circuits to understand the actions of others" (Hill et al., 2019, p. 1087).
5. The N400 wave is an ERP measured using EEG. N400 refers to a negative ERP occurring at about 400 ms after the onset of a stimulus. It indexes cognitive load and is used to investigate semantic processing and the degree to which people predict meaning based on immediate context and general knowledge (Kuperberg & Jaeger, 2016; Kutas & Federmeier, 2011).
6. An intonation phrase is delimited by a low or high boundary tone (Beckman & Pierrehumbert, 1986; Beckman et al., 2005). In addition to its role in speech production, the intonation phrase also represents a unit that Chafe (1994) considered to be an optimal size for processing by a perceiver's echoic memory, and that Wennerstrom (2001) described as "the unit at which the cognition, physics, syntax, phonetics, and phonology of speech converge" (p. 28).
7. A mora is a unit of timing important in the perception and production of Japanese. Unlike consonant-vowel morae, special morae such as geminates and the second half of long vowels do not constitute syllables by themselves, and they are not accent-bearing units (Kubozono, 1999; Tsujimura, 2013).
8. The premotor area integrates auditory, visual, and somatosensory stimuli in the selection, initiation, and performance of movement-related tasks (Hill et al., 2019); it contains mirror neurons.
9. Although Maynard (1987) expressed some concern about using the term *nod* because it can also imply pragmatic meanings such as agreement and acknowledgment, the term is frequently used in the literature with reference to vertical head movement.

Chapter 7

Multimodal Foundations of Pronunciation Teaching and Learning

Learn to observe *the movements of the native's mouth, learn to* control *the movements of your own.*

– Daniel Jones (as cited in Collins & Mees, 2002, Lecture 3)[1]

*****

Background

As with the preceding chapters, this one begins with background on the historical roots of some contemporary topics in the field of pronunciation teaching and learning. Some of what we may consider to be relatively recent trends in the field actually have roots that date back over 100 years, including topics such as (a) the variety of English that may constitute a standard for teaching purposes; (b) attitudes towards accents; (c) the effect of familiarity on understanding an accent; (d) a feasible goal in learning to pronounce another language; and (e) the importance of both auditory and visual input in teaching and learning pronunciation – all of which can be found in the works of Daniel Jones (1881–1967).

Jones was a phonetician and renowned authority on the pronunciation of English and the application of phonetics to language teaching who worked in the first half of the twentieth century. Some of his ideas remained constant, but there is evidence from his published lectures and informal correspondence (Collins & Mees, 2002) that some of his viewpoints evolved from the early 1900s to the final revision he made of his book *The Pronunciation of English* (D. Jones, 1956), originally published in 1909. The book is a detailed description of the phonetics of English written for the English learner at home and abroad. Although the book focused primarily on varieties of English in England, Jones also made reference to the varieties spoken in Scotland, Ireland, Australia, and America. This broader scope provided a platform for his views on the viability of a standard pronunciation, the acceptance of different English accents, and what the primary goal in learning the pronunciation of another language should be, in addition to his recommendations for how speakers should approach the pronunciation learning task. As the epigraph at the start of this chapter suggests, Jones took a multimodal approach to the task. These issues continue to be important today; consequently, this chapter presents details of these concepts followed by a consideration of their role in language teacher education and on-the-job training.

Is There a Standard Pronunciation?

The field of L2 pronunciation teaching and learning has long wrestled with the issue of which variety of a language to teach, which, in turn, is linked to the issue of a standard pronunciation – if one exists. Jones's view on a standard English pronunciation for teaching purposes evolved over the years. In the first edition of his book *The Pronunciation of English*, published in 1909, Jones maintained that there was a standard English pronunciation, which should be the target of learning. A few years later, however, in a lecture to French students about English phonetics, instead of recommending one standard pronunciation, Jones urged students to learn the pronunciation of those English speakers whom they were likely to meet or with whom they would like to associate. He surmised that if they expected to interact only with Americans, it was better for them to learn AE pronunciation. However, Jones added that in the absence of a particular target variety, the French students could adopt the pronunciation of well-educated speakers in Southern England, which would "pass as good English in any society" (Collins & Mees, 2002, Lecture 2).[2]

As a result of additional experience with a range of varieties of English, Jones acknowledged in 1927 that his earlier concept of the variety that constituted the standard was not, in fact, a variety used by as many people as he had originally thought. He also noted that although the existence of a standard pronunciation might be desirable for ease of communication across regional varieties and for teaching English to speakers of other languages, it was difficult, if not impossible, to choose one variety that would meet with universal acceptance. By 1946, after years of observing the speech of others, Jones concluded "that an absolute standard is not really necessary – that there is no harm in the pronunciation of our language varying within pretty wide limits" (as cited in Collins & Mees, 2002, Lecture 12). Although some accents may be difficult to understand, "their difficulty is to be attributed to unfamiliarity with that manner of speech and not to any inherent 'badness' in the sounds" (D. Jones, 1956, p. 5). Jones also attributed negative attitudes towards some accents to their association with specific people or unpleasant circumstances the listener had recalled (Collins & Mees, 2002, Lecture 11). In the last revised edition of his book, he concluded with reference to English that "it can no longer be said that any standard exists, nor do I think it desirable to attempt to establish one" (D. Jones, 1956, p. vi).

Intelligibility

In 1946, Jones set aside the notion of a standard form as the goal in pronunciation learning and decided that the primary goal should simply be intelligibility, specifically "easy intelligibility" (as cited in Collins & Mees, 2002, Lecture 11), which is likely similar to "comfortable intelligibility" (Kenworthy, 1987, p. 16). These terms suggest a level at which both listener and speaker can communicate with relative ease or comfort, which Kenworthy asserted must be the goal of pronunciation. Today, easy or comfortable intelligibility might be considered a merging of two concepts: comprehensibility, defined as a listener's impression of the ease of understanding a speaker, and intelligibility, defined as a listener's actual understanding of what a speaker has said (e.g., Derwing & Munro, 1997). The latter concept in L2 pronunciation learning is now generally recognized as the *Intelligibility Principle*, that is, "learners simply need to be understandable" (Levis, 2005, p. 370).

Although these definitions of comprehensibility and intelligibility add some clarity to the issue of what the goal should be in pronunciation teaching, they also introduce another important variable, specifically, the listeners (Pennington & Rogerson-Revell, 2019, chapter 3). Do the listeners share the speaker's L1, or are they L2 listeners, and, if so, at what level of proficiency? The listener is the decision-maker in the assessment of comprehensibility and intelligibility (e.g., Gagnon & Hardison, 2022). In many contexts, including those in which English serves as a lingua franca, communication may involve the challenge of comprehending an unfamiliar accent (Algana & Hardison, 2024; Ballard & Winke, 2017). Although accentedness and intelligibility can coexist, accentedness can impact both intelligibility and comprehensibility (e.g., Derwing & Munro, 1997). Even though a substantial number of learners of English want to acquire a native accent (e.g., Derwing, 2003; Timmis, 2002), others want to maintain aspects of their L1 accent as an overt marker of their identity (e.g.,

Gatbonton et al., 2005), underscoring the need for a tolerance of accented speech. In addition, the assessment of accentedness can be impacted by a listener's negative attitude (Lippi-Green, 2012) and stereotyping (Kang & Rubin, 2014).

Role of Visual Input

As expressed in the chapter's opening epigraph, in becoming an intelligible speaker of another language, there is an important role for visual input. Jones made several recommendations for language learners, including (a) observing the mouth movements of a native speaker of the target language to understand how sounds are produced; (b) using a mirror to monitor articulations; and (c) understanding and using phonetic transcription (Collins & Mees, 2002). In his earliest extant lecture on the teaching of English pronunciation to French speakers, delivered to multiple audiences throughout 1912–13, Jones encouraged the audience members to study the way sounds were formed by the mouths of "good" speakers and imitate them, but qualified the value of this approach by stating, "In England we speak without moving our lips very much" (as cited in Collins & Mees, Lecture 1).

Jones learned firsthand of the value of attending to mouth movements in learning to pronounce sounds in another language. In a lecture delivered in 1916 (Collins & Mees, 2002, Lecture 3) on the use of phonetics to learn lesser known languages in Africa, Jones described having watched the lip movements and tongue positions of his native-speaking informant of Sechuana (now known as Setswana), a South African Bantu language, in order to experiment more effectively with pronunciation. He emphasized the effectiveness of this approach in contrast to just listening to recordings or reading books. At that time, technology was not available to provide a view of the movement of internal articulators during speech, though such a view is now available with real-time magnetic resonance imaging (see, e.g., the website SPAN, https://sail.usc.edu/span).

Teachers and learners should be aware that visual speech input is variable across language varieties (e.g., Hardison, 2007); talkers (e.g., Conrey & Gold, 2006; Gagné et al., 1994; Hardison, 2003; Kricos & Lesner, 1982); sounds (e.g., Binnie et al., 1976; Fisher, 1968); rates and styles of speech (e.g., Gagné et al., 1994; Hardison, 2005b; Picheny et al., 1986); and phonetic contexts (e.g., Benguerel & Pichora-Fuller, 1982; Franks & Kimble, 1972; Hardison, 2003, 2005b, 2018b; Owens & Blazek, 1985; see also chapter 1).

Articulatory Settings

Jones recognized variable articulatory settings across languages and varieties of English. An articulatory setting can be defined as the set of postural configurations (e.g., tongue, jaw, and lip positions) and mechanics that serve as a framework for the vocal tract articulators to produce fluent and natural speech (Honikman, 1964; Sweet, 1890). O'Connor (1973) referred to the concept as the different *bases of articulation* of different languages. In noting their importance in foreign language teaching, O'Connor stated that "better results are achieved when the learner gets the basis of articulation right rather than trying for the foreign sound sequences from the basis of his own language" (p. 289). This assertion implies that learners may expect to face difficult challenges in trying to pronounce the sounds of another language intelligibly if the topic of articulatory settings does not receive the pedagogical attention it deserves.

Learners may also have a tendency to regard L2 sounds as a set of individual elements when they really need to "weld them into a consistent whole" (Honikman, 1964, p. 74) within a new articulatory setting. This tendency may be influenced by the way sounds are presented individually in pronunciation textbooks. At first glance, it may not seem to be an optimal approach towards achieving the ultimate goal of producing and understanding *connected speech* – that is, the continuous sequence of speech sounds characterized by phenomena such as vowel reduction, consonant deletion, and changes in one sound's production in anticipation of another sound (see chapter 8). However, there is an advantage to addressing L2 sounds individually, at least in the early stages of learning when attention can be focused more easily and the overall task may be less daunting from the learners' perspective. Using the guideline of a pedagogical norm (e.g., Gass et al., 2002), beginning learners can be presented with L2 sounds that correspond to citation forms as the initial targets of learning with the addition of variability over time.

The articulatory setting for a language depends on the most frequently occurring sounds and sound combinations. Because English consonants are articulated at the alveolar ridge behind the upper front teeth more frequently than at any other place of articulation, the alveolar ridge "should be regarded as the basis of the internal articulatory setting of English utterance" (Honikman, 1964, p. 76). Alveolar consonants include [t] (e.g., *top*), [d] (e.g., *dog*), [n] (e.g., *night*), [s] (e.g., *sound*), [z] (e.g., *zip*), and the flap/tap[3] [ɾ] (e.g., *city*). In particular, [t] and [n] are the most frequent alveolar consonants, followed by [s].

If we consider the external (visible) manifestations of articulatory setting, AE is roughly in the middle of a continuum stretching from French on one end as a language exhibiting substantial lip movement in articulation, to Japanese on the opposite end as a language with comparatively less movement (Vance, 1987). O'Connor (1973) described English sound production as involving more relaxed cheeks, a tenser tongue tip, and less movement of the lips and jaw as compared to French, which is characterized as involving tense cheeks, a more dominant tongue blade (behind the tip), and "vigorous lip-rounding and spreading" (p. 289).

We now know more about the variability of articulatory settings because of the advent of real-time MRI. In a study conducted by Ramanarayanan et al. (2013), real-time MRI was used to analyse the articulatory setting of the vocal tract of five female native AE speakers during speech production. Frames were extracted that corresponded to inter-speech pauses, speech-ready positions, and absolute rest positions from sequences of read and spontaneous speech. To elicit read speech, the speakers were recorded/imaged during a scan while reading sentences and the *rainbow* passage, a brief passage in which the first four lines capture a wide variety of sounds and thus mouth movements that occur in unscripted English speech.[4] To elicit spontaneous speech, the participants were then engaged in a dialogue with the experimenter on general topics, such as their preferred type of music. For each speech turn, audio responses and MRI videos of vocal tract articulation were recorded. Mid-sagittal real-time images of the vocal tract were analysed and various measurements were taken, including lip aperture (i.e., the minimum distance between the upper and lower lip); velic aperture (i.e., the minimum distance between the velum and the pharyngeal wall); tongue tip constriction degree; tongue dorsum constriction degree; and tongue root constriction degree.

Ramanarayanan et al. (2013) discovered statistically significant differences between the vocal tract postures that speakers adopted during inter-speech pauses and those at absolute rest before speaking; the postures at absolute rest also exhibited greater speaker variability. In addition, there was a distinction between the articulatory settings adopted during inter-speech pauses in read versus spontaneous speech such that spontaneous settings had a slightly higher jaw and lower tongue position. Ramanarayanan et al. proposed that the differences in vocal tract postures during rest positions, speech-ready positions, and inter-speech pauses might reflect an increasing degree of active control by the cognitive speech planning processes, in that order, which would assign the greatest cognitive control to inter-speech pauses. They also proposed that supralaryngeal articulatory settings in combination with laryngeal articulatory settings might generate the formant structure and *harmonic* structure (i.e., a structure dependent on the waveform generated by vibrating vocal folds) of the acoustic speech signal that creates what is heard as a particular voice quality (see "Voice Quality" below).

In a communication theoretic framework, such as that proposed by Traunmüller (1994), speech signals result from the modulation by a speaker's articulatory gestures of a phonetically neutral signal that has the voice quality and articulatory setting of the speaker. Ramanarayanan et al. (2013) pointed out that an understanding of articulatory settings contributes to an understanding of the characteristics of speech that both depend on and are independent of a given speaker. Gick et al. (2004) further noted that the neutral position of articulators is language-specific; postural bias depends on the speech patterns of the language variety that the speaker has learned.

Voice Quality

Articulatory settings serve as the basis of voice quality, which is composed of supralaryngeal settings (i.e., those above the larynx involving the positioning of active or movable articulators such as the lips, lower jaw, and tongue) and phonatory or laryngeal settings (i.e., the way in which the vocal folds are made to vibrate; e.g., Laver, 1980). Voice quality comprises the settings that define the voice of an individual and the accent of that person's L1 variety, and it may also signal mood or emotion in conversation or serve to identify the talker (Esling & Wong, 1983). When we recognize people by their voices, we are responding to the most persistent or long-lasting speech cues that make up their accent (Esling et al., 2019).

Voice quality, as a relatively non-fluctuating long-term characteristic of a person's speech, contrasts with a person's rapidly fluctuating segmental (i.e., consonant and vowel) articulations and prosodic patterns (Abercrombie, 1967). The vibrations generated by the vocal folds constitute the *phonation type*, or *phonatory quality*, that underlie the voiced sounds that speakers produce. Beginning in the larynx, the speech signal is then modified through the shapes created by the position of the articulators above the larynx and throughout the upper vocal tract. The long-term setting or posture has an effect on the segments in a stretch of speech; for example, a speaker with a generally close (vs. open), rounded (vs. spread) labial setting produces on average more sounds with more lip rounding than would occur in the speech of a speaker who does not employ such a vocal setting (Esling et al., 2019).

Esling et al. (2019, pp. 123–43) have provided a range of examples to illustrate different types of voice quality and articulatory settings. Among the examples most recognizable to readers are (a) *nasal voice*, often associated with French but also evident in Bluegrass music and American folk music, such as in the recitative singing style of Bob Dylan (e.g., Dylan, 1963); (b) *breathy voice*, produced when vibration for voicing occurs at the anterior portion of the glottis while air escapes at the wider posterior portion, associated with the actress Marilyn Monroe (e.g., Monroe, 1959); (c) *close jaw* setting (limited jaw movement during speaking) combined with spread lips, characteristic of Rod Serling's commentary in the *Twilight Zone* television series (e.g., Serling, 1959–1964); (d) *open jaw* setting, which may involve an exaggerated jaw opening, as in Frank Sutton's characterization of the sergeant in the *Gomer Pyle* television series (Ruben, 1964–69), and (e) the *laterally offset jaw* posture or movement of the jaw from side to side, such as that used to humorous effect by the comedian Jim Carrey (e.g., Howard, 2000).

In adopting specific articulatory and voice quality settings, performers make use of the relationship between popular stereotypes and accents (Pratt & D'Onofrio, 2017), although not all speakers follow a stereotypical pattern. For example, Jones's comments, noted earlier, on the limited lip movement (close jaw posture) of speakers in England did not apply to all speakers of British English; however, as Esling et al. (2019) pointed out, "there are dialect affinities. The retroflex accents of the south coast of England tend to jaw opening – a plausible historical source for many North American speech settings" (p. 139).

Mouth Gymnastics

In several lectures, Jones summarized succinctly the pedagogical application of the notion of articulatory setting when he stated that

> in addition to *ear training* we give our students [at the London School of Phonetics] plenty of *mouth-training*. To learn to pronounce a foreign language really well involves doing a great deal of *mouth gymnastics* – to get into the way of using the vocal organs in the unaccustomed foreign manner. (as cited in Collins & Mees, 2002, Lecture 13)

Jones provided specific English pronunciation exercises with a visual component for learners to use. For example, to learn to produce the English rounded vowel /u/ (e.g., *boot*) and unrounded vowel /i/ (e.g., *beet*), he recommended that learners use a mirror and watch their production of [u-i-u-i-u], which he promoted as an "exercise for the lips" (as cited in Collins & Mees, 2002, Lecture 1), then repeat the same lip movements without any sound before moving to a different vowel contrast.

Jones's writings also included sketches of lip positions or lip shapes (Pennington, 1996) that influence vowel quality, such as the lip spreading in *see* (/i/), open-mouth neutral position in *ah* (/ɑ/), open-mouth lip rounding in *talk* (/ɔ/), and closed-mouth lip rounding in *boot* (/u/) (D. Jones, 1956). There were also diagrams of the mid-sagittal view of the head that have often been used in various forms in phonetics and pronunciation textbooks over the years (e.g., L. Grant, 2017; Ladefoged & Johnson, 2015; Prator & Robinett, 1985). Most of these diagrams focus on tongue position, with some showing the graduated height of the tongue body for pronouncing low, mid, and high vowels. In his writings, Jones frequently recommended having a mental picture of the tongue position for each sound that one is learning to produce.

To the suggestion of developing a mental picture of tongue position, one could add the recommendation for language learners to develop a mental picture of the external articulatory gesture for a sound. This could be based on learners' observations of natural speech or online media, as books often omit this detail. For example, although Jones (1956) included diagrams that were related to the production of consonants such as /ʃ/ (e.g., <u>sh</u>*ip*), these diagrams focused only on tongue position and excluded lip protrusion, as do some contemporary textbooks (e.g., L. Grant, 2017; Orion, 2012). To produce sounds such as /ʃ/ and /r/, Jones recommended that learners observe the various degrees of lip protrusion exhibited by speakers.[iv] It is important to note the difference between protrusion and rounding. Protrusion involves movement forward; for example, the articulation of the initial sound /ʃ/ (e.g., <u>sh</u>*ip*) and medial /ʒ/ (e.g., *mea<u>s</u>ure*) may involve protrusion with a larger lip opening as compared to rounding (Toda et al., 2003), whereas the articulation of /w/ (e.g., <u>w</u>*et*) involves lip

iv. Editor's Note: It should be remembered that Daniel Jones was describing British English, whose speakers I have noted tend to produce /ʃ/ and /ʒ/ with lip protrusion to a greater extent than American English speakers, whom I have observed to produce these consonants with a different type of lip gesture, or labialization. I have observed some American English speakers produce /ʃ/ and /ʒ/, as well as /r/, with the corners of the lips pulled back a bit rather than protruded. Also, as I have observed, AE /ʃ/ and /ʒ/ may anticipate the lip gesture of a following vowel or be produced with no distinctive lip gesture. I do not think a detailed study of these variants has yet been made. – MCP protrusion with rounding that creates a small opening. Interestingly, the final edition of Jones's book in 1956 included something infrequently seen even in contemporary pronunciation textbooks (but see McCormack et al., 2010): two photographs (albeit black and white) demonstrating lateral spreading and contracting of the tongue, which Jones recommended as exercises to improve control over tongue movements in speech.

Such awareness of visual speech cues, articulatory settings, and mouth gymnastics should be incorporated into language teacher education. Following some observations on multisensory elements in language teaching materials, suggestions are provided for emphasizing these elements in teacher education (and ideas for their implementation in language classes are presented in chapter 8).

Teaching Materials

Textbooks currently in use for the teaching of English pronunciation vary in their acknowledgment of visual speech cues and the multimodal nature of speech (e.g., Celce-Murcia et al., 2010). Some books emphasize such points as the importance of eye contact with interlocutors to establish a rapport (e.g., S.F. Miller, 2006); the use of a mirror to monitor articulations (e.g., Orion, 2012); the benefit of shadowing speakers for practice (e.g., S.F. Miller, 2006); and the value of paying attention to television newscasters' pronunciation during English-language news programs (e.g., Dale & Poms, 2005).

The pedagogical value of diagrams in books also varies. Materials range from simple sketches of mouth shapes for English vowels that exhibit different degrees of lip rounding and lower jaw positions (Prator & Robinett, 1985) to mid-sagittal diagrams focused on tongue position that may ignore lip position, omitting the salient gesture of protrusion from the diagrams for some sounds (e.g., L. Grant, 2017; Orion, 2012). Animation mouth shapes can represent relative degrees of mouth opening (i.e., the position of the lower jaw) fairly well, but they do not represent the degree of lip spreading and lip rounding well, nor do they distinguish rounding from protrusion (e.g., Celce-Murcia et al., 2010; Dale & Poms, 2005; Gilbert, 2012). The most accurate and informative still images are colour photographs of the mouth area (e.g., McCormack et al., 2010). Even though diagrams and photos can show one point in the articulatory process, they cannot show the movement of articulators, either external or internal, which is important in the production of a speech sound. To fill this gap, there are websites, such as those described below, that demonstrate articulatory gestures, and in some cases the displays include motion of the less visible internal articulators. To use the following sites, individuals should have knowledge of the International Phonetic Alphabet (IPA).

1. Sounds of Speech (https://soundsofspeech.uiowa.edu): This tool, developed at the University of Iowa, has undergone some changes since its inception. Of the languages that it addresses (English, German, and Spanish), English is currently available only as a mobile app. Audio and video examples (e.g., animation and a human face) demonstrate the production of consonants and vowels in isolation and in words (see Figure 7.1).

FIGURE 7.1 Screenshot from the Sounds of Speech Mobile App

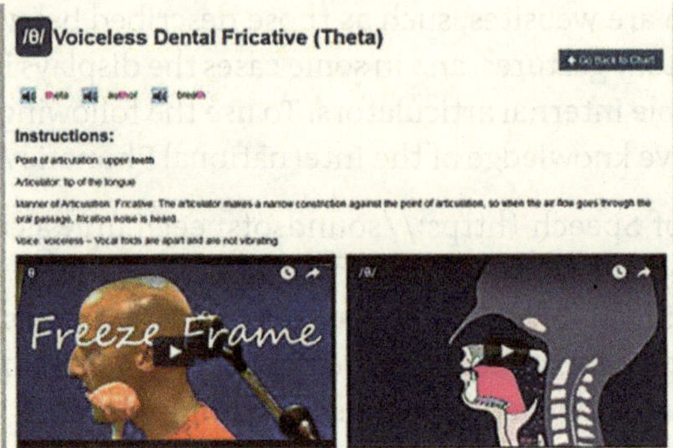

FIGURE 7.2 Screenshot from the eNunciate! Website Showing an Ultrasound Overlay (Left) and Animation Video (Right) for Production of the Voiceless Interdental Fricative

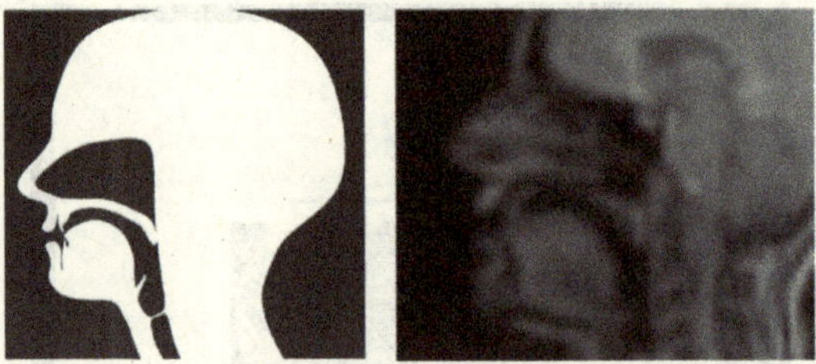

FIGURE 7.3 Screenshots from the Seeing Speech Website Showing Animation View (Left) and MRI (Right) for Production of the Voiced Interdental Fricative

2. eNunciate! (https://enunciate.arts.ubc.ca): This site, developed at the University of British Columbia, is described as a visual language learning tool that provides ultrasound overlay videos in which ultrasound images of tongue movements in speech are superimposed on videos of a face so users can see how the facial and tongue muscles coordinate with each other. For example, the consonant sound /θ/ (e.g., think) is produced in a CV syllable and then in a VCV syllable with the open-mouth vowel /ɑ/ (see Figure 7.2). Vowels are produced following a consonant. An animation video shows tongue movement and airflow.
3. Seeing Speech (https://seeingspeech.ac.uk): This resource, developed at the University of Glasgow, offers several types of display for the articulation of speech sounds (see Figure 7.3). For consonants, animation, MRI, and ultrasound images are available with accompanying audio. The phonetic context in which each consonant is produced varies but often includes the target sound produced between vowels such as [ɑ] and/or [i]. For vowels, MRI and ultrasound images are available.

4. SPAN (https://sail.usc.edu/span): The Speech Production and Articulation Knowledge Group (SPAN) out of the University of Southern California provides real-time MRI data from several phoneticians producing the consonant and vowel sounds represented in an IPA chart (see Figure 7.4). Each consonant is produced in the frame [hɑ_ɑ]. Each vowel is produced in isolation with a prolonged articulation and then in words, short sentences, and passages. Double-clicking on an MRI video permits the user to control the speed of the video playback in order to focus on the movement of the internal articulators.

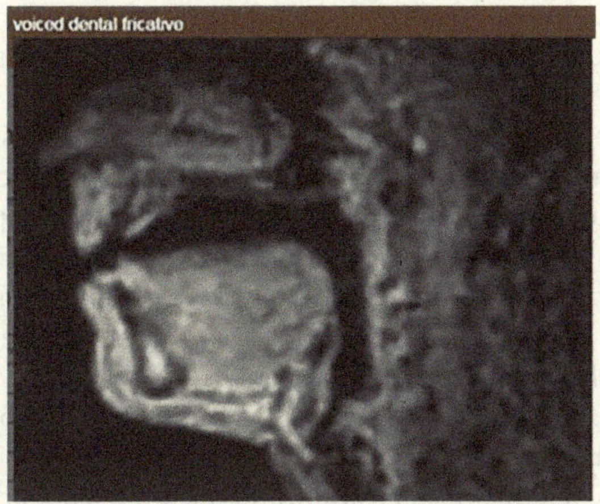

FIGURE 7.4 Screenshot from the SPAN Website Showing an MRI for the Production of the Voiced Interdental Fricative

Choosing the Target Sounds to Teach

Teachers are often challenged to find sufficient class time for pronunciation. To determine the sounds to teach, they may rely on existing textbooks and/or the results of an analysis of the needs of a particular group of learners that might not be available far enough in advance for planning purposes. Teachers may also be inclined to make decisions on the sounds to address in class based on one of the following concepts: *functional load* (e.g., A. Brown, 1988; Munro & Derwing 2006); *error gravity* (e.g., Gagnon & Hardison, 2022; Munro, 2018); or the *Lingua Franca Core* (J. Jenkins, 2002). Each is discussed here in turn.

Functional Load

Functional load has been defined different ways (for a review, see A. Brown, 1988). The simplest determination of the functional load of a given phonemic contrast (e.g., AE /m/ and /n/) is the number of *minimal pairs* that this pair of sounds distinguishes. Minimal pairs are words that differ in meaning but involve the contrast of a pair of phonetically similar sounds (e.g., /m/ and /n/ are both nasal consonants) in the same position in words such as *mine* and *nine*. However, Avram (1964) emphasized the need to have additional criteria to interpret functional load by pointing out that one phonemic contrast for which there are 10 minimal pairs versus another contrast for which there are 20 minimal pairs should not necessarily be interpreted as evidence of greater importance for the second contrast based solely on the number of minimal pairs.

To evaluate functional load, Munro and Derwing (2006) used the following criteria: (a) the number of minimal pairs; (b) the range of positions in which the sounds can occur within a word (e.g., in initial position, *mine* and *nine*; in medial position, *dimmer* and *dinner*; in final position, *sum* and *sun*); and (c) the probability of the occurrence of either member of the minimal pair. For example, Munro and Derwing considered the /l/-/n/ (e.g., *l̲ight*, *n̲ight*) contrast to have a higher functional load than the /ð/-/d/ (e.g., *t̲h̲ough*, *d̲ough*) contrast based on the greater number of minimal pairs, the higher frequency of occurrence of the contrast in word-initial and word-final (e.g., *fil̲e*, *fin̲e*) position, and the low likelihood that the contrast would be neutralized (no perceptible difference) in any regional variety of English. The /ð/-/d/ contrast is neutralized in some regions of the US.[v] Errors involving a high functional load had a relatively large effect on listeners' ratings of the comprehensibility and accentedness of learner speech. The effect on comprehensibility of errors involving low functional load was small as compared to the effect of such errors on accentedness. Munro and Derwing concluded that listeners' ratings of comprehensibility are related to their difficulties in processing learner speech, whereas their ratings of accentedness are related to the relative perceptual salience of the errors in learners' speech. The study left open questions concerning the differing effects of errors involving vowels versus the consonants tested, and of errors according to their location within words. In addition,

v. Editor's Note: The contrast is also commonly neutralized in rapid speech as well as in many varieties of English outside the US. – MCP

the presence of supportive semantic context may impact the effect of functional load on listeners' comprehension.

The relative roles of functional load and accent familiarity on native listeners' judgments of learner speech were investigated by Pfau (2020) using corpus analysis tools. Two groups of native English listeners provided assessments of intelligibility and comprehensibility for speech samples provided by L1 Japanese learners of English in the US. One group involved students on a large university campus who were regularly exposed to a range of accents, including Japanese; the other group included members of the general community who had little exposure to foreign accents. Minimal pairs involving the contrasts /r/-/l/ and /s/-/θ/ were selected. Although both pairs of sounds were challenging for the learners, they exhibited different functional load values. The /r/-/l/ load was considered the highest, whereas the /s/-/θ/ load was relatively low according to Phonological CorpusTools (Hall et al., 2017) using the Irvine Phonotactic Online Dictionary (Vaden et al., 2009) as the corpus. The words containing the target sounds were embedded in short carrier sentences in which either member of a minimal pair was acceptable. This approach controlled the influence of semantic context on word identification. In the intelligibility task, after listeners heard each sample, they saw the sentence frame on a computer screen and typed the missing target word in the space provided. After listening to a sample a second time, listeners used a 9-point scale to provide a rating of comprehensibility.

Results for the student listener group in the Pfau (2020) study revealed 62% correct identification of the /s/-/θ/ words but only 45% of the /r/-/l/ words. The accuracy of the general community members was lower overall, demonstrating little influence of functional load values (i.e., 41% accuracy for /s/-/θ/ and 39% for /r/-/l/). In terms of comprehensibility, both listener groups reported more difficulty understanding the /r/-/l/ speech samples. In sum, "FL [functional load] alone as a device for developing instructional materials does not paint a complete picture of how listeners will respond to that speech" (Pfau, 2020, p. 42).

Error Gravity

In contrast to functional load, the concept of error gravity takes a more subjective approach from the listeners' perspective and may help determine priorities for instruction. Error gravity recognizes a larger impact on comprehensibility for some errors versus others (Munro, 2018). Gagnon and Hardison (2022) found variability in comprehensibility ratings for

L1 English learners' recorded productions of six L2 Korean phonological processes according to the process, presentation condition (i.e., excised from connected speech or presented in context), and rater group (i.e., native Korean listeners or advanced non-native listeners). Learners at the novice-high to intermediate-mid American Council on the Teaching of Foreign Languages (ACTFL) proficiency levels were asked to read a passage in Korean and then discuss it with a native speaker of Korean. This dictogloss type of task, coined a *DictoSpeak*, facilitated discussion between the native speaker and each learner to ensure the occurrence of lexical items involving the target phonological processes.

Overall, native Korean listeners in the Gagnon and Hardison (2022) study rated samples more negatively than the advanced non-native listeners. Mean comprehensibility ratings from the native listeners were lowest for the excised tokens that involved lateralization (i.e., production of a nasal /n/ as [l] when the nasal is preceded or followed by /l/ in final consonant position). Assessments from both rater groups increased (i.e., tokens were easier to understand) for all phonological processes when the tokens were presented in their semantic context. Context appeared to have had a moderating effect on the assessment of comprehensibility by both groups of raters, and it emphasized the importance of giving learners opportunities to practise pronouncing phonological processes in communicative contexts.

Lingua Franca Core

Based on interactions between non-native speakers in international contexts, J. Jenkins (2002) proposed the Lingua Franca Core (LFC), which included features whose presence was thought to act as "safeguards of mutual intelligibility" in lingua franca interactions and thus should be addressed in instruction (p. 96). Core elements, mostly segmental issues, were considered crucial for intelligibility; non-core elements, including suprasegmental and connected speech phenomena, were not considered to be crucial. The LFC was based on the analysis of 27 episodes of communicative breakdowns between upper-intermediate to low-advanced L2 English speakers. Deterding (2013) reported comparable findings among non-native speakers for a corpus of 183 instances of misunderstandings in interactions, 158 (86.3%) of which were related to pronunciation. There were several methodological issues surrounding the LFC studies, including the difficulty in defining intelligibility, identification of the precise causes of misunderstandings (i.e., speaker's pronunciation or listener's lack of familiarity with the accent), and the disproportionate number of contributions across speakers.

Setting aside those concerns, general adoption of LFC guidelines for instruction of L2 learners who might be communicating with L1 and/or highly proficient L2 English speakers could be problematic in terms of both intelligibility and socio-affective concerns. The core elements in the LFC omitted the interdental fricatives /θ/ (*th̲ink*) and /ð/ (*th̲is*). Mispronunciations involving these fricatives might elicit a negative affective response from a more proficient interlocutor to utterances such as what sounds like *sink* for *think*, *sum* for *thumb*, or *mouse* for *mouth*. Even if semantic context facilitates listening comprehension, the interlocutor's reaction could have a negative and longer-lasting impact on the learner's affect and subsequent willingness to communicate. In the absence of sufficient support from semantic context, listeners' word recognition could also be slowed or derailed by mispronunciations depending on variables such as the target sound's position in the word. The first two sounds in a word are crucial to the word recognition process (e.g., Fort et al., 2012; Hardison, 2005b, 2018b; Skipper, van Wassenhove et al., 2007; Tyler, 1984).

The non-core elements in the LFC included suprasegmental issues and connected speech. Relegating connected speech phenomena to a non-core status may have resulted from their absence in the non-native speech corpus (Sewell, 2017). In interactions between native and non-native speakers, however, mutual intelligibility could be challenged by (a) the absence in non-native speech of features that native listeners expect and may rely on; and (b) the presence of these features in native speech that may cause perceptual difficulty for learners who have not received any instruction on them. On this point, J.D. Brown and Crowther (2023) argued that

> the reality of L2 English usage is that CS [connected speech] is a key feature of native–nonnative interaction and has significant implications for the attainment of mutual understanding. The teaching of CS should thus benefit nonnative users of English both perceptually and productively, and at the same time, should in no way hinder, and maybe even enhance, nonnative–nonnative English interactions. (p. 8)

Preparing Teachers to Teach Pronunciation

This section outlines some important issues that impact the preparation of teachers to take a multimodal approach to teaching pronunciation, including confidence, awareness of visual cues and articulatory settings, knowledge of pronunciation learning strategies and phonetic transcription, and recognition of the benefits of practice in analysing L2 speech samples.

Lack of Teacher Confidence and Training

In addition to issues related to materials for teaching pronunciation, classroom teachers have also expressed concerns about their ability to carry out the task. Some teachers, including L1 speakers of the target language, lack confidence and sometimes accurate information about articulatory phonetics when they address pronunciation issues, and they often want more training. In a survey of teachers in 67 ESL programs across Canada, only 30% reported having received any formal training for teaching pronunciation (Breitkreutz et al., 2001).

A follow-up study was conducted in Canada in 2010 by Foote et al. (2011) involving surveys completed by 159 teachers, 82% of whom were L1 English speakers. There was no substantial change in pronunciation instruction, although the teachers reported implementing a slightly greater focus on the teaching of segmentals. In addition, 86% of the teachers reported that they regularly integrated pronunciation into their general ESL classes and corrected mispronunciations. Their preferred pedagogical activities included the use of minimal pairs (e.g., in a game), learner repetition following teacher modelling, and learners' self-assessment of their recorded speech. Of particular relevance to this chapter were the teachers' recommendations that learners use mirrors to see their own articulations and become aware of *proprioceptive feedback* (i.e., a talker's sense of the position and movement of the articulators in the vocal tract). The teachers also used diagrams of the mouth to teach correct articulation. A clear majority (89%) of the teachers agreed that pronunciation instruction should help make learners "comfortably intelligible" to their listeners; however, only slightly more than half of the teachers (58%) were "completely comfortable" teaching segmentals or all aspects of prosody (56%), and 75% wanted more training in teaching pronunciation (Foote et al., 2011, p. 14).

The perception of insufficient training also emerged in an online survey by A. Henderson et al. (2012) of English pronunciation teaching in seven European countries (Finland, France, Germany, Macedonia, Poland, Spain, and Switzerland). A total of 459 respondents rated the quality of their training on average as 2.91 on a 5-point scale (1 = *extremely poor*, 5 = *excellent*). The source of this perception was unclear. The relatively low rating did not appear to be a reflection of their mean self-assessed pronunciation skill of 4.17 on the same 5-point scale. It also did not appear to stem from the importance the respondents attached to English ($M = 4.66$) or to pronunciation as compared to other language skills ($M = 4.17$) measured on a 5-point scale (1 = *not important at all*, 5 = *extremely important*). The authors commented that the lack of training was not compatible with the emphasis placed on English pronunciation in commonly used assessment tools such as the International English Language Testing System (IELTS), the Test of English as a Foreign Language (TOEFL), or CEFR.

In general, some of the lack of teaching comfort reported by teachers appears to arise from gaps and inaccuracies in their knowledge of such features as (a) the production of individual sounds; (b) the pattern of stressed and unstressed syllables in a word; and (c) the impact on meaning of the placement of focal stress in a sentence such that misplacement might result in misunderstanding (Couper, 2021). For many teachers, these challenges constitute a narrative of insufficiency in education and/or support. Whether teachers speak English as an L1 or L2, they often express frustration related to (a) insufficient support from books, including suggestions on how to integrate pronunciation into classes; (b) the amount of time needed to find extra materials; and (c) insufficient time to address pronunciation in the classroom. In Couper's study, L2 English-speaking teachers lacked confidence in their own pronunciation, asked questions about how they could improve it, and about how they could teach pronunciation if they were not confident in their own ability (e.g., to teach intonation). In addition, the teachers reported a lack of knowledge of phonetics and phonology. In sum, sufficient access to accurate knowledge and materials is crucial in teacher education and contributes to increased confidence.

Awareness of Visual Cues

All the above issues strongly support the inclusion of a course on pronunciation teaching in teacher education programs involving relevant research findings, curriculum development, and an opportunity for teaching practice (Derwing, 2008). To this list can be added an awareness of the sources of visual cues in communication, such as a talker's lip movements, brow raise, and other muscular facial movements associated with speech as well as hand-arm gestures, body position, and head movement (Hardison & Pennington, 2021). These cues establish a rapport between interlocutors and are important in the exchange of information (see chapter 6). It is also important to acknowledge the different cultural norms that may be present in a classroom that can affect eye gaze behaviour (Blais et al., 2008), and to encourage discussion of their implications for interaction and teaching. Teachers can show some recordings from various media sources in audio-only, video-only, and then audiovisual modalities to demonstrate the overall contribution of each modality to comprehension, and they can emphasize the variability in articulatory gestures and voices across talkers.

Multimodal elements are also involved in applications of theatre voice training to language pedagogy. This approach emphasizes raising awareness of the physiological components of speech, such as articulatory setting and voice quality, before proceeding to linguistic elements (Hardison & Sonchaeng, 2005). Techniques at the preparation stage address expansion of the vowel space, breathing linked to rhythm and pausing, voice projection and flow, and enhancement of pitch range, followed by the practice stage, which includes shadowing a speaker (i.e., imitating the speech) and then mirroring (i.e., shadowing plus imitation of facial expression, gestures, posture, etc.), with the ultimate goal of practising monologues and dialogues in meaningful contexts (see also LaScotte et al., 2023).

Awareness of Different Articulatory Settings

Students should be aware of different articulatory settings across languages. For example, English is among those languages in which spread lips occur with front tongue raising, as in the vowel /i/ (e.g., *heed*), and rounded lips occur with back tongue raising, as in the vowel /u/ (e.g., *boot*). Other commonly learned languages such as French have front tongue raising with both spread lips (e.g., /i/ *l̲ivre*, "book") and rounded lips (e.g., /y/ *tu̲*, "you").

Web-based tools, such as those described earlier (e.g., SPAN), may be useful for both native and non-native English-speaking teachers so they can show learners what the internal articulators are doing during speech production to help them develop proprioceptive intelligence; or, as Underhill (2012) put it, "Know your mouth." It is challenging for teachers to explain how a sound is produced while simultaneously producing it!

For some L2 learners of English, producing English sounds is uncomfortable or awkward because the production of sounds in their L1 may not involve as much movement of the mouth (Honikman, 1964; Vance, 1987). Honikman (1964) recounted remarks made by foreign students in England who had studied English in their home countries. When asked for their impressions of English spoken in England, they often commented that English speakers didn't move their mouths when they spoke, echoing Jones's caution to French students learning English phonetics (Collins & Mees, 2002, Lecture 1). In contrast, I have heard the opposite observation in the US from East Asian students, specifically that Americans move their mouths a lot when they talk. Implicit in these learners' comments is the characterization of the visible articulatory settings of L1 speakers of English, whether British or American, as not only different from their own but also apparently in some cases not what they had expected prior to arriving in the host country.

Following awareness raising, the next step involves Jones's notion of mouth gymnastics (Collins & Mees, 2002, Lecture 9) and Pennington's (1996, p. 79) tongue calisthenics. Students should become comfortable with the range of motion of the movable articulators, notably the lips, jaw, and tongue. Beginning with the most visible, address the visual salience of lip rounding by producing /u/ (e.g., *hoot*) and then spreading the lips by producing /i/ (e.g., *heat*) – then continue to repeat the sequence of sounds. At this point, these movements can be treated as gymnastics, not necessarily as speech sounds.

Pronunciation Learning Strategies

Both teachers and learners should be aware of pronunciation learning strategies involving visual input, which learners can test for themselves to determine the strategies that work best for them. In studies exploring pronunciation learning strategies, there is little mention of articulatory setting or visual speech cues. Of the 100 adult ESL learners (immigrants) interviewed in Canada about their pronunciation needs and strategies, 60 reported that they could control their accents, and of those, about 21 reported using "miscellaneous strategies," which included moving their mouths more (Derwing & Rossiter, 2002, p. 161).

Eckstein (2007) examined the correlations between the pronunciation learning strategies reported by 183 adult ESL learners enrolled at a university in the US and their pronunciation scores obtained in spontaneous speech. Of the 28 strategies reported, none mentioned attention to talkers' visual cues, and only one learner made reference to articulatory setting by reporting the adjustment of facial muscles to produce new sounds. Results showed a significant correlation between higher pronunciation scores and respondents' reported noticing of others' English mistakes, asking for pronunciation help, and adjustment of their facial muscles. Of these three strategies, only one – asking for pronunciation help – was widely used (by 81% of the participants); adjusting facial muscles on a regular basis was reported by only 48%.

In a more recent study, Szyszka (2015) found that survey respondents, who were advanced L2 English speakers working as higher education specialists in EFL, envisioned important roles for awareness-raising and instruction in developing their phonological competence. They also described active learning strategies such as imitating native speakers and singing English songs in addition to shadowing actors and singers. The respondents' interest in the speech field may have influenced their strategy use.

Although there was no specific mention of attention to talkers' visual cues in the Szyszka (2015) study, other research involving participants in a short-term study abroad program to Germany reported a significant increase in (a) the amount of attention L1 AE learners of L2 German reported paying to the facial cues and gestures of native German speakers while abroad; and (b) the frequency with which they imitated native speech (Hardison, 2014a). In contrast, L1 AE and L1 Chinese sojourners on an 8-week study abroad program to Japan showed only a slight, non-significant increase in their reported strategies involving attention to the lip and/or head movements of native speakers of Japanese in order to imitate their speech (Hardison & Okuno, 2022). This finding might be a reflection of the perceived information value of the lip movements in Japanese, which Vance (1987) placed on the low end of the continuum of articulatory movement across languages.

Multisensory Approach to Using Phonetic Transcription

A multisensory approach to speech learning includes the use of phonetic transcription, which has a pedagogical application beyond the study of phonetics (Baker, 2014). A knowledge of articulatory phonetics and the IPA is critical to the development of phonological literacy among language teachers and learners (Couper, 2021; Hardison, 2014b; Mompean & Fouz-González, 2021). As a component of pronunciation instruction, it can raise learners' awareness and noticing of L2 sounds in an effort to encourage output (Saito, 2013), and it may facilitate memory recall of L2 sounds (Mompean & Lintunen, 2015). For both learners and teachers, phonetic symbols and articulatory descriptions serve as a metalanguage to use to conceptualize speech (Mompean & Fouz-González, 2021) as well as a means by which to communicate more precisely about L2 sounds (Couper, 2021).

The IPA, which crosses linguistic and geographical boundaries, represents a one-to-one correspondence between sound and symbol and makes salient the features that may be hidden in orthography. These features include (a) the AE flap (e.g., the medial consonant sound in words such as *pre<u>tt</u>y*); (b) the frequently occurring processes involved in the pronunciation of connected speech (e.g., the palatalization involved in pronouncing /s/ in *miss* as *sh* /ʃ/ when preceding a palatal glide [j] in *<u>y</u>ou*, such as in the phrase *miss you* [mɪʃu]); (c) and differences in the way a word is pronounced across speakers (e.g., *huge* with /h/ [hjudʒ] or without /h/ [judʒ]). Already 40 years ago, with reference to the benefits of being able to read the phonetic transcription of natural speech, Prator and Robinett (1985) made the following observation:

> Your attention may not be called to these [unstressed vowels] at all when you *hear* a word spoken, but you can *see* them as clearly as the stressed vowels in a phonetic transcription. The eye is more analytical than the ear. We can see separately all the symbols that make up a written word, but we can hardly hear individually all the sounds that compose it as it is normally spoken.... There is every advantage in being able to have your eye aid your ear. Something learned in two different ways is probably four times as well learned. (p. 2)

In addition, learners may benefit from taking a kinesthetic approach to working with phonetic symbols. Celce-Murcia et al. (2010, p. 338) recommended that for learners familiar with the symbols, teachers could display large cards, each with a symbol, a word containing the sound, and a picture. Learners could then group the cards in various combinations to transcribe words.

Tactual reinforcement is particularly important for some learner populations who cannot rely on vision. In a study by Medina González and Hardison (2022), adult L1 Spanish low vision and blind learners of English improved their pronunciation of English consonants and vowels through a set of tools called ADEPT: Assistive Design for English Phonetic Tools. ADEPT involves auditory-visual-tactual integration through the use of visual-tactile IPA symbol cards and an auditory-visual companion website based on the Universal Design for Learning (CAST, 2018). Each card includes a symbol, description, and website reference number, all with braille notations. The website includes printed and audio-recorded information on the articulation of AE consonants and vowels with audio recordings of each sound in isolation, in syllables, and in words. The multisensory nature of ADEPT was designed to promote inclusion in the classroom for low vision and blind learners and collaboration with sighted learners. The study participants demonstrated a significant improvement in their production of AE vowels and reported a sense of accomplishment in learning phonetic terminology that allowed them to interact with each other and share their views on learning the sounds.

Analysis of L2 Speech Samples

Finally, as part of teacher preparation and an effective prelude to a teaching practicum, there may also be a benefit from coursework that involves experience in analysing L2 speech samples, including a discussion of the potential impact on easy or comfortable intelligibility of the speakers' misarticulations, and suggestions that teachers could offer for improvement using auditory, visual, and proprioceptive information. An available database of speech samples is The Speech Accent Archive (http://accent.gmu.edu), developed by Steven H. Weinberger at George Mason University. This is a growing online archive of audio samples obtained from a wide range of L2 English learners and can be searched according to biographical data (e.g., L1, age at the onset of English learning), language learning method (i.e., academic vs. naturalistic), and specific consonant, vowel, or syllable issue (e.g., /r/-/l/ problems). The recorded speech samples were provided by learners who read the same paragraph, which contains most of the AE consonants, vowels, and consonant clusters. The linguistic focus of this archive involves segmental and syllable structure issues versus suprasegmental elements (e.g., intonation).

In addition, a good exercise for pre- and in-service teachers is a critical review of various types of instructional materials, including web-based tools. In fact, it is important for teachers to evaluate all types of teaching materials critically before using them because errors do occur. Instructions in textbooks for how a sound is produced may be accompanied by an incorrect diagram, such as one that does not show a lowered velum for the production of the velar nasal /ŋ/ as in *si<u>ng</u>* (e.g., Dale & Poms, 2005, p. 224). In addition, the labelling of places of articulation along the upper surface of the vocal tract and the principal regions of the dorsum of the tongue is not consistent across instructional materials, which also vary in the phonetic notation systems they use.

Chapter 7 in Review

This chapter began with a look to the past at Daniel Jones, in whose work we can find the roots of numerous contemporary topics on the teaching of pronunciation, including (a) setting aside the notion of a standard to focus on the goal of easy or comfortable intelligibility; (b) accepting different accents; (c) being aware of the important role of visual cues and proprioceptive intelligence; (d) having knowledge of the articulatory setting of a language; and (e) practising mouth gymnastics before tackling the production of consonants and vowels. These elements can be part of a language class and can serve as the foundation for teacher education, which should also encourage teachers to engage in the analysis of L2 speech samples and critical review of teaching materials.

Throughout this chapter there has also been a general theme of maximizing input from more than one sensory modality – a theme that has not always received sufficient attention in the teaching and learning of second-language speech. Better knowledge of the multimodal factors involved in the acquisition of second-language speech should help build confidence in pronunciation teaching. Chapter 8 next presents details of a multisensory approach to the teaching of speech sounds in a stand-alone pronunciation course and in a course more broadly focused on the development of oral communication skills.

Chapter 7 Notes

1. The volume by Collins and Mees (2002) contains the writings (e.g., lectures, correspondence, etc.) of Daniel Jones; however, it does not have any page numbers. For reader reference, the lecture number accompanies all quotes from the book. Each lecture is only a few pages in length.
2. This lecture does not have a known date, but Collins and Mees determined that it was delivered prior to 1916.
3. The terms *tap* and *flap* are often used interchangeably; in this book, *flap* is used to refer to a rapid striking of the tongue tip against the alveolar area behind the upper front teeth.
4. The rainbow passage is available at https://www.york.ac.uk/media/languageandlinguistics/documents/currentstudents/linguisticsresources/Standardised-reading.pdf.

Chapter 8

A Multisensory Approach to Teaching and Learning Speech Sounds

It is likely that the human brain has evolved to develop, learn and operate optimally in multisensory environments.

– Shams & Seitz (2008, p. 411)

*****

Background

The previous chapter focused on the historical roots of some current issues in pronunciation teaching and their role in language teacher training. A key player was Daniel Jones, a prominent phonetician and authority on the pronunciation of English and the application of phonetics to language teaching in the first half of the 20th century. There were other players, of course, who also contributed to the development of the field.

In a review of 150 years of pronunciation teaching, Murphy and Baker (2015) outlined four waves of change and some of their instructional innovators. The first wave began in the 1850s with Berlitz and Dubois (1882), who were interested in teaching learners to converse extemporaneously in the target language. An important inspirational element in the second wave was the establishment in the mid-1880s of the International Phonetic Association with well-known supporters such as Henry Sweet and Daniel Jones in England. This period of time saw the development of the International Phonetic Alphabet (IPA), which Jones promoted as a critical part of pronunciation learning and teaching (see chapter 7). In the third wave in the 1980s, classroom teachers were introduced to communicative means of teaching pronunciation (e.g., Celce-Murcia, 1983). Murphy and Baker (2015) marked the beginning of the fourth wave in the mid-1990s with the emergence of empirical research involving three areas of ESL pronunciation teaching: (a) phonological features that need to be taught; (b) effective teaching methods; and (c) teachers' and learners' beliefs about pronunciation instruction. Among these waves and their leading scholars, Jones appeared to be the only one to recognize explicitly the value of visual cues.[1]

The current chapter builds on the foundation laid by the previous chapters in continuing the theme of a multisensory approach to the teaching and learning of speech sounds. I have used the content as part of a course on phonetics and phonology for pre-service ESL/EFL teachers in both in-person and virtual instructional formats. The basic goals of the course are to:

- raise awareness to the multisensory nature of speech, emphasizing how consonants and vowels look, sound, and feel;
- develop phonetic knowledge;
- demonstrate the use of technological tools (for reviews, see Bliss et al., 2018; Hardison, 2018a), especially those that make the internal articulators visible;
- practise speech sounds in the classroom to promote proprioceptive intelligence; and
- provide encouragement for students to practise beyond the classroom.

Although the course includes a discussion of word-level and sentence-level stress, rhythm, and intonation, among other topics (see also Murphy, 2018; Pennington & Rogerson-Revell, 2019; Rogerson-Revell, 2011), the focus of the current chapter is a multisensory approach to teaching the segmental level of speech and common phonological processes of connected speech that affect perception and production using AE examples. The chapter is designed to contribute to the knowledge base of teacher trainers as well as pre- and in-service teachers.

We begin with an overview of the vocal organs followed by specifics on the articulation of speech sounds, an explanation of common processes in connected speech, issues to consider in teaching connected speech to L2 learners (see J.D. Brown & Crowther, 2023), and, finally, ideas for a stand-alone pronunciation course for L2 learners and for incorporating pronunciation into a course more broadly focused on the development of L2 oral skills.

The Vocal Organs

The vocal organs or organs of speech (e.g., vocal folds, tongue) play important roles in speech production (see Figure 8.1). In this process, the stream of air from the lungs can be interrupted by other organs to create audible sound. Air must pass through the trachea, at the top of which is a box-like structure, the larynx, "the engine of the phonatory system" (Collins et al., 2019, p. 32). The larynx surrounds the vocal folds (also referred to in some works as "vocal cords" or "vocal bands") of membranous tissue, which are part of the glottis (see Figure 8.2).

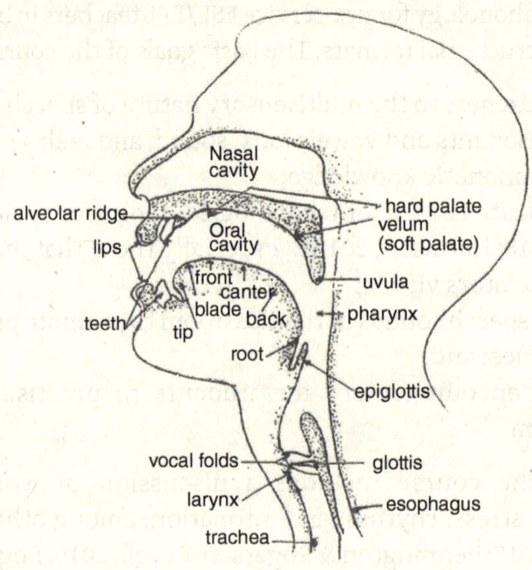

FIGURE 8.1 Mid-Sagittal View of the Major Vocal Organs

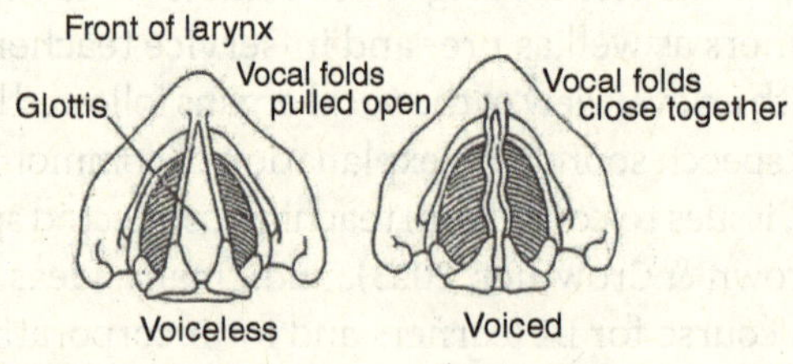

FIGURE 8.2 Glottis and Vocal Folds

The Glottis

The glottis is the first element that shapes a person's speech (Esling et al., 2019). The vocal folds are situated opposite one another at the top of the larynx to form an opening across the glottis. They are fixed adjacent to each other at the front (the palpable *Adam's apple*) but are horizontally movable at the back where they are attached to the arytenoid cartilages. When the arytenoids are drawn together, the vocal folds may come together firmly and block the airstream, as in the production of the glottal stop ([ʔ]), commonly associated with a Cockney accent. The glottal stop may occur in some AE contexts, including the post-vocalic position preceding a syllable-final voiceless consonant such as /p, t, k, ʧ/ (e.g., *stop* [stɑʔp]). In glottal stopping, pressure builds up beneath the vocal folds and is then released when they separate.[vi] Students may be able to feel the vocal folds opening and closing by producing a series of very weak coughs (O'Connor, 1973). In contrast, the folds are wide apart in producing *Sh!*; the sound that we hear is created by the obstruction in the mouth. Between these two extreme positions of the vocal folds is the setting for [h] (e.g., *hot*), where the folds are close enough to cause slight turbulence but not stoppage of the airflow.

When the airstream passes through the vocal folds and the muscles tighten and move closer together, the folds vibrate and produce a voiced sound, as shown in Figure 8.2. Students can experience the proprioceptive feedback of voicing in one of several ways: (a) by placing their fingers gently over the front of their throats and saying *aaah* to feel the vibration; (b) by covering their ears while humming to hear and feel the vibrations; or (c) by contrasting a prolonged hissing sound *ssss* with a buzzing sound *zzzz* and paying attention to the sound and feel of the off and on of voicing. When the vocal folds are relaxed, air moves up from the lungs through the glottis freely, producing a voiceless sound. The voicing distinction serves a critical function in the description of English consonants. It can create differences in meaning between many pairs of words (e.g., *pit*, *bit*; *time*, *dime*; *fine*, *vine*; *sip*, *zip*).

With this foundation, students can now become aware of the nasal and oral cavities in the vocal tract, the concept of resonance, the function of the tongue, and points of articulation for consonant production, including an emphasis on the visual element and proprioceptive feedback, as they become more familiar with movement of the articulators.

---

vi. Editor's Note: Specifically, substitution of a glottal stop for medial /t/ is associated with a Cockney accent, as in *water* [wɑʔə] or *bottle* [bɔʔl̩]. Unlike in Cockney, in which the oral stop is replaced by a glottal stop, in AE the oral stop is usually retained – though in the case of post-vocalic /t/, substitution of glottal stop is spreading among young people in the US (see Editor's Note xii below). When a glottal stop precedes a voiceless (oral) consonant, that consonant is said to be (pre-)glottalized. The release of a glottalized stop can be realized as aspiration on the glottalized consonant, as in *stop* [stɑʔp^{h}]. However, the built-up air pressure can be carried over into following linguistic context, so that the release occurs on a later consonant, as in *Stop it!* [stɑʔpɪt^{h}]; or the pressurized air can be expelled after vocalization has ceased, that is, during pause, as in [stɑʔp #] followed by an expulsion of breath. – MCP

The Vocal Tract

Above the larynx is a single cavity known as the pharynx, which branches into two other cavities, the nasal and the oral, as shown in Figure 8.1. The vibration (*resonance*) of the air in these cavities co-occurs with vibrations from the vocal folds. The shape of the oral cavity can be changed substantially, and this results in changes in the sounds that are produced.

The nasal cavity's role in speech production is one of resonance. When the vocal folds are vibrating, if the velum (or soft palate) is lowered, the pharynx, nasal cavity, and oral cavity are connected, and the air vibrates throughout. Have students place their hands over their ears while humming to get a better understanding of the resonating quality of the vocal tract when producing the continuous non-turbulent airflow that characterizes nasals ([m] <u>m</u>y, [n] <u>n</u>o, [ŋ] si<u>ng</u>), approximants ([ɹ] <u>r</u>*ock*, [l] <u>l</u>*ock*, [j] <u>y</u>*es*, [w] <u>w</u>*in*), and vowels. Then have students place their lips together and, while humming, have them pinch the nose to demonstrate that production of nasal sounds involves air escaping through the nose. In addition to the role of nasal resonance in distinguishing /m/, /n/, and /ŋ/ from other phonemes, the degree of nasality in AE speech is often considered an indicator of social or regional background (Esling et al., 2019).

The oral cavity is variable in size and shape, and it houses the mobile articulators of the tongue, teeth, and lips. The positioning of the internal movable organs of the mouth to produce a natural (i.e., unexaggerated) utterance influences the external, visible manifestations of an articulatory setting. As O'Connor (1973) noted, "The tongue is the organ of speech *par excellence*; in many languages 'tongue' is synonymous with 'language' itself and we can speak of 'the tongues of men and of angels,' being 'tongue-tied' and 'having a silver tongue'" (p. 34). Take advantage of the agility of the tongue to familiarize students with the primary points of articulation, starting with the lips placed together to produce *bilabial* (*bi*: two; *labial*: pertaining to the lips) sounds and then moving backwards to points on the upper surface of the oral tract. This will set the stage for later introduction of the individual consonant sounds at these points of articulation. Include mention of the principal parts of the tongue: the tip, blade (behind the tip), front (partly beneath the hard palate at rest), centre (partly beneath the hard palate and soft palate/*velum*), and back (partly beneath the velum). The tip and blade are the most mobile. Using a mirror, students can see some of their tongue movements. For example, to say *ahk* [ɑk], the vowel portion is produced with a flat tongue, the back of which then rises to meet the velum to produce [k].

Have students make contact between the lower lip and upper front teeth (*labiodental* position). Then insert the tongue between the teeth (amount of protrusion varies across talkers, phonetic contexts, speech rates, etc.) for the *interdental* position. Move the tongue tip or blade back slowly to just behind the upper teeth to make contact with the *alveolar ridge* (also referred to as the *teeth ridge*). Students may be able to feel the ridge's bumpy nature, which also varies across individuals. A bony structure, the *hard palate*, is next, followed by the soft palate or velum at the back of the roof of the mouth. Students should be able to move the tongue tip over the hard palate, which can be ticklish, but may not be able to reach the velum comfortably with the tongue.

Students can now look at the diagram of the typical mid-sagittal view of the head (Figure 8.1) to see these major features of the vocal tract. To review these topics outside of class, students can also use a variety of media resources (e.g., YouTube) to: (a) shadow talkers silently to get used to their own internal and external articulatory movements before adding sound; (b) observe and make notes of the movements of the lips and jaw of different people speaking the target language (Honikman, 1964); and (c) access a range of models of various accents so they can choose one(s) they expect to be exposed to the most (Esling & Wong, 1983).

Articulation of Speech Sounds

Sequence of Instruction

Ideally, time should be set aside to address all sounds in order to ensure accurate knowledge of their articulation because this cannot be assumed, especially when students come from a variety of instructional backgrounds. They will benefit from correct knowledge as a foundation for continued practice on their own. More time can be spent on sounds that pose the most problems for individuals or specific L1 groups in a particular class.

Although some textbooks begin with vowels, starting with consonants has several advantages. Consonants involve more precision in their articulation, which is reflected in their phonetic descriptions. They generally convey more linguistic information and are typically easier to speechread because observers can watch for the movement of the lips and jaw, whereas vowels are formed by the overall shape of the mouth (see chapter 1). Learning consonants first is also easier for students because the IPA symbols for many sounds are the same as the letters that tend to represent the sounds in standard orthography. In addition, consonants do not differ as much across varieties of English as vowels do; vowels are the major carriers of accent. Finally, on a typical consonant chart (see Figure 8.3), the sounds that teachers start with in the upper left corner (i.e., stops or nasals) are usually ones that do not present a substantial challenge, so starting here may also serve as a source of positive affect at the beginning of the task. Less challenging tasks may increase motivation to learn and provide a foundation for progressing to more difficult sounds.

As discussion of consonants proceeds, for reference, students can complete a chart as each sound and symbol is introduced. For individual reference outside of class, students can look at the online chart of the International Phonetic Alphabet (International Phonetic Association, 2004–9). On that site, moving the mouse over a symbol displays the symbol's name and character code for word processing purposes.

Phonemes

To native listeners of a language, the acoustic signal may sound like an invariable sequence of discrete sounds, but, in fact, it is a signal filled with overlapping acoustic cues that vary from one utterance to the next. The sounds we hear (i.e., *phones*) are the product of variability, the sources of which include the phonetic context and prosodic structure of the utterance, talker characteristics, speech rate, speech style, and so forth. Closely related phones (variants) that do not distinguish meaning between words in a language are related at a more abstract level to a *phoneme*. For example, the /p/ sounds in *pot* and *spot* differ phonetically. In *pot*, there is aspiration (a puff of air) after the release of the stop; in *spot*, there is no aspiration. Aspirated and unaspirated sounds have similar characteristics but do not occur in the same environments in English. They therefore cannot contrast meaning and are treated as allophonic variants of the same phoneme, in this case /p/; they occur in *complementary distribution* (i.e., in specific phonetic and/or prosodic contexts, described in the "Prosodic Phonology" section below). However, the phonemes /p/ and /b/, which share place and manner of articulation, contrast meaning by creating numerous minimal pairs (e.g., *pat, bat*; *tap, tab*). The difference between these two phonemes is one of voicing (i.e., /p/ is voiceless and /b/ is voiced). In summary, Figure 8.3 shows the symbols for consonant phonemes, or the basic, functional AE consonantal units. Phonemes, as the most meaningful, functionally distinctive sounds in the ambient language environment, are the focus of the human perceptual system's attunement process during the first year of life (e.g., Kuhl et al., 2006; see also chapter 2).

Describing Consonants

Elements to keep in mind when describing the articulation of sounds include: (a) the overall articulatory setting; (b) the general position of the jaw; (c) muscular tension of the tongue, lips, cheeks, jaw, and pharynx; (d) tongue shape; (e) lip position; and (f) pressure exerted by the articulators. With the presentation of each sound and IPA symbol in class, familiar words can be used as examples with associated images to facilitate comprehension and memory recall (e.g., Celce-Murcia et al., 2010, p. 337). Students can take an active role in this process by suggesting some words that are familiar to them.

Consonants are described according to three characteristics: (a) place of articulation (where they are produced in the mouth); (b) manner of articulation (how they are produced); and (c) voicing (whether the vocal folds are vibrating or not). Practise each consonant sound in a CV syllable and sample words while noting any phonotactic constraints, such as the absence in syllable-initial position of the velar nasal [ŋ], which is frequently represented orthographically as the *-ng* ending (e.g., *si<u>ng</u>*). For practice, use choral response first as students look in their mirrors to watch their articulations, followed by individual responses.

	bilabial	labio-dental	inter-dental	alveolar	palato-alveolar	palatal	velar
stop	p b			t d			k g
nasal	m			n			ŋ
fricative		f v	θ ð	s z	ʃ ʒ		
affricate					tʃ dʒ		
approximant				ɹ		j	w (labio-velar)
lateral approximant				l			

Note. In cells with two symbols, the voiceless one is on the left and the voiced one is on the right.

FIGURE 8.3 Consonant Phonemes of American English

After acquainting students with the places of consonant articulation and voicing while building their proprioceptive knowledge, focus on individual sounds and their IPA symbols according to manner of articulation as shown in the leftmost column in Figure 8.3. The symbols in the chart represent AE consonant phonemes.

Based on manner of articulation, consonants can be grouped into the following natural classes: (a) *obstruents* (characterized by obstructed airflow), including stops, fricatives, and affricates; (b) *sonorants* (characterized by continuous non-turbulent airflow), including nasals and approximants (and vowels); (c) *continuants* (characterized by incomplete closure of the vocal tract), including approximants, fricatives (and vowels); (d) *approximants* (liquids: /r/, /l/; and glides: /w/, /j/); and (e) *sibilants* (hissing sounds), which include the fricatives /s/, /z/, /ʃ/, and /ʒ/ and the affricates /tʃ/ and /dʒ/ (see more below).[vii]

In Figure 8.3, in cells with two symbols, the symbol on the left represents the voiceless sound and the one on the right represents the voiced sound. In English, the nasals and approximants are voiced. Voiced sounds are produced with vibrating vocal folds, which can be felt by placing the fingers on the front of the throat during production. For voiceless sounds, the folds do not vibrate.

Consonant sounds may be classified as *fortis* or *lenis*. Articulation of fortis sounds (/p, t, k, f, θ, s, ʃ, ʧ/) is stronger, produced with more energetic tensing of muscles, and they are voiceless. In some contexts, the fortis stops (/p, t, k/) are followed by aspiration, as noted above. These contexts often involve the stop in the onset position of a stressed syllable (but see "Prosodic Phonology" below for a full explanation). Articulation of lenis sounds (/b, d, g, v, ð, z, ʒ, ʤ/) is weaker and produced with less energy. The lenis stops (/b, d, g/) are unaspirated and voiced when produced in isolation or in voiced phonetic environments, such as between vowels or other voiced sounds; however, before a pause or fortis consonant, some degree of voicing is usually lost.

See if students can distinguish the members of the minimal pair *heed* /hid/ and *heat* /hit/ based on visual information only (i.e., no sound). Make the closure for the final stop but do not release it in order to avoid making any sound. If students can distinguish these words, it signals an ability to use only visual information to detect the longer vowel before the lenis consonant (i.e., [d]).[2]

How Consonants Look, Sound, and Feel

In this chapter, the discussion of consonants and vowels is focused on a description of how each one looks, sounds, and feels. Multisensory

vii. Editor's Note: Some phoneticians differentiate /s, z/ from /ʃ, ʒ/ as sibilants versus shibilants, though the latter term is not in widespread use. – MCP training protocols are more effective for human learning in general than those that depend on only one sensory modality (Shams & Seitz, 2008). In addition, increasing proficiency in identifying L2 contrasts in one modality (i.e., visual or auditory) is associated with increased proficiency in the other (Hardison, 2003; Hazan et al., 2006; see also chapter 3).

The following manners of articulation follow the sequence in Figure 8.3, starting with the top leftmost cell:

1. *Stop* (or plosive): Stops are made by blocking the air from the lungs (i.e., creating an obstruction) and then releasing this closure, which produces the sound. Stops may be voiceless or voiced. The stops shown in Figure 8.3 occur at the bilabial, alveolar, and velar points of articulation (e.g., voiceless: [p] *spot*, [t] *stop*, [k] *scan*; voiced: [b] *bait*, [d] *date*, [g] *gate*).

   Fortis stops are followed by aspiration (a puff of air) after their release in some contexts (see "Prosodic Phonology" below). When aspiration occurs, the sounds are transcribed with a superscript [h] (e.g., [p^h]). Aspiration can often be felt on the back of the hand when placed in front of the mouth. Individuals who produce considerable aspiration may extinguish a lit match held in front of the mouth when the aspirated sound is produced. Because of aspiration, the above examples of voiceless unaspirated stops are *spot*, *stop*, and *scan* versus *pot*, *top*, and *can*; the latter three begin with aspirated stops.
2. *Nasal*: In English, the nasal sounds are voiced and occur in the same places of articulation as the (oral) stops. A nasal sound is created when the velum is lowered and air from the lungs escapes through the nose (e.g., [m] *might*, [n] *night*). The bilabial nasal and the bilabial oral stops are visually salient articulations, whereas the alveolar and velar nasals [n, ŋ] and stops [t, d, k, g] are less visually salient. The symbol for the velar nasal is known as *eng* or *angma*.
3. *Fricative*: There are several fricatives in English, which are produced when articulators are close enough to form a narrow channel creating a turbulent airflow and audible noise. Fricatives differ from stops because there is no complete closure or obstruction of the airflow, which continues during production.
   (a) Beginning at the front of the mouth, labiodentals are produced when the lower lip and upper teeth create the channel for air, as in *five*, which includes both the voiceless [f] and voiced [v] fricatives.
   (b) The next fricatives are the interdentals, which are produced with the tongue tip between the teeth: theta [θ] (e.g., *think*) is voiceless and eth [ð] (e.g., *the*) is voiced. The degree to which the tongue

is visible between the teeth varies according to factors such as talker, phonetic context, speech rate, and speech style.

(c) Moving back in the mouth are the alveolar fricatives. The voiceless [s] (e.g., *sip*) and voiced [z] (e.g., *zip*) fricatives are produced with the tongue tip below the ridge, with the sides of the tongue in contact with the sides of the palate. Have students place the articulators in this position, produce [s], and while holding that position, breathe in through the mouth. Cold air moves over the middle part of the tongue blade.

(d) The last pair of fricatives is often described as palato-alveolar (also known as post-alveolar or alveopalatal) because the narrow channel occurs between the tongue blade and the back part of the alveolar ridge extending towards the palate: esh [ʃ] (e.g., *ship*) is voiceless and yogh [ʒ] (e.g., *measure*) is voiced. The voiced sound [ʒ] does not occur in word-initial position in English. The palato-alveolar fricatives involve protrusion with a larger lip opening than for rounding. This protrusion may lower the frequency of the fricative noise, enhancing the contrast with the alveolar fricatives /s/ and /z/, which have no protrusion (Toda et al., 2003).

4. *Affricate*: An affricate is made when there is a closure as if to produce a stop, but that closure is released into a fricative. The affricates are visually salient articulations made with lip protrusion. There are different views on the transcription of the affricates. This chapter follows Ladefoged's guidelines (e.g., Ladefoged & Ferrari-Disner, 2012; Ladefoged & Johnson, 2015) for transcription of the voiceless sound as the t-esh ligature [tʃ] (e.g., *church*) and of the voiced sound as the d-yogh ligature [dʒ] (e.g., *judge*), both representing the two elements that are present in the production of each affricate.

5. *Approximant*: Approximants are produced when one articulator is brought close to another without causing audible friction. English approximants are voiced. This category includes two sounds described as *glides* or *semivowels* ([w] *win*, [j] *yes*), and two sounds that are described as *liquids* ([ɹ] *rock*, [l] *lock*). The terms *glide* and *liquid* are indicative of the fluid-like continuous articulation involved in producing these sounds.

(a) The labiovelar glide [w] involves a salient protrusion of the lips (hence the term *labio*) with rounding and raising of the back of the tongue towards the velum.

(b) The palatal glide [j] is made when the body of the tongue is high in the mouth near the palate and the sides of the tongue press against the inside of the upper teeth.

(c) The /r/ sound is among the most challenging sounds for L2 English learners. There are different /r/-like sounds (i.e., *rhotics*) across languages and within AE (Lindau, 1985). In some pronunciation books, the articulation of /r/ may be characterized as retroflex, as shown in Figure 8.4.

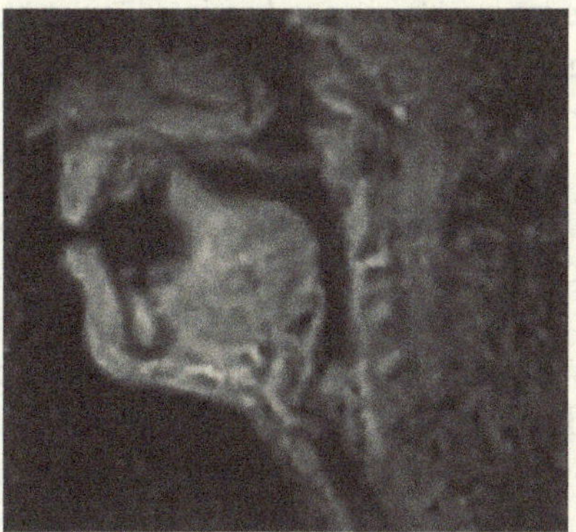

FIGURE 8.4 Screenshot from the SPAN Website Showing an MRI for the Articulation of a Retroflex /r/

Across varieties of English, there is variability in the articulatory gesture for both the retroflex /r/, which is produced with the tongue tip raised towards the alveolar ridge and the dorsum lowered, and the *bunched* /r/, which is produced with the tongue tip lowered and the dorsum raised, as shown in Figure 8.5.

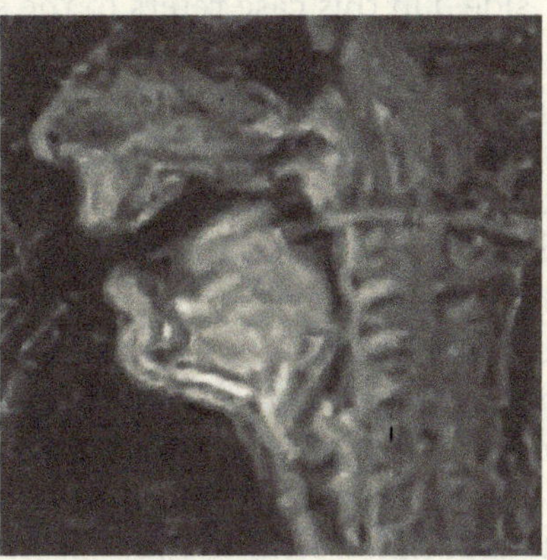

FIGURE 8.5 Screenshot from the SPAN Website Showing an MRI for the Articulation of a Bunched /r/

Based on MRI scans of the vocal tract, individuals who use either the retroflex or bunched tongue configuration tend to show three supraglottal constrictions along the vocal tract: in the pharynx, in the hard palate region, and at the lips. The precise location, degree, and length of these constrictions can differ significantly (Zhou et al., 2008), though listeners do not appear to perceive a difference between these types of /r/ production (Twist et al., 2007).

For L2 learners, the benefit of producing the bunched /r/ is the greater separation between tongue tip and alveolar ridge. Contact between these articulators could result in the production of /l/ instead of /r/, especially in the context of a high vowel such as /i/, which is produced with a high tongue body, narrowing the gap between the tongue and the ridge. L1 English speakers vary in their lip position in producing /r/; many show some degree of protrusion (versus rounding). If the lip position is rounded, it might result in the production of a sound perceived as /w/. A bunched articulation of /r/ is easier for learners following these guidelines:

i. Do not curl up the tip of the tongue.
ii. Do not confuse protrusion or movement forward of the lips with lip rounding, which may produce [w].
iii. Feel the sides of the tongue pressing against the gap between the upper and lower teeth.
iv. Raise and retract (i.e., bunch) the body of the tongue as if to produce the voiced velar stop [g] (e.g., *good*), but do not make the closure.

(d) The other liquid, /l/, is called a *lateral* approximant. Lateral (meaning "side") in this case refers to the sides of the tongue. There are two AE variants of /l/: the *light* or *clear* /l/ ([l]) and the *dark* or *velarized* /l/ ([ɫ]). The clear [l] is made by touching the tip of the tongue to the alveolar area and allowing the air to flow over the sides of the tongue to create the sound. Have students produce [l], and then while holding that position, breathe in. They should feel cold air on the sides and underside of the tongue; the sides are not in contact with the palate. The velarized /l/ is produced with *apical* (i.e., formed with the tongue tip) contact farther back than the alveolar ridge.

To help students recognize and produce the difference in lip movements associated with the /r/-/l/ contrast, Pennington (1996, Appendix C, pp. 258–66) suggested that teachers display a set of minimal pairs contrasting the liquids in word-initial position (e.g., *rock* and *lock*) and silently model each word while pointing to it. Teachers should then visually model one of the words at random and have students determine which one it is. This task can progress to the use of other minimal pairs with different vowels and the liquids in different positions in words. Both word position and adjacent vowel significantly affect the visual discernibility and auditory perceptual accuracy of the liquids, which can be enhanced by multiple AV exemplars in training (Hardison, 2003). Then practice AV word identification. Improved segmental perception contributes to earlier identification of words beginning with the sounds that are the target of instruction (Hardison, 2005b, 2005c, 2018b; see also chapter 3).

Other Consonant Sounds

There are three consonant sounds that are not shown in Figure 8.3: the flap [ɾ] (discussed under "Prosodic Phonology" below), the glottal stop [ʔ], and [h]. As noted earlier, the glottal stop, which is not a phoneme in English, involves complete closure of the glottal opening. It often occurs prior to a vowel sound in utterance-initial position, especially in a word produced emphatically (e.g., [ʔaʊt] *Out!*), and in a post-vocalic syllable-final position preceding a fortis stop (e.g., [stɛʔp] *step*).

The other sound that does not appear in Figure 8.3 is [h]. Although students may find it in the glottal fricative cell of other charts, the source of the slight turbulence when this sound is produced is the movement of air between the vocal folds and across other surfaces of the vocal tract, not from the movement of air through a narrow channel typical of fricatives (e.g., Esling et al., 2019). It lacks the place and manner of articulation of a typical consonant or the characteristics (e.g., height and backness) of a typical vowel. It has been described as the voiceless counterpart of the vowel that follows it with the shape of the vocal tract reflecting that of the surrounding sounds. Ladefoged and Maddieson (1996) stated that it might be more appropriate to consider [h] in languages such as English as a segment with only a laryngeal specification.

Syllable Structure

As noted earlier, aspiration, flapping, and l-velarization are common AE phenomena. Understanding their occurrence requires an understanding of the basic structure of the syllable, the concept of syllable weight, and the contribution of prosodic phonology, a theory of domains, to an accurate description of their occurrence (e.g., Nespor & Vogel, 1986).

Minimally, a syllable has a nucleus that consists of a vowel or vowel-like element. A syllabic liquid or nasal is a vowel-like element, transcribed with a short vertical line beneath the consonant symbol. It can constitute a syllable by itself or the nucleus of one (e.g., *whistle* [wɪsl̩], *prism* [pʰɹɪzm̩]; see the section "Other Sandhi Phenomena" below). Figure 8.6 shows the structure of the monosyllabic word *dog*, which has a filled onset [d], and in the rhyme (or rime) there is a nucleus [ɔ] and a simple filled coda [g].

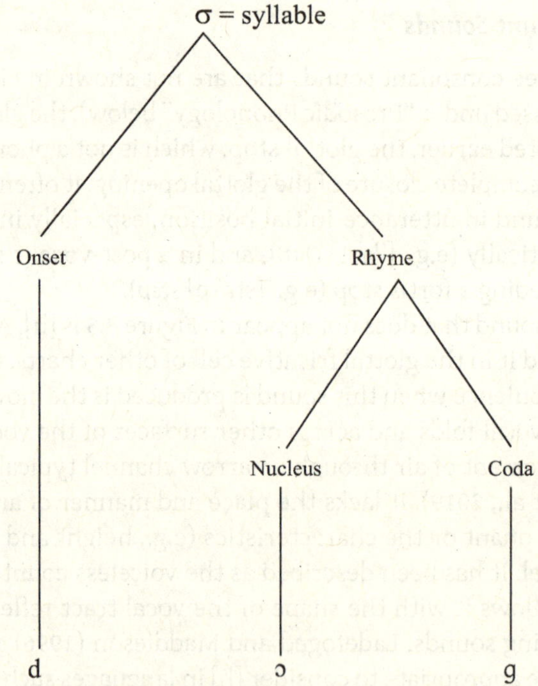

FIGURE 8.6 Basic Syllable Structure

The structure of a syllable is often more complex. English allows as many as three consonant sounds before a vowel, and as many as four after the vowel in the same syllable. Syllable boundaries are drawn in English on the basis of the *Maximal Onset Principle* (e.g., Selkirk, 1984), which assigns the maximum allowable number of consonants to the syllable on the right. Taking the word tun.dra as an example, the syllable boundary (indicated by the dot) is drawn between [n] and [d]. Although [nd] is a possible sequence for the coda of a syllable (e.g., *kind* [kʰaɪnd]), it is not a permissible syllable onset sequence in English, so [n] remains in the coda position of the first syllable. However, [dɹ] is an allowable sequence for a syllable onset, and following the Maximal Onset Principle, both [d] and [ɹ] are assigned to the syllable on the right.

Syllable Weight

Of particular importance is the concept of syllable weight. The weight (heavy or light) of a syllable is determined by its rhyme structure and is language-specific. In English, a heavy syllable has a branching rhyme, which is created by a filled coda (e.g., the second syllable of the word *finish* [fɪ.nɪʃ]) or a *diphthong*. In contrast to a *monophthong*, which is a vowel with a single non-dynamic quality, a diphthong is a vowel with continuously changing quality within one syllable (e.g., the second syllable of *meadow* [mɛ.doʊ]). The front and back mid AE vowels are transcribed as diphthongs (e.g., *may* [eɪ] and *no* [oʊ]; Ladefoged & Johnson, 2015; see also "Describing Vowels" below). A light syllable has a non-branching rhyme (e.g., the initial syllable in *finish* [fɪ] or *meadow* [mɛ]).

Prosodic Phonology

To provide an explanation for the occurrence of phenomena such as aspirated voiceless stops, flapping, and l-velarization (i.e., dark /l/), consider a structural unit beyond the syllable. To do this, we look briefly at prosodic phonology, a theory of domains in which the representation of speech is divided into hierarchically structured chunks (Harris, 2004; Jensen, 2000; Nespor & Vogel, 1986). In this framework, a prosodic constituent (or unit) can be the domain for specific processes. The following are the most applicable domains to the explanation of the common processes that characterize spoken English: the *prosodic word*, *foot*, *syllable*, *mora*, and *segment*.

In this framework, as shown in Figure 8.7, the prosodic word (ω, also known as the phonological word), consists minimally of a foot (F) in English. Harris (2004) described the foot as "the minimal utterable domain in the production of English" (p. 106). The foot contains one and only one stressed syllable (σ_s). The requirement that a foot have two morae (i.e., that it be *bimoraic*) gives it weight. The mora (m) is a unit of syllable weight; for example, in the heavy syllables shown in Figure 8.7, the consonant [ʃ] in the coda position in *finish* creates a second mora, and the diphthong [oʊ] in *meadow* creates a second mora. In this theory, all syllables must be footed.

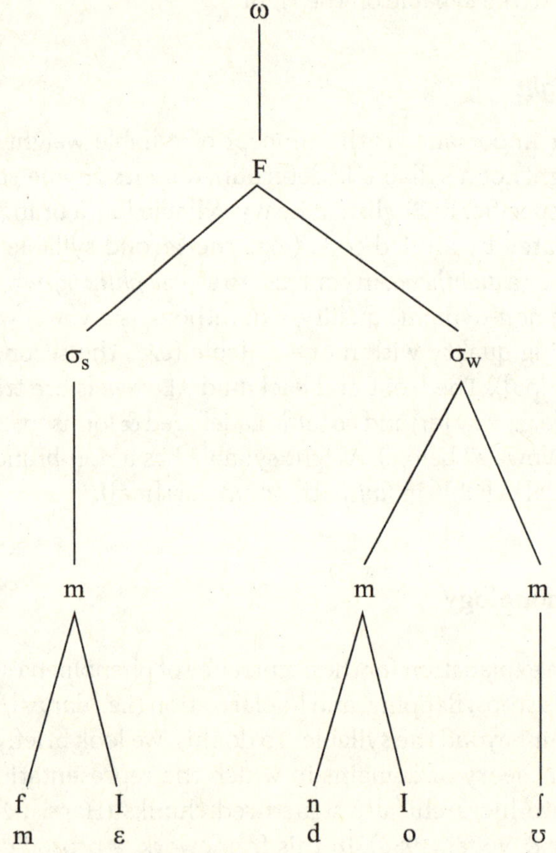

FIGURE 8.7 Basic Prosodic Word Structure

The Domain of the Foot

Each of the units (e.g., prosodic word, foot, syllable, mora, and segment) in the hierarchical structure is a domain. The question arises as to which domain is the most appropriate to account for processes such as aspiration, flapping, and l-velarization.

Consider the structure of the word *potato* [pʰətʰeɪɾoʊ], shown in Figure 8.8, which can be produced with two aspirated stops ([pʰ] and [tʰ]) and a flap ([ɾ]).[viii] In *potato*, the stress is on the syllable [tʰeɪ] leaving an unstressed word-initial syllable [pʰə]. Because all syllables need to be footed and a foot must contain two morae, the initial syllable, which has one mora, is adjoined to the right. In words such as these with an initial unstressed syllable, another layer in the structure is needed. Adding another layer preserves the structure of the original (minimal) foot and creates a new (maximal) foot to dominate the adjoined syllable and the original foot – a process called *stray syllable adjunction*. Typically in English, adjunction is carried out to the left when a stray unstressed syllable following a stressed one is adjoined to an adjacent foot to the left that dominates the stressed syllable. This adjunction follows from a structure preservation principle based on the consideration of feet in English as basically *trochaic* (i.e., composed of a stressed syllable followed by an unstressed one), although additional weak syllables can be adjoined. When the word-initial unstressed light syllable [pʰə] in *potato* is adjoined to the right, a *maximal* foot (a foot not dominated by another foot) is created to preserve the trochaic structure of the lower foot. The lower foot is called a *minimal* foot (i.e., a foot that does not dominate another foot), and the process creates *nested feet*.

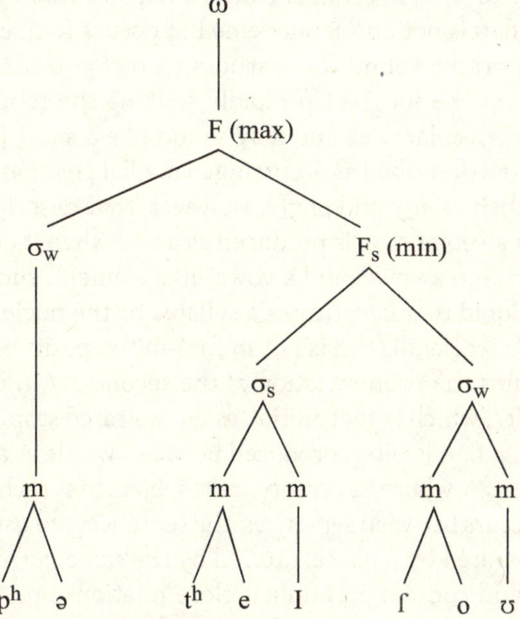

FIGURE 8.8 Prosodic Word Structure for *potato*

viii. Editor's Note: *Potato* may also be pronounced with non-aspirated stops in the first two syllables (i.e., [pəteɪroʊ]), or even with a (voiced) flap occurring between the first two vowels of the word (i.e., [pəɾeɪroʊ]). – MCP

Aspiration

To account for aspiration of a voiceless stop, prosodic phonology fills a gap created by the traditional explanation, which states that the stop occurs in the non-branching onset position of a stressed syllable. Although that explanation accounts for aspiration of the /p/ in *pot* [pʰɑt] versus *spot* [spɑt], it does not explain aspiration of the /p/ in a word like *potato* or *pronunciation*. In neither of those words is /p/ in a stressed syllable, and in *pronunciation*, the stop is in a syllable with a branching onset /pr/. A prosodic approach offers a better explanation. Voiceless stops aspirate if they are in initial position of the syllable onset and initial position of the foot. The stops /p/ and /t/ in *potato* are both foot-initial, even though /p/ is foot-initial as a result of adjunction. The syllable [pʰə] is in initial position of the new maximal foot and [tʰeɪ] is in initial position of the minimal foot. The foot-initial position is a strong one for a consonant. Because of the structural position of these stops, aspiration can occur.

Flapping

The final syllable [ɾoʊ] in *potato* includes a flap, a variant of the alveolar stop /t/. The flap is not an AE phoneme but occurs frequently in speech and is an important sound for learners to recognize. Articulation of the flap involves the tongue tip rapidly striking the roof of the mouth in roughly the alveolar area and may sound like a short [d]. The flap is voiced. It is often described as occurring in medial position between vowels in words such as *city* and *pretty*. However, that description needs to be refined. An alveolar stop is produced as a flap when it occurs between vowels, or between a vowel and a vowel-like element, such as a syllabic liquid (i.e., a liquid that constitutes a syllable or the nucleus of one; e.g., *butter* [bʌɾɹ̩], *letter* [lɛɾɹ̩]), and is not in foot-initial position. Reference to the foot explains the pronunciation of the second /t/ in *potato* as a flap and the first /t/, which is foot-initial, as an aspirated stop.[ix]

In addition, a flap is often produced between words in a sentence and between sentences, where its occurrence is subject to speech rate and style. When a flap occurs between sentences, the sentences are usually relatively short, not separated by a pause, uttered by the same person to the same interlocutor, and contain an implicit close relationship. A flap can also occur between words, as in *he caught a* [kʰɔɾə] *cold*. Recognition of the flap is important because of its frequency of occurrence in oral communication.

ix. Editor's Note: Though a different explanation is needed for the unaspirated stop pronunciation of the first two consonants of *potato* referred to in the previous Editor's Note. – MCP

l-Velarization

The final process to consider is l-velarization. Many AE speakers produce a light or clear /l/ ([l]) in words such as *leaf* and *like*, and a dark or velarized /l/ ([ɫ]) in words such as *feel* and *dull*. A velarized /l/ is commonly described in pronunciation textbooks as being in the coda position of a syllable following a vowel. But [ɫ] also occurs in *valley* and *yellow*, where it is in the onset position of the second syllable following the Maximal Onset Principle (see Figure 8.9). Some works have described the /l/ in words such as *valley* and *yellow* as *ambisyllabic*, or belonging to two syllables: the coda position of the first syllable and the onset position of the second syllable. However, reference to ambisyllabicity is not independently well motivated, especially for English, which does not have contrastive segmental duration (e.g., Jensen, 2000). Therefore, to describe the occurrence of [ɫ] in words such as *feel*, *dull*, *valley*, and *yellow*, the domain of the foot offers a tentative explanation: [ɫ] does not occur in foot-initial position, but [l] does.

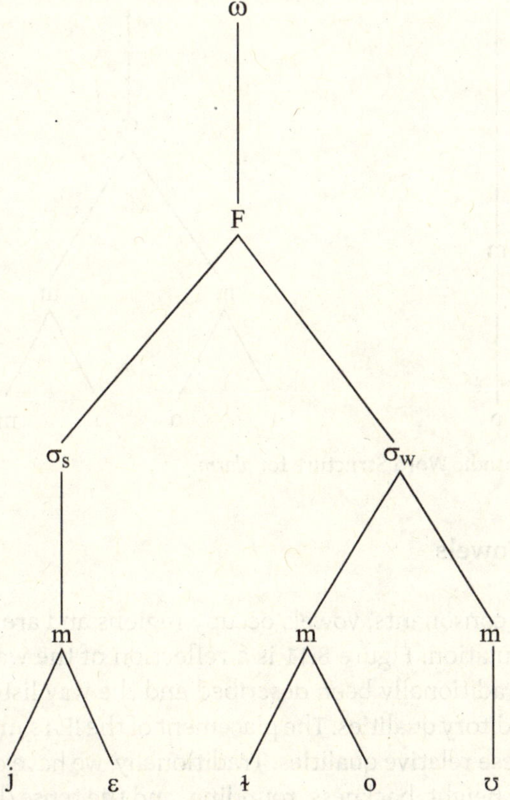

FIGURE 8.9 Prosodic Word Structure for *yellow*

However, speakers may also produce [ɫ] in words such as *alarm* and *allow*, where it is in the onset position of the stressed syllable and in foot-initial position; therefore, the description of where [ɫ] occurs needs to be refined. As shown in Figure 8.10, words such as *alarm* begin with an unstressed syllable. This is an example of stray syllable adjunction. To clarify the description of the occurrence of these variants of /l/, the velarized /l/ ([ɫ]) occurs in initial position of a minimal foot, and [l] is restricted to the maximal foot.

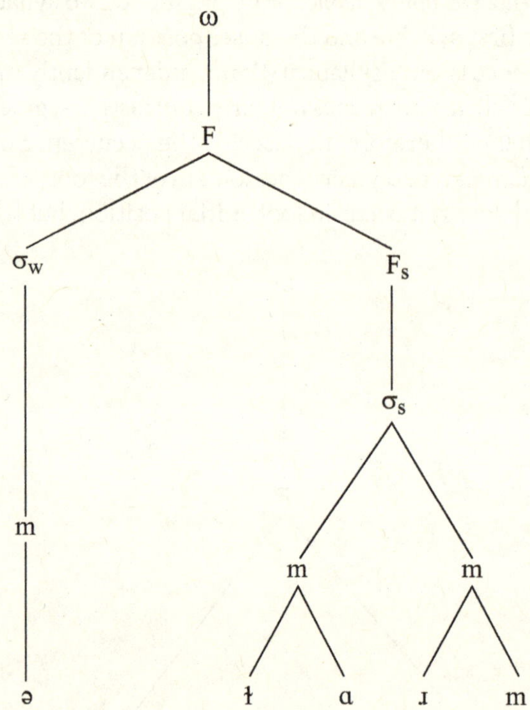

FIGURE 8.10 Prosodic Word Structure for *alarm*

Describing Vowels

In contrast to consonants, vowels occupy regions and are less precise in terms of articulation. Figure 8.11 is a reflection of the way in which AE vowels have traditionally been described and the way listeners perceive the relative auditory qualities. The placement of the IPA symbols in the figure follows these relative qualities. Traditionally, we have described vowels in terms of height, backness, rounding, and the tense/lax distinction, and these terms are still useful pedagogically. As compared to their lax counterparts, tense vowels require more muscular effort to produce, have a higher tongue position, may have a more advanced tongue root position, and may have a longer duration.

Some pronunciation textbooks and websites describe the difference between the vowel /i/ in *heed* or *heat* and the vowel /ɪ/ in *hid* or *hit* as one of length: long and short, respectively. Although the length of AE vowels does vary, and the tense vowels (e.g., /i/) may be longer than their lax counterparts (e.g., /ɪ/), vowel duration is not a distinctive/contrastive feature in English; that is, vowel length alone does not create minimal pairs of words that contrast meaning. Vowel length in English is affected by factors such as talker intent (a longer vowel may signal emphasis) and phonetic context (vowels tend to be longer before lenis obstruents). Consequently, reference to segmental duration as a general descriptor may be misleading for both teachers and learners.

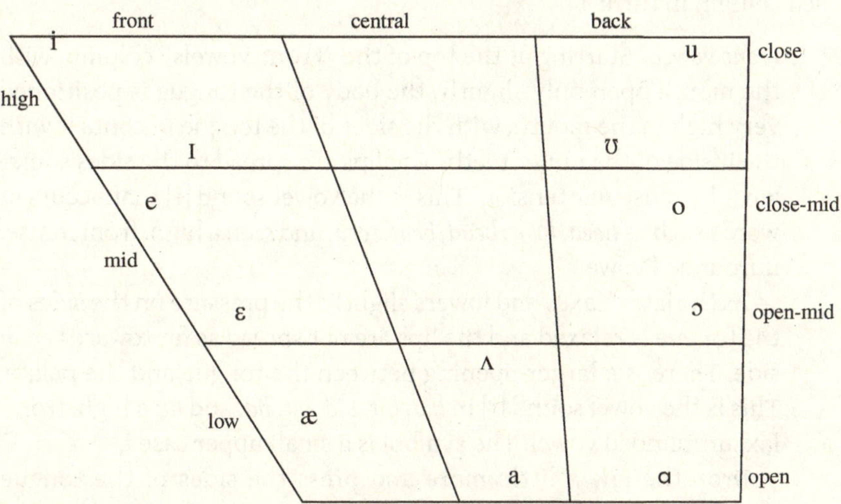

FIGURE 8.11 Relative Qualities of American English Vowels

Vowel height is often broadly described as high, mid, or low from a pedagogical perspective, as shown on the left side of Figure 8.11. High vowels are produced with a fairly closed-mouth position. Mid vowels are produced with a lowering of the jaw, which corresponds to a wider vertical opening of the mouth. Low vowels have the lowest jaw and the most open-mouth position. As shown on the right side of Figure 8.11, vowel height is labelled in more detail from close (/klos/) to close-mid, open-mid, and finally open (versus high to low) – typical of an IPA chart – in order to reflect the critical role of jaw opening on vowel quality, and thus the influence of jaw posture on the perception of voice quality. Backness refers to the relative front or back position of the tongue in the mouth when the vowel is produced. The characteristic of backness is described as front, central, or back. Rounding, which does not appear explicitly in the figure, refers to lip position. As noted earlier, vowels can also be classified as monophthongs or diphthongs. The front (e.g., [eɪ] *bait*) and back (e.g., [oʊ] *boat*) AE mid vowels are generally transcribed as diphthongs in which the tongue glides from the first component to the second in a single syllable.

How Vowels Look, Sound, and Feel

The chart in Figure 8.11 is typically read by starting in the upper left area of the first column and moving downward and then rightward to review each column in turn:

1. *Front Vowels.* Starting at the top of the "Front Vowels" column, with the mouth open only slightly, the body of the tongue is positioned very high in the mouth, with the sides of the tongue in contact with the inside of the upper teeth. The lips are spread to the sides somewhat by muscular tension. This is the vowel sound [i] that occurs in words such as *heed*, *heat*, *bead*, *beat*, *seed*, and *seat*: a high, front, tense, unrounded vowel.

   As the jaw relaxes and lowers slightly, the pressure on the sides of the tongue is relaxed and the lips are not spread as far towards each side. There is a larger opening between the tongue and the palate. This is the vowel sound [ɪ] in *hid*, *hit*, *bid*, *bit*, *lid*, and *lit*: a high, front, lax, unrounded vowel. The symbol is a small upper case i.

   Drop the jaw a little more and press the sides of the tongue slightly against the sides of the upper teeth. The opening between the tongue and the palate is larger and the lips are open. This AE vowel sound is typically produced and transcribed as a diphthong [eɪ] because there is an upward movement of the tongue, pushing it closer to the palate. This is the vowel in words such as *hade*, *hate*, *bade*, *bait*, *fade*, and *fate*: a mid, front, tense, unrounded vowel. The symbol is a lowercase e plus a small upper case i.

   Lower the jaw a little more and release the pressure that the tongue was placing on the teeth. The lips are open and still spread somewhat but not as much. This is the vowel sound [ɛ] that occurs in such words as *head, bed, bet, said*, and *set*: a mid, front, lax, unrounded vowel. The symbol is the epsilon.

The last of the front vowels is formed by lowering the jaw quite a bit until the mouth is open without muscular effort. The lips are spread somewhat to the sides. This is the vowel sound [æ] that occurs in words such as *had, hat, bad, bat, sad*, and *sat*: a low, front, unrounded vowel. The symbol is called an ash.

2. *Central Vowels*. Moving to the middle column, that of "Central Vowels," no phonological distinction is generally made between an AE *turned v* [ʌ] and a *schwa* [ə]. In some descriptions, the turned v has a value of lower-mid back, but in others it is considered lower-mid central (e.g., Ladefoged & Johnson, 2015; Pike, 1947). Some linguists use [ʌ] in a stressed syllable and [ə] in a reduced (unstressed) syllable (e.g., *abut* [əbʌt]). They are used in this manner in this chapter.
3. *Back Vowels*. Starting at the bottom of the "Back Vowel" column, the vowel sound [ɑ] is perhaps the easiest vowel to produce. The mouth is opened more widely than for any other sound. The jaw is low and the tongue is lower in the mouth than for any other vowel. It occurs in words such as *hod, hot, pod, pot, cod*, and *cot*: a low, back, unrounded vowel. The symbol is the script a.

   English rounded vowels are all mid back and upper back vowels. Moving up the chart, the next vowel is /ɔ/ (open-o), which some AE speakers do not have in their vowel inventory. The lips are slightly rounded and protruded with the tongue remaining bunched towards the back of the mouth. If speakers do not produce this vowel, they usually substitute one that is close to /ɑ/. There are few minimal pairs involving /ɔ/ and /ɑ/, so the possibility of confusion is limited. Those pairs include (with /ɔ/ listed first): *caught, cot*; *naught, not/knot*; *stalk, stock*; *dawn, Don*; *walk, wok*; *talk, tock* (as in *tick-tock*); and *taught/taut, tot*.[x]

   Next, create an opening with the lips shaped like a little circle. Like the front, mid, tense vowel, this AE vowel sound [oʊ] is also a diphthong. The tongue is pulled back or bunched. When this diphthong is produced, the lips lose some of their rounding and the back of the tongue moves upward and backward. This is the sound in

x. Editor's Note: Some AE speakers make a stronger contrast in these pairs, using /ɔ/ in the first member of the pair (e.g., in *talk* or *taught*), but a more fronted low vowel /a/ in the other member of the pair (e.g., in *tock* or *tot*, as in the side dish alternative to fries, often abbreviated as *tots*). But many AE speakers do not consistently differentiate the pronunciation of the listed pairs. – MCP

words such as *hoed, bode, boat, code,* and *coat*: a mid, back, rounded, tense vowel. The symbol is the lowercase o plus the upsilon.

There are two high back vowels. To pronounce the first one, the lower jaw is raised a bit from the starting position for [oʊ] and the lips are less rounded, but there is some protrusion with relatively little muscular tension. The tongue is still pulled back. This is the vowel sound [ʊ] that occurs in such words as *hood, hook, book, good, could,* and *cook*: a high, back, lax, rounded vowel. The symbol is the upsilon.

Round the lips as much as possible, leaving only a small opening. The sides of the tongue press firmly against the inside of the upper teeth and the tongue is pulled back. This is the vowel sound [u] that occurs in such words as *who'd, hoot, booed, boot, sued,* and *suit*: a high, back, tense, rounded vowel. The symbol is the lowercase u.

Students should be aware that the vowel dimensions of height and rounding influence the visual articulation of the surrounding consonants (e.g., Benguerel & Pichora-Fuller, 1982; Owens & Blazek, 1985). The lip rounding gesture for /u/ can extend over as many as four consonants preceding the vowel (Daniloff & Moll, 1968; see also chapter 1).

Other Diphthongs

There are three other commonly occurring AE diphthongs. The first is [aɪ], which starts with a low central unrounded articulation, more forward in the mouth than [ɑ], with the jaw rising until the sides of the tongue come in contact with the sides of the upper teeth. This is the vowel sound in words such as *hide, height, bide, bite, tied,* and *tight*. The symbol is the script a plus the small upper case i.

The second diphthong is the sound [aʊ], which also starts with a low central unrounded articulation, with the jaw rising as the lips round and move forward in a visually salient gesture while the tongue pulls back. This is the vowel sound in the words that make up the well-known phrase *How now brown cow*, used to demonstrate the movement from an open-mouth position to create a rounded vowel. The symbol is the script a plus the upsilon.

Finally, the diphthong [ɔɪ] begins at the open-o position with rounded lips, and then the lips are unrounded while the tongue rises and moves forward. This is the vowel sound in words such as *boy, toy,* and *joy*. The symbol is the open *o* plus the small upper case i.

Rhotacized or r-Coloured Vowels

A vowel followed by [ɹ] in the same syllable (i.e., *tautosyllabic*) has a different auditory quality called *r-colouring* or *rhotacization*. In words such as *beer*, *bear*, *bar*, and *bore*, the rhotacization of the vowel may not be very evident at the beginning of the vowel, and something of the vowel quality remains (Ladefoged & Johnson, 2015, p. 101). In words such as *heard*, *work*, *bird*, and *fur*, the whole vowel (mid-central) is rhotacized. These r-coloured AE vowels are written with vowel-r digraphs: [ɝ] in a stressed syllable (e.g., *heard*, *work*), and [ɚ] in an unstressed/reduced syllable (e.g., *sister*, *teacher*). For a real-time MRI of [ɝ] produced in *bird*, you can visit the website SPAN (https://sail.usc.edu/span).

Practising Vowel Production

To emphasize the continuous quality of vowel production, teachers can begin by producing the vowel sounds starting at the top left of Figure 8.11 with [i] and working as slowly as possible down the front vowels to [æ]. Then reduce the lip spread and lower the jaw a bit more to produce [ɑ] and work continuously up to [u]. Do the same thing in reverse order. To practise vowels in class, it is helpful to begin with the target vowel following /h/ and preceding a stop consonant, as in the frame [h_d] or [h_t], and then work around the chart. One possible sequence is as follows: *heed* [i], *hid* [ɪ], *hade* [eɪ], *head* [ɛ], *had* [æ], *hod* [ɑ], *hawed* [ɔ], *hoed* [oʊ], *hood* [ʊ], and *who'd* [u] (*hud* [ʌ] can also be added). Real-time MRIs, such as those available on SPAN, are particularly helpful for showing the movement of the internal articulators involved in the production of sounds, including the movement characterizing the front and back mid vowel diphthongs *hade* [eɪ] and *hoed* [oʊ], as well as the diphthongs in *hide* [aɪ], *bowed* [aʊ], and *Boyd* [ɔɪ].

As a pedagogical technique, Elliott (2018) urged learners to associate the typical quadrilateral (see Figure 8.11) with a "Vowel Elevator" to create a visual-kinesthetic approach to expanding the vowel space. In this approach, learners visualize the mouth as a building with elevators that move between floors to represent the height dimension of vowel production. As learners produce a sequence of vowel sounds, they visualize the elevator stopping at each floor while watching the teacher's corresponding hand-arm gesture. In this approach, AE has a front and back elevator (front-back dimension) with a *service* elevator in the middle (for a central vowel).

Teachers should be aware that the velar nasal [ŋ] (e.g., *bang*) and velar stop [g] (e.g., *bag*) often raise the articulation of preceding non-high vowels (e.g., /æ/); this raising is subject to geographical variation across North America (Mielke et al., 2017). Therefore, teachers may want to avoid these phonetic contexts at first when focusing on vowels in class.

In addition, to address challenges that students might experience producing a high unrounded vowel (e.g., [i]) or rounded vowel (e.g., [u]) before the liquids, Prator and Robinett (1985, pp. 116–17) suggested having students insert a short off-glide (shown as a superscript) in words such as *feel* [fiʲəl] and *fool* [fuʷəl] in which the glide is followed by a schwa [ə], essentially creating two syllables. This approach could also apply to high vowels before [ɹ] (e.g., *fear*). In the case of words with a rounded vowel, the objective is to reduce the influence of rounding on the articulation of the liquids. There is a caveat to using this technique, however: learners need to understand that the glide and schwa are not emphasized in natural speech.

Connected Speech

In preparing teachers to teach English pronunciation, it is important to raise awareness about the most frequently occurring phenomena of connected speech. This style of speech has been referred to by different names, including *sandhi* (from Sanskrit, meaning "placing together"; Prator & Robinett, 1985), *reduced forms* (e.g., J.D. Brown & Hilferty, 1986), and *connected speech* (e.g., J.D. Brown & Crowther, 2023). Other labels provided by nonlinguists for these phenomena may include "sloppy," "lazy," or "careless," suggesting a relationship to a non-prestige or substandard form of speech. As Richards and Schmidt (2011) have suggested, however, "educated L1 speakers of a language normally use colloquial speech in informal situations with friends, fellow workers, and members of the family" (p. 96). Some of these forms are more perceptible to AE listeners than others. They are pervasive in the language, challenging for learners, and often not apparent in orthography.

Native English-speaking teachers are not always aware of the phonological processes involved in connected speech or the constraints on their usage; non-native teachers may need guidance in understanding these elements, and both groups can benefit from suggestions on teaching them. J.D. Brown and Crowther (2023) argued for the importance of going beyond the expectation that L2 learners can simply use metacognitive strategies (e.g., predicting, monitoring) to understand connected speech (e.g., Vandergrift, 2002) and emphasized the explicit teaching of connected speech. Specifically, "if learners struggle to initially decode an incoming message at the phonemic level, they may be unable to make use of these metacognitive strategies" (J.D. Brown & Crowther, 2023, p. 6).

This section of the chapter on connected speech begins with a discussion of secondary articulations followed by other connected speech phenomena, such as coarticulation, reduction, and linking.

Secondary Articulations

Secondary articulations may pose challenges both auditorily and visually, but because of their frequent occurrence in daily communication, they should be addressed. A secondary articulation occurs with a lesser degree of closure at the same time as another (primary) articulation. Examples involving consonants include *labialization*, *palatalization*, and *velarization*.

A sound may become labialized (i.e., have lip rounding) in its articulation because of the influence of neighbouring labial sounds. Some speakers may have a labialized /l/ [lʷ] (the superscript [w] is added to the symbol) when pronouncing sound sequences such as the suffix *-ble* (e.g., *livable, flexible*) because of the bilabial stop /b/. This is particularly common among L1 English children in the early stages of phonological development but also occurs in the speech of some adults.

A consonant such as [k], which has a velar place of articulation, may be palatalized [kʲ] (the superscript [j] is added to the symbol) when it occurs before a front vowel, as in the word *keep*. The palatal glide closes the articulatory gap between the consonant and vowel.

In some contexts, /l/ can have a secondary articulation of velarization [ɫ] because the back of the tongue approaches the velum. Have students contrast the point of contact of the tongue tip as they pronounce the /l/ in *lawn* [lɔn] and the /l/ in *fill* [fɪɫ]. (The occurrence of l-velarization was described in more detail under "Prosodic Phonology" above.)

The next two sections on "Coarticulatory Phenomena" and "Other Sandhi Phenomena" outline some of the most common examples of connected speech involving AE consonants and vowels (for an extensive review, see J.D. Brown & Crowther, 2023).[3]

Coarticulatory Phenomena

Variable ways of pronouncing a phoneme can arise from *coarticulatory phenomena* – the overlapping of adjacent articulations – that typify natural colloquial or casual speech such as each of the following.

Vowel Nasalization

Vowels become nasalized when they occur before a nasal consonant; however, nasal vowels are not phonemic (i.e., they do not serve a contrastive function) in English as they are in some other languages, such as French. Non-phonemic nasalization occurs because the timing of the lowering of the velum is not perfectly synchronized with the tongue movement for the consonant. In a narrow phonetic transcription, the vowel in a word such as *dream* would be transcribed as [ĩ].

Assimilation

Consonants may vary in their place of articulation so they become more like (i.e., similar to) the next sound; that is, they undergo the process of *assimilation*. There are several types of frequently occurring assimilation phenomena:

1. *Anticipatory* (regressive): The articulation of a sound changes in anticipation of the following sound. This is the most common type of assimilation. Examples include the following:
   (a) *ten bikes* [tʰɛmbaɪks]: the alveolar nasal /n/ at the end of *ten* changes its place of articulation but not its manner (i.e., a partial assimilation) to the bilabial nasal [m] in anticipation of the bilabial stop [b] at the beginning of *bikes*.
   (b) *horse show* [hɔɹʃːoʊ]: the alveolar fricative /s/ at the end of *horse* is pronounced as the palato-alveolar fricative [ʃ] (shown as a lengthened consonant), which is the initial sound in *show*.
   (c) *grandpa* [ɡɹæmpə]: the /d/ is deleted and the /n/ is pronounced as the bilabial nasal [m] in anticipation of the bilabial stop /p/.
   (d) *destroyed* [dəʃtɹɔɪd]: the alveolar fricative /s/ can become a palatal fricative [ʃ]. This phenomenon is not as pervasive as others but has been occurring in the speech of some AE speakers in words such as *de<u>str</u>oyed*, *<u>str</u>eet*, *<u>str</u>ike*, *re<u>str</u>icted*, *<u>str</u>ong*, *history* (when pronounced as two syllables, *hi<u>s.tr</u>y*), and *<u>str</u>ucture* that contain a three-member consonant cluster [stɹ]. It may also occur across word boundaries (e.g., *parent<u>s tr</u>ying*). The trigger may be the lip protrusion and tongue position for [ɹ]. Other factors may also contribute to this phenomenon, such as the lip protrusion associated with a following palato-alveolar affricate [dʒ] (e.g., *stran<u>g</u>e*, *strate<u>g</u>y*).
2. *Progressive* (lag or perseverative): The articulation of a sound changes because of the preceding sound. For example, <u>*What's the*</u> *problem?* /wʌtsðə.../ may be pronounced as [wʌtzə...]. The interdental fricative

/ð/ is deleted, but the fricative /s/ may adopt its voicing feature and become [z].

3. *Reciprocal*: Two sounds mutually influence each other, as in the following examples:
   (a) Fricative change: The alveolar fricative /s/ or /z/ plus the glide /j/ result in a palato-alveolar fricative with the voicing feature of the fricative, either [ʃ] as in *miss‿you* [mɪʃu], or [ʒ] as in *as‿yet* [æʒɛt], *raise‿your hand*, *lose‿your shirt*, and *when's‿your appointment*. Some speakers retain production of the glide when pronouncing *miss you* (*miss you* [mɪʃju]), creating an anticipatory assimilation.
   (b) Stop changes to an affricate: The alveolar stop /t/ or /d/ plus the palatal glide /j/ result in a palato-alveolar affricate with the voicing feature of the stop, either [tʃ] as in *want‿you* [wantʃu], *what's‿your* [wʌtʃɚ] *name*, *eat‿your vegetables*, *why don't‿you come*, and *finished‿yet*; or [dʒ] as in *need‿you* [nidʒu], *did‿you go*, and *would‿you like*.

There are other sandhi phenomena in natural speech that depart from the citation form of words and may challenge the L2 learner visually and auditorily because the boundaries between sounds and words are blurred. These include vowel and consonant reductions and deletions, contractions, consonant substitutions, insertions, and linking.

Other Sandhi Phenomena

Reductions

1. Vowel reduction: Many vowels, including those in pronouns, prepositions, and conjunctions, reduce to a *schwa* [ə] in unstressed syllables, such as *you* [jə], *them* [ðəm], *at* [ət] (e.g., *Who's at the door?*), *to* [tə] (e.g., *They went to the store*), and *than* [ðən] (e.g., *more than that*).
2. Reduction of verbs + *to* has become so commonplace that informal spelling conventions exist; however, the use of these reduced forms is limited to specific meanings. Examples include *gonna* (*going* + *to*) to express intention (e.g., *I'm gonna look for my keys*) and *hafta* (*have* + *to*) to express necessity (e.g., *What do they hafta say at the meeting?*). (For a list of such reduced forms, see Prator & Robinett, 1985, pp. 195–6.)

Consonant Deletion

1. Deletion of /t/: The alveolar stop /t/ is often deleted in the environment shown in the following words: *winter* [wɪnɹ̩] (sounds like *winner*), *planter* (sounds like *planner*), *twenty*, *plenty*, *Santa Claus*, *Atlantic*, *county*, and *quantity*. In each case, the stop follows an [n] (both are

alveolar), and the [n] is in the coda position of the stressed syllable. After producing the nasal, the tongue tip leaves the alveolar ridge weakly so there is no release burst for the stop, and the following unstressed vowel or syllabic liquid is produced.

2. Other consonant deletions make words and phrases easier to produce:
   (a) Deletion of the second /f/ in *fifth* [fɪθ], the second /t/ in *tempts* [tʰɛmps], the /k/ in *asked* [æst], and the /ð/ in *like that* [laɪkæt] can facilitate production.
   (b) Deletion of the final /t/ in the following phrases allows a more fluid transition from the continuant /s/ to the consonant at the beginning of the next word: *jus~~t~~ right*, *las~~t~~ time*, and *las~~t~~ minute.* Some speakers might delete the final /t/ regardless of the type of sound that follows.
   (c) The following two phrases can sound the same when the initial consonant of the pronoun is not pronounced: *give ~~h~~im* and *give ~~th~~em* [gɪvm̩]. Some frequently used reduced forms appear in advertising, as in the National Work Zone Safety program "Give 'Em A Brake," reminding drivers to slow down and move over when workers are present on the roadway.
   (d) Deletion of /f/ in the preposition *of* frequently occurs in phrases such as *cup o~~f~~ tea* where *cup of* is pronounced as [kʰʌpə], sometimes written as *cuppa.*
   (e) Deletions may also produce a coarticulated sound that is not phonemic in English: *comfortable* [kʰʌɱtɚbl̩],[xi] where [ɱ] is a voiced labiodental nasal.

Vowel Deletion Creating Syllabic Liquids and Nasals

1. Liquids and nasals may be syllabic when they occur at the end of a word; that is, they may constitute a syllable or the nucleus of one. In transcription, a short vertical line beneath the symbol indicates syllabicity.
   (a) Syllabic liquids following nasals: *hammer* [hæmɹ̩] and *channel* [ʧænl̩].
   (b) Syllabic liquid following another liquid: *tailor* [tʰeɪɫɹ̩].
   (c) Syllabic liquids and nasals following fricatives: *razor* [ɹeɪzɹ̩], *whistle* [wɪsl̩], and *prism* [pʰɹɪzm̩].

xi. Editor's Note: The word *comfortable* is sometimes pronounced [kʰʌɱɚbl̩] (i.e., without the /t/). – MCP

(d) Syllabic liquids and nasals in reduced forms of words such as
   i. conjunctions: *black and* [n̩] *white, here and* [n̩] *there*, and *this or* [ɹ̩] *that*;
   ii. the modal auxiliary verb *can*, in which the final sound may be pronounced as a syllabic alveolar nasal (e.g., in the phrase *I can* [kn̩] *see*) or velar nasal (e.g., in the phrase *I can* [kŋ̍] *go*), depending on the place of articulation of the following consonant;
   iii. the progressive *-ng* ending in words such as *talking* and *walking*, resulting in *talkin'* and *walkin'* produced with a syllabic /n/: [tʰɔkn̩] and [wɔkn̩].

(e) The flap and syllabic liquids: *butter* [bʌɾɹ̩], *bottle* [baɾl̩], and *little* [lɪɾl̩]. For some speakers, *writer* may sound like *rider*, and *latter* may sound like *ladder* because of the medial flap.

(f) The flap and syllabic bilabial nasal: *bottom* [baɾm̩].

(g) The glottalized alveolar stop and syllabic alveolar nasal: A syllabic nasal can occur in a word such as *button*, which can be produced as [bʌʔtn̩] if both a glottal closure and an alveolar closure are made for the voiceless stop, or as [bʌʔn̩] if a glottal closure is made without any oral stop closure. In these situations, the air pressure builds up behind the closure and is then released through the nose (i.e., *nasal plosion*) by lowering the velum for the nasal consonant (e.g., Ladefoged & Johnson, 2015, p. 66). If students follow the first transcription of *button* and pronounce it slowly, pausing articulation at the stop closure, they can feel the nasal plosion and hear the onset of voicing.[xii]

---

xii. Editor's Note: Increasingly, a glottal stop is being substituted in English words for /t/ preceding any of the syllabic consonants – as in *bottle, letter, mitten*, and *bottom*. The glottal pronunciation of medial (intervocalic) /t/, which was once a stereotype of Cockney, is becoming common in other varieties of English. In American English, I have heard it especially in the speech of the under-30 generation. Of special note are cases when /t/ follows /n/ in a stressed syllable and begins a weakly stressed syllable with /n/ – in words such as *mountain, fountain*, and *sentence*, and in colloquial pronunciations of words such as *wanting* (*wantin'*) and *planting* (*plantin'*). Like other cases of /t/ preceding a syllabic (e.g., *bottle, letter, mitten, bottom*), the /t/ in *mountain, fountain, sentence, wantin'*, and *plantin'* may be glottalized. When the /t/ is glottalized in the latter cases, the /n/ preceding it may be deleted (i.e., [maʊʔtn̩] or [maʊʔn̩], [faʊʔtn̩] or [faʊʔn̩], [sɛʔtn̩s] or[sɛʔn̩s], [waʔtn̩] or [waʔn̩], [plæʔtn̩] or [plæʔn]). However, the latter cases generally do not admit of consonant deletion (either glottal or alveolar stop) before the weak syllable, thus contrasting with the cases of the two-syllable words with /t/ following /n/ and preceding a weak syllable

Vowel/Syllable Deletion

1. In two-syllable words, the initial unstressed vowel may be deleted when followed by a liquid, as in the following examples: *parade, police, believe, terrific*, and *collision*. The deletion creates an acceptable syllable-onset cluster, such as *pr, pl, bl, tr*, or *cl*. This deletion process can also occur with an unstressed r-coloured vowel, as in the first syllable of *surprise!* [spɹaɪz] (J.D. Brown & Crowther 2023, p. 115).[xiii]
2. In words with more than two syllables in their citation form, vowel deletion results in the loss of a syllable: *average, different, every, evening, interesting, several, chocolate, vegetable, temperature*. Such internal vowel deletion can create consonant clusters, which can be challenging for L2 speakers of English.[xiv]

Contractions

J.D. Brown and Crowther (2023) describe contractions as a subset of *blendings*. Both involve an adjustment in pronunciation because something has been dropped.

1. Contractions are so commonplace they have a corresponding written form. Examples include *I've* (*I have*), *you're* (*you are*), and *couldn't* (*could not*).
2. Blendings are defined as forms that are more common in spoken than written English: *there're* (*there are*) and *this's* (*this is*). Many contractions cannot occur when they conclude a phrase; for example, English speakers say *Yes, I am* but not *Yes, I'm*.

---

noted in point 1 above ("Deletion of /t/"), such as *winter* [wɪnɹ̩] that becomes homophonous with *winner* and *planter* that becomes homophonous with *planner*. The word *sentence* is, however, an exception, since it may have /t/ deleted if a vowel is retained in the second syllable. Any of the following pronunciations are thus possible for sentence: [sɛntʰəns], [sɛnəns], [sɛntʰn̩s], [sɛʔtn̩s], [sɛʔn̩s]. – MCP

xiii. Editor's Note: Although syllabicity is not generally recognized for nonresonant consonants, rather than creating a cluster when the following weak vowel is lost, the remaining initial /s/ in *surprise* may be syllabic (i.e., a voiceless syllabic sibilant). Although not common, I think there are other cases of voiceless syllabics in AE (e.g., *Shazam!* can be pronounced with only a syllabic /ʃ/ for the first syllable). – MCP

xiv. Editor's Note: Some of these clusters occur in English and so present no problem for native speakers but may for L2 speakers of English (e.g., /fr/ for *different*, /tr/ for *interesting*, /pr/ for *temperature*, and /kl/ for *chocolate*). Others, although they do not otherwise occur in English, do not present much difficulty for native speakers, though they may be problematic for L2 speakers (e.g., /vr/ for *average, every*, and *several*). Other difficult combinations are avoided by maintaining the two consonants that remain after vowel deletion in separate syllables (e.g., *eve.ning, vege.table*). – MCP

Consonant Substitutions

Just as deletions can facilitate production, substitutions of some consonants can play the same role. Substitution of [t] for [θ] in *months* [mʌnts] is easier to produce.

Insertions

In natural speech, a consonant may be inserted to facilitate production. In the pronunciation of words such as *warmth, prince,* and *strength,* a voiceless stop is inserted in the final consonant cluster as follows: *warmth* [wɔɹmpθ], *prince* [pʰɹĩnts] (sounds like *prints*), and *strength* [stɹɛ̝ŋkθ] (the diacritic under the epsilon indicates raising of the vowel before the velar nasal).[xv] This insertion phenomenon occurs most regularly when a nasal is present in a final cluster where it is followed by a voiceless sound, usually also a continuant. The place of articulation of the stop matches that of the preceding nasal, but the stop is voiceless, like the fricative at the end.

Transitions or Linking Phenomena

1. Consonant-to-consonant: Stops may be unreleased (and, optionally, pre-glottalized) before another consonant, as in *caught̲ fire, street̲ sign, lat̲e night, lock̲ box* where the underlined stop is unreleased.
2. Consonant-to-vowel transition: Between closely related words within the same thought group (e.g., verb + object, auxiliary + main verb, modifying adverb + adjective), the final consonant of one word is linked to the vowel that begins the next word, as if the consonant were in the onset position of the following syllable, so that the production of *loans‿it* approximates *loan zit.* Prator and Robinett (1985) referred to this as *phonetic syllabification.*
3. Vowel-to-vowel transition: Linking also occurs with glides (semivowels), as in *too‿often, do‿I, see‿it, be‿on time.* The vowel in the first word in each of these phrases can be followed by a glide (semivowel): a [w] (labiovelar) sound in the case of the rounded vowel [u] in *too* and *do,* and a [j] (palatal) sound in the case of the front unrounded vowel [i] in *be* and *see.* Speakers make use of these glides to create a smoother transition to the following vowel (e.g., *do‿* I [duʷaɪ] *see‿it* [siʲɪt]).

xv. Editor's Note: Consonantal transitions occur in words of more than one syllable as well, such as *comfort* [khʌmpfɚt] or [khʌʔmpfɚt]. – MCP

Connected Speech, Colloquialisms, and L2 Learners

To place the above forms of connected speech in the context of L2 pedagogy, consider the following comment from prominent phonetician Peter Ladefoged:

> There is, of course, nothing slovenly or lazy about using weak forms and assimilations. Only people with artificial notions about what constitutes so-called good speech could use adjectives such as these to label the kind of speech I have been describing.... Weak forms and assimilations are common in the speech of every sort of speaker in both Britain and America. Foreigners who make insufficient use of them sound stilted. (as cited in Ladefoged & Johnson, 2015, p. 119)

However, the situation is not so clearcut for "foreigners," who may be confronted with the dilemma of either avoiding connected speech and sounding stilted, or adopting the phenomena and producing them incorrectly and/or in inappropriate contexts.

Connected speech is a common part of colloquial speech, which encompasses phonological, grammatical, and lexical characteristics of informal conversation. L1 listeners vary in their receptiveness to L2 speakers' use of colloquial speech. In some reports, L1 listeners are critical (e.g., Ruivivar & Collins, 2018), while in others more positive comments have appeared (e.g., Beaulieu, 2016). Beaulieu (2016) investigated the attitudes of 42 L1 French-speaking patients in Western Canada towards the stylistic variations used by nurses who spoke French as an L2. A *matched-guise* technique was used in which the same speaker recorded the two types of speech samples characteristic of nurse–patient interactions: variants used by L1 French nurses that matched the target community's informal stylistic norm (*informal* guise), and variants typically found in textbooks for L2 French nursing students, which promoted the use of formal features (*formal* guise).[4] Variants consisted of phonological, grammatical, and lexical items. After listening to the recordings, 24 of the 42 patients described the speaker in the formal guise as "cold, distant, [and] authoritative," among other generally negative descriptors; however, seven patients responded positively, describing the speech as more professional. Beaulieu proposed that the more positive attitude might have stemmed from the fact that these seven patients had grown up in a French-majority environment (Quebec or France), where prescriptive language norms were highly valued in a professional setting.

In contrast, the informal guise received a clear majority of positive reactions (from 35 of 42 patients), attributing to the speakers such characteristics as "warmth, kindness, [and] adaptability." These patients commented that professionalism entailed adapting to patients by using informal words. However, this same accommodation to the local norm was described as "patronizing, condescending," and "highly unprofessional" by the seven participants who had favoured the formal guise. Beaulieu (2016) argued that social norms in particular environments play an important role in how receptive listeners are to more colloquial features of speech, and that successful L2 learners should control both formal and informal varieties.

In a review of the literature, DuBois (2019) summarized several concerns expressed by learners of a range of second languages about the use of phonological variant forms in their L2 speech.

1. Learners described having:
   a. negative attitudes towards a variant form and concern for a possible stigma attached to it (e.g., Nagy et al., 2003);
   b. a lack of confidence in knowledge of variants, how they're used appropriately, and their ability to produce the forms accurately (e.g., Ringer-Hilfinger, 2012); and
   c. a sense of awkwardness about producing the language in a native-like way when they are not native speakers and do not belong to the culture (e.g., Ringer-Hilfinger, 2012).
2. Learners expressed concerns, such as:
   a. not having "the right to the full range of L2 mastery" (DuBois, 2019, p. 49);
   b. the impractical nature of learning something that may not be appropriate in all areas or contexts in which the language is used (e.g., George, 2014);
   c. an increased chance of being misunderstood when using less formal speech (e.g., Beaulieu, 2016);
   d. a negative or distrustful reaction from native speakers (e.g., Ruivivar & Collins, 2018); and
   e. the potential for a loss of L1 identity from using L2 casual speech (e.g., Gatbonton et al., 2005; Lybeck, 2002).

As noted above, there is the question of how L1 speakers may perceive L2 speakers' use of forms that deviate from the citation forms. In recent study abroad research, L1 Japanese raters of speech samples from L2 Japanese sojourners commented that the L2 speakers tended to overuse features of native speech in their oral proficiency interviews such as the particle *ne*, which has many nuanced meanings, including those similar to the tags *right?* or *isn't it?* on an English question (Hardison & Okuno, 2022).

The raters were also teachers and emphasized that advanced L2 speakers might overuse particles to sound more like a native speaker of Japanese. In the interviews conducted in that study, there was also evidence of the overuse of *eeto*, a hesitation filler, and *chotto*, to express "a little/a little bit/somewhat." Nevertheless, the raters preferred this use over the insertion of English expressions such as *uhm* in Japanese conversation.[xvi]

DuBois (2019) explored native listener responses to the use of colloquial lexical items by L1 and L2 speakers of Peninsular Spanish. Although the use of colloquial language did not correlate significantly with higher or lower linguistic proficiency, native listener assessments of recorded speech samples revealed a double standard in attitudes towards colloquial language use based on the speaker's L1. The L2 speakers were downgraded in ratings of personality characteristics associated with status (e.g., success, intelligence), but they did not receive the same consideration

---

xvi. Editor's Note: The term "overuse" is a subjective term that implies exceeding some baseline of "normal" or "acceptable" use. Establishing a baseline of use for any feature of language is difficult, since there is usually a wide range in contextual variation. And establishing even a rough boundary between a "normal" or "acceptable" amount of use, or frequency of occurrence, and "overuse" of a feature requires speaker judgments. The conversational particles *ne*, *eeto*, and *chotto* – like many discourse markers in other languages (e.g., *you know* or *like* in English) – are typical of informal language (e.g., everyday speech or conversation) and so are often stereotyped as not "proper" language. Although discourse markers serve specific purposes (see Schiffrin, 1987, for specific functions of a range of English discourse markers), using them more than infrequently in one interaction may be perceived as "sloppy speech" or "overuse." When I travelled to Japan, I noticed some L1 speakers of Japanese using *ne* – and sometimes *eeto* and *chotto* – frequently in some interactions with other L1 Japanese speakers. Like discourse markers such as English *you know* and *like* that are commonly criticized for their "overuse," it can be assumed that L1 Japanese speakers – and perhaps especially teachers of Japanese who see themselves as "gatekeepers" of the language – would consider more than infrequent use of *ne*, *eeto*, or *chotto* to be overuse. Granted that discourse markers can be overused – either in the sense that they are used so frequently as to lose their functionality and thus become essentially meaningless or so frequently as to become annoying or distracting – it is not clear whether an L1 speaker's perceived "overuse" of discourse markers would be interpreted in the same way as an L2 speaker's perceived "overuse." Given that they are not members of the L1 speech community, L2 speakers may make frequent use of conversational particles or discourse markers as a deliberate interactional strategy for reaching out to L1 speakers – such as to indicate friendliness or solidarity, to solicit responses from their L1 interlocutors, or to hold their attention. Such usage may help to compensate for less than full competence or fluency in the L2 and yet may backfire if L1 speakers view the L2 speaker's efforts as inappropriate or "overkill." – MCP

as L1 speakers in terms of traits indicating solidarity (e.g., being sociable, friendly). The post-study debriefing revealed at least some degree of a favourable attitude towards colloquial language use on the part of L2 speakers by 186 of the 216 respondents. Based on the results, DuBois (2019) commented that "so long as L2 users are aware of the potential risks associated with using such language, there seems to be no reason to discourage its production" (p. viii). The requirements of a particular communicative situation are important considerations regarding such usage.

A Stand-Alone Pronunciation Course

If teachers have the opportunity to teach a stand-alone pronunciation course for L2 speakers, the information presented in this chapter can serve as a guideline for developing course content (for a discussion of the effectiveness of pronunciation instruction, see Derwing, 2018).[5] The amount of detail that can be included in such a course will depend on the amount of time available and on the learners' proficiency level and needs. Minimally, learners should be introduced to visual cues, articulatory settings, mouth gymnastics, and the nature and functioning of the basic vocal organs before they focus on and practise the articulation of individual consonants and vowels.[xvii]

A frank discussion in the classroom of the prevalence and role of forms of connected speech within speech communities may assuage some concerns about and set the stage for the presentation and practice of these forms. Raising awareness is a critical first step. J.D. Brown and Crowther (2023) recommend having students (a) listen to a speech sample produced without connected speech; (b) listen to the same sample with features of connected speech; (c) listen to the second sample again with a transcript and mark where the speech does not align with the written version; and (d) consider the processes involved in the differences that students identified (e.g., deletion of sounds).

---

xvii. Editor's Note: It makes good sense to introduce these features at the outset of a pronunciation course and before the individual consonants and vowels. In addition to providing necessary background for demonstration as well as for explanation and feedback, doing so can help avoid the tendency of learners to base pronunciation on the L1 or to avoid coarticulation. However, introducing these features before the individual consonant and vowel phonemes is different from the order of instruction in most textbooks and courses, if the features are included at all, and will present a challenge for most pronunciation teachers. – MCP

There is a role here for the transcription of connected speech without using spaces for word boundaries to emphasize the difference between the written language, in which word boundaries are obvious, and the spoken language, in which they are not necessarily clear – especially in the presence of connected speech. Through transcription, teachers can show students the various stages of change; for example, in the pronunciation of *Did you ever meet her?*, speakers might say [dɪdʒuɛvɹ̩miɾɹ̩], which shows reciprocal assimilation of the stop /d/ at the end of *did* and the glide /j/ at the beginning of *you*. They might also reduce the vowel /u/ to a schwa [ə] or continue the reduction by pronouncing the question as [dʒɛvɹ̩miɾɹ̩], in which *did you* is reduced to an affricate. At minimum, connected speech should be presented to L2 learners for *receptive knowledge* in order to facilitate listening comprehension so that the learners can determine for themselves, depending on personality and communicative context, if their goal is *productive control* of this style of speech.

Assessment in a pronunciation course can include the submission of portfolios that learners assemble using recorded samples of their speech in various contexts from controlled syllable-level utterances to longer stretches of speech in discourse contexts at different points in time throughout a course. Learners' recordings might be accompanied by (a) their (written or audio-recorded) reflections on improvements that they noted over time; (b) strategies that they developed in learning English pronunciation; (c) changes that they made in articulatory setting; (d) observations (based on visual and auditory perception) that they made of other speakers; (e) proprioceptive knowledge that they developed; and (f) issues that they will continue to address. AV recordings demonstrating interaction skills, including negotiation for meaning, especially stemming from mispronunciations, might be more beneficial for both the learners' reflections and the instructors' assessments (e.g., Nambiar & Goon, 1993). These reflections are also an indication of the learners' self-perception ability.

If pronunciation issues are not the sole focus of a course, they can be dealt with on an incidental basis, as Couper (2021) suggested, allowing them "to arise out of a listening-focused lesson, which could lead into a focus on perception, then production, and then be integrated into a speaking activity" (p. 139). Pronunciation may also be embedded in communicative tasks (e.g., expressing opinions), which can include the provision of corrective feedback (e.g., Darcy et al., 2021). However, teachers may be concerned that incidental approaches could relegate pronunciation to an "if-we-have-time status" (Hardison, 2010, p. 3). To ensure that particular sounds are addressed, teachers can seed the content of a lesson with words containing a targeted segmental issue (e.g., the /r/-/l/ contrast) or sentences exhibiting a specific suprasegmental feature (e.g., intonation in questions, contrastive stress in making comparisons); in doing so, the elements would be presented and practised in contextualized, meaningful communication.

Pronunciation in an Oral Skills Development Course

Following are some ideas for incorporating pronunciation into a course for L2 learners focused more broadly on the development of oral communication skills for adult L2 learners of English. These suggestions are adapted from a community-based ESL course I coordinate and conduct at a US university. Participants generally represent a range of L1s, needs, and goals. Some participants are members of the primary and extended university community, including students, their spouses, and visiting scholars; others are members of the general non-academic community. Since 2020, the course has been offered in in-person, virtual, and blended formats.[6] Typically, there are five or six levels of oral proficiency, each taught by a team of teachers. There are often 15–20 learners per level. Placement interviews are conducted by the coordinator.

Individual lessons are scheduled in 2-hour blocks, including a break. Each lesson focuses on a topic chosen for its relevance to the daily lives of the participants. The course follows the principle of goal-driven lesson planning, an integrated teaching framework in which the goals or outcomes of a lesson are the driving force for all of its components (Reed & Michaud, 2010). This approach requires teachers to *begin* lesson planning with the *end* (i.e., lesson outcomes/goals) in mind and to reverse-engineer the lesson to determine the content, activities, and organization that will best meet those goals.

Across the lessons in this course, there are five categories of learning goals: (a) vocabulary and grammatical structures; (b) pronunciation; (c) communication strategies; (d) non-verbal communication; and (e) culture. The following example is taken from a two-part lesson on "What color is your personality?" (adapted from Ritberger, 2000) and its potential effect on how one approaches conflict resolution. Although this lesson's content was designed for an upper-intermediate level of proficiency, it is adaptable to other levels. With respect to each of the learning goals, this lesson had the following specific learning objectives: (a) broaden vocabulary to describe personality characteristics; (b) practise vowel sounds with an emphasis on visual cues and proprioceptive feedback; (c) practise ways to ask for clarification, express agreement/disagreement, and resolve conflict based on suggestions in a related video; (d) use gestures to facilitate communication and be aware of eye contact; and (e) become aware of differences in personality characteristics that are valued in different cultures.

The suggestions presented here are confined to the pronunciation learning objective (b) focused on vowels. Before presenting and practising the vowel sounds, the teachers set aside some time to set the stage for teaching specific vowel sounds by addressing the segments described earlier in this chapter dealing with the awareness of visual cues, articulatory setting, mouth gymnastics, and the vocal tract, if these topics have not already been covered.

In this lesson, the perception and production of vowel sounds are merged with colours and key words for focused practice using choral and then individual response guided by the Color Vowel Chart (Taylor & Thompson, 2020), a chart that uses a different colour for each vowel. This chart includes some of the following phrases: *green tea* [i], *silver pin* [ɪ], *gray day* [eɪ], *red dress* [ɛ], *black cat* [æ], and so on. Visual cues for each vowel and proprioceptive feedback should be emphasized.[7] The association of the vowel sounds with colour, frequently occurring nouns, and images facilitates memory recall (e.g., Macedonia & Kepler, 2013).

Communicative practice is then provided through discussion of how colour can relate to personality type. Briefly, a colour is assigned to each personality type based on the results of a questionnaire completed by each learner. The questionnaire involves statements addressing multiple personality traits (e.g., "I am able to develop strategies to solve problems" or "I welcome change"). Using a 5-point scale, respondents indicate how often each statement pertains to them. As an example, "green" personality types are said to have their strength in knowledge. They feel best about themselves when they are solving problems, demonstrating analytical ability, and so forth. They have a variety of interests, tend to be perfectionists, are curious, and value efficiency. Their leadership style is described as expecting competence from others and encouraging change for improvement.

A possible sequence of tasks is the following:

1. Learners complete the questionnaire, which can be done in advance of the class.

2. In class, learners are divided into groups according to their predominant personality colour based on the questionnaire results. Each group gets a copy of the definitions of each personality colour and discusses how accurate the definitions are of them.
3. Learners are then placed in small groups so that each group has a mix of personality colours. Each learner receives a handout with two columns of descriptors as end points of a continuum. The descriptors vary across learners. These can be adjectives (e.g., *quiet—talkative, cooperative—competitive*) or verb phrases (e.g., *want facts—want opinions, focus on the big picture—try to attend to many details*). Taking turns, each learner asks another a question based on one of the scales, for example, "Are you often quiet or talkative?" For verb phrases, one question can be "Do you tend to want facts or opinions?" In each case, the response must be sufficiently detailed, including an example, to place the individual somewhere along the continuum between the two end points. At the end of this task, learners should be able to provide a summary of their strongest traits and those of another member of the group. If participants feel uncomfortable about sharing personal details, they may prefer to adopt a different identity for this activity.
4. Teachers circulate among the groups to offer assistance, if needed, and make a note of pronunciation issues, especially for the vowels, which are the focus of this topic. At the end of the class, these issues are reviewed for all learners.

The information obtained from the above tasks can serve as a foundation for additional discussions on topics such as the participants' preferred strategies for conflict resolution, which are related to personality type.

Other sounds can be the focus of this type of lesson. As the coordinator of the program in which these materials have been used, I have observed similar classes focused on different sounds, including /r/ and /l/ and the interdental fricatives /θ, ð/. For example, one teaching team seeded their lesson with words containing /r/ and /l/ in different phonetic environments. During communicative activities that took place in small groups of students, the teachers circulated around the room, offering guidance and answering questions. At the same time, they were taking note of the words that seemed to be more challenging than others for the students to produce. Towards the end of the class, the teachers went over the pronunciation of those words with the whole class, focusing on how /r/ and /l/ look and sound, and how the articulation feels to them (e.g., position of the tongue in the mouth).

Chapter 8 in Review

This chapter has outlined the basics of a multisensory approach to the teaching and learning of AE speech sounds as they are produced in isolation and in connected speech. It is important for teachers and learners to know how consonants and vowels look, sound, and feel in order to maximize the value of visual cues to guide perception and production, and to maximize proprioceptive feedback to guide production. The content was designed for teacher trainers and pre- and in-service teachers to address the gap that teachers often say they have in their knowledge base with regard to phonetics and its application to language teaching and learning. The information, on a more limited scale, has also been included in a stand-alone pronunciation course for ESL learners. Suggestions were also provided for incorporating pronunciation into a course designed more broadly for the development of L2 oral communication skills.

Chapters 1 through 7 explored a variety of visual cues to speech provided by a talker's movements (e.g., lip movements, hand-arm gestures, head nods). They also explored (a) the process of AV integration of speech cues from behavioural and neurophysiological perspectives; (b) the application of lip movements to L2 perception training; and (c) the contributions of eye-movement research to deciphering where and when perceivers look on a talker's face. On this basis, chapter 8 presented information on preparing teachers to take a multisensory approach to teaching speech sounds. Next, chapter 9 will conclude the book with an emphasis on a key theme that ran throughout the chapters: variability.

Chapter 8 Notes

1. The chapter by Murphy and Baker (2015) mentions an audiovisual method used in France for language teaching (e.g., Centre de recherche et d'étude pour la diffusion du français, 1962); however, further investigation revealed that *audiovisual* in that case referred to imagery (e.g., pictures) to provide a context for language.
2. Early in my language teaching career, I discovered ESL learners' speechreading abilities in distinguishing vowel length before voiced and voiceless consonants when my English pronunciation class was held in an old building with huge windows that produced a howling sound in the wind and blocked learners' auditory perception of what was being said. The learners honed their speechreading skills considerably during that semester!
3. Audio examples referred to in J.D. Brown and Crowther (2023) are available as downloadable files at https://www.routledge.com/9780367697570 under "Support Material."

4. In this use of the matched-guise technique, distractor speech samples were inserted in the recordings to minimize the chances of listeners becoming aware that the same speaker was producing the experimental items.
5. The content of this chapter, though with less detail, was used in a stand-alone pronunciation course I taught for upper-intermediate and advanced adult L2 English learners in the US. In addition to segmental issues, that course addressed word- and sentence-level stress, rhythm, and intonation. For these suprasegmental topics, computer-based displays, such as those for pitch, constituted the visual input. For a discussion of the use of technology in language teaching, see Chun and Jiang (2022), Hardison (2004, 2005a, 2018a), O'Brien (2022), and O'Brien et al. (2018).
6. The different instructional formats were started in response to institutional restrictions on in-person instruction during COVID-19 and were continued in order to address the needs of adult ESL learners at a distance.
7. Teaching ideas for using the colour chart are also available at https://americanenglish.state.gov/resources/color-vowel-chart.

Chapter 9

Conclusion: The Keyword Is Variability

One thing that puzzled us from the outset was why normally hearing individuals are influenced by the facial information, when the visual stimulus is not necessary to perceive the auditory speech. We formulated this as "Why does the brain do this when it generally doesn't need to?" . . . For a number of reasons I think this question is misconceived, and it should be framed as "Why would the brain not use such available information when it is built so to do?"

– MacDonald (2017, p. 9)

*****

Background

The above epigraph from John MacDonald is part of his reflections on his discussions with Harry McGurk regarding the origins of the perceptual illusion, published in 1976, that bears their names (see Chapter 2). Since that time, behavioural and neurophysiological studies have provided further evidence that speech processing involves both the eyes and the ears (and sometimes the sense of touch). This book adopted the perspective that multimodal/multisensory speech – whether auditory-visual, auditory-(aero)tactile, or visual-(aero)tactile – is the baseline condition; therefore, unimodal input removes something that for many people is naturally present and part of their daily interactions in multisensory environments.

Publications starting in the early 1900s set the stage for AV speech perception research. Gutzmann (1912) emphasized the roles of both vision and audition in perception (see also chapter 1); Jones (1956) advocated for the importance of a talker's facial cues to L2 pronunciation; classic studies by Sumby and Pollack (1954) and G.A. Miller and Nicely (1955) uncovered the value of seeing a talker's face in noisy environments, such as military and industrial settings; and Walden et al. (1977, 1981) documented the value of speechreading training for participants with hearing loss. Subsequent research with other populations underscored the value for perceivers of visual cues from a talker's face when comprehending a semantically complex message or their L1 spoken with an accent (Reisberg et al., 1987); when learning to perceive and produce L2 sounds in English (e.g., Hardison, 2003, 2005b) and French (Inceoglu, 2014); and, more recently, when trying to deal with the absence of facial cues while communicating with individuals wearing masks because of COVID-19. Yet, despite the general value of multimodal speech cues, they exhibit considerable variability.

Variability

The early lectures by Jones (see Collins & Mees, 2002), the clinical research by Walden et al. (1977), and the speechreading studies in the literature by numerous researchers, as reviewed in chapter 1, acknowledged the existence of variability. Speechreading ability varied with the visual discernibility of consonants as influenced by phonetic context (e.g., Benguerel & Pichora-Fuller, 1982; Berger, 1972; Franks & Kimble, 1972); talker (e.g., Kricos & Lesner, 1982; Walden et al., 1977); the amount of noise added to the signal (Binnie et al., 1974; Summerfield, 1987); and, later, individual perceiver characteristics (e.g., Bernstein et al., 2000; Tye-Murray et al., 2016; see chapter 1).

Beginning in the 1970s, numerous studies involving the McGurk–MacDonald effect uncovered several sources of variability in the strength of that perceptual illusion, including talker familiarity, angle of view, and language and cultural issues, among others (see chapter 2). Over the years, research on the factors that affect L1 and L2 speech processing has highlighted the variable nature of natural speech and of perceivers' responses to it. Successful L2 auditory perception training paradigms revealed that incorporating stimulus variability is beneficial for language learners (see chapter 3). Multiple voices producing multiple exemplars improved L2 challenges, such as the perception and production of Chinese tone (Leather, 1990). Placing words contrasting AE /r/ and /l/ in a range of phonetic contexts spoken by multiple talkers promoted the development of robust perceptual categories for L2 AE learners (L1 Japanese), allowing improved perceptual abilities to generalize to the task of perceiving novel stimuli spoken by unfamiliar voices, and to transfer to improvement in production (e.g., Bradlow et al., 1999; Lively et al., 1993; Logan et al. 1991). This approach to auditory perception training using multiple voices later became known as high variability perception training (HVPT).

Combining speech cues from a talker's face with auditory cues in an HVPT paradigm produced findings in L2 studies demonstrating a significant advantage for AV versus A-only training in the improvement of perceptual identification accuracy. In keeping with the hallmarks of successful perception training, the benefits extended to production and earlier word identification in connected speech (e.g., Hardison, 2003, 2005b, 2005c, 2018b). Yet there was variability in the findings of this research, as some studies did not find a similar advantage (e.g., Hazan et al., 2005; Sekiyama & Tohkura, 1993), possibly due to differences in methodological details and talker characteristics (see chapter 3).

Several decades ago when HVPT experiments first appeared in the published literature (e.g., Lively et al., 1993; Logan et al., 1991), the researchers proposed that an episodic view of the memory encoding of speech could accommodate the findings that showed context- and talker-dependent speech processing (see chapter 3). An episodic view posits that the memory encoding of speech involves storage of the attended perceptual details of individual episodes that retain the contextual features and indexical properties of speech. This view, which preserves the variability present in the speech signal, challenged the abstractionist view of phonological representations, which held that such details are discarded and input is matched to a prototype concept for identification. In an adaptation of multiple-trace memory theory (e.g., Hintzman, 1986), Hardison (2003, 2012) proposed that the exemplars of episodic models and prototypes could coexist, as Pierrehumbert (2016) later also suggested (see chapter 3).

Variability also occurs in the attention paid to a talker's manual gestures in face-to-face interactions, which may be explained by differences in their informativeness to perceivers, which may, in turn, be related to different cultural practices. For example, if a talker's gestures are not compatible with a perceiver's culture, focusing on them may demand too many attentional resources during listening comprehension – at which point the gestures may become more fatiguing, even annoying, than beneficial, especially in the presence of an additional challenge such as that presented by unfamiliar accented speech (Algana & Hardison, 2024; see chapter 6).

Eye-movement research demonstrated that variability also exists in the areas of a talker's face that capture perceivers' attention. For example, Lansing and McConkie (2003) proposed the eye primacy effect to account for participants having fixated the eyes of a talker during the silence before speech periods (see chapter 4). However, a talker's eyes do not always attract initial fixations. As described in chapter 5, the likelihood of initial fixations to the eyes of a talker sharing the perceivers' L1 (AE) was lower as compared to fixations to the mouth and nose in AV, AVn, and

V-only stimulus conditions; in contrast, the likelihood of initial fixations to the eyes was greater in both the AV and AVn conditions involving an L2 French talker.

Lansing and McConkie (2003) also proposed an information source attraction effect for L1 perceivers because of the availability of speech information in the mouth region of a talker's face. However, the information must be usable by the perceiver, and this might not always occur in either an L1 or L2 situation. If the target of fixation is not informative for a task, gaze may be redirected, suggesting that perhaps the effect could be relabelled the *informative* source attraction effect. Analyses of gaze behaviour in chapter 5 established that much of the variance in the areas of a talker's face that were fixated initially and for the longest duration was explained by the random effects (i.e., differences across participants) rather than the fixed effects of language (L1, L2), stimulus condition (AV, AVn, V-only), and their interactions. In contrast, the differences across participants explained very little of the variance in vowel identification accuracy. For the participants engaged in the task of identifying vowels, variability in their gaze behaviour did not come at the expense of accuracy.

Researchers are encouraged to offer participants in their studies the opportunity to comment on their participation experiences and elaborate on their responses to tasks by completing questionnaires. The insightful comments provided by the L2 French learners following data collection in the eye-tracking study (see chapter 5), and those given by participants in other studies (e.g., Algana & Hardison, 2024; Hardison, 2003; Reisberg et al., 1987; Summerfield, 1979; Walden et al., 1977), emphasize the importance of including this source of information in the interpretation of the results.

Given the considerable variability in the targets of fixation on a talker's face in AV contexts (see chapter 5), I return to the earlier question: *Do the eyes really have it?* The answer appears to be "sometimes" – but it varies! This variability suggests the need for more research, especially on the contribution of the features of individual talkers' faces and behaviours to speech perception. In addition, given that the literature is heavily focused on English, much more research is needed on multimodal speech perception in various languages and cultures. As technology progresses, research should also continue on the neuroarchitecture of auditory-visual integration.

Variability within the multimodal context of speech has a role in teacher education and in language teaching. To build more confidence, pre- and in-service teachers need to be aware of the value of multimodal input in the presentation of new speech sounds to learners for practice in the classroom and beyond. Teachers are encouraged to exploit the variability in speech through their audiovisual presentation of content and selection of pedagogic materials to help learners practise their perception and production skills with sounds in isolation and connected speech in addition to prosodic and non-verbal features of communication (see chapter 8). Although instructors will need to determine how much variability their learners are able to accept at particular stages of interlanguage development, the benefits to phonological learning are worth the effort.

As some studies have shown (e.g., Couper, 2021; Foote et al., 2011), language teachers often report inadequate preparation for teaching pronunciation. Although there are numerous textbooks available that address pronunciation either as their sole focus or as part of the overall development of speaking skills, they may lack sufficient details on the phenomena of connected speech in context and how to incorporate them into lessons (J.D. Brown & Crowther, 2023; see chapter 8). Print materials can be supplemented with video resources that are widely available on the internet to maximize multimodal input. Teachers, both native and non-native speakers of English, need guidance on how to select materials and include their content in lessons to emphasize the way the language is spoken in the natural language environment. Minimally, learners need to understand the speech that is addressed to them, and often they want to produce it in order to interact with other speakers beyond the classroom. Teacher educators and materials developers have a role to play in guiding a multisensory approach to teaching and learning speech sounds in context.

References

Abercrombie, D. (1967). *Elements of general phonetics*. Edinburgh University Press.

Alcorn, S. (1932). The Tadoma method. *Volta Review*, *34*, 195–8.

Algana, M., & Hardison, D.M. (2024). Variable effects of speakers' visual cues and accentedness on L2 listening comprehension: A mixed-methods approach. *Language Teaching Research*. Advance online publication. https://doi.org/10.1177/13621688241246106.

Alibali, M.W., Heath, D.C., & Myers, H.J. (2001). Effects of visibility between speaker and listener on gesture production: Some gestures are meant to be seen. *Journal of Memory and Language*, *44*(2), 169–88. https://doi.org/10.1006/jmla.2000.2752.

Alsius, A., Paré, M., & Munhall, K.G. (2018). Forty years after hearing lips and seeing voices: The McGurk effect revisited. *Multisensory Research*, *31*(1–2), 111–44. https://doi.org/10.1163/22134808-00002565.

Alsius, A. & Soto-Faraco, S. (2011). Searching for audiovisual correspondence in multiple speaker scenarios. *Experimental Brain Research*, *213*(2–3), 175–83. https://doi.org/10.1007/s00221-011-2624-0.

Alsubhi, M. S. (2017). *How language and culture shape gesture in English, Arabic and second language speakers* [Doctoral dissertation, University of Birmingham]. University of Birmingham Research Archive. https://etheses.bham.ac.uk/id/eprint/8296/1/Alsubhi18PhD.pdf.

Apoux, F., & Bacon, S.P. (2004). Relative importance of temporal information in various frequency regions for consonant identification in quiet and in noise. *Journal of the Acoustical Society of America*, *116*(3), 1671–80. https://doi.org/10.1121/1.1781329.

Arbona, E., Seeber, K.G., & Gullberg, M. (2023). Semantically related gestures facilitate language comprehension during simultaneous interpreting. *Bilingualism: Language and Cognition*, *26*(2), 425–39. https://doi.org/10.1017/S136672892200058X.

Argyle, M. (1967). *The psychology of interpersonal behaviour*. Penguin Books.

Argyle, M., & Cook, M. (1976). *Gaze and mutual gaze*. Cambridge University Press.

Armann, R., & Bülthoff, I. (2009). Gaze behavior in face comparison: The roles of sex, task, and symmetry. *Attention, Perception, & Psychophysics*, *71*(5), 1107–26. https://doi.org/10.3758/APP.71.5.1107.

Aronson, E., & Rosenbloom, S. (1971). Space perception in early infancy: Perception within a common auditory-visual space. *Science*, *172*(3988), 1161–3. https://doi.org/10.1126/science.172.3988.1161.

Asher, J.J. (1966). The learning strategy of the total physical response: A review. *Modern Language Journal*, *50*(2), 79–84. https://doi.org/10.1111/j.1540-4781.1966.tb03573.x.

Auer, E.T. (2002). The influence of the lexicon on speechread word recognition: Contrasting segmental and lexical distinctiveness. *Psychonomic Bulletin & Review*, *9*(2), 341–7. https://doi.org/10.3758/BF03196291.

Auer, E.T., & Bernstein, L.E. (2007). Enhanced visual speech perception in individuals with early-onset hearing impairment. *Journal of Speech, Language, and Hearing Research, 50*(5), 1157–65. https://doi.org/10.1044/1092-4388.

Auer, P. (2018). Gaze, addressee selection and turn-taking in three-party interaction. In G. Brône & B. Oben (Eds.), *Eye-tracking in interaction: Studies on the role of eye gaze in dialogue* (pp. 197–231). John Benjamins. https://doi.org/10.1075/ais.10.09aue.

Avram, A. (1964). Some thoughts on the functional yield of phonemic oppositions. *Linguistics, 2*(5), 40–7. https://doi.org/10.1515/ling.1964.2.5.40.

Bahrick, LE., & Lickliter, R. (2000). Intersensory redundancy guides attentional selectivity and perceptual learning in infancy. *Developmental Psychology, 36*(2), 190–201. https://doi.org/10.1037//0012-1649.36.2.190.

Bailey, K.M. (1982). *Teaching in a second language: The communicative competence of non-native speaking assistants* [Unpublished doctoral dissertation]. University of California.

Baills, F. (2022). *Using the hands to embody prosody boosts phonological learning in a foreign language* [Doctoral dissertation, Universitat Pompeu Fabra]. Tesis Doctorals en Xarxa. http://hdl.handle.net/10803/673777.

Baker, A. (2014). Exploring teachers' knowledge of second language pronunciation techniques: Teacher cognitions, observed classroom practices, and student perceptions. *TESOL Quarterly, 48*(1), 136–63. https://doi.org/10.1002/tesq.99.

Ballard, L., & Winke, P. (2017). Students' attitudes towards English teachers' accents: The interplay of accent familiarity, comprehensibility, intelligibility, perceived native speaker status, and acceptability as a teacher. In T. Isaacs & P. Trofimovich (Eds.), *Second language pronunciation assessment: Interdisciplinary perspectives* (pp. 121–40). Multilingual Matters. https://doi.org/10.21832/9781783096855-009.

Barenholtz, E., Mavica, L., & Lewkowicz, D.J. (2016). Language familiarity modulates relative attention to the eyes and mouth of a talker. *Cognition, 147*, 100–5. https://doi.org/10.1016/j.cognition.2015.11.013.

Bates, D., Mächler, M., Bolker, B., & Walker, S. (2015). Fitting linear mixed-effects models using lme4. *Journal of Statistical Software, 67*(1), 1–48. https://doi.org/10.18637/jss.v067.i01.

Batty, A.O. (2021). An eye-tracking study of attention to visual cues in L2 listening tests. *Language Testing, 38*(4), 511–35. https://doi.org/10.1177/0265532220951504.

Bavelas, J.B., Coates, L., & Johnson, T. (2002). Listener responses as collaborative process: The role of gaze. *Journal of Communication, 52*(3), 566–80. https://doi.org/10.1111/j.1460-2466.2002.tb02562.x.

Beauchamp, M.S. (2016). Audiovisual speech integration: Neural substrates and behavior. In G. Hickok & S.L. Small (Eds.), *Neurobiology of language* (pp. 515–26). Academic Press. https://doi.org/10.1016/B978-0-12-407794-2.00042-0.

Beauchamp, M.S., Argall, B.D., Bodurka, J., Duyn, J.H., & Martin, A. (2004) Unraveling multisensory integration: Patchy organization within human STS multisensory cortex. *Nature Neuroscience, 7*(11), 1190–2. https://doi.org/10.1038/nn1333.

Beauchamp, M.S., Nath, A.R., & Pasalar, S. (2010). fMRI-guided transcranial magnetic stimulation reveals that the superior temporal sulcus is a cortical locus of the McGurk effect. *Journal of Neuroscience, 30*(7), 2414–17. https://doi.org/10.1523/JNEUROSCI.4865-09.2010.

Beaulieu, S. (2016). Prescriptivism and French L2 instruction. *Journal of Multilingual and Multicultural Development, 37*(3), 274–85. https://doi.org/10.1080/01434632.2015.1068786.

Beckman, M.E., Hirschberg, J., & Shattuck-Hufnagel, S. (2005). The original ToBI system and the evolution of the ToBI framework. In S. Jun (Ed.), *Prosodic typology: The phonology of intonation and phrasing* (pp. 9–54). Oxford University Press. https://doi.org/10.1093/acprof:oso/9780199249633.003.0002.

Beckman, M.E., & Pierrehumbert, J. (1986). Intonational structure in Japanese and English. *Phonology Yearbook*, *3*, 255–309. https://doi.org/10.1017/S095267570000066X.

Benguerel, A.P., & Pichora-Fuller, M.K. (1982). Coarticulation effects in lipreading. *Journal of Speech and Hearing Research*, *25*(4), 600–7. https://doi.org/10.1044/jshr.2504.600.

Benoît, C., Mohamadi, T., & Kandel, S. (1994). Effects of phonetic context on audio-visual intelligibility of French. *Journal of Speech, Language, and Hearing Research*, *37*(5), 1195–1203. https://doi.org/10.1044/jshr.3705.1195.

Berger, K.W. (1972). *Speechreading: Principles and methods*. National Education Press.

Berger, K.W. (1973). Consonant confusions in speechreading. *Ohio Journal of Speech and Hearing*, *8*(1), 10–18.

Bergeson, T.R., Pisoni, D.B., & Davis, R.A.O. (2003). A longitudinal study of audiovisual speech perception by children with hearing loss who have cochlear implants. *Volta Review*, *103*(4), 347–70. PMID: 21743753.

Berlitz, M., & Dubois, E. (1882). *Méthode pour l'enseignement la langue française dans les écoles Berlitz, première partie*. Karl Schoenhof.

Berman, J. (2008, February 8). *Anderson Cooper 360 Degrees* [TV broadcast transcript]. CNN. https://transcripts.cnn.com/show/acd/date/2022-02-08/segment/01.

Bernstein, L.E., Auer, E.T., & Eberhardt, S.P. (2022). During lipreading training with sentence stimuli, feedback controls learning and generalization to audiovisual speech in noise. *American Journal of Audiology*, *31*(1), 57–77. https://doi.org/10.1044/2021_AJA-21-00034.

Bernstein, L.E., Auer, E.T., Wagner, M., & Ponton, C.W. (2008). Spatiotemporal dynamics of audiovisual speech processing. *NeuroImage*, *39*(1), 423–35. https://doi.org/10.1016/j.neuroimage.2007.08.035.

Bernstein, L.E., Demorest, M.E., & Tucker, P.E. (2000). Speech perception without hearing. *Perception & Psychophysics*, *62*(2), 233–52. https://doi.org/10.3758/BF03205546.

Bernstein, L.E., Jiang, J., Pantazis, D., Lu, Z.L., & Joshi, A. (2011). Visual phonetic processing localized using speech and nonspeech face gestures in video and point-light displays. *Human Brain Mapping*, *32*, 1660–76. https://doi.org/10.1002/hbm.21139.

Bernstein, L.E., & Liebenthal, E. (2014). Neural pathways for visual speech perception. *Frontiers in Neuroscience*, *8*, Article 386. https://doi.org/10.3389/fnins.2014.00386.

Bertelson, P., & Aschersleben, G. (1998). Automatic visual bias of perceived auditory location. *Psychonomic Bulletin & Review*, *5*(3), 482–9. https://doi.org/10.3758/BF03208826.

Best, C.T., & Tyler, M.D. (2007). Nonnative and second-language speech perception: Commonalities and complementarities. In M.J. Munro & O.-S. Bohn (Eds.), *Language experience in second language speech learning: In honor of James Emil Flege* (pp. 13–34). John Benjamins. https://doi.org/10.1075/lllt.17.07bes.

Bicevskis, K., Derrick, D., & Gick, B. (2016). Visual-tactile integration in speech perception: Evidence for modality neutral speech primitives. *Journal of the Acoustical Society of America*, *140*(5), 3531–9. https://doi.org/10.1121/1.4965968.

Binnie, C.A., Jackson, P.L., & Montgomery, A.A. (1976). Visual intelligibility of consonants: A lipreading screening test with implications for aural rehabilitation. *Journal of Speech and Hearing Disorders*, *41*(4), 530–9. https://doi.org/10.1044/jshd.4104.530.

Binnie, C.A., Montgomery, A.A., & Jackson, P.L. (1974). Auditory and visual contributions to the perception of consonants. *Journal of Speech and Hearing Research*, *17*(4), 619–30. https://doi.org/10.1044/jshr.1704.619.

Birch, H.G., & Lefford, A. (1967). Visual differentiation, intersensory integration, and voluntary motor control. *Monographs of the Society for Research in Child Development, 32*(2), 1–87. https://doi.org/10.2307/1165792.

Birdwhistell, R.L. (1970). *Kinesics and context: Essays on body motion communication.* University of Pennsylvania Press. https://doi.org/10.9783/9780812201284.

Birulés, J., Bosch, L., Pons, F., & Lewkowicz, D.J. (2020). Highly proficient L2 speakers still need to attend to a talker's mouth when processing L2 speech. *Language, Cognition and Neuroscience, 35*(10), 1314–25. https://doi.org/10.1080/23273798.2020.1762905.

Blackwood, D.H., & Muir, W.J. (1990). Cognitive brain potentials and their application. *British Journal of Psychiatry, 157*(S9), 96–101. https://doi.org/10.1192/S0007125000291897.

Blais, C., Jack, R.E., Scheepers, C., Fiset, D., & Caldara, R. (2008). Culture shapes how we look at faces. *PLoS ONE, 3*(8), Article e3022. https://doi.org/10.1371/journal.pone.0003022.

Bliss, H., Abel, J., & Gick, B. (2018). Computer-assisted visual articulation feedback in L2 pronunciation instruction: A review. *Journal of Second Language Pronunciation, 4*(1), 129–53. https://doi.org/10.1075/jslp.00006.bli.

Boersma, P., & Weenink, D. (2022). Praat: Doing phonetics by computer (Version 6.2.21) [Computer software]. Paul Boersma. http://www.fon.hum.uva.nl/praat.

Bohn, O.S. (1995). Cross-language perception in adults: First language transfer doesn't tell it all. In W. Strange (Ed.). *Speech perception and linguistic experience: Theoretical and methodological issues* (pp. 370–410). York Press.

Bojko, A. (2009). Informative or misleading? Heatmaps deconstructed. In J.A. Jacko (Ed.), *Human-computer interaction: New trends* (pp. 30–9). Springer. https://doi.org/10.1007/978-3-642-02574-7_4.

Bolinger, D. (1985). *Intonation and its parts: Melody in spoken English.* Stanford University Press.

Bond, R. (2014). The eyes have it. In *Falling in love again: Stories of love and romance* (pp. 1–5). Rupa Publications India.

Bonda, E., Petrides, M., Ostry, D., & Evans, A. (1996). Specific involvement of human parietal systems and the amygdala in the perception of biological motion. *Journal of Neuroscience, 16*(11), 3737–44. https://doi.org/10.1523/JNEUROSCI.16-11-03737.1996.

Bovo, R., Ciorba, A., Prosser, S., & Martini, A. (2009). The McGurk phenomenon in Italian listeners. *Acta Otorhinolaryngologica Italica, 29*(4), 203–8. PMID: 20161878.

Bower, T.G.R. (1974). The evolution of sensory systems. In R.B. MacLeod & H.L. Pick (Eds.), *Perception: Essays in honor of James G. Gibson* (pp. 141–65). Cornell University Press.

Bradlow, A.R., Akahane-Yamada, R., Pisoni, D.B., & Tohkura, Y. (1999). Training Japanese listeners to identify English /r/ and /l/: Long-term retention of learning in perception and production. *Perception & Psychophysics, 61*(5), 977–85. https://doi.org/10.3758/BF03206911.

Bradlow, A.R., Toretta, G.M., & Pisoni, D.B. (1996). Intelligibility of normal speech I: Global and fine-grained acoustic-phonetic talker characteristics. *Speech Communication, 20*(3–4), 255–72. https://doi.org/10.1016/S0167-6393(96)00063-5.

Breitkreutz, J.A., Derwing, T.M., & Rossiter, J. (2001). Pronunciation teaching practices in Canada. *TESL Canada Journal, 19*(1), 51–61. https://doi.org/10.18806/tesl.v19i1.919.

Broaders, S.C., Cook, S.W., Mitchell, Z., & Goldin-Meadow, S. (2007). Making children gesture brings out implicit knowledge and leads to learning. *Journal of Experimental Psychology: General, 136*(4), 539–50. https://doi.org/10.1037/0096-3445.136.4.539.

Brône, G., & Oben, B. (2018). Introduction: Gaze, interaction and eye-tracking: A multidisciplinary endeavor. In G. Brône & B. Oben (Eds.), *Eye-tracking in interaction: Studies on the role of eye gaze in dialogue* (pp. 1–18). John Benjamins. https://doi.org/10.1075/ais.10.01bro.

Brooks, R., & Meltzoff, A.N. (2005). The development of gaze following and its relation to language. *Developmental Science*, *8*(6), 535–43. https://doi.org/10.1111/j.1467-7687.2005.00445.x.

Brown, A. (1988). Functional load and the teaching of pronunciation. *TESOL Quarterly*, *22*(4), 593–606. https://doi.org/10.2307/3587258.

Brown, J.D., & Crowther, D. (2023). *Shaping learners' pronunciation: Teaching the connected speech of North American English*. Routledge. https://doi.org/10.4324/9781003144779.

Brown, J.D., & Hilferty, A. (1986). The effectiveness of teaching reduced forms for listening comprehension. *RELC Journal*, *17*(2), 59–70. https://doi.org/10.1177/003368828601700204.

Bruce, V., & Green, P. (1985). *Visual perception: Physiology, psychology and ecology*. Erlbaum.

Buchan, J.N., Paré, M., & Munhall, K.G. (2007). Spatial statistics of gaze fixations during dynamic face processing. *Social Neuroscience*, *2*(1), 1–13. https://doi.org/10.1080/17470910601043644.

Buchan, J.N., Paré, M., & Munhall, K.G. (2008). The effect of varying talker identity and listening conditions on gaze behavior during audiovisual speech perception. *Brain Research*, *1242*, 162–71. https://doi.org/10.1016/j.brainres.2008.06.083.

Bull, P., & Connelly, G. (1985). Body movement and emphasis in speech. *Journal of Nonverbal Behavior*, *9*(3), 169–87. https://doi.org/10.1007/BF01000738.

Burnham, K.P., Anderson, D.R., & Huyvaert, K.P. (2011). AIC model selection and multimodel inference in behavioral ecology: Some background, observations, and comparisons. *Behavioral Ecology and Sociobiology*, *65*(1), 25–35. https://doi.org/10.1007/s00265-010-1029-6.

Burnham, D., Lau, S., Tam, H., & Schoknecht, C. (2001). Visual discrimination of Cantonese tone by tonal but non-Cantonese speakers, and by non-tonal language speakers. In D.W. Massaro, K. Geraci, & J. Light (Eds.), *Proceedings of the Auditory-Visual Speech Perception Conference 2001 (AVSP 2001)* (pp. 155–60). Causal Productions. https://www.isca-archive.org/avsp_2001/burnham01_avsp.html.

Callan, D.E., Jones, J.A., Munhall, K., Callan, A.M., Kroos, C., & Vatikiotis-Bateson, E. (2003). Neural processes underlying perceptual enhancement by visual speech gestures. *Neuroreport*, *14*(17), 2213–18. https://doi.org/10.1097/00001756-200312020-00016.

Calvert, G.A., Bullmore, E.T., Brammer, M.J., Campbell, R., Williams, S.C., McGuire, P.K., Woodruff, P.W.R., Iversen, S.D., & David, A.S. (1997). Activation of auditory cortex during silent lipreading. *Science*, *276*(5312), 593–6. https://doi.org/10.1126/science.276.5312.593.

Calvert, G.A., & Campbell, R. (2003). Reading speech from still and moving faces: The neural substrates of visible speech. *Journal of Cognitive Neuroscience*, *15*(1), 57–70. https://doi.org/10.1162/089892903321107828.

Canolty, R.T., Soltani, M., Dalal, S.S., Edwards, E., Dronkers, N.F., Nagarajan, S.S., Kirsch, H.E., Barbaro, N.M., & Knight, R.T. (2007). Spatiotemporal dynamics of word processing in the human brain. *Frontiers in Neuroscience*, *1*(1), 185–96. https://doi.org/10.3389/neuro.01.1.1.014.2007.

Carota, F., Moseley, R., & Pulvermüller, F. (2012). Body-part-specific representations of semantic noun categories. *Journal of Cognitive Neuroscience*, *24*(6), 1492–1509. https://doi.org/10.1162/jocn_a_00219.

Carton, F. (1974). *Introduction à la phonétique du français*. Bordas.

CAST. (2018). The Universal Design for Learning (UDL) guidelines (Version 2.2). https://udlguidelines.cast.org/static/udlg2.2-text-a11y.pdf.

Cecchetti, L., Kupers, R., Ptito, M., Pietrini, P., & Ricciardi, E., (2016). Are supramodality and cross-modal plasticity the yin and yang of brain development? From blindness to rehabilitation. *Frontiers in Systems Neuroscience, 10*, Article 89. https://doi.org/10.3389/fnsys.2016.00089.

Celce-Murcia, M. (1983, May). Activities for teaching pronunciation communicatively. *CATESOL News*, 10–11.

Celce-Murcia, M., Brinton, D.M., Goodwin, J.M., & Griner, B. (2010). *Teaching pronunciation: A course book and reference guide* (2nd ed.). Cambridge University Press.

Centre de recherche et d'étude pour la diffusion du français (CREDIF). (1962). *Voix et images de France: Cours audio-visuel de français premier degré*. Harrap.

Chafe, W. (1994). *Discourse, consciousness, and time: The flow and displacement of conscious experience in speaking and writing*. University of Chicago Press.

Chandrasekaran, C., Trubanova, A., Stillittano, S., Caplier, A., & Ghazanfar, A.A. (2009). The natural statistics of audiovisual speech. *PLoS Computational Biology*, *5*(7), Article e1000436. https://doi.org/10.1371/journal.pcbi.1000436.

Cho, T. (2006). Manifestation of prosodic structure in articulation: Evidence from lip kinematics in English. In L.M. Goldstein, D.H. Whalen, & C.T. Best (Eds.), *Laboratory phonology 8: Varieties of phonological competence* (pp. 519–48). De Gruyter Mouton. https://doi.org/10.1515/9783110197211.

Chun, D.M., & Jiang, Y. (2022). Using technology to explore L2 pronunciation. In J. Levis, T. Derwing, & S. Sonsaat-Hegelheimer (Eds.), *Second language pronunciation: Bridging the gap between research and teaching* (pp. 129–50). Wiley. https://doi.org/10.1002/9781394259663.ch7.

Clark, H.H. (1996). *Using language*. Cambridge University Press. https://doi.org/10.1017/CBO9780511620539.

Cohen, R.L. (1981). On the generality of some memory laws. *Scandinavian Journal of Psychology*, *22*(1), 267–81. https://doi.org/10.1111/j.1467-9450.1981.tb00402.x.

Collins, B., & Mees, I.M. (Eds.). (2002). *Daniel Jones, selected works: Vol. 8. Unpublished writings and correspondence*. Routledge.

Collins, B., Mees, I.M., & Carley, P. (2019). *Practical English phonetics and phonology: A resource book for students* (4th ed.). Routledge. https://doi.org/10.4324/9780429490392.

Condon, W.S. (1976). An analysis of behavioral organization. *Sign Language Studies*, *13*, 285–318. https://www.jstor.org/stable/26203180.

Conrey, B., & Gold, J.M. (2006). An ideal observer analysis of variability in visual-only speech. *Vision Research*, *46*(19), 3243–58. https://doi.org/10.1016/j.visres.2006.03.020.

Cook, S.W., & Tanenhaus, M.K. (2009). Embodied communication: Speakers' gestures affect listeners' actions. *Cognition*, *113*(1), 98–104. https://doi.org/10.1016/j.cognition.2009.06.006.

Council of Europe. (2001). *Common European framework of reference for languages: Learning, teaching, assessment*. Cambridge University Press.

Couper, G. (2021). Pronunciation teaching issues: Answering teachers' questions. *RELC Journal*, *52*(1), 128–43. https://doi.org/10.1177/0033688220964041.

Crowther, D.J. (2018). *Linguistic measures of second language speech: Moving from monologic to interactive speech* (Publication No. 10808765) [Doctoral dissertation, Michigan State University]. ProQuest Dissertations and Theses Global.

Cutler, A., & Jesse, A. (2021). Word stress in speech perception. In J.S. Pardo, L.C. Nygaard, & D.B. Pisoni (Eds.), *The handbook of speech perception* (2nd ed., pp. 239–65). John Wiley & Sons. https://doi.org/10.1002/9781119184096.ch9.

Dahl, C.D., Logothetis, N.K., & Kayser, C. (2009). Spatial organization of multisensory responses in temporal association cortex. *Journal of Neuroscience*, *29*(38), 11924–32. https://doi.org/10.1523/JNEUROSCI.3437-09.2009.

Dahl, T.I., & Ludvigsen, S. (2014). How I see what you're saying: The role of gestures in native and foreign language listening comprehension. *Modern Language Journal*, *98*(3), 813–33. https://doi.org/10.1111/modl.12124.

Dale, P., & Poms, L. (2005). *English pronunciation made simple*. Pearson Education.

Daniloff, R.G., & Hammarberg, R.E. (1973). On defining coarticulation. *Journal of Phonetics*, *1*(3), 239–48. https://doi.org/10.1016/S0095-4470(19)31388-9.

Daniloff, R.G., & Moll, K. (1968). Coarticulation of lip rounding. *Journal of Speech and Hearing Research*, *11*(4), 707–21. https://doi.org/10.1044/jshr.1104.707.

Darcy, I., Rocca, B., & Hancock, Z. (2021). A window into the classroom: How teachers integrate pronunciation instruction. *RELC Journal*, *52*(1), 110–27. https://doi.org/10.1177/0033688220964269.

Darwin, C. (1899). *The expression of the emotions in man and animals*. D. Appleton and Company. https://www.gutenberg.org/files/1227/1227-h/1227-h.htm. (Original work published 1872)

de Barros, P.C.M. (2010). *"It's easier to understand": The effect of a speaker's accent, visual cues, and background knowledge on listening comprehension* [Master's thesis, Kansas State University]. Kansas State University Libraries. http://hdl.handle.net/2097/4492.

Degutyte, Z., & Astell, A. (2021). The role of eye gaze in regulating turn taking in conversations: A systematized review of methods and findings. *Frontiers in Psychology*, *12*, Article 616471. https://doi.org/10.3389/fpsyg.2021.616471.

deHahn, P. (2020, April 16). Face masks are excluding the deaf and hard of hearing community. *Quartz*. https://qz.com/1839479/covid-19-face-masks-exclude-the-deaf-and-hard-of-hearing.

de Jong, K.J. (1995). The supraglottal articulation of prominence in English: Linguistic stress as localized hyperarticulation. *Journal of the Acoustical Society of America*, *97*(1), 491–504. https://doi.org/10.1121/1.412275.

Dekle, D.J., Fowler, C.A. & Funnell, M.G. (1992). Audiovisual integration in perception of real words. *Perception & Psychophysics*, *51*(4), 355–62. https://doi.org/10.3758/BF03211629.

Denis, M., Engelkamp, J., & Mohr, G. (1991). Memory of imagined actions: Imagining oneself or another person. *Psychological Research*, *53*(3), 246–50. https://doi.org/10.1007/BF00941394.

D'Entremont, B., Hains, S.M.J., & Muir, D.W. (1997). A demonstration of gaze following in 3- to 6-month-olds. *Infant Behavior and Development*, *20*(4), 569–72. https://doi.org/10.1016/S0163-6383(97)90048-5.

Derrick, D., Anderson, P., Gick, B., & Green, S. (2009). Characteristics of air puffs produced in English "pa": Data and simulation. *Journal of the Acoustic Society of America*, *125*, 2272–81. https://doi.org/10.1121/1.3081496.

Derwing, T.M. (2003). What do ESL students say about their accents? *Canadian Modern Language Review*, *59*(4), 547–67. https://doi.org/10.3138/cmlr.59.4.547.

Derwing, T.M. (2008). Curriculum issues in teaching pronunciation to second language learners. In J.G. Hansen Edwards & M.L. Zampini (Eds.), *Phonology and second language acquisition* (pp. 347–69). John Benjamins. https://doi.org/10.1075/sibil.36.17der.

Derwing, T.M. (2018). The efficacy of pronunciation instruction. In O. Kang, R.I. Thomson, & J.M. Murphy (Eds.), *The Routledge handbook of contemporary English pronunciation* (pp. 320–34). Routledge. https://doi.org/10.4324/9781315145006.

Derwing, T.M., & Munro, M.J. (1997). Accent, intelligibility, and comprehensibility: Evidence from four L1s. *Studies in Second Language Acquisition, 19*(1), 1–16. https://doi.org/10.1017/S0272263197001010.

Derwing, T.M., & Rossiter, M.J. (2002). ESL learners' perceptions of their pronunciation needs and strategies. *System, 30*, 155–66. http://dx.doi.org/10.1016/S0346-251X(02)00012-X.

Deterding, D. (2013). *Misunderstandings in English as a lingua franca: An analysis of ELF interactions in South-East Asia*. De Gruyter. https://doi.org/10.1515/9783110288599.

Deubel, H., & Schneider, W.X. (1996). Saccade target selection and object recognition: Evidence for a common attentional mechanism. *Vision Research, 36*(12), 1827–37. https://doi.org/10.1016/0042-6989(95)00294-4.

Dias, J.W., McClaskey, C.M., & Harris, K.C. (2021). Audiovisual speech is more than the sum of its parts: Auditory-visual superadditivity compensates for age-related declines in audible and lipread speech intelligibility. *Psychology and Aging, 36*(4), 520–30. https://doi.org/10.1037/pag0000613.

Dick, P.K. (1953). The eyes have it. In *Science fiction stories* (pp. 128–30). Columbia Publications.

Dimitrova, D., Chu, M., Wang, L., Özyürek, A., & Hagoort, P. (2016). Beat that word: How listeners integrate beat gesture and focus on multimodal speech discourse. *Journal of Cognitive Neuroscience, 28*(9), 1255–69. https://doi.org/10.1162/jocn_a_00963.

Dodd, B. (1977). The role of vision in the perception of speech. *Perception, 6*(1), 31–40. https://doi.org/10.1068/p060031.

Dodd, B. (1979). Lip-reading in infants: Attention to speech presented in-and out-of-synchrony. *Cognitive Psychology, 11*(4), 478–84. https://doi.org/10.1016/0010-0285(79)90021-5.

Dodd, B. (1987). The acquisition of lip-reading skills by normally hearing children. In B. Dodd & R. Campbell (Eds.), *Hearing by eye: The psychology of lip-reading* (pp. 163–75). Erlbaum.

DuBois, S.K. (2019). *Are L2 speakers allowed to use colloquialisms? L1 attitudes toward Spanish L2 speakers' use of informal lexical items* (Publication No. 13900640) [Doctoral dissertation, University of California, Santa Barbara]. ProQuest Dissertations and Theses Global.

Dylan, B. (1963). Blowin' in the wind [Song]. On *The Freewheelin' Bob Dylan*. Columbia.

Easton, R.D., & Basala, M. (1982). Perceptual dominance during lipreading. *Perception & Psychophysics, 32*(6), 562–70. https://doi.org/10.3758/BF03204211.

Eckstein, G.T. (2007). *A correlation of pronunciation learning strategies with spontaneous English production of adult ESL learners* [Master's thesis, Brigham Young University]. Brigham Young University Scholars Archive. https://scholarsarchive.byu.edu/etd/973.

Elff, M. (2013). mclogit: Mixed Conditional Logit, R package (Version 0.2–7) [Computer software]. Martin Elff. https://doi.org/10.32614/CRAN.package.mclogit.

Elliott, N.C. (2018). Teaching tip: The vowel elevator: A visual-kinesthetic way to expand the vowel space. In J. Levis (Ed.), *Proceedings of the 9th Pronunciation in Second Language Learning and Teaching Conference* (pp. 239–44). Iowa State University. https://apling.engl.iastate.edu/wp-content/uploads/sites/221/2018/09/PSLLT-Proceedings-9_9-14-18_2.pdf.

Emery, N.J. (2000). The eyes have it: The neuroethology, function and evolution of social gaze. *Neuroscience and Biobehavioral Reviews, 24*(6), 581–604. https://doi.org/10.1016/S0149-7634(00)00025-7.

Engelkamp, J., & Krumnacker, H. (1980). Image- and motor-processes in the retention of verbal materials. *Zeitschrift für Experimentelle und Angewandte Psychologie, 27*(4), 511–33.

Engelkamp J., & Zimmer, H.D. (1994). Motor similarity in subject-performed tasks. *Psychological Research, 57*, 47–53. https://doi.org/10.1007/bf00452995.

Erber, N.P. (1969). Interaction of audition and vision in the recognition of oral speech stimuli. *Journal of Speech and Hearing Research, 12*(2), 423–5. https://doi.org/10.1044/jshr.1202.423.

Esling, J.H., Moisik, S.R., Benner, A., & Crevier-Buchman, L. (2019). *Voice quality: The laryngeal articulator model*. Cambridge University Press. https://doi.org/10.1017/9781108696555.

Esling, J.H., & Wong, R.F. (1983). Voice quality settings and the teaching of pronunciation. *TESOL Quarterly, 17*(1), 89–95. https://doi.org/10.2307/3586426.

Everdell, I.T., Marsh, H., Yurick, M.D., Munhall, K.G., & Paré, M. (2007). Gaze behaviour in audiovisual speech perception: Asymmetrical distribution of face-directed fixations. *Perception, 36*(10), 1535–45. https://doi.org/10.1068/p5852.

Fairhurst, M.T., Travers, E., Hayward, V., & Deroy, O. (2018). Confidence is higher in touch than in vision in cases of perceptual ambiguity. *Scientific Reports, 8*(1), Article 15604. https://doi.org/10.1038/s41598-018-34052-z.

Faraco, M., & Kida, T. (2008). Gesture and the negotiation of meaning in a second language classroom. In S.G. McCafferty & G. Stam (Eds.), *Gesture: Second language acquisition and classroom research* (pp. 280–97). Routledge.

Findlay, J.M. (1982). Global visual processing for saccadic eye movements. *Vision Research, 22*(8), 1033–45. https://doi.org/10.1016/0042-6989(82)90040-2.

Fisher, C.G. (1968). Confusions among visually perceived consonants. *Journal of Speech and Hearing Research, 11*(4), 796–804. https://doi.org/10.1044/jshr.1104.796.

Flecha-García, M.L. (2010). Eyebrow raises in dialogue and their relation to discourse structure, utterance function and pitch accents in English. *Speech Communication, 52*(6), 542–54. https://doi.org/10.1016/j.specom.2009.12.003.

Flege, J.E., & Bohn, O. (2021). The Revised Speech Learning Model (SLM-r). In R. Wayland (Ed.), *Second language speech learning: Theoretical and empirical progress* (pp. 3–83). Cambridge University Press. https://doi.org/10.1017/9781108886901.002.

Flege, J.E., & Liu, S. (2001). The effect of experience on adults' acquisition of a second language. *Studies in Second Language Acquisition, 23*(4), 527–52. https://doi.org/10.1017/S0272263101004041.

Fletcher, M.D., Mills, S.R., & Goehring, T. (2018). Vibro-tactile enhancement of speech intelligibility in multi-talker noise for simulated cochlear implant listening. *Trends in Hearing*, 22, 1–11. https://doi.org/10.1177/2331216518797838.

Flinker, A., Korzeniewska, A., Shestyuk, A., Franaszczuk, P.J., Dronkers, N.F., Knight, R.T., & Crone, N.E. (2015). Redefining the role of Broca's area in speech. *Proceedings of the National Academy of Sciences, 112*(9), 2871–5. https://doi.org/10.1073/pnas.1414491112.

Floyd, S., Manrique, E., Rossi, G., & Torreira, F. (2016). Timing of visual bodily behavior in repair sequences: Evidence from three languages. *Discourse Processes, 53*(3), 175–204. https://doi.org/10.1080/0163853X.2014.992680.

Foote, J.A., Holtby, A.K., & Derwing, T.M. (2011). Survey of the teaching of pronunciation in adult ESL programs in Canada, 2010. *TESL Canada Journal, 29*(1), 1–22. https://doi.org/10.18806/tesl.v29i1.1086.

Formisano, E., de Martino, F., Bonte, M., & Goebel, R. (2008). "Who" is saying "what"? Brain-based decoding of human voice and speech. *Science, 322*(5903), 970–3. https://doi.org/10.1126/science.1164318.

Fort, M., Kandel, S., Chipot, J., Savariaux, C., Granjon, L., & Spinelli, E. (2012). Seeing the initial articulatory gestures of a word triggers lexical access. *Language and Cognitive Processes, 28*(8), 1207–23. http://dx.doi.org/10.1080/01690965.2012.701758.

Fowler, C. (2004). Speech as a supramodal or amodal phenomenon. In G.A. Calvert, C. Spence, & B.E. Stein (Eds.), *The handbook of multisensory processes* (pp. 189–201). Boston Review. https://doi.org/10.7551/mitpress/3422.003.0016.

Fowler, C., & Dekle, D.J. (1991). Listening with eye and hand: Cross-modal contributions to speech perception. *Journal of Experimental Psychology: Human Perception and Performance, 17*(3), 816–28. https://doi.org/10.1037/0096-1523.17.3.816.

Fraisse, P. (1982). Rhythm and tempo. In D. Deutsch (Ed.), *The psychology of music* (pp. 149–80). Academic Press. https://doi.org/10.1016/B978-0-12-213562-0.50010-3.

Franks, J.R., & Kimble, J. (1972). The confusion of English consonant clusters in lipreading. *Journal of Speech and Hearing Research, 15*(3), 474–82. https://doi.org/10.1044/jshr.1503.474.

Friston, K.J. (2009). Modalities, modes, and models in functional neuroimaging. *Science, 326*(5951), 399–403. https://doi.org/10.1126/science.1174521.

Fromkin, V. (1964). Lip positions in American English vowels. *Language and Speech, 7*(4), 215–25. https://doi.org/10.1177/002383096400700402.

Fuster-Duran, A. (1996). Perception of conflicting audio-visual speech: An examination across Spanish and German. In D.G. Stork & M.E. Hennecke (Eds.), *Speechreading by humans and machines: Models, systems, and applications* (pp. 135–43). Springer. https://doi.org/10.1007/978-3-662-13015-5_9.

Gagné, J.P., Masterson, V., Munhall, K.G., Bilida, N., & Querengesser, C. (1994). Across talker variability in auditory, visual, and audiovisual speech intelligibility for conversational and clear speech. *Journal of the Academy of Rehabilitative Audiology, 27*, 135–58.

Gagnon, S.G., & Hardison, D.M. (2022). Hidden in plain sight: An exploration of learner productions of phonological processes in Korean and their impact on comprehensibility to the native and non-native ear. *Korean Language in America, 26*(1–2), 22–46. https://doi.org/10.5325/korelangamer.26.1-2.0022.

Galley, N., Betz, D., & Biniossek, C. (2015). Fixation durations: Why are they so highly variable? In T. Heinen (Ed.), *Advances in visual perception research* (pp. 1–26). Nova Science Publishers. https://doi.org/10.13140/RG.2.1.3128.1769.

Gass, S.M. (2017). *Input, interaction, and the second language learner* (2nd ed.). Routledge. https://doi.org/10.4324/9781315173252.

Gass, S.M., Bardovi-Harlig, K., Sieloff Magnan, S., & Walz, J. (Eds.). (2002). *Pedagogical norms for second and foreign language learning and teaching: Studies in honour of Albert Valdman.* John Benjamins. https://doi.org/10.1075/lllt.5.

Gass, S.M., & Varonis, E.M. (1984). The effect of familiarity on the comprehensibility of nonnative speech. *Language Learning, 34*(1), 65–89. https://doi.org/10.1111/j.1467-1770.1984.tb00996.x.

Gatbonton, E., Trofimovich, P., & Magid, M. (2005). Learners' ethnic group affiliation and L2 pronunciation accuracy: A sociolinguistic investigation. *TESOL Quarterly*, *39*(3), 489–511. https://doi.org/10.2307/3588491.

Geisler, W.S. (2004). Ideal observer analysis. In L.M. Chalupa & J.S. Werner (Eds.), *The visual neurosciences* (pp. 825–37). MIT Press. https://doi.org/10.7551/mitpress/7131.003.0061.

George, A. (2014). Study abroad in central Spain: The development of regional phonological features. *Foreign Language Annals*, *47*(1), 97–114. https://doi.org/10.1111/flan.12065.

Gibson, J.J. (1966). *The senses considered as perceptual systems*. Houghton Mifflin.

Gick, B., & Derrick, D. (2009). Aero-tactile integration in speech perception. *Nature*, *462*(7272), 502–4. https://doi.org/10.1038/nature08572.

Gick, B., Ikegami, Y., & Derrick, D. (2010). The temporal window of audio-tactile integration in speech perception. *Journal of the Acoustical Society of America*, *128*(5), EL342–6. https://doi.org/10.1121/1.3505759.

Gick, B., Jóhannsdóttir, K.M., Gibraiel, D., & Mühlbauer, J. (2008). Tactile enhancement of auditory and visual speech perception in untrained perceivers. *Journal of the Acoustical Society of America*, *123*(4), EL72–6. https://doi.org/10.1121/1.2884349.

Gick, B., Wilson, I., Koch, K., & Cook, C. (2004). Language-specific articulatory settings: Evidence from inter-utterance rest position. *Phonetica*, *61*, 220–33. https://doi.org/10.1159/000084159.

Gilbert, J.B. (2012). *Clear Speech* (4th ed.). Cambridge University Press.

Gliga, T., & Csibra, G. (2009). One-year-old infants appreciate the referential nature of deictic gestures and words. *Psychological Science*, *20*(3), 347–53. https://doi.org/10.1111/j.1467-9280.2009.02295.x.

Glover, G.H. (2011). Overview of functional magnetic resonance imaging. *Neurosurgery Clinics of North America*, *22*(2), 133–9. https://doi.org/10.1016/j.nec.2010.11.001.

Goldinger, S.D. (1997). Words and voices: Perception and production in an episodic lexicon. In K. Johnson & J.W. Mullennix (Eds.), *Talker variability in speech processing* (pp. 33–66). Academic Press.

Goldinger, S.D. (2007). A complementary-systems approach to abstract and episodic speech perception. In J. Trouvain & W.J. Berry (Eds.), *Proceedings of the 16th International Congress of Phonetic Sciences* (pp. 49–54). Saarland University Press.

Goldin-Meadow, S. (1999). The role of gesture in communication and thinking. *Trends in Cognitive Sciences*, *3*(11), 419–29. https://doi.org/10.1016/S1364-6613(99)01397-2.

Goldin-Meadow, S., Nusbaum, H., Kelly, S.D., & Wagner, S. (2001). Explaining math: Gesturing lightens the load. *Psychological Science*, *12*(6), 516–22. https://doi.org/10.1111/1467-9280.00395.

Golinkoff, R.M., Hirsh-Pasek, K., Cauley, K.M., & Gordon, L. (1987). The eyes have it: Lexical and syntactic comprehension in a new paradigm. *Journal of Child Language*, *14*(1), 23–45. https://doi.org/10.1017/S030500090001271X.

Goodwin, M.H., & Goodwin C. (1986). Gesture and coparticipation in the activity of searching for a word. *Semiotica*, *62*(1–2), 51–75. https://doi.org/10.1515/semi.1986.62.1-2.51.

Goto, H. (1971). Auditory perception by normal Japanese adults of the sounds "l" and "r." *Neuropsychologia*, *9*(3), 317–23. https://doi.org/10.1016/0028-3932(71)90027-3.

Grant, K.W., Walden, B.E., & Seitz, P.F. (1998). Auditory-visual speech recognition by hearing-impaired subjects: Consonant recognition, sentence recognition, and auditory-visual integration. *Journal of the Acoustical Society of America, 103*(5), 2677–90. https://doi.org/10.1121/1.422788.

Grant, L. (2017). *Well said: Pronunciation for clear communication* (4th ed.). Cengage Learning.

Gratiolet, L. (1865). *De la physionomie et des mouvements d'expression*. J. Hetzel.

Green, K.P., Kuhl, P.K., & Meltzoff, A.N. (1988). Factors affecting the integration of auditory and visual information in speech: The effect of vowel environment. *Journal of the Acoustical Society of America, 84*(S1), S155. https://doi.org/10.1121/1.2025888.

Green, K.P., Kuhl, P.K., Meltzoff, A.N., & Stevens, E.B. (1991). Integrating speech information across talkers, gender, and sensory modality: Female faces and male voices in the McGurk effect. *Perception & Psychophysics, 50*(6), 425–536. https://doi.org/10.3758/BF03207536.

Gregersen, T. (2005). Nonverbal cues: Clues to the detection of foreign language anxiety. *Foreign Language Annals, 38*(3), 388–400. https://doi.org/10.1111/j.1944-9720.2005.tb02225.x.

Gregersen, T., Olivares-Cuhat, G., & Storm, J. (2009). An examination of L1 and L2 gesture use: What role does proficiency play? *Modern Language Journal, 93*(2), 195–208. https://doi.org/10.1111/j.1540-4781.2009.00856.x.

Grosjean, F. (1980). Spoken word recognition processes and the gating paradigm. *Perception & Psychophysics, 28*(4), 267–83. https://doi.org/10.3758/BF03204386.

Grüter, T., Kim. J., Nishizawa, H., Wang, J., Alzahrani, R., Chang, Y-T., Nguyen, H., Nuesser, M., Ohba, A., Roos, S., & Yusa, M. (2023). Language proficiency modulates listeners' selective attention to a talker's mouth: A conceptual replication of Birulés et al. (2020). *Studies in Second Language Acquisition, 45*(4), 1074–89. https://doi.org/10.1017/S0272263123000086.

Gullberg, M. (1998). *Gesture as a communication strategy in second language discourse: A study of learners of French and Swedish* [Doctoral dissertation, Lund University]. Lund University Press. https://lucris.lub.lu.se/ws/portalfiles/portal/4825091/3912717.pdf.

Gullberg, M. (2006). Some reasons for studying gesture and second language acquisition (Hommage à Adam Kendon). *International Review of Applied Linguistics in Language Teaching, 44*(2), 103–24. https://doi.org/10.1515/IRAL.2006.004.

Gullberg, M. (2011). Multilingual multimodality: Communicative difficulties and their solutions in second language use. In J. Streeck, C. Goodwin, & C. LeBaron (Eds.), *Embodied interaction: Language and body in the material world* (pp. 137–51). Cambridge University Press.

Gullberg, M., & Holmqvist, K. (1999). Keeping an eye on gestures: Visual perception of gestures in face-to-face communication. *Pragmatics & Cognition, 7*(1), 35–63. https://doi.org/10.1075/pc.7.1.04gul.

Gullberg, M., & Holmqvist, K. (2006). What speakers do and what addressees look at: Visual attention to gestures in human interaction live and on video. *Pragmatics & Cognition, 14*(1), 53–82. https://doi.org/10.1075/pc.14.1.05gul.

Gullberg, M., Roberts, L., Dimroth, C., Veroude, K., & Indefrey, P. (2010). Adult language learning after minimal exposure to an unknown natural language. *Language Learning, 60*(s2), 5–24. https://doi.org/10.1111/j.1467-9922.2010.00598.x.

Guo, K., Meints, K., Hall, C., Hall, S., & Mills, D. (2009). Left gaze bias in humans, rhesus monkeys and domestic dogs. *Animal Cognition, 12*(3), 409–18. https://doi.org/10.1007/s10071-008-0199-3.

Guo, K., Smith, C., Powell, K., & Nicholls, K. (2012). Consistent left gaze bias in processing different facial cues. *Psychological Research, 76*, 263–9. https://doi.org/10.1007/s00426-011-0340-9.

Gurler, D., Doyle, N., Walker, E., Magnotti, J., & Beauchamp, M. (2015). A link between individual differences in multisensory speech perception and eye movements. *Attention, Perception, & Psychophysics, 77*, 1333–41. https://doi.org/10.3758/s13414-014-0821-1.

Gustafsson, E., Brisson, J., Beaulieu, C., Mainville, M., Mailloux, D., & Sirois, S. (2015). How do infants recognize joint attention? *Infant Behavior and Development, 40*, 64–72. https://doi.org/10.1016/j.infbeh.2015.04.007.

Gutzmann, H. (1912). *Sprachheilkunde: Vorlesungen über die Störungen der Sprache mit besondere Berücksichtigung der Therapie*. Kornfeld.

Hadar, U., Dar, R., & Teitelman, A. (2001). Gesture during speech in first and second language: Implications for lexical retrieval. *Gesture, 1*(2), 151–65. https://doi.org/10.1075/gest.1.2.04had.

Hadar, U. Steiner, T.J., Grant, E.C., & Rose, F.C. (1983). Head movement correlates of juncture and stress at sentence level. *Language and Speech, 26*(2), 117–29. https://doi.org/10.1177/002383098302600202.

Hall, K.C., Allen, B., Fry, M., Johnson, K., Lo, R., Mackie, S., & McAuliffe, M. (2017). Phonological CorpusTools (Version 1.3). [Computer software]. University of British Columbia. http://phonologicalcorpustools.github.io/CorpusTools.

Hanzawa, C. (2012). *Listening behaviors in Japanese: Aizuchi and head nod use by native speakers and second language learners* [Doctoral dissertation, University of Iowa]. Iowa Research Online. https://doi.org/10.17077/etd.p4yv50ow.

Hardison, D.M. (1996). Bimodal speech perception by native and nonnative speakers of English: Factors influencing the McGurk effect. *Language Learning, 46*(1), 3–73. https://doi.org/10.1111/j.1467-1770.1996.tb00640.x.

Hardison, D.M. (2003). Acquisition of second-language speech: Effects of visual cues, context, and talker variability. *Applied Psycholinguistics, 24*(4), 495–522. https://doi.org/10.1017/S0142716403000250.

Hardison, D.M. (2004). Generalization of computer-assisted prosody training: Quantitative and qualitative findings. *Language Learning & Technology, 8*(1), 34–52. http://dx.doi.org/10125/25228.

Hardison, D.M. (2005a). Contextualized computer-based L2 prosody training: Evaluating the effects of discourse context and video input. *CALICO Journal*, 22, 175–90. https://doi.org/10.1558/cj.v22i2.175-190.

Hardison, D.M. (2005b). Second-language spoken word identification: Effects of perceptual training, visual cues, and phonetic environment. *Applied Psycholinguistics, 26*(4), 579–96. https://doi.org/10.1017/S0142716405050319.

Hardison, D.M. (2005c). Variability in bimodal spoken language processing by native and nonnative speakers of English: A closer look at effects of speech style. *Speech Communication, 46*(1), 73–93. https://doi.org/10.1016/j.specom.2005.02.002.

Hardison, D.M. (2006). Effects of familiarity with faces and voices on L2 spoken language processing: Components of memory traces. In *Interspeech 2006: Proceedings of the Ninth International Conference on Spoken Language Processing* (pp. 2462–5). International Speech Communication Association. https://doi.org/10.21437/Interspeech.2006-617.

Hardison, D.M. (2007). The visual element in phonological perception and learning. In M.C. Pennington (Ed.), *Phonology in context* (pp. 135–58). Palgrave Macmillan. https://doi.org/10.1057/9780230625396_6.

Hardison, D.M. (2010). *Trends in teaching pronunciation. CLEAR News, 14*(2), 1, 3–5. http://clear.web.cal.msu.edu/wp-content/uploads/sites/22/2018/10/fall2010.pdf.

Hardison, D.M. (2012). Second-language speech perception: A cross-disciplinary perspective on challenges and accomplishments. In S.M. Gass & A. Mackey (Eds.), *The Routledge handbook of second language acquisition* (pp. 349–63). Routledge. https://doi.org/10.4324/9780203808184.

Hardison, D.M. (2014a). Changes in second-language learners' oral skills and socio-affective profiles following study abroad: A mixed-methods approach. *Canadian Modern Language Review, 70*(4), 415–44. https://doi.org/10.3138/cmlr.2202.

Hardison, D.M. (2014b). Phonological literacy in L2 learning and teacher training. In J. Levis & A. Moyer (Eds.), *Social dynamics in second language accent* (pp. 195–218). De Gruyter Mouton. https://doi.org/10.1515/9781614511762.195.

Hardison, D.M. (2018a). Computer-assisted pronunciation training. In O. Kang, R.I. Thomson, & J.M. Murphy (Eds.), *The Routledge handbook of contemporary English pronunciation* (pp. 478–94). Routledge. https://doi.org/10.4324/9781315145006.

Hardison, D.M. (2018b). Effects of contextual and visual cues on spoken language processing: Enhancing L2 perceptual salience through focused training. In S.M. Gass, P. Spinner, & J. Behney (Eds.), *Salience in second language acquisition* (pp. 201–20). Routledge. https://doi.org/10.4324/9781315399027.

Hardison, D.M. (2018c). Visualizing the acoustic and gestural beats of emphasis in multimodal discourse: Theoretical and pedagogical implications. *Journal of Second Language Pronunciation, 4*(2), 231–58. https://doi.org/10.1075/jslp.17006.har.

Hardison, D.M. (2023). *Relationships among gesture type, pitch, and segmental duration in the speech of teachers of Japanese* [Manuscript in preparation]. Department of Linguistics, Languages, and Cultures, Michigan State University.

Hardison, D.M., & Okuno, T. (2022). Changes in second language learners' oral skills and socio-affective profile following short-term study abroad to Japan. *Study Abroad Research in Second Language Acquisition and International Education, 7*(2), 204–39. https://doi.org/10.1075/sar.21023.har.

Hardison, D.M., & Pennington, M.C. (2021). Multimodal second-language communication: Research findings and pedagogical implications. *RELC Journal, 51*(1), 62–76. https://doi.org/10.1177/0033688220966635.

Hardison, D.M., & Sonchaeng, C. (2005). Theatre voice training and technology in teaching oral skills: Integrating components of a speech event. *System, 33*(4), 593–608. https://doi.org/10.1016/j.system.2005.02.001.

Harris, J. (2004). Release the captive coda: The foot as a domain of phonetic interpretation. In J. Local, R. Ogden, & R. Temple (Eds.), *Phonetic interpretation: Papers in laboratory phonology VI* (pp. 103–29). Cambridge University Press. https://doi.org/10.1017/CBO9780511486425.007.

Hattori, T. (1987). A study of nonverbal intercultural communication between Japanese and Americans: Focusing on the use of the eyes. *Japan Association of Language Teachers, 8*(2), 109–18. https://jalt-publications.org/sites/default/files/pdf-article/jj-8.2-art1.pdf.

Hauk, O., Johnsrude, I., & Pulvermüller, F. (2004). Somatotopic representation of action words in human motor and premotor cortex. *Neuron, 41*(2), 301–7. http://dx.doi.org/10.1016/S0896-6273(03)00838-9.

Hayhoe, M., & Ballard, D. (2005). Eye movements in natural behavior. *Trends in Cognitive Sciences, 9*(4), 188–94. https://doi.org/10.1016/j.tics.2005.02.009.

Hazan, V., Kim, J., & Chen, Y. (2010). Audiovisual perception in adverse conditions: Language, speaker and listener effects. *Speech Communication, 52*(11–12), 996–1009. https://doi.org/10.1016/j.specom.2010.05.003.

Hazan, V., Sennema, A., Faulkner, A., & Ortega-Llebaria, M. (2006). The use of visual cues in the perception of non-native consonant contrasts. *Journal of the Acoustical Society of America, 119*(3), 1740–51. https://doi.org/10.1121/1.2166611.

Hazan, V., Sennema, A., Iba, M., & Faulkner, A. (2005). Effect of audiovisual perceptual training on the perception and production of consonants by Japanese learners of English. *Speech Communication, 47*(3), 360–78. https://doi.org/10.1016/j.specom.2005.04.007.

Heald, S.L.M., & Nusbaum, H.C. (2014). Talker variability in audio-visual speech perception. *Frontiers in Psychology, 5*, Article 698. https://doi.org/10.3389/fpsyg.2014.00698.

Heimler, B., Striem-Amit, E., & Amedi, A. (2015). Origins of task-specific sensory-independent organization in the visual and auditory brain: Neuroscience evidence, open questions and clinical implications. *Current Opinion in Neurobiology, 35*, 169–77. https://doi.org/10.1016/j.conb.2015.09.001.

Helstrup T. (1987). One, two, or three memories? A problem-solving approach to memory for performed acts. *Acta Psychologica, 66*(1), 37–68. https://doi.org/10.1016/0001-6918(87)90017-5.

Henderson, A., Frost, D., Tergujeff, E., Kautzsch, A., Murphy, D., Kirkova-Naskova, A., Waniek-Klimezak, E., Levey, D., Cunningham, U., & Curnick, L. (2012). The English pronunciation teaching in Europe survey: Selected results. *Research in Language, 10*(1), 5–27. https://doi.org/10.2478/v10015-011-0047-4.

Henderson, J.M. & Hollingworth, A (1999). High-level scene perception. *Annual Review of Psychology, 50*, 243–71. https://doi.org/10.1146/annurev.psych.50.1.243.

Herlofsky, W.J. (1985). Gaze as a regulator in Japanese conversation. *Papers in Japanese Linguistics, 10*(1–2), 16–33. https://doi.org/10.1515/jjl-1985-1-204.

Hickok, G., Buchsbaum, B., Humphries, C., & Muftuler, T. (2003). Auditory-motor interaction revealed by fMRI: Speech, music, and working memory in area Spt. *Journal of Cognitive Neuroscience, 15*(5), 673–82. https://doi.org/10.1162/089892903322307393.

Hickok, G., & Poeppel, D. (2000). Towards a functional neuroanatomy of speech perception. *Trends in Cognitive Sciences, 4*(4), 131–8. https://doi.org/10.1016/s1364-6613(00)01463-7.

Hickok, G., Rogalsky, C., Matchin, W., Basilakos, A., Cai, J., Pillay, S., Ferrill, M., Mickelsen, S., Anderson, S.W., Love, T., Binder, J., & Fridriksson, J. (2018). Neural networks supporting audiovisual integration for speech: A large-scale lesion study. *Cortex, 103*, 360–71. https://doi.org/10.1016/j.cortex.2018.03.030.

Hill, V.B., Cankurtaran, C.Z., Liu, B.P., Hijaz, T.A., Naidich, M., Nemeth, A., Gastala, J., Krumpelman, C., McComb, E.N., & Korutz, A.W. (2019). A practical review of functional MRI anatomy of the language and motor systems. *American Journal of Neuroradiology, 40*(7), 1084–90. https://doi.org/10.3174/ajnr.A6089.

Hintzman, D.L. (1986). "Schema abstraction" in a multiple-trace memory model. *Psychological Review, 93*(4), 411–28. https://doi.org/10.1037/0033-295X.93.4.411.

Hirata, Y., & Kelly, S.D. (2010). Effects of lips and hands on auditory learning of second-language speech sounds. *Journal of Speech, Language, and Hearing Research, 53*(2), 298–310. https://doi.org/10.1044/1092-4388(2009/08-0243).

Hirata, Y., Kelly, S.D., Huang, J., & Manansala, M. (2014). Effects of hand gestures on auditory learning of second-language vowel length contrasts. *Journal of Speech,*

Language, and Hearing Research, *57*(6), 2090–101. https://doi.org/10.1044/2014_JSLHR-S-14-0049.

Hisanaga, S., Sekiyama, K., Igasaki, T., & Murayama, N. (2016). Language/culture modulates brain and gaze processes in audiovisual speech perception. *Scientific Reports*, *6*, Article 35265. https://doi.org/10.1038/srep35265.

Holle, H., Gunter, T.C., Rüschemeyer, S.-A., Hennenlotter, A., & Iacoboni, M. (2008). Neural correlates of the processing of co-speech gestures. *NeuroImage*, *39*(4), 2010–24. https://doi.org/10.1016/j.neuroimage.2007.10.055.

Holmes, N.P., Calvert, G.A., & Spence, C. (2009). Multimodal integration. In M.D. Binder, N. Hirokawa, & U. Windhorst (Eds.), *Encyclopedia of neuroscience* (pp. 2457–61). Springer. https://doi.org/10.1007/978-3-540-29678-2_3640.

Holmqvist, K., & Andersson, R. (2017). *Eye tracking: A comprehensive guide to methods, paradigms, and measures* (2nd ed.). Lund Eye-Tracking Research Institute.

Homa, D., & Cultice, J.C. (1984). Role of feedback, category size, and stimulus distortion on the acquisition and utilization of ill-defined categories. *Journal of Experimental Psychology: Learning, Memory, and Cognition*, *10*(1), 83–94. https://doi.org/10.1037/0278-7393.10.1.83.

Honikman, B. (1964). Articulatory settings. In D. Abercrombie, D.B. Fry, P.A.D. MacCarthy, N.C. Scott, & J.L.M. Trimm (Eds.), *In honour of Daniel Jones: Papers contributed on the occasion of his eightieth birthday, 12 September 1961* (pp. 73–84). Longmans, Green and Co.

Howard, R. (Director). (2000). *How the Grinch stole Christmas* [Film]. Universal Pictures.

Hualde, J.I. (2005). *The sounds of Spanish*. Cambridge University Press.

Hunt, A.R., & Kingstone, A. (2003). Covert and overt voluntary attention: Linked or independent? *Cognitive Brain Research*, *18*(1), 102–5. https://doi.org/10.1016/j.cogbrainres.2003.08.006.

Hyrskykari, A., Ovaska, S., Majaranta, P., Räihä, K., & Lehtinen, M. (2008). Gaze path stimulation in retrospective think-aloud. *Journal of Eye Movement Research*, *2*(4), 1–18. https://doi.org/10.16910/jemr.2.4.5.

Inceoglu, S. (2014). *Effect of multimodal training on the perception and production of French nasal vowels by American English learners of French* (Publication No. 3623317) [Doctoral dissertation, Michigan State University]. ProQuest Dissertations and Theses Global.

Ingram, J.C.L., & Park, S.-G. (1998). Language, context, and speaker effects in the identification and discrimination of English /r/ and /l/ by Japanese and Korean listeners. *Journal of the Acoustical Society of America*, *103*(2), 1161–74. https://doi.org/10.1121/1.421225.

International Phonetic Association. (2004–9). The International Phonetic Alphabet (revised to 2005). http://westonruter.github.io/ipa-chart/keyboard.

Iverson, J.M., & Goldin-Meadow, S. (1998). Why people gesture when they speak. *Nature*, *396*(6708), 228. https://doi.org/10.1038/24300.

Jacobs, M.A. (1982). Visual communication (speechreading) for the severely and profoundly hearing-impaired adult. In D.G. Sims, G.G. Walter, & R.L. Whitehead (Eds.), *Deafness and communication: Assessment and training* (pp. 271–95). Williams and Wilkins.

Jenkins, J. (2002). A sociolinguistically based, empirically researched pronunciation syllabus for English as an international language. *Applied Linguistics*, *23*(1), 83–103. https://doi.org/10.1093/applin/23.1.83.

Jenkins, S., & Parra, I. (2003). Multiple layers of meaning in an oral proficiency test: The complementary roles of nonverbal, paralinguistic, and verbal behaviors in assessment decisions. *Modern Language Journal, 87*(1), 90–107. https://doi.org/10.1111/1540-4781.00180.

Jensen, J.T. (2000). Against ambisyllabicity. *Phonology, 17*(2), 187–235. https://doi.org/10.1017/S0952675700003912.

Jesse, A., & Massaro, D.W. (2010). The temporal distribution of information in audiovisual spoken-word identification. *Attention, Perception, & Psychophysics, 72*(1), 209–25. https://doi.org/10.3758/APP.72.1.209.

Jewitt, C. (2014). An introduction to multimodality. In C. Jewitt (Ed.), *The Routledge handbook of multimodal analysis* (2nd ed., pp. 15–30). Routledge.

Jia, G., Strange, W., Wu, Y., Collado, J., & Guan, Q. (2006). Perception and production of English vowels by Mandarin speakers: Age-related differences vary with amount of L2 exposure. *Journal of the Acoustical Society of America, 119*(2), 1118–30. https://doi.org/10.1121/1.2151806.

Johnson, K., & Mullennix, J.W. (Eds.). (1997). *Talker variability in speech processing.* Academic Press.

Jones, D. (1956). *The pronunciation of English* (4th ed.). Cambridge University Press.

Jones, M.R. (1986). Attentional rhythmicity in human perception. In J.R. Evans & M. Clynes (Eds.), *Rhythm in psychological, linguistic, and music processes* (pp. 13–40). Charles C. Thomas.

Jusczyk, P.W. (1993). Sometimes it pays to look back before you leap ahead. In B. de Boysson-Bardies, S. de Schonen, P.W. Jusczyk, P. MacNeilage, & J. Morton (Eds.), *Developmental neurocognition: Speech and face processing in the first year of life* (pp. 227–36). Kluwer Academic. https://doi.org/10.1007/978-94-015-8234-6_19.

Just, M.A., & Carpenter, P.A. (1980). A theory of reading: From eye fixations to comprehension. *Psychological Review, 87*(4), 329–54. https://doi.org/10.1037/0033-295X.87.4.329.

Kamiya, N. (2022). The limited effects of visual and audio modalities on second language listening comprehension. *Language Teaching Research.* Advance online publication. https://doi.org/10.1177/13621688221096213.

Kanan, C., Bseiso, D.N.F., Ray, N.A., Hsiao, J.H., & Cottrell, G.W. (2015). Humans have idiosyncratic and task-specific scanpaths for judging faces. *Vision Research, 108*, 67–76. https://doi.org/10.1016/j.visres.2015.01.013.

Kang, O., & Rubin, D. (2014). Listener expectations, reverse linguistic stereotyping, and individual background factors in social judgments and oral performance assessment. In J.M. Levis & A. Moyer (Eds.), *Social dynamics in second language accent* (pp. 239–53). De Gruyter Mouton. https://doi.org/10.1515/9781614511762.239.

Kaukomaa, T., Peräkylä, A., & Ruusuvuori, J. (2013). Turn-opening smiles: Facial expression constructing emotional transition in conversation. *Journal of Pragmatics, 55*, 21–42. http://dx.doi.org/10.1016/j.pragma.2013.05.006.

Kawase, S., Hannah, B., & Wang, Y. (2014). The influence of visual speech information on the intelligibility of English consonants produced by non-native speakers. *Journal of the Acoustical Society of America, 136*(3), 1352–62. https://doi.org/10.1121/1.4892770.

Kellerman, S. (1992). "I see what you mean": The role of kinesic behaviour in listening and implications for foreign and second language learning. *Applied Linguistics, 13*(3), 239–58. https://doi.org/10.1093/applin/13.3.239.

Kelly, S.D., Barr, D.J., Church, R.B., & Lynch, K. (1999). Offering a hand to pragmatic understanding: The role of speech and gesture in comprehension and memory. *Journal of Memory and Language, 40*(4), 577–92. https://doi.org/10.1006/jmla.1999.2634.

Kelly, S.D., Kravitz, C., & Hopkins, M. (2004). Neural correlates of bimodal speech and gesture comprehension. *Brain and Language*, *89*(1), 253–60. https://doi.org/10.1016/S0093-934X(03)00335-3.

Kelly, S.D., Manning, S.M., & Rodak, S. (2008). Gesture gives a hand to language and learning: Perspectives from cognitive neuroscience, developmental psychology and education. *Language and Linguistics Compass*, *2*(4), 569–88. https://doi.org/10.1111/j.1749-818X.2008.00067.x.

Kelly, S.D., McDevitt, T., & Esch, M. (2009). Brief training with co-speech gesture lends a hand to word learning in a foreign language. *Language and Cognitive Processes*, *24*(2), 313–34. https://doi.org/10.1080/01690960802365567.

Kelly, S.D., Özyürek, A., & Maris, E. (2010). Two sides of the same coin: Speech and gesture mutually interact to enhance comprehension. *Psychological Science*, *21*(2), 260–7. https://doi.org/10.1177/0956797609357327.

Kelly, S.D., & Tran, Q-A.N. (2023). Exploring the emotional functions of co-speech hand gesture in language and communication. *Topics in Cognitive Science*. Advance online publication. https://doi.org/10.1111/tops.12657.

Kendon, A. (1967). Some functions of gaze-direction in social interaction. *Acta Psychologica*, *26*, 22–63. https://doi.org/10.1016/0001-6918(67)90005-4.

Kendon, A. (1972). Some relationships between body motion and speech: An analysis of an example. In A.W. Siegman & B. Pope (Eds.), *Studies in dyadic communication* (pp. 177–210). Pergamon Press. https://doi.org/10.1016/B978-0-08-015867-9.50013-7.

Kendon, A. (1981). The study of gesture: Some remarks on its history. In J.N. Deely & M.D. Lenhart (Eds.), *Semiotics* (pp. 153–64). Springer. https://doi.org/10.1007/978-1-4615-9328-7_15.

Kendon, A. (2004). *Gesture: Visible action as utterance*. Cambridge University Press. https://doi.org/10.1017/CBO9780511807572.

Kenworthy, J. (1987). *Teaching English pronunciation*. Longman.

Kimmelman, V., & Pfau, R. (2016). Information structure in sign languages. In C. Féry & S. Ishihara (Eds.), *The Oxford handbook of information structure* (pp. 814–34). Oxford University Press. https://doi.org/10.1093/oxfordhb/9780199642670.013.001.

Kim-Renaud, Y.-K. (1974). *Korean consonantal phonology* [Unpublished doctoral dissertation]. University of Hawaii.

Kipp, M. (2001). Anvil: A generic annotation tool for multimodal dialogue. In *Proceedings of the 7th European Conference on Speech Communication and Technology* (pp. 1367–70). International Speech Communication Association. https://michaelkipp.de/publication/Kipp2001_ANVIL.pdf.

Kita, S. (2009). Cross-cultural variation of speech-accompanying gesture: A review. *Language and Cognitive Processes*, *24*(2), 145–67. https://doi.org/10.1080/01690960802586188.

Kita, S., & Ide, S. (2007). Nodding, *aizuchi*, and final particles in Japanese conversation: How conversation reflects the ideology of communication and social relationships. *Journal of Pragmatics*, *39*(7), 1242–54. https://doi.org/10.1016/j.pragma.2007.02.009.

Knapp, M.L., Cody, M.J., & Reardon, K.K. (1987). Nonverbal signals. In C.R. Berger & S.H. Chafee (Eds.), *Handbook of communication science* (pp. 385–418). Sage.

Kogure, M. (2007). Nodding and smiling in silence during the loop sequence of backchannels in Japanese conversation. *Journal of Pragmatics*, *39*(7), 1275–89. https://doi.org/10.1016/j.pragma.2007.02.011.

Krahmer, E., & Swerts, M. (2007). The effects of visual beats on prosodic prominence: Acoustic analyses, auditory perception and visual perception. *Journal of Memory and Language*, *57*(3), 396–414. https://doi.org/10.1016/j.jml.2007.06.005.

Kramer, A.F., Cassavaugh, N.D., Irwin, D.E., Peterson, M.S., & Hahn, S. (2001). Influence of single and multiple onset distractors on visual search for singleton targets. *Perception & Psychophysics*, *63*(6), 952–68. https://doi.org/10.3758/BF03194515.

Krasotkina, A., Götz, A., Höhle, B., & Schwarzer, G. (2021). Perceptual narrowing in face- and speech-perception domains in infancy: A longitudinal approach. *Infant Behavior and Development*, *64*, Article 101607. https://doi.org/10.1016/j.infbeh.2021.101607.

Krauss, R.M., & Hadar, U. (1999). The role of speech-related arm/hand gestures in word retrieval. In L. Messing & R. Campbell (Eds.), *Gesture, speech, and sign* (pp. 93–116). Oxford University Press. https://doi.org/10.1093/acprof:oso/9780198524519.003.0006.

Kricos, P.B., & Lesner, S.A. (1982). Differences in visual intelligibility across talkers. *Volta Review*, *84*(4), 219–25.

Król, M.E. (2018). Auditory noise increases the allocation of attention to the mouth, and the eyes pay the price: An eye-tracking study. *PLoS One*, *13*(3), Article e0194491. https://doi.org/10.1371/journal.pone.0194491.

Kubozono, H. (1999). Mora and syllable. In N. Tsujimura (Ed.), *The handbook of Japanese linguistics* (pp. 31–61). Blackwell. https://doi.org/10.1002/9781405166225.ch2.

Kuczkowski, J., Cieszyńska, J., Plichta, Ł., Tretiakow, D., & Stodulski, D. (2015). Hermann Gutzmann (1865–1922): The father of phoniatrics, an independent specialty. *Journal of Voice*, *29*(3), 263–4. https://doi.org/10.1016/j.jvoice.2014.09.001.

Kuhl, P.K., Andruski, J.E., Chistovich, I.A., Chistovich, L.A., Kozhevnikova, E.V., Ryskina, V.L., Stolyarova, E.I., Sundberg, U., & Lacerda, F. (1997). Cross-language analysis of phonetic units in language addressed to infants. *Science*, *277*(5326), 684–6. https://doi.org/10.1126/science.277.5326.684.

Kuhl, P.K., Green, K.P., & Meltzoff, A.N. (1988). Factors affecting the integration of auditory and visual information in speech: The level effect. *Journal of the Acoustical Society of America*, *83*(S1), S86. https://doi.org/10.1121/1.2025560.

Kuhl, P.K., & Meltzoff, A.N. (1984). The intermodal representation of speech in infants. *Infant Behavior and Development*, *7*(3), 361–81. https://doi.org/10.1016/S0163-6383(84)80050-8.

Kuhl, P.K., Stevens, E., Hayashi, A., Deguchi T., Kiritani, S., & Iverson, P. (2006). Infants show a facilitation effect for native language phonetic perception between 6 and 12 months. *Developmental Science*, *9*(2), F13–21. https://doi.org/10.1111/j.1467-7687.2006.00468.x.

Kuperberg, G.R., & Jaeger, T.F. (2016). What do we mean by prediction in language comprehension? *Language, Cognition and Neuroscience*, *31*(1), 32–59. https://doi.org/10.1080/23273798.2015.1102299.

Kutas, M., & Federmeier, K.D. (2011). Thirty years and counting: Finding meaning in the N400 component of the event-related brain potential (ERP). *Annual Review of Psychology*, *62*(1), 621–47. https://doi.org/10.1146/annurev.psych.093008.131123.

Ladefoged, P., & Ferrari-Disner, S. (2012). Vowels and consonants (3rd ed.). Wiley-Blackwell.

Ladefoged, P., & Johnson, K. (2015). *A course in phonetics* (7th ed.). Cengage Learning.

Ladefoged, P., & Maddieson, I. (1996). *The sounds of the world's languages*. Blackwell.

Land, M.F., & Hayhoe, M. (2001). In what ways do eye movements contribute to everyday activities? *Vision Research*, *41*(25–6), 3559–65. https://doi.org/10.1016/S0042-6989(01)00102-X.

Langton, S.R.H., Watt, R.J., & Bruce, V. (2000). Do the eyes have it? Cues to the direction of social attention. *Trends in Cognitive Sciences*, *4*(2), 50–9. https://doi.org/10.1016/s1364-6613(99)01436-9.

Lansing, C.R., & McConkie, G.W. (1994). A new method for speechreading research: Tracking observers' eye movements. *Journal of the Academy of Rehabilitative Audiology*, *27*, 25–43.

Lansing, C.R., & McConkie, G.W. (1999). Attention to facial regions in segmental and prosodic visual speech perception tasks. *Journal of Speech, Language, and Hearing Research*, *42*(3), 526–39. https://doi.org/10.1044/jslhr.4203.526.

Lansing, C.R., & McConkie, G.W. (2003). Word identification and eye fixation locations in visual and visual-plus-auditory presentations of spoken sentences. *Perception & Psychophysics*, *65*(4), 536–52. https://doi.org/10.3758/BF03194581.

Large, E.W., & Jones, M.R. (1999). The dynamics of attending: How people track time-varying events. *Psychological Review*, *106*(1), 119–59. https://doi.org/10.1037/0033-295X.106.1.119.

LaScotte, D., Meyers, C., & Tarone, E. (2023). *Voice and mirroring in L2 pronunciation instruction*. Equinox.

Laver, J. (1980). *The phonetic description of voice quality*. Cambridge University Press.

Lazaraton, A. (2004). Gesture and speech in the vocabulary explanations of one ESL teacher: A microanalytic inquiry. *Language Learning*, *54*(1), 79–117. https://doi.org/10.1111/j.1467-9922.2004.00249.x.

Leather, J. (1990). Perceptual and productive learning of Chinese lexical tone by Dutch and English speakers. In J. Leather & A. James (Eds.), *New sounds 90: Proceedings of the Amsterdam Symposium on the Acquisition of Second Language Speech* (pp. 72–97). University of Amsterdam.

Legerstee, M. (1990). Infants use multimodal information to imitate speech sounds. *Infant Behavior and Development*, *13*(3), 343–54. https://doi.org/10.1016/0163-6383(90)90039-B.

Lenth, R.V. (2023). emmeans: Estimated Marginal Means, aka Least-Squares Means. R package (Version 1.8.5) [Computer software]. Russell V. Lenth. https://doi.org/10.32614/CRAN.package.emmeans.

Léon, P. (1983). Les voyelles nasales et leurs réalisations dans les parlers français du Canada. *Langue Française*, *60*, 48–64. https://doi.org/10.3406/lfr.1983.5175.

Lesner, S.A. (1988). The talker. *Volta Review*, *90*(5), 89–98.

Lesner, S.A., & Hardick, E.J. (1982). An investigation of spontaneous eye blinks during lipreading. *Journal of Speech, Language, and Hearing Research*, *25*(4), 517–20. https://doi.org/10.1044/jshr.2504.517.

Levis, J. (2005). Changing contexts and shifting paradigms in pronunciation teaching. *TESOL Quarterly*, *39*(3), 369–77. https://doi.org/10.2307/3588485.

Lewkowicz, D.J. (2021, February 11). Masks can be detrimental to babies' speech and language development. *Scientific American*. https://www.scientificamerican.com/article/masks-can-be-detrimental-to-babies-speech-and-language-development1.

Lewkowicz, D.J., & Hansen-Tift, A.M. (2012). Infants deploy selective attention to the mouth of a talking face when learning speech. *Proceedings of the National Academy of Sciences*, *109*(5), 1431–6. https://doi.org/10.1073/pnas.1114783109.

Liberman, A. (2014, November 19). The ayes have it. *OUPblog*. https://blog.oup.com/2014/11/aye-yes-etymology-word-origin.

Liberman, Akiva M. (2005). How much more likely? The implications of odds ratios for probabilities. *American Journal of Evaluation*, *26*(2), 253–66. https://doi.org/10.1177/1098214005275825.

Liberman, Alvin M. (1982). On finding that speech is special. *American Psychologist*, *37*(2), 148–67. https://doi.org/10.1037/0003-066X.37.2.148.

Liberman, Alvin M., Miyawaki, K., Jenkins J.J., & Fujimura, O. (1973). Cross-language study of the perception of the F3 cue for [r] vs. [l] in speech-and nonspeech-like patterns. *Journal of the Acoustical Society of Japan*, *29*(5), 315. https://doi.org/10.20697/jasj.29.5_315.

Light, G.A., Williams, L.E., Minow, F., Sprock, J., Rissling, A., Sharp, R., Swerdlow, N.R., & Braff, D.L. (2010). Electroencephalography (EEG) and event-related potentials (ERPs) with human participants. *Current Protocols in Neuroscience*, *52*(1), 6.25.1–24. https://doi.org/10.1002/0471142301.ns0625s52.

Lindau, M. (1985). The story of /r/. In V.A. Fromkin (Ed.), *Phonetic linguistics: Essays in honor of Peter Ladefoged* (pp. 157–68). Academic Press.

Lippi-Green, R. (2012). *English with an accent: Language, ideology and discrimination in the United States* (2nd ed.). Routledge. https://doi.org/10.4324/9780203348802.

Lively, S.E., Logan, J.S., & Pisoni, D.B. (1993). Training Japanese listeners to identify English /r/and /l/. II: The role of phonetic environment and talker variability in learning new perceptual categories. *Journal of the Acoustical Society of America*, *94*(3), 1242–55. https://doi.org/10.1121/1.408177.

Lively, S.E., Pisoni, D.B., Yamada, R.A., Tohkura, Y., & Yamada, T. (1994). Training Japanese listeners to identify English /r/ and /l/. III. Long-term retention of new phonetic categories. *Journal of the Acoustical Society of America*, *96*(4), 2076–87. https://doi.org/10.1121/1.410149.

Loehr, D. (2007). Aspects of rhythm in gesture and speech. *Gesture*, *7*(2), 179–214. https://doi.org/10.1075/gest.7.2.04loe.

Logan, J.S., Lively, S.E., & Pisoni, D.B. (1991). Training Japanese listeners to identify English /r/ and /l/: A first report. *Journal of the Acoustical Society of America*, *89*(2), 874–86. https://doi.org/10.1121/1.1894649.

London, J. (2012). *Hearing in time: Psychological aspects of musical meter* (2nd ed.). Oxford University Press. https://doi.org/10.1093/acprof:oso/9780199744374.001.0001.

Luce, P.A. (1986). A computational analysis of uniqueness points in auditory word recognition. *Perception & Psychophysics*, *39*(3), 155–8. https://doi.org/10.3758/Bf03212485.

Luce, P.A., & Pisoni, D.B. (1998). Recognizing spoken words: The neighborhood activation model. *Ear and Hearing*, *19*(1), 1–36. https://doi.org/10.1097/00003446-199802000-00001.

Lüdecke, D., Ben-Shachar, M.S., Patil, I., Waggoner, P., & Makowski, D. (2021). Performance: An R package for assessment, comparison and testing of statistical models. *Journal of Open Source Software*, *6*(60), Article 3139. https://doi.org/10.21105/joss.03139.

Lusk, L.G., & Mitchel, A.D. (2016). Differential gaze patterns on eyes and mouth during audiovisual speech segmentation. *Frontiers in Psychology*, *7*, Article 52. https://doi.org/10.3389/fpsyg.2016.00052.

Lybeck, K. (2002). Cultural identification and second language pronunciation of Americans in Norway. *Modern Language Journal*, *86*(2), 174–91. https://doi.org/10.1111/1540-4781.00143.

MacDonald, J. (2017). Hearing lips and seeing voices: The origins and development of the "McGurk effect" and reflections on audio-visual speech perception over the last 40 years. *Multisensory Research*, *31*(1–2), 7–18. https://doi.org/10.1163/22134808-00002548.

MacDonald, J., Andersen, S., & Bachmann, T. (2000). Hearing by eye: How much spatial degradation can be tolerated? *Perception*, *29*(10), 1155–68. https://doi.org/10.1068/p3020.

MacDonald, J., & McGurk, H. (1978). Visual influences on speech perception processes. *Perception & Psychophysics*, *24*(3), 253–7. https://doi.org/10.3758/BF03206096.

Macedonia, M., & Kepler, J. (2013). Three good reasons why foreign language instructors need neuroscience. *Journal of Studies in Education*, *3*(4), 1–20. https://doi.org/10.5296/jse.v3i4.4168.

Macedonia, M., Müller, K., & Friederici, A.D. (2011). The impact of iconic gestures on foreign language word learning and its neural substrate. *Human Brain Mapping*, *32*(6), 982–98. https://doi.org/10.1002/hbm.21084.

MacLeod, A., & Summerfield, Q. (1987). Quantifying the contribution of vision to speech perception in noise. *British Journal of Audiology*, *21*(2), 131–41. https://doi.org/10.3109/03005368709077786.

Magnotti, J.F., & Beauchamp, M.S. (2017). A causal inference model explains perception of the McGurk effect and other incongruent audiovisual speech. *PLoS Computational Biology*, *13*(2), Article e1005229. https://doi.org/10.1371/journal.pcbi.1005229.

Major, R.C., Fitzmaurice, S.M., Bunta, F., & Balasubramanian, C. (2005). Testing the effects of regional, ethnic, and international dialects of English on listening comprehension. *Language Learning*, *55*(1), 37–69. https://doi.org/10.1111/j.0023-8333.2005.00289.x.

Mallick, D.B., Magnotti, J.F., & Beauchamp, M.S. (2015). Variability and stability in the McGurk effect: Contributions of participants, stimuli, time, and response type. *Psychonomic Bulletin Review*, *22*, 1299–307. https://doi.org/10.3758/s13423-015-0817-4.

Marks, L.E. (1978). *The unity of the senses: Interrelations among the modalities*. Academic Press. https://doi.org/10.1016/C2013-0-11140-3.

Marslen-Wilson, W., & Tyler, L.K. (1980). The temporal structure of spoken language understanding. *Cognition*, *8*(1), 1–71. https://doi.org/10.1016/0010-0277(80)90015-3.

Martin, P., Beaudoin-Bégin, A., Goulet, M.-J., & Roy, J. (2001). Les voyelles nasales en français du Québec. *La Linguistique*, *37*(2), 49–70. https://doi.org/10.3917/ling.372.0049.

Martinet, A. (1988). The internal conditioning of phonological changes. *La Linguistique*, *24*(2), 17–26. http://www.jstor.org/stable/30248579.

Masao, K. (1976). The Japanese language and intercultural communication. *Japan Interpreter*, *10*, 267–83.

Massaro, D.W. (1998). *Perceiving talking faces: From speech perception to a behavioral principle*. MIT Press.

Massaro, D.W., Cohen, M.M., Gesi, A., Heredia, R., & Tsuzaki, M. (1993). Bimodal speech perception: An examination across languages. *Journal of Phonetics*, *21*(4), 445–78. https://doi.org/10.1016/S0095-4470(19)30230-X.

Massaro, D.W., & Light, J. (2003). Read my tongue movements: Bimodal learning to perceive and produce non-native speech /r/ and /l/. In *Proceedings of the 8th European Conference on Speech Communication and Technology* (pp. 2249–52). Eurospeech. https://doi.org/10.21437/Eurospeech.2003-629.

Mattys, S.L., Bernstein, L.E., & Auer, E.T. (2002). Stimulus based lexical distinctiveness as a general word-recognition mechanism. *Perception & Psychophysics, 64*(4), 667–79. https://doi.org/10.3758/BF03194734.

Mayer, C., Abel, J., Barbosa, A.V., Black, A., & Vatikiotis-Bateson, E. (2011). The labial viseme reconsidered: Evidence from production and perception. *Journal of the Acoustical Society of America, 129*(4), 2456. https://doi.org/10.1121/1.3588075.

Maynard, S.K. (1986). On back-channel behavior in Japanese and English casual conversation. *Linguistics, 24*(6), 1079–108. https://doi.org/10.1515/ling.1986.24.6.1079.

Maynard, S.K. (1987). Interactional functions of a nonverbal sign: Head movement in Japanese dyadic casual conversation. *Journal of Pragmatics, 11*(5), 589–606. https://doi.org/10.1016/0378-2166(87)90181-0.

Maynard, S.K. (1989). *Japanese conversation: Self-contextualization through structure and interactional management.* Ablex.

Maynard, S.K. (1993). *Discourse modality: Subjectivity, emotion and voice in the Japanese language.* John Benjamins. https://doi.org/10.1075/pbns.24.

McCafferty, S.G. (2002). Gesture and creating zones of proximal development for second language learning. *Modern Language Journal, 86*(2), 192–203. https://doi.org/10.1111/1540-4781.00144.

McCandliss, B.D., Fiez, J.A., Protopapas, A., Conway, M., & McClelland, J. (2002). Success and failure in teaching the [r]-[l] contrast to Japanese adults: Tests of a Hebbian model of plasticity and stabilization in spoken language perception. *Cognitive, Affective, & Behavioral Neuroscience, 2*, 89–108. https://doi.org/10.3758/CABN.2.2.89.

McClave, E. (1994). Gestural beats: The rhythm hypothesis. *Journal of Psycholinguistic Research, 23*(1), 45–66. https://doi.org/10.1007/BF02143175.

McClave, E. (2000). Linguistic functions of head movements in the context of speech. *Journal of Pragmatics, 32*(7), 855–78. https://doi.org/10.1016/S0378-2166(99)00079-X.

McCormack, J., Watkins, S., Smith, J., & Margolis, A. (2010). *Speaking and pronunciation.* Garnet Publishing.

McCroskey, J.C., Richmond, V.P., Sallinen, A., Fayer, J.M., & Barraclough, R.A. (1995). A cross-cultural and multi-behavioral analysis of the relationship between nonverbal immediacy and teacher evaluation. *Communication Education, 44*(4), 281–91. https://doi.org/10.1080/03634529509379019.

McDonough, K., Trofimovich, P., Lu, L., & Abashidze, D. (2019). The occurrence and perception of listener visual cues during nonunderstanding episodes. *Studies in Second Language Acquisition, 41*(5), 1151–65. https://doi.org/10.1017/S0272263119000238.

McGowen, C. (2012, November 8). The eyes have it: The key to unlocking a diagnosis. *American Policy Roundtable.* https://aproundtable.org/blog/the-eyes-have-it-the-key-to-unlocking-a-diagnosis.

McGurk, H. (1972). Infant discrimination of orientation. *Journal of Experimental Child Psychology, 14*(1), 151–64. https://doi.org/10.1016/0022-0965(72)90040-9.

McGurk, H. (1981). Listening with eye and ear [Paper discussion]. In T. Meyers, J. Laver, & J. Anderson (Eds.), *The cognitive representation of speech* (pp. 336–7). North-Holland.

McGurk, H. (1988). Developmental psychology and the vision of speech (McGurk's inaugural lecture in 1988). In *Proceedings of the Auditory-Visual Speech Processing Conference, the Ninth International Conference* (pp. 3–20). International Speech Communication Association. https://www.isca-speech.org/archive/avsp_1998/mcgurk98_avsp.html.

McGurk, H., & Lewis, M. (1974). Space perception in early infancy: Perception within a common auditory-visual space? *Science, 186*(4164), 649–50. https://doi.org/10.1126/science.186.4164.649.

McGurk, H., & MacDonald, J. (1976). Hearing lips and seeing voices. *Nature, 264*, 746–8. https://doi.org/10.1038/264746a0.

McGurk, H., & MacDonald, J. (1978). Auditory-visual coordination in the first year of life. *International Journal of Behavioral Development, 1*(3), 229–39. https://doi.org/10.1177/016502547800100303.

McNeill, D. (1992). *Hand and mind: What gestures reveal about thought*. University of Chicago Press.

McNeill, D. (2005). *Gesture and thought*. University of Chicago Press. https://doi.org/10.7208/chicago/9780226514642.001.0001.

McNeill, D. (2006). Gesture and communication. In K. Brown (Ed.), *The encyclopedia of language and linguistics* (2nd ed., pp. 58–66). Elsevier.

McNeill, D., Levy, E.T., & Duncan, S.D. (2015). Gesture in discourse. In D. Tannen, H.E. Hamilton, & D. Schiffrin (Eds.), *The handbook of discourse analysis* (2nd ed., pp. 262–89). John Wiley & Sons. https://doi.org/10.1002/9781118584194.ch12.

McNeill, D., Levy, E.T., & Pedelty, L.L. (1990). Speech and gesture. In G.E. Hammond (Ed.), *Cerebral control of speech and limb movements* (pp. 203–56). North-Holland.

Medina González, M., & Hardison, D.M. (2022). Assistive Design for English Phonetic Tools (ADEPT) in language learning. *Language Learning & Technology, 26*(1), 1–23. https://doi.org/10125/73493.

Mehoudar, E., Arizpe, J., Baker, C.I., & Yovel, G. (2014). Faces in the eye of the beholder: Unique and stable eye scanning patterns of individual observers. *Journal of Vision, 14*(6), 1–11. https://doi.org/10.1167/14.7.6.

Meltzoff, A.N., & Kuhl, P.K. (1994). Faces and speech: Intermodal processing of biologically relevant signals in infants and adults. In D.J. Lewkowitz & R. Lickliter (Eds.), *The development of intersensory perception: Comparative perspectives* (pp. 335–39). Erlbaum. https://doi.org/10.4324/9780203773079.

Meltzoff, A.N., & Moore, M.K. (1977). Imitation of facial and manual gestures by human neonates. *Science, 198*(4312), 74–8. https://doi.org/10.1126/science.897687.

Meltzoff, A.N., & Moore, M.K. (1993). Why faces are special to infants: On connecting the attraction of faces and infants' ability for imitation and cross-modal processing. In B. de Boysson-Bardies, S. de Schonen, P. Jusczyk, P. McNeilage, & J. Morton (Eds.), *Developmental neurocognition: Speech and face processing in the first year of life* (pp. 211–25). Kluwer Academic. https://doi.org/10.1007/978-94-015-8234-6_18.

Merker, B.H., Madison, G.S., & Eckerdal, P. (2009). On the role and origin of isochrony in human rhythmic entrainment. *Cortex, 45*(1), 4–17. https://doi.org/10.1016/j.cortex.2008.06.011.

Mielke, J., Carignan, C., & Thomas, E.R. (2017). The articulatory dynamics of pre-velar and pre-nasal /æ/-raising in English: An ultrasound study. *Journal of the Acoustical Society of America, 142*(1), 332–49. https://doi.org/10.1121/1.4991348.

Miller, S.F. (2006). *Targeting pronunciation: Communicating clearly in English* (2nd ed.). Houghton Mifflin.

Miller, G.A., & Nicely, P.E. (1955). An analysis of perceptual confusions among some English consonants. *Journal of the Acoustical Society of America, 27*(2), 338–52. https://doi.org/10.1121/1.1907526.

Mills, A.E. (1987). The development of phonology in the blind child. In B. Dodd & R. Campbell (Eds.), *Hearing by eye: The psychology of lip-reading* (pp. 145–61). Erlbaum.

Mills, A.E., & Thiem, R. (1980). Auditory-visual fusions and illusions in speech perception. *Linguistische Berichte, 68*, 85–108.

Mishra, J., Martinez, A., Sejnowski, T.J., & Hillyard, S.A. (2007). Early cross-modal interactions in auditory and visual cortex underlie a sound-induced visual illusion. *Journal of Neuroscience*, *27*(15), 4120–31. https://doi.org/10.1523/JNEUROSCI.4912-06.2007.

Miyawaki, K., Jenkins, J.J., Strange, W., Liberman, A.M., Verbrugge, R., & Fujimura, O. (1975). An effect of linguistic experience: The discrimination of [r] and [l] by native speakers of Japanese and English. *Perception & Psychophysics*, *18*(5), 331–40. https://doi.org/10.3758/BF03211209.

Mizutani, N. (1982). The listener's responses in Japanese conversation. *Sociolinguistic Newsletter*, *13*(1), 33–8.

Mochizuki, M. (1981). The identification of /r/ and /l/ in natural and synthesized speech. *Journal of Phonetics*, *9*(3), 283–303. https://doi.org/10.1016/S0095-4470(19)30972-6.

Mompean, J.A., & Fouz-González, J. (2021). Phonetic symbols in contemporary pronunciation instruction. *RELC Journal*, *52*(1), 155–68. https://doi.org/10.1177/0033688220943431.

Mompean, J.A., & Lintunen, P. (2015). Phonetic notation in foreign language teaching and learning: Potential advantages and learners' views. *Research in Language*, *13*(3), 292–314. https://doi.org/10.1515/rela-2015-0026.

Monroe, M. (1959). I wanna be loved by you [Song]. In B. Wilder (Director), *Some Like It Hot*. United Artists.

Morett, L.M. (2014). When hands speak louder than words: The role of gesture in the communication, encoding, and recall of words in a novel second language. *Modern Language Journal*, *98*(3), 834–53. https://doi.org/10.1111/modl.12125.

Morett, L.M., & Chung, L.-Y. (2015). Emphasizing sound and meaning: Pitch gestures enhance Mandarin lexical tone acquisition. *Language, Cognition and Neuroscience*, *30*(3), 347–53. https://doi.org/10.1080/23273798.2014.923105.

Morett, L.M., & Fraundorf, S.H. (2019). Listeners consider alternative speaker productions in discourse comprehension and memory: Evidence from beat gesture and pitch accenting. *Memory & Cognition*, *47*(8), 1515–30. https://doi.org/10.3758/s13421-019-00945-1.

Morett, L.M., Fraundorf, S.H., & McPartland J.C. (2021). Eye see what you're saying: Contrastive use of beat gesture and pitch accent affects online interpretation of spoken discourse. *Journal of Experimental Psychology: Learning, Memory, and Cognition*, *47*(9), 1494–1526. https://doi.org/10.1037/xlm0000986.

Morin-Lessard, E., Poulin-Dubois, D., Segalowitz, N., & Byers-Heinlein, K. (2019). Selective attention to the mouth of talking faces in monolinguals and bilinguals aged 5 months to 5 years. *Developmental Psychology*, *55*(8), 1640–55. http://dx.doi.org/10.1037/dev0000750.

Morosan, D.E., & Jamieson, D.G. (1989). Evaluation of a technique for training new speech contrasts: Generalization across voices, but not word-position or task. *Journal of Speech and Hearing Research*, *32*(3), 501–11. https://doi.org/10.1044/jshr.3203.501.

Morrel-Samuels, P., & Krauss, R.M. (1992). Word familiarity predicts temporal asynchrony of hand gestures and speech. *Journal of Experimental Psychology: Learning, Memory and Cognition*, *18*(3), 615–62. https://doi.org/10.1037/0278-7393.18.3.615.

Morsbach, H. (1982). Aspects of nonverbal communication in Japan. In L.A. Samovar & R.E. Porter (Eds.), *Intercultural communication: A reader* (3rd ed., pp. 300–19). Wadsworth Publishing.

Moussu, L. (2010). Influence of teacher-contact time and other variables on ESL students' attitudes towards native- and nonnative-English-speaking teachers. *TESOL Quarterly*, *44*(4), 746–68. https://doi.org/10.5054/tq.2010.235997.

Munhall, K.G., Gribble, P.L., Sacco, L., & Ward, M. (1996). Temporal constraints on the McGurk effect. *Perception & Psychophysics*, *58*(3), 351–62. https://doi.org/10.3758/BF03206811.

Munhall, K.G., Jones, J.A., Callan, D.E., Kuratate, T., & Vatikiotis-Bateson, E. (2004). Visual prosody and speech intelligibility: Head movement improves auditory speech perception. *Psychological Science*, *15*(2), 133–7. https://doi.org/10.1111/j.0963-7214.2004.01502010.x.

Munhall, K.G., & Tohkura, Y. (1998). Audiovisual gating and the time course of speech perception. *Journal of the Acoustical Society of America*, *104*(1), 530–9. https://doi.org/10.1121/1.423300.

Munro, M.J. (2018). How well can we predict second language learners' pronunciation difficulties? *CATESOL Journal*, *30*(1), 267–81. https://doi.org/10.5070/B5.35975.

Munro, M.J., & Derwing, T.M. (2006). The functional load principle in ESL pronunciation instruction: An exploratory study. *System*, *34*(4), 520–31. https://doi.org/10.1016/j.system.2006.09.004.

Munro, M.J., & Derwing, T.M. (2008). Segmental acquisition in adult ESL learners: A longitudinal study of vowel production. *Language Learning*, *58*(3), 479–502. https://doi.org/10.1111/j.1467-9922.2008.00448.x.

Murphy, J.M. (2018). Teacher training in the teaching of pronunciation. In O. Kang, R.I. Thomson, & J.M. Murphy (Eds.), *The Routledge handbook of contemporary English pronunciation* (pp. 298–319). Routledge. https://doi.org/10.4324/9781315145006.

Murphy, J.M., & Baker, A.A. (2015). History of ESL pronunciation teaching. In M. Reed & J.M. Levis (Eds.), *The handbook of English pronunciation* (pp. 36–65). Wiley-Blackwell. https://doi.org/10.1002/9781118346952.ch3.

Nagy, N., Blondeau, H., & Auger, J. (2003). Second language acquisition and "real" French: An investigation of subject doubling in the French of Montreal Anglophones. *Language Variation and Change*, *15*(1), 73–103. https://doi.org/10.1017/S0954394503151034.

Nakagawa, S., Johnson, P.C.D., Schielzeth, H. (2017). The coefficient of determination R2 and intra-class correlation coefficient from generalized linear mixed-effects models revisited and expanded. *Journal of the Royal Society Interface*, *14*(134), Article 20170213. https://doi.org/10.1098/rsif.2017.0213.

Nakano, T., Kato, M., Morito, Y., Itoi, S., & Kitazawa, S. (2013). Blink-related momentary activation of the default mode network while viewing videos. *Proceedings of the National Academy of Sciences*, *110*(2), 702–6. https://doi.org/10.1073/pnas.1214804110.

Nambiar, M.K., & Goon, C. (1993). Assessment of oral skills: A comparison of scores obtained through audio recordings to those obtained through face-to-face evaluation. *RELC Journal*, *24*(1), 15–31. https://doi.org/10.1177/003368829302400010.

Nath, A.R., & Beauchamp, M.S. (2011). Dynamic changes in superior temporal sulcus connectivity during perception of noisy audiovisual speech. *Journal of Neuroscience*, *31*(5), 1704–14. https://doi.org/10.1523/JNEUROSCI.4853-10.2011.

Nath, A.R., & Beauchamp, M.S. (2012). A neural basis for interindividual differences in the McGurk effect, a multisensory speech illusion. *NeuroImage*, *59*(1), 781–7. https://doi.org/10.1016/j.neuroimage.2011.07.024.

Navarra, J., Alsius, A., Velasco, I., Soto-Faraco, S., & Spence, C. (2010). Perception of audiovisual speech synchrony for native and non-native language. *Brain Research* *6*(1323), 84–93. https://doi.org/10.1016/j.brainres.2010.01.059.

Nespor, M., & Vogel, I. (1986). *Prosodic phonology*. Foris Publications.

Neu, J. (1990). Assessing the role of nonverbal communication in the acquisition of communicative competence in L2. In R.C. Scarcella, E.S. Andersen, & S.D. Krashen (Eds.), *Developing communicative competence in a second language* (pp. 121–38). Heinle & Heinle.

Nielsen, G.S. (1962). *Studies in self-confrontation: Viewing a sound motion picture of self and another person in a stressful dyadic interaction*. Munksgaard.

Nosofsky, R.M. (1986). Attention, similarity, and the identification–categorization relationship. *Journal of Experimental Psychology: General, 115*(1), 39–57. https://doi.org/10.1037/0096-3445.115.1.39.

Nuthmann, A., Schütz, I., & Einhäuser, W. (2020). Salience-based object prioritization during active viewing of naturalistic scenes in young and older adults. *Scientific Reports, 10*(1), Article 22057. https://doi.org/10.1038/s41598-020-78203-7.

Nygaard, L.C. (2005). The integration of linguistic and non-linguistic properties of speech. In D. Pisoni & R. Remez (Eds.), *The handbook of speech perception* (pp. 390–414). Blackwell. https://doi.org/10.1002/9780470757024.ch16.

Nygaard, L.C., Sommers, M.S., & Pisoni, D.B. (1995). Effects of stimulus variability on perception and representation of spoken words in memory. *Perception & Psychophysics, 57*(7), 989–1001. https://doi.org/10.3758/BF03205458.

Oben, B. (2018). Gaze as a predictor for lexical and gestural alignment. In G. Brône & B. Oben (Eds.), *Eye-tracking in interaction: Studies on the role of eye gaze in dialogue* (pp. 223–63). John Benjamins. https://doi.org/10.1075/ais.10.10obe.

O'Brien, M.G. (2022). Making the teaching of suprasegmentals accessible. In J. Levis, T. Derwing, & S. Sonsaat-Hegelheimer (Eds.), *Second language pronunciation: Bridging the gap between research and teaching* (pp. 85–106). Wiley. https://doi.org/10.1002/9781394259663.ch5.

O'Brien, M.G., Derwing, T.M., Cucchiarini, C., Hardison, D.M., Mixdorff, H., Thomson, R.I., Strik, H., Levis, J.M., Munro, M.J., Foote, J.A., & Muller Levis, G. (2018). Directions for the future of technology in pronunciation research and teaching. *Journal of Second Language Pronunciation, 4*(2), 182–206. https://doi.org/10.1075/jslp.17001.obr.

O'Connor, J.D. (1973). *Phonetics*. Penguin Books.

Orion, G.F. (2012). *Pronouncing American English: Sounds, stress, and intonation* (3rd ed.). Heinle & Heinle.

Oshima, D.Y. (2014). On the morphological status of *-te, -ta*, and related forms in Japanese: Evidence from accent placement. *Journal of East Asian Linguistics, 23*(3), 233–65. https://doi.org/10.1007/s10831-014-9120-z.

Owens, E., & Blązek, B. (1985). Visemes observed by hearing-impaired and normal hearing adult viewers. *Journal of Speech and Hearing Research, 28*(3), 381–93. https://doi.org/10.1044/jshr.2803.381.

Özçalişkan, S., & Goldin-Meadow, S. (2005). Gesture is at the cutting edge of early language development. *Cognition, 96*(3), B101–13. https://doi.org/10.1016/J.Cognition.2005.01.001.

Ozker, M., Yoshor, D., & Beauchamp, M.S. (2018). Frontal cortex selects representations of the talker's mouth to aid in speech perception. *eLife, 7*, Article e30387. https://doi.org/10.7554/eLife.30387.001.

Paré, M., Richler, R.C., ten Hove, M., & Munhall, K.G. (2003). Gaze behavior in audiovisual speech perception: The influence of ocular fixations on the McGurk effect. *Perception & Psychophysics, 65*(4), 553–67. https://doi.org/10.3758/BF03194582.

Partridge, E. (1959). *Origins: A short etymological dictionary of modern English*. Macmillan.

Pascual-Leone, A., & Hamilton, R. (2001). The metamodal organization of the brain. In C. Casanova & M. Ptito (Eds.), *Progress in brain research: Vol. 134. Vision: From neurons to cognition* (pp. 427–45). Elsevier. https://doi.org/10.1016/S0079-6123(01)34028-1.

Pascual-Leone, A., & Torres, F. (1993). Plasticity of the sensorimotor cortex representation of the reading finger in Braille readers. *Brain, 116*(1), 39–52. https://doi.org/10.1093/brain/116.1.39.

Pascual-Leone, A., Walsh, V., & Rothwell, J. (2000). Transcranial magnetic stimulation in cognitive neuroscience-virtual lesion, chronometry, and functional connectivity. *Current Opinion in Neurobiology, 10*(2), 232–7. https://doi.org/10.1016/s0959-4388(00)00081-7.

Peduzzi, P., Concato, J., Kemper, E., Holford, T.R., & Feinstein, A.R. (1996). A simulation study of the number of events per variable in logistic regression analysis. *Journal of Clinical Epidemiology, 49*(12), 1373–9. https://doi.org/10.1016/s0895-4356(96)00236-3.

Peelle, J.E., & Sommers, M.S. (2015). Prediction and constraint in audiovisual speech perception. *Cortex, 68*, 169–81. http://dx.doi.org/10.1016/j.cortex.2015.03.006.

Pelphrey, K.A., Morris, J.P., Michelich, C.R., Allison, T., & McCarthy, G. (2005). Functional anatomy of biological motion perception in posterior temporal cortex: An fMRI study of eye, mouth and hand movements. *Cerebral Cortex, 15*(12), 1866–76. https://doi.org/10.1093/cercor/bhi064.

Pennington, M.C. (1996). *Phonology in English language teaching: An international approach*. Longman.

Pennington, M.C., & Rogerson-Revell, P. (2019). *English pronunciation teaching and research*. Palgrave Macmillan. https://doi.org/10.1057/978-1-137-47677-7.

Pennycook, A. (1985). Actions speak louder than words: Paralanguage, communication, and education. *TESOL Quarterly, 19*(2), 259–82. https://doi.org/10.2307/3586829.

Perry, L.K., Mech, E.N., MacDonald, M.C., & Seidenberg, M.S. (2018). Influences of speech familiarity on immediate perception and final comprehension. *Psychonomic Bulletin and Review, 25*, 431–9. https://doi.org/10.3758/s13423-017-1297-5.

Pfau, A. (2020). *Re-examining functional load in light of raters' perception of error gravity in second language speech* (Publication No. 27961707) [Master's thesis, Michigan State University]. ProQuest Dissertations and Theses Global.

Piaget, J. (1952). *The origins of intelligence in children* (M. Cook, Trans.). W.W. Norton & Co. https://psycnet.apa.org/doi/10.1037/11494-000.

Picheny, M.A., Durlach, N.I., & Braida, L.D. (1986). Speaking clearly for the hard of hearing. II: Acoustic characteristics of clear and conversational speech. *Journal of Speech and Hearing Research, 29*(4), 434–46. https://doi.org/10.1044/jshr.2904.434.

Pierrehumbert, J. (2016). Phonological representation: Beyond abstract versus episodic. *Annual Review of Linguistics, 2*(1), 33–52. https://doi.org/10.1146/annurev-linguist-030514-125050.

Pike, K. (1947). *Phonemics: A technique for reducing languages to writing*. University of Michigan Press.

Pisoni, D.B. (1973). Auditory and phonetic memory codes in the discrimination of consonants and vowels. *Perception & Psychophysics, 13*(2), 253–60. https://doi.org/10.3758/BF03214136.

Pisoni, D.B. (1997). Some thoughts on "normalization" in speech perception. In K. Johnson & J.W. Mullennix (Eds.), *Talker variability in speech processing* (pp. 9–32). Academic Press.

Pisoni, D.B., Aslin, R.N., Perey, A.J., & Hennessy, B.L. (1982). Some effects of laboratory training on identification and discrimination of voicing contrasts in stop consonants. *Journal of Experimental Psychology: Human Perception and Performance, 8*(2), 297–314. https://doi.org/10.1037/0096-1523.8.2.297.

Pisoni, D.B., Nusbaum, H.C., Luce, P.A., & Slowiaczek, L.M. (1985). Speech perception, word recognition and the structure of the lexicon. *Speech Communication, 4*(1–3), 75–95. https://doi.org/10.1016/0167-6393(85)90037-8.

Pons, F., Bosch, L., & Lewkowicz, D.J. (2015). Bilingualism modulates infants' selective attention to the mouth of a talking face. *Psychological Science, 26*(4), 490–8. https://doi.org/10.1177/0956797614568320.

Posner, M.I. (1980). Orienting of attention. *Quarterly Journal of Experimental Psychology, 32*(1), 3–25. https://doi.org/10.1080/00335558008248231.

Posner, M.I., & Raichle, M.E. (1994). *Images of mind.* Scientific American Library.

Posner, M.I., Walker, J.A., Friedrich, F.J., & Rafal, R.D. (1984). Effects of parietal injury on covert orienting of attention. *Journal of Neuroscience, 4*(7), 1863–74. https://doi.org/10.1523/JNEUROSCI.04-07-01863.

Powers, A.R., III, Hevey, M.A., & Wallace, M.T. (2012). Neural correlates of multisensory perceptual learning. *Journal of Neuroscience, 32*(18), 6263–74. https://doi.org/10.1523/JNEUROSCI.6138-11.2012.

Powers, A.R., III, Hillock, A.R., & Wallace, M.T. (2009). Perceptual training narrows the temporal window of multisensory binding. *Journal of Neuroscience, 29*(39), 12265–74. https://doi.org/10.1523/JNEUROSCI.3501-09.2009.

Prator, C.H., & Robinett, B.W. (1985). *Manual of American English pronunciation* (4th ed.). Harcourt Brace & Company.

Pratt, T., & D'Onofrio, A. (2017). Jaw setting and the California vowel shift in parodic performance. *Language in Society, 46*(3), 283–312. https://doi.org/10.1017/S0047404517000227.

Price, P.J. (1981). *A cross-linguistic study of flaps in Japanese and in American English* [Unpublished doctoral dissertation]. University of Pennsylvania.

Prieto, P., Cravotta, A., Kushch, O., Rohrer, P.L., & Vilà-Giménez, I. (2018). Deconstructing beat gestures: A labelling proposal. In K. Klessa, J. Bachan, A. Wagner, M. Karpiński, & D. Śledziński (Eds.), *Proceedings of the 9th International Conference on Speech Prosody* (pp. 201–5). International Speech Communication Association. https://doi.org/10.21437/SpeechProsody.2018-41.

Puce, A., Epling, J.A., Thompson, J.C., & Carrick, O.K. (2007). Neural responses elicited to face motion and vocalization pairings. *Neuropsychologia, 45*(1), 93–106. https://doi.org/10.1016/j.neuropsychologia.2006.04.017.

Pullum, G.K., & Ladusaw, W.A. (1996). *Phonetic symbol guide* (2nd ed.). University of Chicago Press.

Purves, D., Augustine, G.J., Fitzpatrick, D., Hall, W.C., LaMantia, A.-S., McNamara, J.O., & Williams, S.M. (Eds.). (2004). *Neuroscience* (3rd ed.). Sinauer Associates.

Raizada, R.D.S., Tsao, F.-M., Liu, H.-M., & Kuhl, P.K. (2010). Quantifying the adequacy of neural representations for a cross-language phonetic discrimination task: Prediction of individual differences. *Cerebral Cortex, 20*(1), 1–12. https://doi.org/10.1093/cercor/bhp076.

Ramanarayanan, V., Goldstein, L., Byrd, D., & Narayanan, S. (2013). An investigation of articulatory setting using real-time magnetic resonance imaging. *Journal of the Acoustical Society of America, 134*(1), 510–19. https://doi.org/10.1121/1.4807639.

Rayner, K., Smith, T.J., Malcolm, G.L., & Henderson, J.M. (2009). Eye movements and visual encoding during scene perception. *Psychological Science*, *20*(1), 6–10. https://doi.org/10.1111/j.1467-9280.2008.02243.x.

Reed, M., & Michaud, C. (2010). *Goal-driven lesson planning for teaching English to speakers of other languages*. University of Michigan Press. https://doi.org/10.3998/mpub.1425013.

Reichle, E.D., Pollatsek, A., & Rayner, K. (2006). E-Z reader: A cognitive-control, serial-attention model of eye-movement behavior during reading. *Cognitive Systems Research*, *7*(1), 4–22. https://doi.org/10.1016/j.cogsys.2005.07.002.

Reichle, E.D., Pollatsek, A., & Rayner, K. (2012). Using E-Z reader to simulate eye movements in nonreading tasks: A unified framework for understanding the eye-mind link. *Psychological Review*, *119*(1), 155–85. https://doi.org/10.1037/a0026473.

Reinagel, P., & Zador, A.M. (1999). Natural scene statistics at the centre of gaze. *Network: Computation in Neural Systems*, *10*(4), 341–50. PMID: 10695763.

Reisberg, D., McLean, J., & Goldfield, A. (1987). Easy to hear but hard to understand: A lip-reading advantage with intact auditory stimuli. In B. Dodd & R. Campbell (Eds.), *Hearing by eye: The psychology of lip-reading* (pp. 97–113). Erlbaum.

Reisberg, D., Scheiber, R., & Potemken, L. (1981). Eye position and the control of auditory attention. *Journal of Experimental Psychology: Human Perception and Performance*, *7*(2), 318–23. https://doi.org/10.1037/0096-1523.7.2.318.

Remez, R.E., Pardo, J.S., Piorkowski, R.L., & Rubin, P.E. (2001). On the bistability of sine wave analogues of speech. *Psychological Science*, *12*(1), 24–9. https://doi.org/10.1111/1467-9280.00305.

Rennig, J., & Beauchamp, M.S. (2018). Free viewing of talking faces reveals mouth and eye preferring regions of the human superior temporal sulcus. *NeuroImage*, *183*, 25–36. https://doi.org/10.1016/j.neuroimage.2018.08.008.

Rennig, J., Wegner-Clemens, K., & Beauchamp, M.S. (2020). Face viewing behavior predicts multisensory gain during speech perception. *Psychonomic Bulletin & Review*, *27*, 70–7. https://doi.org/10.3758/s13423-019-01665-y.

Richards, J.C., & Schmidt, R. (2011). *Longman dictionary of language teaching and applied linguistics* (4th ed.). Longman. https://doi.org/10.4324/9781315833835.

Ringer-Hilfinger, K. (2012). Learner acquisition of dialect variation in a study abroad context: The case of the Spanish [θ]. *Foreign Language Annals*, *45*(3), 430–46. https://doi.org/10.1111/j.1944-9720.2012.01201.x.

Ritberger, C. (2000). *What color is your personality? Red, orange, yellow, green*. Hay House.

Robert-Ribes, J., Schwartz, J., Lallouache, T., & Escudier, P. (1998). Complementarity and synergy in bimodal speech: Auditory, visual, and audio-visual identification of French oral vowels in noise. *Journal of the Acoustical Society of America*, *103*(6), 3677–89. https://doi.org/10.1121/1.423069.

Robinson, G.S., & Casali, J.G. (2003). Speech communications and signal detection in noise. In E.H. Berger, L.H. Royster, J.D. Royster, D.P. Driscoll, & M. Layne (Eds.), *The noise manual* (5th ed., pp. 567–600). American Industrial Hygiene Association.

Rogerson-Revell, P. (2011). *English phonology and pronunciation teaching*. Continuum.

Rohrer, P.L., Delais-Roussarie, E., & Prieto, P. (2020). Beat gestures for comprehension and recall: Differential effects of language learners and native listeners. *Frontiers in Psychology*, *11*, Article 575929. https://doi.org/10.3389/fpsyg.2020.575929.

Rosen, S.M., Fourcin, A.J., & Moore, B.C. (1981). Voice pitch as an aid to lipreading. *Nature*, *291*(5811), 150–2. https://doi.org/10.1038/291150a0.

Rosenblum, L.D. (2005). Primacy of multimodal speech perception. In D.B. Pisoni & R.E. Remez (Eds.), *The handbook of speech perception* (pp. 51–78). Blackwell. https://doi.org/10.1002/9780470757024.ch3.

Rosenblum, L.D. (2010). *See what I'm saying: The extraordinary powers of our five senses.* W.W. Norton & Co.

Rosenblum, L.D., Dias, J.W., & Dorsi, J. (2017). The supramodal brain: Implications for auditory perception. *Journal of Cognitive Psychology, 29*(1), 65–87. https://doi.org/10.1080/20445911.2016.1181691.

Rosenblum, L.D., & Dorsi, J. (2021). Primacy of multimodal speech perception for the brain and science. In J.S. Pardo, L.C. Nygaard, R.E. Remez, & D.B. Pisoni (Eds.), *The handbook of speech perception* (2nd ed., pp. 28–57). John Wiley & Sons. https://doi.org/10.1002/9781119184096.ch2.

Rosenblum, L.D., Johnson, J.A., & Saldaña, H. (1996). Point-light facial displays enhance comprehension of speech in noise. *Journal of Speech and Hearing Research, 39*(6), 1159–70. https://doi.org/10.1044/jshr.3906.1159.

Rosenblum, L.D., Miller, R.M., & Sanchez, K. (2007). Lip-read me now, hear me better later: Cross-modal transfer of talker-familiarity effects. *Psychological Science, 18*(5), 392–6. https://doi.org/10.1111/j.1467-9280.2007.01911.x.

Rosenblum, L.D., & Saldaña, H.M. (1996). An audiovisual test of kinematic primitives for visual speech perception. *Journal of Experimental Psychology: Human Perception and Performance, 22*(2), 318–31. https://doi.org/10.1037/0096-1523.22.2.318.

Rosenblum, L.D., Schmuckler, M.A., & Johnson, J.A. (1997). The McGurk effect in infants. *Perception & Psychophysics, 59*(3), 347–57. https://doi.org/10.3758/BF03211902.

Ross, L.A., Saint-Amour, D., Leavitt, V.M., Javitt, D.C., & Foxe, J.J. (2007). Do you see what I am saying? Exploring visual enhancement of speech comprehension in noisy environments. *Cerebral Cortex, 17*(5), 1147–53. https://doi.org/10.1093/cercor/bhl024.

Rossano, F. (2013). Gaze in conversation. In J. Sidnell & T. Stivers (Eds.), *The handbook of conversation analysis* (pp. 308–29). Wiley-Blackwell. https://doi.org/10.1002/9781118325001.ch15.

Rouger, J., Lagleyre, S., Fraysse, B., Denève, S., Deguine, O., & Barone, P. (2007). Evidence that cochlear-implanted deaf patients are better multisensory integrators. *Proceedings of the National Academy of Sciences, 104*(17), 7295–300. https://doi.org/10.1073/pnas.0609419104.

Ruben, A. (Creator). (1964–9). *Gomer Pyle, U.S.M.C.* [TV series]. Andy Griffith Enterprises; CBS.

Ruivivar, J., & Collins, L. (2018). The effects of foreign accent on perceptions of nonstandard grammar: A pilot study. *TESOL Quarterly, 52*(1), 187–98. https://doi.org/10.1002/tesq.374.

Saito, K. (2013). Reexamining effects of form-focused instruction on L2 pronunciation development: The role of explicit phonetic information. *Studies in Second Language Acquisition, 35*(1), 1–29. https://doi.org/10.1017/S0272263112000666.

Sams, M., Aulanko, R., Hämäläinen, M., Hari, R., Lounasmaa, O.V., Lu, S.-T., & Simola, J. (1991). Seeing speech: Visual information from lip movements modifies activity in the human auditory cortex. *Neuroscience Letters, 127*(1), 141–5. https://doi.org/10.1016/0304-3940(91)90914-f.

Scarborough, R., Keating, P., Mattys, S.L., Cho, T., & Alwan, A. (2009). Optical phonetics and visual perception of lexical and phrasal stress in English. *Language and Speech, 52*(2–3), 135–75. https://doi.org/10.1177/0023830909103165.

Schiffrin, D. (1987). *Discourse markers*. Cambridge University Press. https://doi.org/10.1017/CBO9780511611841.

Schwartz, J.L., & Savariaux, C. (2014). No, there is no 150 ms lead of visual speech on auditory speech, but a range of audiovisual asynchronies varying from small audio lead to large audio lag. *PLoS Computational Biology*, *10*(7), Article e1003743. https://doi.org/10.1371/journal.pcbi.1003743.

Sedley, W., & Cunningham, M.O. (2013). Do cortical gamma oscillations promote or suppress perception? An under-asked question with an over-assumed answer. *Frontiers in Human Neuroscience*, *7*, Article 595. https://doi.org/10.3389/fnhum.2013.00595.

Sekiyama, K. (1997). Cultural and linguistic factors in audiovisual speech processing: The McGurk effect in Chinese subjects. *Perception & Psychophysics*, *59*(1), 73–80. https://doi.org/10.3758/BF03206849.

Sekiyama, K., & Burnham, D. (2008). Impact of language on development of auditory-visual speech perception. *Developmental Science*, *11*(2), 306–20. https://doi.org/10.1111/j.1467-7687.2008.00677.x.

Sekiyama, K., Kanno, I., Miura, S., & Sugita, Y. (2003). Auditory-visual speech perception examined by fMRI and PET. *Neuroscience Research*, *47*(3), 277–87. https://doi.org/10.1016/s0168-0102(03)00214-1.

Sekiyama, K., & Tohkura, Y. (1991). McGurk effect in non-English listeners: Few visual effects for Japanese subjects hearing Japanese syllables of high auditory intelligibility. *Journal of the Acoustical Society of America*, *90*(4), 1797–805. https://doi.org/10.1121/1.401660.

Sekiyama, K., & Tohkura, Y. (1993). Inter-language differences in the influence of visual cues in speech perception. *Journal of Phonetics*, *21*(4), 427–44. https://doi.org/10.1016/S0095-4470(19)30229-3.

Selkirk, E. (1984). On the major class features and syllable theory. In M. Aronoff & R.T. Oehrle (Eds.), *Language sound structure* (pp. 107–36). MIT Press.

Serling, R. (Creator). (1959–1964). *The twilight zone* [TV series]. Paramount; CBS.

Sewell, A. (2017). Functional load revisited: Reinterpreting the findings of "lingua franca" intelligibility studies. *Journal of Second Language Pronunciation*, *3*(1), 57–79. https://doi.org/10.1075/jslp.3.1.03sew.

Shadle, C.H. (2007). Speech production and speech intelligibility. In M.J. Crocker (Ed.), *Handbook of noise and vibration control* (pp. 293–300). Wiley. https://doi.org/10.1002/9780470209707.ch22.

Shams, L., Kamitani, Y., & Shimojo, S. (2002). Visual illusion induced by sound. *Cognitive Brain Research*, *14*, 147–52. https://doi.org/10.1016/s0926-6410(02)00069-1.

Shams, L., & Seitz, A.R. (2008). Benefits of multisensory learning. *Trends in Cognitive Sciences*, *12*(11), 411–17. https://doi.org/10.1016/j.tics.2008.07.006.

Shimojo, S., & Shams, L. (2001). Sensory modalities are not separate modalities: Plasticity and interactions. *Current Opinion in Neurobiology*, *11*(4), 505–9. https://doi.org/10.1016/s0959-4388(00)00241-5.

Shinohara, Y. (2021). Audiovisual English /r/-/l/ identification training for Japanese-speaking adults and children. *Journal of Speech, Language, and Hearing Research*, *64*(7), 2529–38. https://doi.org/10.1044/2021_JSLHR-20-00506.

Sime, D. (2008). "Because of her gesture, it's very easy to understand": Learners' perceptions of teachers' gestures in the foreign language class. In S.G. McCafferty & G. Stam (Eds.), *Gesture: Second language acquisition and classroom research* (pp. 259–79). Routledge.

sixesfullofnines. (2016, March 16). *McGurk effect - auditory illusion - BBC Horizon clip* [Video]. YouTube. https://youtu.be/2k8fHR9jKVM.

Skipper, J.I. (2015). The NOLB model: A model of the natural organization of language and the brain. In R.M. Willems (Ed.), *Cognitive neuroscience of natural language use* (pp. 101–34). Cambridge University Press. https://doi.org/10.1017/CBO9781107323667.006.

Skipper, J.I., Goldin-Meadow, S., Nusbaum, H.C., & Small, S.L. (2007). Speech-associated gestures, Broca's area, and the human mirror system. *Brain and Language*, *101*(3), 260–77. https://doi.org/10.1016/j.bandl.2007.02.008.

Skipper, J.I., Goldin-Meadow, S., Nusbaum, H.C., & Small, S.L. (2009). Gestures orchestrate brain networks for language understanding. *Current Biology*, *19*(8), 661–7. https://doi.org/10.1016/j.cub.2009.02.051.

Skipper, J.I., van Wassenhove, V., Nusbaum, H.C., & Small, S.L. (2007). Hearing lips and seeing voices: How cortical areas supporting speech production mediate audiovisual speech perception. *Cerebral Cortex*, *17*(10), 2387–99. https://doi.org/10.1093/cercor/bhl147.

Smotrova, T. (2017). Making pronunciation visible: Gesture in teaching pronunciation. *TESOL Quarterly*, *51*(1), 59–89. https://doi.org/10.1002/tesq.276.

Sommers, M.S. (2021). Santa Claus, the Tooth Fairy, and auditory-visual integration: Three phenomena in search of empirical support. In J.S. Pardo, L.C. Nygaard, R.E. Remez, & D.B. Pisoni (Eds.), *The handbook of speech perception* (2nd ed., pp. 517–39). John Wiley & Sons. https://doi.org/10.1002/9781119184096.ch19.

Sommers, M.S., Tye-Murray, N., & Spehar, B. (2005). Auditory-visual speech perception and auditory-visual enhancement in normal-hearing younger and older adults. *Ear and Hearing*, *26*(3), 263–75. https://doi.org/10.1097/00003446-200506000-00003.

Soto-Faraco, S., Kvasova, D., Biau, E., Ikumi, N., Ruzzoli, M., Morís-Fernández, L., & Torralba, M. (2019). *Multisensory interactions in the real world*. Cambridge University Press. https://doi.org/10.1017/9781108578738.

Sparks, D.W., Kuhl, P.A., Edmonds, A.E., & Gray, G.P. (1978). Investigating the MESA (Multipoint Electrotactile Speech Aid): The transmission of segmental features of speech. *Journal of the Acoustical Society of America*, *63*(1), 246–57. https://doi.org/10.1121/1.381720.

Staudte, M., & Crocker, M.W. (2018). On the role of gaze for successful and efficient communication. In G. Brône & B. Oben (Eds.), *Eye-tracking in interaction: Studies on the role of eye gaze in dialogue* (pp. 91–106). John Benjamins. https://doi.org/10.1075/ais.10.05sta.

Stein, B.E., Stanford, T.R., & Rowland, B.A. (2009). The neural basis of multisensory integration in the midbrain: Its organization and maturation. *Hearing Research*, *258*(1–2), 4–15. https://doi.org/10.1016/j.heares.2009.03.012.

Stephan, K.E., & Friston, K.J. (2009). Functional connectivity. In L.R. Squire (Ed.), *Encyclopedia of neuroscience* (pp. 391–7). Academic Press. https://doi.org/10.1016/B978-008045046-9.00308-9.

Strand, J.F., & Sommers, M.S. (2011). Sizing up the competition: Quantifying the influence of the mental lexicon on auditory and visual spoken word recognition. *Journal of the Acoustical Society of America*, *130*(3), 1663–72. https://doi.org/10.1121/1.3613930.

Strange, W., & Dittmann, S. (1984). Effects of discrimination training on the perception of /r-l/ by Japanese adults learning English. *Perception & Psychophysics*, *36*(2), 131–45. https://doi.org/10.3758/BF03202673.

Sueyoshi, A., & Hardison, D.M. (2005). The role of gestures and facial cues in second-language listening comprehension. *Language Learning, 55*(4), 661–99. https://doi.org/10.1111/j.0023-8333.2005.00320.x.

Suh, M.-W., Lee, H.-J., Kim, J.S., Chung, C.K., & Oh, S.-H. (2009). Speech experience shapes the speechreading network and subsequent deafness facilitates it. *Brain, 132*(10), 2761–71. https://doi.org/10.1093/brain/awp159.

Sumby, W.H., & Pollack, I. (1954). Visual contribution to speech intelligibility in noise. *Journal of the Acoustical Society of America, 26*(2), 212–15. https://doi.org/10.1121/1.1907309.

Summerfield, Q. (1979). Use of visual information for phonetic perception. *Phonetica, 36*(4–5), 314–31. https://doi.org/10.1159/000259969.

Summerfield, Q. (1987). Some preliminaries to a comprehensive account of audio-visual speech perception. In B. Dodd & R. Campbell (Eds.), *Hearing by eye: The psychology of lipreading* (pp. 3–51). Erlbaum.

Summerfield, Q. (1992). Lipreading and audio-visual speech perception. *Philosophical Transactions: Biological Sciences, 335*(1273), 71–8. https://doi.org/10.1098/rstb.1992.0009.

Summerfield, Q., MacLeod, A.M., McGrath, M., & Brooke, M. (1989). Lips, teeth, and the benefits of lipreading. In A.W. Young & H.D. Ellis (Eds.), *Handbook of research on face processing* (pp. 223–33). North-Holland. https://doi.org/10.1016/B978-0-444-87143-5.50019-6.

Summerfield, Q., & McGrath, M. (1984). Detection and resolution of audio-visual incompatibility in the perception of vowels. *Quarterly Journal of Experimental Psychology, 36*(1), 51–74. https://doi.org/10.1080/14640748408401503.

Sweet, H. (1890). *A primer of spoken English.* Clarendon Press.

Szyszka, M. (2015). Good English pronunciation users and their pronunciation learning strategies. *Research in Language, 13*(1), 93–106. https://doi.org/10.1515/rela-2015-0017.

Tatler, B.W. (2007). The central fixation bias in scene viewing: Selecting an optimal viewing position independently of motor biases and image feature distributions. *Journal of Vision, 7*(14), 1–17. https://doi.org/10.1167/7.14.4.

Tatler, B.W., Wade, N.J., Kwan, H., Findlay, J.M., & Velichkovsky, B.M. (2010). Yarbus, eye movements, and vision. *I-Perception, 1*(1), 7–27. https://doi.org/10.1068/i0382.

Taylor, K., & Thompson, S. (2020). *The color vowel chart.* American English. https://americanenglish.state.gov/resources/color-vowel-chart.

Telestream, Inc. (2020). ScreenFlow (Version 0.0.5) [Computer software]. Telestream, Inc. http://www.telestream.net/screenflow.

Theeuwes, J. (1993). Visual selective attention: A theoretical analysis. *Acta Psychologica, 83*(2), 93–154. https://doi.org/10.1016/0001-6918(93)90042-p.

Theeuwes, J., Kramer, A.F., Hahn, S., & Irwin, D.E. (1998). Our eyes do not always go where we want them to go: Capture of the eyes by new objects. *Psychological Science, 9*(5), 379–85. https://doi.org/10.1111/1467-9280.00071.

Timmis, I. (2002). Native-speaker norms and international English: A classroom view. *ELT Journal, 56*(3), 240–9. https://doi.org/10.1093/elt/56.3.240.

Toda, M., Maeda, S., Carlen, A.J., & Meftahi, L. (2003). Lip protrusion/rounding dissociation in French and English consonants: /w/ vs. /ʃ/ and /ʒ/. In *Proceedings of the 15th International Congress of Phonetic Sciences* (pp. 1763–6). Universitat Autònoma de Barcelona. https://www.internationalphoneticassociation.org/icphs-proceedings/ICPhS2003/papers/p15_1763.pdf.

Traunmüller, H. (1994). Conventional, biological and environmental factors in speech communication: A modulation theory. *Phonetica*, *51*(1–3), 170–83. https://doi.org/10.1159/000261968.

Treffner, P., Peter, M., & Kleidon, M. (2008). Gestures and phases: The dynamics of speech-hand communication. *Ecological Psychology*, *20*(1), 32–64. https://doi.org/10.1080/10407410701766643.

Triesch, J., Ballard, D.H., Hayhoe, M.M., & Sullivan, B.T. (2003). What you see is what you need. *Journal of Vision*, *3*(1), 86–94. https://doi.org/10.1167/3.1.9.

Troille, E., Cathiard, M.-A., & Abry, C. (2010) Speech face perception is locked to anticipation in speech production. *Speech Communication*, *52*(6), 513–24. https://doi.org/10.1016/j.specom.2009.12.005.

Trubetzkoy, N.S. (1969). *Principles of phonology* (C.A.M. Baltaxe, Trans.). University of California Press. (Original work published 1939)

Tsujimura, N. (2013). *An introduction to Japanese linguistics* (3rd ed.). Wiley-Blackwell.

Tuite, K. (1993). The production of gesture. *Semiotica*, *93*(1–2), 83–106. https://doi.org/10.1515/semi.1993.93.1-2.83.

Twist, A., Baker, A., Mielke, J., & Archangeli, D. (2007). Are "covert" /ɹ/ allophones really indistinguishable? *University of Pennsylvania Working Papers in Linguistics*, *13*(2), Article 16. https://repository.upenn.edu/pwpl/vol13/iss2/16.

Tye-Murray, N., Sommers, M.S., & Spehar, B. (2007). Audiovisual integration and lipreading abilities of older adults with normal and impaired hearing. *Ear and Hearing*, *28*(5), 656–68. https://doi.org/10.1097/AUD.0b013e31812f7185.

Tye-Murray, N., Spehar, B., Myerson, J., Hale, S., & Sommers, M. (2016). Lipreading and audiovisual speech recognition across the adult lifespan: Implications for audiovisual integration. *Psychology and Aging*, *31*(4), 380–9. https://doi.org/10.1037/pag0000094.

Tyler, L.K. (1984). The structure of the initial cohort: Evidence from gating. *Perception & Psychophysics*, *36*(5), 417–27. https://doi.org/10.3758/BF03207496.

Underhill, A. (2012, August 28). Proprioception and pronunciation: The physicality of pronunciation and proprioception. *Adrian Underhill's Pronunciation Site*. https://adrianunderhill.com/2012/08/28/proprioception-and-pronunciation.

Uther, M., Knoll, M., & Burnham, D. (2007). Do you speak E-NG-L-I-SH? A comparison of foreigner- and infant-directed speech. *Speech Communication*, *49*(1), 2–7. https://doi.org/10.1016/j.specom.2006.10.003.

Vaden, K.I., Halpin, H.R., & Hickock, G.S. (2009). Irvine phonotactic online dictionary (Version 2.0) [Data file]. http://www.iphod.com.

Vance, T.J. (1987). *An introduction to Japanese phonology*. State University of New York Press.

Vandergrift, L. (2002). "It was nice to see that our predictions were right": Developing metacognition in L2 listening comprehension. *Canadian Modern Language Review*, *58*(4), 555–75. https://doi.org/10.3138/cmlr.58.4.555.

van Engen, K.J., Phelps, J.E.B., Smiljanic, R., & Chandrasekaran, B. (2014). Enhancing speech intelligibility: Interactions among context, modality, speech style, and masker. *Journal of Speech, Language, and Hearing Research*, *57*(5), 1908–18. https://doi.org/10.1044/JSLHR-H-13-0076.

van Engen, K.J., Xie, Z. & Chandrasekaran, B. (2017). Audiovisual sentence recognition not predicted by susceptibility to the McGurk effect. *Attention, Perception, & Psychophysics*, *79*(2), 396–403. https://doi.org/10.3758/s13414-016-1238-9.

van Wassenhove, V. (2013). Speech through ears and eyes: Interfacing the senses with the supramodal brain. *Frontiers in Psychology*, *4*, Article 388. https://doi.org/10.3389/fpsyg.2013.00388.

van Wassenhove, V., Grant, K.W., & Poeppel, D. (2005). Visual speech speeds up the neural processing of auditory speech. *Proceedings of the National Academy of Sciences of the United States of America, 102*(4), 1181–6. https://doi.org/10.1073/pnas.0408949102.

van Wassenhove, V., Grant, K.W., & Poeppel, D. (2007). Temporal window of integration in auditory-visual speech perception. *Neuropsychologia, 45*(3), 598–607. https://doi.org/10.1016/j.neuropsychologia.2006.01.001.

Vatakis, A., & Spence, C. (2007). Crossmodal binding: Evaluating the "unity assumption" using audiovisual speech stimuli. *Perception & Psychophysics, 69*(5), 744–56. https://doi.org/10.3758/BF03193776.

Vatikiotis-Bateson, E., Eigsti, I., Yano, S., & Munhall, K.G. (1998). Eye movement of perceivers during audiovisual speech perception. *Perception & Psychophysics, 60*(6), 926–40. https://doi.org/10.3758/BF03211929.

Vatikiotis-Bateson, E., & Yehia, H. (1996). Physiological modeling of facial motion during speech. *Transactions of the Technical Committee on Psychological and Physiological Acoustics, H-96*(65), 1–8.

Vecera, S.P., Cosman, J.D., Vatterott, D.B., & Roper, Z.J.J. (2014). The control of visual attention: Toward a unified account. In B.H. Ross (Ed.), *The psychology of learning and motivation* (Vol. 60, pp. 303–47). Academic Press. https://doi.org/10.1016/B978-0-12-800090-8.00008-1.

Venezia, J.H., Fillmore, P., Matchin, W., Isenberg, A.L., Hickok, G., & Fridriksson, J. (2016). Perception drives production across sensory modalities: A network for sensorimotor integration of visual speech. *NeuroImage, 126*, 196–207. https://doi.org/10.1016/j.neuroimage.2015.11.038.

Venezia, J.H., Vaden, K.I., Jr., Rong, F., Maddox D., Saberi, K., & Hickok, G. (2017). Auditory, visual and audiovisual speech processing streams in superior temporal sulcus. *Frontiers in Human Neuroscience, 11*, Article 174. https://doi.org/10.3389/fnhum.2017.00174.

Violin-Wigent, A. (2006). Southeastern French nasal vowels: Perceptual and acoustic elements. *Canadian Journal of Linguistics, 51*(1), 15–43. https://doi.org/10.1353/cjl.2007.0030.

Võ, M.L.-H., Smith, T.J., Mital, P.K., & Henderson, J.M. (2012). Do the eyes really have it? Dynamic allocation of attention when viewing moving faces. *Journal of Vision, 12*(13), 1–14. https://doi.org/10.1167/12.13.3.

von Kriegstein K., Kleinschmidt, A., Sterzer, P., & Giraud A. L. (2005). Interaction of face and voice areas during speaker recognition. *Journal of Cognitive Neuroscience, 17*(3), 367–76. https://doi.org/10.1162/0898929053279577.

von Raffler-Engel, W. (1980). *Aspects of nonverbal communication*. Swets & Zeitlinger.

Wagner, E. (2010). The effect of the use of video texts on ESL listening test-taker performance. *Language Testing, 27*(4), 493–513. https://doi.org/10.1177/0265532209355668.

Walden, B.E., Erdman, S.A., Montgomery, A.A., Schwartz, D.M., & Prosek, R.A. (1981). Some effects of training on speech recognition by hearing-impaired adults. *Journal of Speech and Hearing Research, 24*(2), 207–16. https://doi.org/10.1044/jshr.2402.207.

Walden, B.E., Prosek, R.A., Montgomery, A.A., Scherr, C.K., & Jones, C.J. (1977). Effects of training on the visual recognition of consonants. *Journal of Speech and Hearing Research, 20*(1), 130–45. https://doi.org/10.1044/jshr.2001.130.

Walker, S., Bruce, V., & O'Malley, C. (1995). Facial identity and facial speech processing: Familiar faces and voices in the McGurk effect. *Perception & Psychophysics, 57*(8), 1124–33. https://doi.org/10.3758/BF03208369.

Walsh, V., & Cowey, A. (2000) Transcranial magnetic stimulation and cognitive neuroscience. *Nature Reviews Neuroscience*, *1*(1), 73–9. https://doi.org/10.1038/35036239.

Walter, H. (1977). *La phonologie du français*. Presses Universitaires de France.

Walton, G.E., & Bower, T.G.R. (1993). Amodal representation of speech in infants. *Infant Behavior and Development*, *16*(2), 233–43. https://doi.org/10.1016/0163-6383(93)80019-5.

Wang, Y., Behne, D.M., & Jiang, H. (2009). Influence of native language phonetic system on audio-visual speech perception. *Journal of Phonetics*, *37*(3), 344–56. https://doi.org/10.1016/j.wocn.2009.04.002.

Wang, Y., Jongman, A., & Sereno, J.A. (2003). Acoustic and perceptual evaluation of Mandarin tone productions before and after perceptual training. *Journal of the Acoustical Society of America*, *113*(2), 1033–43. https://doi.org/10.1121/1.1531176.

Wang, Y., Spence, M.M., Jongman, A., & Sereno, J. A. (1999). Training American listeners to perceive Mandarin tones. *Journal of the Acoustical Society of America*, *106*(6), 3649–58. https://doi.org/10.1121/1.428217.

Warren, D.H., Welch, R.B., & McCarthy, T.J. (1981). The role of visual-auditory "compellingness" in the ventriloquism effect: Implications for transitivity among the spatial senses. *Perception & Psychophysics*, *30*(6), 557–64. https://doi.org/10.3758/BF03202010.

Wegner-Clemens, K., Rennig, J., Magnotti, J.F., & Beauchamp, M.S. (2019). Using principal component analysis to characterize eye movement fixation patterns during face viewing. *Journal of Vision*, *19*(13), 1–15. https://doi.org/10.1167/19.13.2.

Weikum, W.M., Vouloumanos, A., Navarra, J., Soto-Faraco, S., Sebastián-Gallés, N., & Werker, J.F. (2007). Visual language discrimination in infancy. *Science*, *316*(5828), 1159. https://doi.org/10.1126/science.1137686.

Welch, R.B., & Warren, D.H. (1980). Immediate perceptual response to intersensory discrepancy. *Psychological Bulletin*, *88*(3), 638–67. https://doi.org/10.1037/0033-2909.88.3.638.

Wennerstrom, A. (2001). *The music of everyday speech: Prosody and discourse analysis*. Oxford University Press. https://doi.org/10.1093/oso/9780195143218.001.0001.

Werker, J.F., & Tees, R.C. (1984). Cross-language speech perception: Evidence for perceptual reorganization during the first year of life. *Infant Behavior and Development*, *7*(1), 49–63. https://doi.org/10.1016/S0163-6383(84)80022-3.

Willems, R.M., Özyürek, A., & Hagoort. P. (2007). When language meets action: The neural integration of gesture and speech. *Cerebral Cortex*, *17*(10), 2322–33. https://doi.org/10.1093/cercor/bhl141.

Wohltjen, S., & Wheatley, T. (2021). Eye contact marks the rise and fall of shared attention in conversation. *Proceedings of the National Academy of Sciences*, *118*(37), Article e2106645118. https://doi.org/10.1073/pnas.2106645118.

Wolfe, J.M., & Horowitz, T.S. (2004). What attributes guide the deployment of visual attention and how do they do it? *Nature Reviews Neuroscience*, *5*(6), 495–501. https://doi.org/10.1038/nrn1411.

Wood, C.C. (1975). Auditory and phonetic levels of processing in speech perception: Neurophysiological and information-processing analyses. *Journal of Experimental Psychology: Human Perception and Performance*, *1*(1), 3–20. https://doi.org/10.1037/0096–1523.1.1.3.

Woodward, M.F., & Barber, C.G. (1960). Phoneme perception in lipreading. *Journal of Speech and Hearing Research*, *3*(3), 212–22. https://doi.org/10.1044/jshr.0303.212.

Yakel, D.A., Rosenblum, L.D., & Fortier, M.A. (2000). Effects of talker variability on speechreading. *Perception & Psychophysics*, *62*(7), 1405–12. https://doi.org/10.3758/BF03212142.

Yamada, R.A. (1995). Age and acquisition of second language speech sounds: Perception of American English /r/ and /l/ by native speakers of Japanese. In W. Strange (Ed.), *Speech perception and linguistic experience: Issues in cross-language research* (pp. 305–20). York Press.

Yamada, R.A., & Tohkura, Y. (1992). The effects of experimental variables on the perception of American English /r/ and /l/ by Japanese listeners. *Perception & Psychophysics, 52*(4), 376–92. https://doi.org/10.3758/BF03206698.

Yantis, S. (1998). Control of visual attention. In H. Pashler (Ed.), *Attention* (pp. 223–56). Psychology Press.

Yantis, S., & Jonides, J. (1984). Abrupt visual onsets and selective attention: Evidence from visual search. *Experimental Psychology: Human Perception and Performance, 10*(5), 601–21. https://doi.org/10.1037/0096-1523.10.5.601.

Yarbus, A.L. (1967). *Eye movements and vision* (B. Haigh, Trans.) Plenum Press. (Original work published 1965)

Yi, A., Wong, W., & Eizenman, M. (2013). Gaze patterns and audiovisual speech enhancement. *Journal of Speech, Language, and Hearing Research, 56*(2), 471–80. https://doi.org/10.1044/1092-4388(2012/10-0288).

Yi, H-G., Phelps, J.E.B., Smiljanic, R., & Chandrasekaran, B. (2013). Reduced efficiency of audiovisual integration for non-native speech. *Journal of the Acoustical Society of America, 134*(5), EL387–93. https://doi.org/10.1121/1.4822320.

Yu, K., & Jamieson, D.G. (1993). Training of the English /r/ and /l/ speech contrasts in Korean listeners. *Canadian Acoustics, 21*(3), 107–8. https://jcaa.caa-aca.ca/index.php/jcaa/article/view/797.

Yum, J-O. (1987). Korean philosophy and communication. In D.L. Kincaid (Ed.), *Communication theory: Eastern and western perspectives* (pp. 71–86). Academic Press. https://doi.org/10.1016/B978-0-12-407470-5.50011-6.

Zerling, J. (1989). The three degrees of labialisation of the French steady-state vowels: A study for 105 speakers. In *Proceedings of the European Conference on Speech Communication and Technology* (pp. 2445–8). International Speech Communication Association.

Zhang, Y., Frassinelli, D., Tuomainen, J., Skipper, J.I., & Vigliocco, G. (2021). More than words: Word predictability, prosody, gesture and mouth movements in natural language comprehension. *Proceedings of the Royal Society B: Biological Sciences, 288*(1955), Article 20210500. https://doi.org/10.1098/rspb.2021.0500.

Zhou, X., Epsy-Wilson, C.Y., Boyce, S., Tiede, M., Holland, C., & Choe, A. (2008). A magnetic resonance imaging-based articulatory and acoustic study of "retroflex" and "bunched" American English /r/. *Journal of the Acoustical Society of America, 123*(6), 4466–81. https://doi.org/10.1121/1.2902168.

Zhu, L.L., & Beauchamp, M.S. (2017). Mouth and voice: A relationship between visual and auditory preference in the human superior temporal sulcus. *Journal of Neuroscience, 37*(10), 2697–708. https://doi.org/10.1523/JNEUROSCI.2914-16.2017.

Author Index

Subject Index

How to use this keepsake

This keepsake is more than just a book_it's an invitation to slow down, reflect, and connect. Inside, you'll find thoughtful, meaningful questions created to help you share your life story in your own words with your daughter or son. There's no rush to finish it all at once. In fact, taking your time will make the experience richer. You might answer a question a day, a few at a time, or revisit the book during quiet moments, rainy afternoons, or even during a heart-to-heart with your child. Let your answers unfold naturally, with honesty and heart. Don't forget a sprinkling of laughter and a dash of motherly wisdom.

There's no such thing as a "perfect" response. Some questions may make you roll your eyes and others might stir deeper memories or emotions. All of it is welcome here. If a question doesn't quite fit or feels too difficult in the moment, skip it and come back later. This keepsake is a personal story, told your way. Feel free to write in the margins, doodle, or even include mementos like photos, letters, or recipes along the way.

To the child gifting this book:

Your curiosity and love have created something truly meaningful_a rare chance to get to know who your father really is, beyond just "Dad." Encourage him to answer freely, without pressure. Let him know how much these memories mean to you and remind him that this isn't about being formal or flawless_it's about being real.

And to the father filling out these pages:

Your words, no matter how ordinary they may seem, will hold extraordinary meaning to the one who gave you this keepsake_and to the generations who will one day read it. This is your story, your legacy, and a gift that will continue to offer comfort, insight, and strength long after it's written.

“As I entered this big world in the tiniest of forms, your fatherly embrace was there to greet and comfort me with love. You have been my security blanket, Guardian Angel, protector, teacher and disciplinarian. You're also my best source of encouragement, cheerleader and counselor. Dad, you're everything to me and I want to know everything about you.

I know how to push your buttons and I think I know how to make you laugh. I know what every facial expression means and even figured out where your secret hiding place was, but I want to know more. I want to know how you became the person you are today. I want to know you when you were younger like me. Tell me stories from your childhood, tell me about Grandma and Grandpa but mostly tell me more about you.

I don't want to let time pass by without getting to know everything there is to know about you. I want to know more about myself through your eyes. I want to spend some time walking in your shoes, if only to see the world from your view. Please take the time to answer each question. No matter how small or insignificant you think it may be, this means everything to me. I want to know it all, the good, bad and in between. Your history will be written in these pages and while it's no substitute for the real you, I can look back and cherish each answer you wrote just for me.

“DAD, YOU'RE EVERYTHING TO ME AND I WANT TO KNOW EVERYTHING ABOUT YOU.”

There's something remarkable about the bond between a father and child. It's often found in quiet moments—a look of approval, a helping hand, an inside joke, or advice shared at just the right time. But before you were "Dad," you were your own person with dreams, struggles, stories, and a life filled with meaning. That's the version I want to know more about.

This collection of questions isn't just about listing facts. It's an invitation—to laugh, to remember, to share. I want to know who you were before fatherhood. What made you tick? What challenges shaped you? What adventures made you feel most alive? Tell me about your parents_my grandparents_and what they passed down to you. Tell me about your friendships, your milestones, the mistakes you learned from, and the moments that taught you how to be strong.

Every answer is a piece of the puzzle that makes up who you are. And someday, when life gets busy or time feels short, I'll have these pages to return to. Your words, your voice, your story_preserved in your own handwriting, reminding me where I come from and how much I am loved.

One day, long after these pages are filled, this keepsake will become more than just a father-to-child gift_it will be a legacy. These stories and reflections will travel across time, guiding future generations with your wisdom, your humor, and your heart. This book is a time capsule, a family history, and a personal treasure, all in one.

As I grow, I know I'll return to your words looking for strength, reassurance, and perspective. And when I become a parent myself, I know I'll hear echoes of your guidance in how I lead, love, and learn. In discovering more about you, I'll uncover more about myself_why I react a certain way, where I get my stubborn streak (or my sense of humor), and how our family's story continues to live in me.

This isn't just about family history_it's about self-discovery. The traditions you've passed down, the expressions, the values and beliefs—

all of it shapes who I am now and who I'll become. These aren't just written words. They're a living reminder of the depth, grit, and love that runs through our lineage.

Photos capture faces, but your words preserve the meaning behind those moments. Long after the years have passed, your story will remain_a compass when I feel lost, a smile when I need to laugh, and a warm reminder that I am never far from your love and the steadfast role model you've been for me.

In a world that's constantly shifting_where values evolve, and noise can drown out what really matters_your words will bring clarity in the confusion and comfort when times get tough. This keepsake will become a source of strength and inspiration not only for me but for everyone it's shared with in generations to come.

You may not be here in a hundred years, but your words will be. They'll allow your future grandchildren and family to walk in your shoes, see life from your perspective, and carry forward the wisdom you so generously shared with me. Your stories will become their stories. Your strength will become their foundation. And your legacy will continue to guide us for years to come.

Thank you for taking the time to share your heart. These pages are part of our family's story now_and part of me forever.

"I CANNOT THINK OF ANY NEED IN CHILDHOOD AS STRONG AS THE NEED FOR A FATHER'S PROTECTION."

-Sigmund Freud

Tools You'll Need for Your Journey Through This Keepsake:

1. **A sense of humor** _ We don't always see eye to eye (shocking, I know), but my goal is always to make you smile—and laughter is a bonus. I hope these questions bring more than a few chuckles, eye-rolls, or even a dad joke or two.

2. **Patience** – Some questions might stretch your memory like an old rubber band, and others may be tough to revisit. But I want the whole story. I want to understand your strength, connect with your past, and_let's be real_I'm also curious if we made the same questionable decisions in our youth. I'm here for both the polished highlight reel and the blooper reel.

3. **Your favorite pen** _ Pick something that feels good in your hand. There's a lot of ground to cover, and a reliable pen can make even the tough stuff feel smoother. Bonus if it makes your handwriting look cool.

4. **Tissues** _ Yes, I'm hoping for laughs, but I know how life works_there may be a few emotional detours. Whether it's tears of joy, grief, or just a tender memory sneaking in, it's all welcome here. No shame in needing a moment.

5. **Memorabilia** _ Since this keepsake is all about you, make it yours. Add in a photo, a memento, a doodle from a childhood notebook, or even a ticket stub from a day you'll never forget. These little details bring your story to life.

6. **A moment to yourself** _ You don't need silence or a fancy setup, but a calm space helps. Find a quiet corner, your favorite chair, or a peaceful moment with coffee (or your go-to drink of choice), and let your thoughts flow.

7. **An open heart** _ Some answers might surprise you. Others might take you deeper than expected. Approach this with an open mind and a real heart. You don't have to be perfect_just present. That's all I ask.

Chapters

CHAPTER I

About Our Family

"A HAPPY FAMILY IS
BUT AN EARLIER HEAVEN."

-George Bernard Shaw

What was the name of your mother and father? Where and when were they born?

"WE NEVER KNOW
THE LOVE OF A PARENT TILL
WE BECOME PARENTS OURSELVES."

-Henry Ward Beecher

Describe your mom, my grandmother. Did she have any funny habits?

Describe your dad, my grandfather. Did he have any funny habits?

Did you have any brothers or sisters, and did you want any? How did that change through time?

"BROTHERS AND SISTERS
ARE AS CLOSE AS HANDS AND FEET."

-Vietnamese Proverb

Who was your favorite family member that wasn't your mom or dad and why were they your favorite?

What was your favorite thing to do with your dad, my grandpa?

What's the best advice you got from your mom and dad?

"DO NOT COMPLAIN BENEATH THE STARS ABOUT THE LACK OF BRIGHT SPOTS IN YOUR LIFE."

-Bjørnstjerne Bjørnson

What is one thing I don't know about our family you think I should know now?

What traditions do you hope to pass down to me and why?

"TRADITION IS NOT
THE WORSHIP OF ASHES,
BUT THE PRESERVATION OF FIRE."

-Gustav Mahler

Is there anything special about our family lineage? Do you know the origin of our family's name on both sides?

"THE ONE THING
I WANT TO LEAVE MY CHILDREN
IS AN HONORABLE NAME."

-Theodore Roosevelt

In our family, who do you have the most in common with and who did you have the biggest connection with?

Do we have any famous people, inventors or influencers in our family tree?

Does our family have any special recipes that have been passed down?

"EVERY MAN IS A QUOTATION
FROM ALL HIS ANCESTORS."

-Gustav Mahler

Do we have any special family antiques or heirlooms that have significant importance?

"OUR MOST TREASURED
FAMILY HEIRLOOMS ARE
OUR SWEET FAMILY MEMORIES."

-*Unknown*

How did your parents, my grandparents meet? How did their parents, my great grandparents meet?

How did you meet my mother? Describe your first encounter and your first date.

Did you ever experience love at first sight? Who was it with and how did you feel? What happened with this person?

"WHO EVER LOVED
THAT LOVED NOT AT FIRST SIGHT?"

- William Shakespeare

Did we lose any family members in a war?

What are some of the most interesting facts about our family?

What was your all-time favorite holiday of us together as a family and why? Before you became a dad, what was your most memorable holiday and why?

"BLESSED IS THE SEASON
WHICH ENGAGES THE WHOLE WORLD
IN A CONSPIRACY OF LOVE."

-Hamilton Wright Mabie

CHAPTER II

When You Were Young

"A YOUTH IS TO BE
REGARDED WITH RESPECT.
HOW DO WE KNOW THAT HIS FUTURE WILL
NOT BE EQUAL TO OUR PRESENT?"

-Confucius

Where were you born? What is the first (earliest) memory you have from your childhood?

"THE TWO MOST IMPORTANT
DAYS IN YOUR LIFE
ARE THE DAY YOU ARE BORN
AND THE DAY YOU FIND OUT WHY."

-*Unknown*

Did you have a favorite thing or toy as a child and why did you love it so much?

Did you have a nickname as a child? If so, how did you get it and how did you feel about it?

What do you remember about your childhood home?

"A MAN TRAVELS THE WORLD OVER
IN SEARCH OF WHAT HE NEEDS AND
RETURNS HOME TO FIND IT."

-George Moore

What was your favorite TV show, song and movie?

"LET YOURSELF BE SILENTLY DRAWN
BY THE STRONGER PULL OF
WHAT YOU REALLY LOVE."

-*Rumi*

Did anyone ever tease you about anything when you were young and what was it?

What did you want to be when you were little? In other words what did you dream about becoming when you grew up?

"IT TAKES COURAGE TO GROW UP
AND BECOME WHO YOU REALLY ARE."

-E.E. Cummings

What was the naughtiest thing you did as a child?

What was your imagination like? Did you ever play pretend and what did you pretend to be?

What did you want most as a child that your mom and dad never gave you?

"IN TRUTH, PEOPLE CAN GENERALLY MAKE TIME
FOR WHAT THEY CHOOSE TO DO;
IT IS NOT REALLY THE TIME BUT
THE WILL THAT IS WANTING."

-John Lubbock

What were you afraid of when you were little (the dark, monsters under the bed, etc.) and how did your mom and dad comfort you?

What do you miss from your childhood?

"WHAT WAS WONDERFUL ABOUT CHILDHOOD
IS THAT ANYTHING IN IT WAS A WONDER.
IT WAS NOT MERELY A WORLD FULL OF MIRACLES;
IT WAS A MIRACULOUS WORLD."

-G.K. Chesterton

Were you spoiled in any way? If so, by whom and how were you spoiled?

"SOME NATURES ARE TOO GOOD
TO BE SPOILED BY PRAISE."

-Ralph Waldo Emerson

Where was your secret hiding spot as a kid?

Where was your favorite place to play and who did you usually play with?

Did you have a favorite family vacation, road trip or outing that you remember fondly from childhood?

What rules or chores did your parents give you that you swore you'd never give your own children (including me)?

"IT IS A GOOD IDEA TO OBEY ALL THE RULES
WHEN YOU'RE YOUNG
JUST SO YOU'LL HAVE THE STRENGTH
TO BREAK THEM WHEN YOU'RE OLD."

-Mark Twain

What was the town/city like that you grew up in? What was there to do there?

"THE STREETS LOOKED SMALL, OF COURSE.
THE STREETS THAT WE HAVE ONLY SEEN AS
CHILDREN ALWAYS DO I BELIEVE
WHEN WE GO BACK TO THEM."

-Charles Dickens

What childhood experiences did you have, that you wish I would have gotten to experience?

What was your favorite food as a child and do you still like it?

Did you ever dress up for Halloween, pull any pranks or did anyone ever scare you? What ghost stories and urban legends haunted your community?

"LISTEN TO THEM, THE CHILDREN OF THE NIGHT. WHAT MUSIC THEY MAKE!"

-Bram Stoker

What were your hobbies when you were young? What did you enjoy?

"WHAT YOU FEED
IN YOURSELF THAT GROWS."

-Johann Wolfgang von Goethe

What was the scariest moment from your childhood?

What's the biggest difference between your childhood and mine?

What was the best moment from your childhood?

"HOW STRANGE IT IS THAT WHEN I WAS A CHILD
I TRIED TO BE LIKE A GROWNUP,
YET AS SOON AS I CEASED TO BE A CHILD
I OFTEN LONGED TO BE LIKE ONE."

-Leo Tolstoy

Chapter III

Your Adolescent Years

"Common sense is the collection of prejudices acquired by age eighteen."

-Albert Einstein

What did you hate/love the most about growing up?

What was the hardest lesson for you to learn as you grew up?

"EVERY FAILURE IS A LESSON LEARNED ABOUT YOUR STRATEGY."

-Thomas A. Edison

Who was your first crush and what happened with them?

"SHE BLUSHED AND SO DID HE.
SHE GREETED HIM IN A FALTERING VOICE,
AND HE SPOKE TO HER
WITHOUT KNOWING WHAT HE WAS SAYING."

- Voltaire

Who was your first kiss? Where was it and what was it like?

Did you have a high school sweetheart? Spill the beans...

What/who influenced your style and taste as a teenager?

"ON MATTERS OF STYLE,
SWIM WITH THE CURRENT,
ON MATTERS OF PRINCIPLE,
STAND LIKE A ROCK."

-Thomas Jefferson

Did you have a/any best friends? If so, who were they and why did you like them so much?

Who was your celebrity crush and where did you first see them?

Did you have any favorite classes or subjects? Do you remember a particular teacher?

"I AM INDEBTED
TO MY FATHER FOR LIVING,
BUT TO MY TEACHER
FOR LIVING WELL."

-Alexander the Great

Did you ever get into trouble at school? What did you do and what was the punishment?

"EVEN A FISH
WOULDN'T GET INTO TROUBLE
IF IT KEPT ITS MOUTH SHUT."

-Korean Proverb

What was your favorite fad from your generation? What fad was the most embarrassing when you look back?

Did you ever skip school? If you did, why?

What's your most memorable school event (dance, game, etc.) and what made it so memorable?

What kind of student were you and did you belong to any groups or cliques?

"WISDOM IS NOT A PRODUCT OF SCHOOLING BUT OF THE LIFELONG ATTEMPT TO ACQUIRE IT."

-Albert Einstein

What does your yearbook say about you?

"I NEVER LET MY SCHOOLING INTERFERE WITH MY EDUCATION."

-Mark Twain

What was your greatest school accomplishment?

Who was the biggest influence on your life growing up and was it positive or negative?

Did you ever have any friends your parents didn't like?

"A FRIENDSHIP THAT CAN END NEVER REALLY BEGAN."

-*Publilius Syrus*

Did your dad, my grandpa ever do anything funny to a date when you began dating?

"IT'S ALL LIFE IS.
JUST GOING 'ROUND KISSING PEOPLE."

-F. Scott Fitzgerald

What was the hardest thing you ever had to tell your parents as a teenager?

What was the biggest lie you ever told growing up and who did you tell it to? Did anything ever happen?

Did you ever experiment with anything? What was it and what happened?

"THE TRUE METHOD OF KNOWLEDGE IS EXPERIMENT."

- William Blake

What is your biggest regret of your teenage years?

"No space of regret
can make amends for one life's
opportunity misused."

-Charles Dickens

Where did you hang out as a teenager and what did you do?

Did you ever think about college and where did you want to go? Why did you want to go there, and did you get to go? Why or why not?

When you got older, how did what you want to be change from when you were younger? What is the dream you wanted most for your life?

"DREAMS ARE THE TOUCHSTONES OF OUR CHARACTERS."

-*Henry David Thoreau*

What was the first car you wanted and why?

"A PEDESTRIAN IS SOMEONE
WHO THOUGHT THERE WERE
A COUPLE OF GALLONS LEFT IN THE TANK."

-Unknown

How did growing up in your decade differ from mine and what's the biggest difference?

Did you ever rebel? If so, what did you do?

Did you have an afterschool job, or did you want one? Tell me more about it...

"YOUR WORK IS TO DISCOVER YOUR WORK
AND THEN WITH ALL YOUR HEART
TO GIVE YOURSELF TO IT."

-Unknown

Did any world events or politics affect you growing up? How did you cope?

"IN POLITICS,
STUPIDITY IS NOT A HANDICAP."

-*Napoléon Bonaparte*

What was your favorite summer vacation? How did you usually spend summers?

What was your most embarrassing moment in high school and how did you survive it?

"IF QUICK, I SURVIVE.
IF NOT QUICK, I AM LOST.
THIS IS DEATH."

-Sun Tzu

What wild and crazy ideas did you have for after high school that you never pursued?

Did you play sports, instruments or participate in school activities? What did you like and what were you good at?

*I*f you were going to pack a time capsule in high school for your future child to open, what do you think you would have packed for me to see and why?

"THE WHOLE PAST IS
THE PROCESSION OF
THE PRESENT."

-Thomas Carlyle

Did you graduate high school? If so, how was it and what was the highlight of graduating?

Did you dream about getting married and what kind of wedding you'd have? Who did you think you'd marry and what kind of wedding did you want?

"To get the full value of joy
you must have someone to
divide it with."

-Mark Twain

What's the most important thing you learned in school that actually helped you in the real world?

"TELL ME AND I FORGET,
TEACH ME AND I MAY REMEMBER,
INVOLVE ME AND I LEARN."

-Benjamin Franklin

What other hopes and dreams did you have for your life?

Chapter IV

Things You Learned About Life

"It is better to live your own destiny imperfectly than to live an imitation of somebody else's life with perfection."

-Anonymous, The Bhagavad Gita

Where did your life take an unexpected turn and how did it happen?

"LIFE BELONGS TO THE LIVING,
AND HE WHO LIVES
MUST BE PREPARED FOR CHANGES."

-Johann Wolfgang von Goethe

What's the most important thing you learned about relationships?

Is there a secret or key to happiness?

What was the hardest period of your life and why?

Was having a family as rewarding as you thought it would be?

"AFTER A GOOD DINNER
ONE CAN FORGIVE ANYBODY,
EVEN ONE'S OWN RELATIONS."

-Oscar Wilde

*W*hat life challenges were the most difficult for you?

"THE GEM CANNOT BE POLISHED
WITHOUT FRICTION,
NOR MAN PERFECTED
WITHOUT TRIALS."

-*Confucius*

Was there any area of your life you neglected that you wish you hadn't?

*W*hat life event brought you the most emotional pain?

What mistake did you make that you'd never want your children to repeat?

"BE PATIENT,
EVEN IF EVERY POSSIBILITY
SEEMS CLOSED."

-Rumi

Did you ever experience peer pressure? What happened and how did you handle it?

What do you think is the root of all evil and why?

What did you learn about becoming a dad and parent?

"THE SOUL IS HEALED
BY BEING WITH CHILDREN."

-Fyodor Dostoevsky

*W*hat was the scariest thing about raising a child?

What did you learn about true friendships?

"WE ARE LIKE ISLANDS IN THE SEA,
SEPARATE ON THE SURFACE
BUT CONNECTED IN THE DEEP."

-William James

Did you learn anything interesting about yourself on your life's journey, what was it?

"A GOOD TRAVELER
HAS NO FIXED PLANS AND IS NOT
INTENT ON ARRIVING."

-Lao Tzu

What is the most important lesson you've learned about people?

Do you think life's fair? Tell me the way it is or isn't...

What golden rule do you want me to live by?

"HAPPINESS IS NOT AN IDEAL OF REASON BUT OF IMAGINATION."

-*Immanuel Kant*

How did you know when you were in love?

"Nobody is perfect until you fall in love with them."

-*Unknown*

What is life's most precious commodity that shouldn't be wasted?

What should I do if I can't forgive someone?

What moments in your life do you relish the most?

"THERE IS NO MOMENT OF DELIGHT
IN ANY PILGRIMAGE
LIKE THE BEGINNING OF IT."

-Charles Dudley Warner

Did you ever feel like giving up? What did you do? What should I do if I ever feel like giving up on something?

"OUR GREATEST WEAKNESS LIES IN GIVING UP.
THE MOST CERTAIN WAY TO SUCCEED
IS ALWAYS TO TRY JUST ONE MORE TIME."

-Thomas Edison

What is most valuable to you in this life?

Tell me about a crossroads in your life and what you did. How did you make a decision about what to do?

"IT DOES NOT MATTER HOW SLOWLY YOU GO AS LONG AS YOU DO NOT STOP."

-*Confucius*

How does the idea of becoming a grandparent make you feel?

Did you ever want to travel the world? If you could go anywhere you wanted, where would you go and why?

How did you handle betrayal in your life?

"IT IS EASIER TO FORGIVE AN ENEMY THAN TO FORGIVE A FRIEND."

-William Blake

What rule did your parents teach you that turned out to be the most important rule of all?

"When I let go of what I am,
I become what I might be."

-Lao Tzu

Has anything from your past haunted you? What was it?

In what ways do you feel blessed?

Did you ever experience a miracle, if so what?

"THERE ARE TWO WAYS TO LIVE:
YOU CAN LIVE AS IF NOTHING IS A MIRACLE;
YOU CAN LIVE AS IF EVERYTHING IS A MIRACLE."

-*Albert Einstein*

What are you most thankful for in your life today?

"LET US BE GRATEFUL TO THE
PEOPLE WHO MAKE US HAPPY;
THEY ARE THE CHARMING GARDENERS
WHO MAKE OUR SOULS BLOSSOM."

-Marcel Proust

Tell me what you know about the phrase "nothing lasts forever" and "don't know what you've got until it's gone."

Dad, is honesty always the best policy?

"HALF THE TRUTH IS OFTEN
A WHOLE LIE."

-Benjamin Franklin

What bad trait do you have that always got you into trouble? Do I have it too?

What should I never waste energy on?

What's one of the hardest things we will have to do in life?

What have you learned about trusting people?

What's your biggest regret in life?

"REMORSE IS
THE POISON OF LIFE."

-*Charlotte Brontë*

CHAPTER V

Growing Older

"I LIVE IN THAT SOLITUDE
WHICH IS PAINFUL IN YOUTH,
BUT DELICIOUS IN THE
YEARS OF MATURITY."

-Albert Einstein

What do you wish someone had told you about life when you were younger?

"WE ARE WHAT WE REPEATEDLY DO.
EXCELLENCE, THEN,
IS NOT AN ACT, BUT A HABIT."

Does life get easier as you grow older?

Looking back, what do you wish you'd made more time for?

*W*hat is your proudest life accomplishment thus far?

"To accomplish great things,
we must dream as well as act."

-Anatole France

What is your favorite memory about fatherhood in general?

"THE HEART OF A FATHER
IS THE MASTERPIECE OF NATURE."

-Antoine François Prévost

What are you currently looking forward to in your life right now?

How much sacrifice did you have to make in life? In what ways and was the reward worth the sacrifice?

Did you ever think you'd end up where you are now in life?

"TWENTY YEARS FROM NOW
YOU WILL BE MORE DISAPPOINTED
BY THE THINGS YOU DIDN'T DO
THAN BY THE ONES YOU DID DO."

-*Mark Twain*

If you could have met anyone famous at any point in your life, who would it have been and why?

"WE ALL CARRY THE SEEDS
OF GREATNESS WITHIN US,
BUT WE NEED AN IMAGE
AS A POINT OF FOCUS IN ORDER
THAT THEY MAY SPROUT."

-Epictetus

Where did you always want to live that you never got the chance?

What should I never forget to do?

Who or what was your best teacher about life?

"A TRUE TEACHER IS ONE WHO,
KEEPING THE PAST ALIVE,
IS ALSO ABLE TO UNDERSTAND
THE PRESENT."

-Confucius

What is one thing that didn't turn out the way you'd hoped and how did you wish it had turned out?

What problems of the world today trouble you?

"OF ALL YOUR TROUBLES,
GREAT AND SMALL,
THE GREATEST ARE THE ONES
THAT DON'T HAPPEN AT ALL."

-*Thomas Carlyle*

Did you ever experience unrequited love?

"'Tis better to have
loved and lost
Than never to have loved at all."

-Alfred Lord Tennyson

Does wisdom come from age?

What was the one thing you always tried to shelter your child/children from?

What are your plans for retirement?

"TIME SPENT IN LAUGHTER
WHEN ONE IS RETIRED
IS WELL INVESTED."

-Unknown

In what ways are you still like a child?

"EVERY CHILD IS AN ARTIST.
THE PROBLEM IS HOW TO REMAIN AN ARTIST
ONCE HE GROWS UP."

-Pablo Picasso

What can you never be too careful about?

What lessons did you learn about money that you want me to know?

What makes you laugh now, that made you furious back then?

What is the one thing you want people (family, friends, etc.) to remember most about you?

“LIFE SHRINKS OR EXPANDS
IN PROPORTION
TO ONE’S COURAGE.”

-*Anaïs Nin*

What can I expect out of life as I grow older?

"Too many of us are not living our dreams because we are living our fears."

-Les Brown

In what way did you wish your life had turned out different?

CHAPTER VI

Becoming a Dad

"A TRULY RICH MAN IS ONE
WHOSE CHILDREN RUN INTO HIS ARMS
WHEN HIS HANDS ARE EMPTY."

-Anonymous

POST PHOTO
HERE

Take your favorite picture of me and post it here. Tell me why you love it so much.

What is one thing you wish we'd done together, that we haven't had a chance to yet?

"THE LURE OF THE DISTANT AND
THE DIFFICULT IS DECEPTIVE.
THE GREAT OPPORTUNITY
IS WHERE YOU ARE."

-John Burroughs

What was the scariest thing about fatherhood?

Did you always know you wanted to become a dad?

How did you feel the first time you found out my mom was pregnant?

What was one of our most special moments as father and child?

"BECOMING A FATHER IS EASY ENOUGH,
BUT BEING ONE CAN BE VERY ROUGH."

-Wilhelm Busch

If you had to do fatherhood all over again, would you change anything? If so, what?

"BLESSED INDEED IS THE MAN
WHO HEARS MANY GENTLE VOICES
CALL HIM FATHER."

-Lydia Maria Francis Child

Give me your best advice about becoming a new parent.

What do you and I have most in common (features, traits, etc.) and how soon did you notice it?

Describe the bond you and I share.

"IT IS A WISE FATHER
THAT KNOWS HIS OWN CHILD."

-William Shakespeare

Tell me your secret thoughts about me as a kid in my most mischievous phase.

"WHEN CHILDREN
ARE DOING NOTHING,
THEY ARE DOING MISCHIEF."

-Henry Fielding

Describe our relationship in your own words.

When I was a child, what were your hopes and dreams for my life?

Looking back, what were our craziest and funniest moments together?

Be honest, what did I do that drove you crazy?

As I was growing up, what career path did you think I'd pursue?

"DREAM BIG
AND DARE TO FAIL."

-Norman Vaughan

What do you hope I learned from and what would you never want me to repeat?

How good of a job do you think you did as a dad?

"NOBLE FATHERS
HAVE NOBLE CHILDREN."

-Euripedes

I could be the biggest brat when...

"I'M ALWAYS DOING THINGS I CAN'T DO. THAT'S HOW I GET TO DO THEM."

-Pablo Picasso

What was the one thing I gave or give you, others can't?

When you think of me, what's the first thing that comes to mind?

How did you pick my name? Did you almost name me something else and what other names did you consider?

What was the one thing you wish you knew before becoming a father?

"IT IS NOT WHAT YOU DO FOR YOUR CHILDREN,
BUT WHAT YOU HAVE TAUGHT THEM
TO DO FOR THEMSELVES,
THAT WILL MAKE THEM SUCCESSFUL HUMAN BEINGS."

-Ann Landers

Tell me about myself as an infant. What funny story should I know that happened when I was really young?

"IT IS A HAPPY TALENT
TO KNOW HOW TO PLAY."

-Ralph Waldo Emerson

Describe my terrible twos.

When I have kids, what karma do you hope comes back to me. What hellishness did I put you through?

What do you think is my best personality trait and who did I get it from?

"PERSONALITY IS ONLY RIPE
WHEN A MAN HAS MADE THE TRUTH HIS OWN."

-*Søren Kierkegaard*

What birthday of mine stands out as most special, why?

"LET US NEVER KNOW WHAT OLD AGE IS.
LET US KNOW THE HAPPINESS TIME BRINGS,
NOT COUNT THE YEARS."

-*Ausonius*

What is your most treasured memory of just you and I?

Looking back on all the bad things I did as a child, which one secretly made you laugh?

When or what time were you the proudest of me?

How did you feel the first time you saw me after I was born?

"MY MOTHER GROANED,
MY FATHER WEPT,
INTO THE DANGEROUS WORLD I LEAPT."

-William Blake

How are we the most different?

"Be yourself.
Everyone else is already taken."

-Oscar Wilde

Tell me about one of my most embarrassing moments in school and how we got through it together?

What was the hardest talk you ever had to have with me?

Did you pass down any advice or techniques that your dad, my grandfather gave you?

"KEEP YOUR FACE
ALWAYS TOWARD THE SUNSHINE—
AND SHADOWS WILL FALL BEHIND YOU."

-Walt Whitman

What things did you have to learn as you went along? Who did you regularly call for advice on being a father?

"THE MORE I READ,
THE MORE I ACQUIRE,
THE MORE CERTAIN I AM
THAT I KNOW NOTHING."

- Voltaire

What was the greatest invention for dads, in your opinion?

What was the one thing you worried about the most where I was concerned?

What moments as a father made you laugh the most?

What life lesson do you feel is most important for me to learn?

"THE BEST AND MOST BEAUTIFUL THINGS
IN THE WORLD CANNOT BE SEEN OR EVEN TOUCHED;
THEY MUST BE FELT WITH THE HEART."

-Helen Keller

Who or what was your biggest helper as a dad?

"YOU HAVE NOT LIVED TODAY
UNTIL YOU HAVE DONE SOMETHING
FOR SOMEONE WHO CAN
NEVER REPAY YOU."

-John Bunyan

What have you always tried to protect me from?

As a father what did you want more of, that you never had enough of?

In what ways was fatherhood not all it was cracked up to be?

Did having a child/children stand in the way of your dreams?

"LIMITATIONS LIVE ONLY IN OUR MINDS.
BUT IF WE USE OUR IMAGINATIONS,
OUR POSSIBILITIES BECOME LIMITLESS."

-Jamie Paolinetti

Were you afraid of becoming like your father?

"ONE FATHER IS MORE THAN
A HUNDRED SCHOOLMASTERS."

-*George Herbert*

What have you always wanted to ask me but never did?

What punishment was the hardest to give me and why?

What do you think is the most important role/task of a father?

Piccadilly®